Mastering Salesforce Administration

An Advanced Administration Certification Handbook

Rakesh Gupta

BIRMINGHAM - MUMBAI

Mastering Salesforce CRM Administration

First published: March 2017

Production reference: 1220317

Published by Packt Publishing Ltd.
Livery Place
35 Livery Street
Birmingham
B3 2PB, UK.
ISBN 978-1-78646-318-0

www.packtpub.com

Credits

Author
Rakesh Gupta

Reviewers
Vinay Chaturvedi
Jitendra Zaa

Commissioning Editor
Aaron Lazar

Acquisition Editor
Chaitanya Nair

Content Development Editor
Nikhil Borkar

Technical Editor
Hussain Kanchwala

Copy Editor
Muktikant Garimella

Project Coordinator
Ulhas Kambali

Proofreader
Safis Editing

Indexer
Aishwarya Gangawane

Graphics
Abhinash Sahu

Production Coordinator
Melwyn Dsa

Foreword

When I started working on Salesforce in 2008, I had no idea where Salesforce is heading. After Apex and Visualforce, Chatter was a big hit and a much needed product of Salesforce. After Chatter, Salesforce started delivering big features and products, such as Salesforce1, Tooling API, Process Builder, Visual Flow, Platform Encryption, Wave, and Lightning, one after another, to name few. Since the Salesforce ecosystem became vast with each release, sometimes, it's hard for the beginners to find a starting point with the latest information. There are many features in Salesforce that get enhanced with each release, resulting in the existing content on the evangelist's websites becoming obsolete or outdated.

Mastering Salesforce CRM Administration would help Salesforce professionals and newbies to learn many features available in Salesforce. Rakesh has done a fantabulous job in writing and tailoring content and group them in logical chapters.

The first chapter talks about enabling Lightning experience, Salesforce editions, objects, and the type of relationships. This chapter will give a firm start to all new professionals who want to start careers in Salesforce. The next chapter goes deeper into the important topics of security by talking about organization-wide defaults, sharing rules, roles, profiles, and field-level security. It also explains multicurrency. The following chapter focuses on the territory management concept and the steps to enable it.

The next chapter leaves no stone unturned to make you an awesome admin by explaining the micro-level details of custom objects, fields, tabs, Lightning applications, Lightning record pages, and so on. It also explains the tools to improve the data quality of Salesforce, such as validation rule, duplicate management, and more.

There are dedicated chapters for Sales Cloud and Service Cloud. If you ask me, even the whole book will not be sufficient enough to cover Sales Cloud and Service Cloud. However, the author has written the content brilliantly in order to cover as many concepts as possible at a high level so that you would not have any difficulty in exploring them in detail later. The next chapter focuses on complete e-mail management stuff such as e-mail deliverability and e-mail to case. It also covers mobile applications offered by Salesforce, such as SalesforceA, Authenticator app, and Salesforce1.

The author is a well-known blogger for Visual flow globally, and this book has a complete chapter on it. This book has a solid punch of basics to start with flow. I will say this chapter is a trump card for all professionals who want to master Visual flow.

The author doesn't want you to stop at being an awesome admin. He has a bigger plan, and to motivate all awesome admins, he has a short and sweet chapter on getting started with Apex and Visualforce.

One of the inimitable features of this book is the knowledge check at the end of every chapter. It will make sure that you understood the concepts well and will help in summarizing the content.

I hope this book will prove to be a springboard to start a career in Salesforce for many professional. After writing many books, Rakesh has a natural talent at keeping you engaged and entertained in every chapter. I promise that you will enjoy this book.

Jitendra Zaa

Salesforce MVP and Technical Architect

About the Author

Rakesh Gupta is a graduate of SRM University, Chennai, with a degree in information technology. He previously worked at iGate Computer System Ltd (now a part of Capgemini). He is a three-time Salesforce MVP, evangelist, Salesforce trainer, blogger, and is working as a Salesforce solution architect. He has been working on the platform of Salesforce.com for 6+ years. He is from Katihar, Bihar, and lives in Mumbai, India. He is the co-author of the books, *Developing Applications with Salesforce Chatter* and *Salesforce.com Customization Handbook* by Packt Publishing. He is the author of *Learning Salesforce Visual Workflow* and *Learning Salesforce Visual Workflow and Process Builder - Second Edition* by Packt Publishing. He is also the technical reviewer of *Learning Force.com Application Development* and *Mastering Application Development with Force.com* by Packt Publishing.

Best known as an automation champion in the Salesforce ecosystem, as he has written over 100+ articles on Visual Workflow and Process Builder to show how someone can use Visual Workflow and Process Builder to minimize code usage. He is one of the Visual Workflow and Process Builder experts from the industry. He has trained more than 700 individual professionals around the globe and conducted corporate training. He currently holds 9 certifications in Salesforce. He works on all the aspects of Salesforce and is an expert in data migration, process automation, configuration, customization, and integration. He is the leader of the Navi Mumbai and Nashik Salesforce developer user groups in India. He is also the initiator of the Mumbai Salesforce user group and the initiator of a biweekly online webinar, Automation Hour (`http://www.automationhour.com`). He is very passionate about Force.com and shares information through various channels, including Salesforce Success Community and his blog at `http://www.automationchampion.com`.

You can follow him on Twitter at `@rakeshistom` / `@automationchamp`.

First and foremost, I would like to thank my parents, Kedar Nath Gupta and Madhuri Gupta, and my sister, Sarika Gupta, for being patient with me for taking yet another challenge, which decreases the amount of time I can spend with them. They have been my inspiration and motivation for continuing to improve my knowledge and move my career forward. I would like to thank Packt Publishing for giving me this opportunity to share my knowledge via this book. I would also like to thank my friend, Meenakshi Kalra, for helping me while I was writing this book. A special thanks to all my well-wishers and friends. I would like to especially thank Jitender Zaa (Salesforce MVP) and Vinay Chaturvedi (Salesforce MVP); without you, this book would never find its way to the Web. In the end, I'm grateful to every member of Salesforce Ohana; hope you will find this book useful!

About the Reviewers

Vinay Chaturvedi is a Salesforce MVP, currently working as a principal consultant. He has been loving and living Salesforce since 2011.

Vinay leads the Salesforce developer and user group in Noida and loves to blog at `vinaychaturvedi.com`.

Vinay is an accomplished developer, consultant, and business analyst with global consultancy experience, designing and implementing solutions for a large number of reputed clients. Being one of the several Salesforce experts trying to help the community, Vinay has an outstanding understanding of Salesforce concepts and implementation experience of several Salesforce projects.

You can follow Vinay on Twitter at `@vinay_sfdc` and on his website at `vinaychaturvedi.com`.

Jitendra Zaa is a Salesforce MVP, author, and a Dreamforce speaker with more than 9 years of experience in web technologies and cloud platforms. He is a manager at Cognizant Technology Solutions and holds 17 Salesforce certifications under his belt. You can follow him at `@JitendraZaa` or on his website, `http://Jitendrazaa.com`.

Writing technical blog articles, learning new programming languages and frameworks, and sharing knowledge with others are some of his hobbies. His experience and projects normally include Salesforce, JAVA, C#, ASP.Net, JIRA, and PHP-based applications. He is the author of the book *Apex Design Patterns* by Packt Publishing. Other books he has reviewed include *Enterprise Patterns in Salesforce, Introduction to Chatter*, and *Visualforce Development Cookbook* by Packt Publishing.

Customer Feedback

Thanks for purchasing this Packt book. At Packt, quality is at the heart of our editorial process. To help us improve, please leave us an honest review on this book's Amazon page at "`Amazon Book URL`".

If you'd like to join our team of regular reviewers, you can e-mail us at `customerreviews@packtpub.com`. We award our regular reviewers with free eBooks and videos in exchange for their valuable feedback. Help us be relentless in improving our products!

Table of Contents

Preface

Salesforce.com is one of the fastest-growing and demanding technologies at the moment. Mastering Salesforce CRM Administration is a hands-on guide helping Salesforce newbies (who have a basic knowledge of Salesforce), new or experienced Salesforce administrators, and developers who want to take their knowledge to the next level to become a Salesforce certified advanced administrator. As you go through the content, you will notice that this book focuses on real-world examples. This book builds upon these examples to help you understand and use the features of the Salesforce.com platform.

This book is all about mastering the Salesforce admin part, taking your skills as an administrator or developer and tuning them for the unique features of the Salesforce platform. We'll discuss the most complex topics in this book, such as territory management, forecasting, quota, knowledge base, and more. It's going to be awesome. So, let's get started!

What this book covers

`Chapter 1`, *A Deep Dive into the Salesforce Lightning Experience*, describes what Lightning Experience is and how it will help sales and support reps to improve their selling experience. Later, we will discuss the basic concepts of Salesforce that will help you understand the next few chapters.

`Chapter 2`, *Security Settings in Salesforce*, describes the concepts of multi currency, followed by the basics of Salesforce platform security and then goes through the various security aspects of Salesforce. At the end of the chapter, you will find key points to remember and a quiz for practice.

`Chapter 3`, *Territory Management*, gives you an understanding of Territory Management with real-time examples. Then, we will take the discussion ahead and discuss how its impact on your current record sharing. This is one of the key chapters in this book. At the end of the chapter, you will find key points to remember and a quiz for practice.

`Chapter 4`, *Extending Salesforce with Custom Objects and Applications*, gives the understanding of how an organization uses custom objects and applications to customize Salesforce CRM as per their business needs. At the end of the chapter, you will find key points to remember and a quiz for practice.

`Chapter 5`, *Getting More Value from Sales Cloud*, describes the Sales Cloud core concepts in Salesforce, including product, price books, quote, and forecasting management. At the end of the chapter, you will find key points to remember and a quiz for practice.

`Chapter 6`, *Increasing Service Agent Productivity by Using Service Cloud*, describes the Service Cloud core concepts in Salesforce, including case management, entitlement management, and knowledge management. At the end of the chapter, you will find key points to remember and a quiz for practice.

`Chapter 7`, *Optimizing Business Processes with Visual Workflow and Approval Processes*, gives a basic knowledge of the Salesforce Visual Workflow and approval process. We will pick up a few business examples and see how to use a flow instead of Apex code to solve it, and we will also discuss the benefits of using Salesforce Visual Workflow. We will also have an overview of the Flow canvas and its elements. At the end of the chapter, you will find key points to remember.

`Chapter 8`, *Automating Complex Business Processes*, enables you to gain a complete understanding of the Process Builder designer and all available actions inside it. At the end of the chapter, you will find key points to remember.

`Chapter 9`, *Analyzing Productivity with Reports and Dashboards*, describes the concepts of report and dashboard in Salesforce. Salesforce reports and dashboards help analyze the information captured in CRM, so it can help in making informed business decisions. At the end of the chapter, you will find key points to remember and a quiz for practice.

`Chapter 10`, *E-mail and Mobile Administration*, helps you understand how you can enable Salesforce1 for limited users, access SalesforceA, and use Chatter action. At the end of the chapter, you will find key points to remember.

`Chapter 11`, *Different Ways of Deploying an Application between Environments*, gives you a brief knowledge of the various ways of deploying metadata components in between environments. At the end of the chapter, you will find key points to remember.

`Chapter 12`, *Basics of Apex and Visualforce Page*, gives you a basic knowledge of Apex and Visualforce page architecture, including MVC pattern and Apex Data types, and so on. At the end of the chapter, you will find key points to remember.

What you need for this book

All you need to get the most out of this book is your brain, your computer with a modern web browser, and a free Salesforce developer org. You can sign up for a free developer org at `https://developer.salesforce.com/signup`.

Who this book is for

This book is aimed for anyone who has a basic knowledge of Salesforce and wants to take their knowledge to the next level to become a Salesforce certified advanced administrator. This book will not only help you clear Salesforce certified advanced administrator exam but also help you understand advanced concepts of Salesforce, such as territory management, forecasting, quota, knowledge base, entitlement process, deploying metadata components through Force.com Migration Tool, and more.

Conventions

In this book, you will find a number of text styles that distinguish between different kinds of information. Here are some examples of these styles and an explanation of their meaning.

Code words in text, database table names, folder names, filenames, file extensions, pathnames, dummy URLs, user input, and Twitter handles are shown as follows: "The next step is to edit `build.properties` file."

A block of code is set as follows:

```
[default]
exten => s,1,Dial(Zap/1|30)
exten => s,2,Voicemail(u100)
```

Any command-line input or output is written as follows:

```
ant -version
```

New terms and **important words** are shown in bold. Words that you see on the screen, for example, in menus or dialog boxes, appear in the text like this: "Once done, click on **Activate**."

Warnings or important notes appear in a box like this.

Tips and tricks appear like this.

Reader feedback

Feedback from our readers is always welcome. Let us know what you think about this book-what you liked or disliked. Reader feedback is important for us as it helps us develop titles that you will really get the most out of. To send us general feedback, simply e-mail `feedback@packtpub.com`, and mention the book's title in the subject of your message. If there is a topic that you have expertise in and you are interested in either writing or contributing to a book, see our author guide at `www.packtpub.com/authors`.

Customer support

Now that you are the proud owner of a Packt book, we have a number of things to help you to get the most from your purchase.

Errata

Although we have taken every care to ensure the accuracy of our content, mistakes do happen. If you find a mistake in one of our books-maybe a mistake in the text or the code-we would be grateful if you could report this to us. By doing so, you can save other readers from frustration and help us improve subsequent versions of this book. If you find any errata, please report them by visiting `http://www.packtpub.com/submit-errata`, selecting your book, clicking on the **Errata Submission Form** link, and entering the details of your errata. Once your errata are verified, your submission will be accepted and the errata will be uploaded to our website or added to any list of existing errata under the Errata section of that title.

To view the previously submitted errata, go to `https://www.packtpub.com/books/content/support`and enter the name of the book in the search field. The required information will appear under the **Errata** section.

Piracy

Piracy of copyrighted material on the Internet is an ongoing problem across all media. At Packt, we take the protection of our copyright and licenses very seriously. If you come across any illegal copies of our works in any form on the Internet, please provide us with the location address or website name immediately so that we can pursue a remedy.

Please contact us at `copyright@packtpub.com` with a link to the suspected pirated material.

We appreciate your help in protecting our authors and our ability to bring you valuable content.

Questions

If you have a problem with any aspect of this book, you can contact us at `questions@packtpub.com`, and we will do our best to address the problem.

1
A Deep Dive into the Salesforce Lightning Experience

This chapter starts with an overview of the Salesforce Lightning Experience and its benefits, which takes the discussion forward to the various business use cases where it can boost the sales representatives' productivity. We will also discuss different Sales Cloud and Service Cloud editions offered by Salesforce. At the end of this chapter, you will learn the different types of objects and fields available in Salesforce.

In the next few chapters, you will be briefed about user and organization administration, territory management, and the key concepts of Sales Cloud and Service Cloud. We will also go through the various ways of streamlining the sales and service processes using Lightning Process Builder and Visual Workflow. In the last few chapters, we will go through data migration concepts, reports and dashboards in Salesforce, Chatter configuration, mobile administration, and various ways of deploying your metadata. The following topics will be covered in this chapter:

- Getting started with Lightning Experience
- Salesforce Lightning Editions
- Types of objects and fields in Salesforce
- Types of relationships in Salesforce

Getting started with Lightning Experience

Lightning Experience is a new generation productive user interface designed to help your sales team to close more deals and sell quicker and smarter. Whereas support team can close a case faster using various tools and Lightning Components. The upswing in mobile usages is influencing the way people work. Sales representatives are now using mobile to research potential customers, get the details of nearby customer offices, socially connect with their customers, and even more. That's why Salesforce synced the desktop Lightning Experience with mobile Salesforce1.

Salesforce Lightning Editions

With its *Summer'16* release, Salesforce announced the Lightning Editions of Sales Cloud and Service Cloud. The Lightning Editions are a completely reimagined packaging of Sales Cloud and Service Cloud, which offer additional functionality to their customers and increased productivity with a relatively small increase in cost.

Sales Cloud Lightning Editions

Sales Cloud is a product designed to automate your sales process. By implementing this, an organization can boost its sales process. It includes **Campaign**, **Lead**, **Account**, **Contact**, **Opportunity**, **Report**, **Dashboard**, and many other features as well, which we will discuss in `Chapter 5`, *Getting More Value from Sales Cloud*. Salesforce offers various Sales Cloud editions, and as per business needs, an organization can buy any of these different editions, which are shown in the following image:

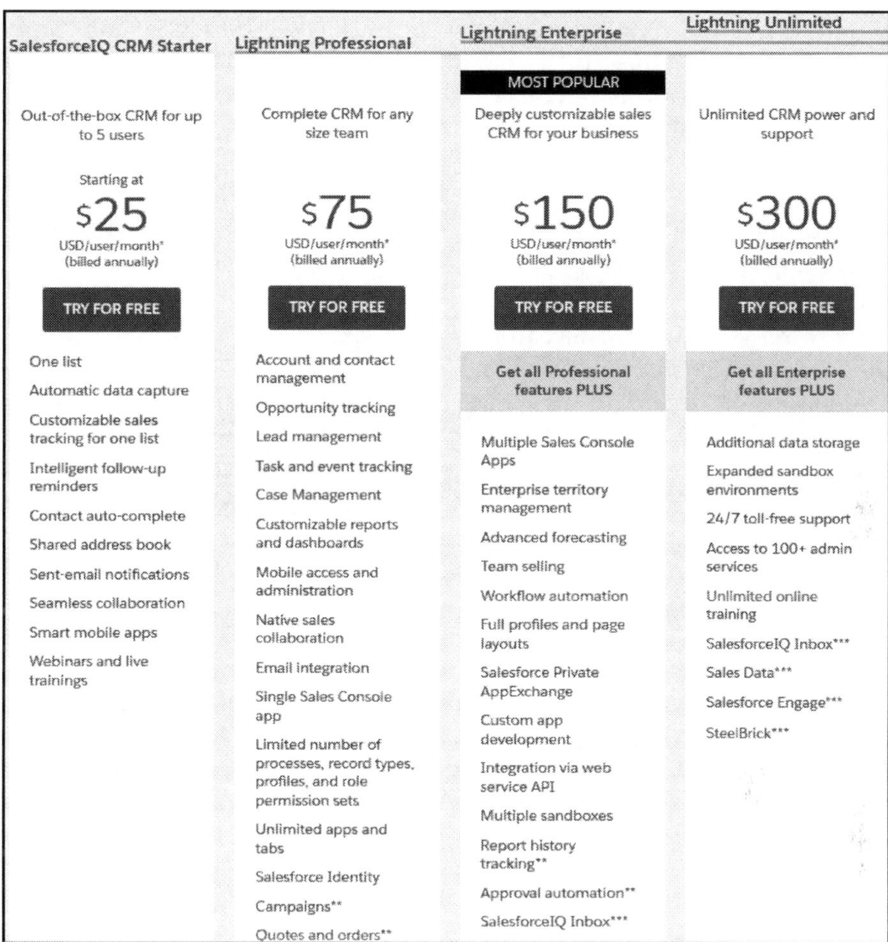

SalesforceIQ CRM Starter
Lightning Professional
Lightning Enterprise
Lightning Unlimited
MOST POPULAR
Out-of-the-box CRM for up to 5 users
Complete CRM for any size team
Deeply customizable sales CRM for your business
Unlimited CRM power and support
Starting at
$25
USD/user/month*
(billed annually)
$75
USD/user/month*
(billed annually)
$150
USD/user/month*
(billed annually)
$300
USD/user/month*
(billed annually)
TRY FOR FREE
One list
Automatic data capture
Customizable sales tracking for one list
Intelligent follow-up reminders
Contact auto-complete
Shared address book
Sent-email notifications
Seamless collaboration
Smart mobile apps
Webinars and live trainings
Account and contact management
Opportunity tracking
Lead management
Task and event tracking
Case Management
Customizable reports and dashboards
Mobile access and administration
Native sales collaboration
Email integration
Single Sales Console app
Limited number of processes, record types, profiles, and role permission sets
Unlimited apps and tabs
Salesforce Identity
Campaigns**
Quotes and orders**
Get all Professional features PLUS
Multiple Sales Console Apps
Enterprise territory management
Advanced forecasting
Team selling
Workflow automation
Full profiles and page layouts
Salesforce Private AppExchange
Custom app development
Integration via web service API
Multiple sandboxes
Report history tracking**
Approval automation**
SalesforceIQ Inbox***
Get all Enterprise features PLUS
Additional data storage
Expanded sandbox environments
24/7 toll-free support
Access to 100+ admin services
Unlimited online training
SalesforceIQ Inbox***
Sales Data***
Salesforce Engage***
SteelBrick***

Let's take a closer look at the three Sales Cloud Lightning Editions:

- **Lightning Professional**: This edition is for **small and medium enterprises (SMEs)**. It is designed for business needs where a full-featured CRM functionality is required. It provides the CRM functionality for marketing, sales, and service automation. Professional Edition is a perfect fit for small- to mid-sized businesses. After the *Summer'16* release, in this edition, you can create a limited number of processes, record types, roles, profiles, and permission sets. For each Lightning Professional Edition license, organizations have to pay USD 75 per month.

- **Lightning Enterprise**: This edition is for businesses with large and complex business requirements. It includes all the features available in the Professional Edition, plus it provides advanced customization capabilities to automate business processes and web service API access for integration with other systems. Enterprise Editions also include processes, workflow, approval process, visual workflow, profile, page layout, and custom app development. In addition, organizations also get the Salesforce Identity feature with this edition. For each Lightning Enterprise Edition license, organizations have to pay USD 150 per month.
- **Lightning Unlimited**: This edition includes all Salesforce.com features for an entire enterprise. It provides all the features of Enterprise Edition and a new level of Platform flexibility for managing and sharing all of their information on demand. The key features of Salesforce.com Unlimited Edition (in addition to Enterprise features) are premier support, full mobile access, and increased storage limits. It also includes Work.com, Service Cloud, knowledge base, live agent chat, multiple sandboxes and unlimited custom app development. For each Lightning Unlimited Edition license, organizations have to pay USD 300 per month.

While purchasing Salesforce.com licenses, organizations have to negotiate with Salesforce to get the maximum number of sandboxes. Salesforce edition prices are subjective to change. Latest information would always available on salesforce official site. To know more about these license types, please visit the Salesforce website at `https://www.salesforce.com/sales-cloud/pricing/`.

Service Cloud Lightning Editions

Service Cloud helps your organization to streamline the customer service process. Users can access it anytime, anywhere, and from any device. It will help your organization to close a case faster. Service agents can connect with customers through the agent console, meaning agents can interact with customers through multiple channels. Customer can also implement Omni-channel to route a customer case to qualified and available support agent. Service Cloud includes case management, **computer telephony integration (CTI)**, Service Cloud console, knowledge base, Salesforce communities, Salesforce Private AppExchange, premier+ success plan, report, and dashboards, with many other analytics features. We will discuss more about Service Cloud in `Chapter 6`, *Increasing Service Agent Productivity by Using Service Cloud.*

The various Service Cloud Lightning Editions are shown in the following image:

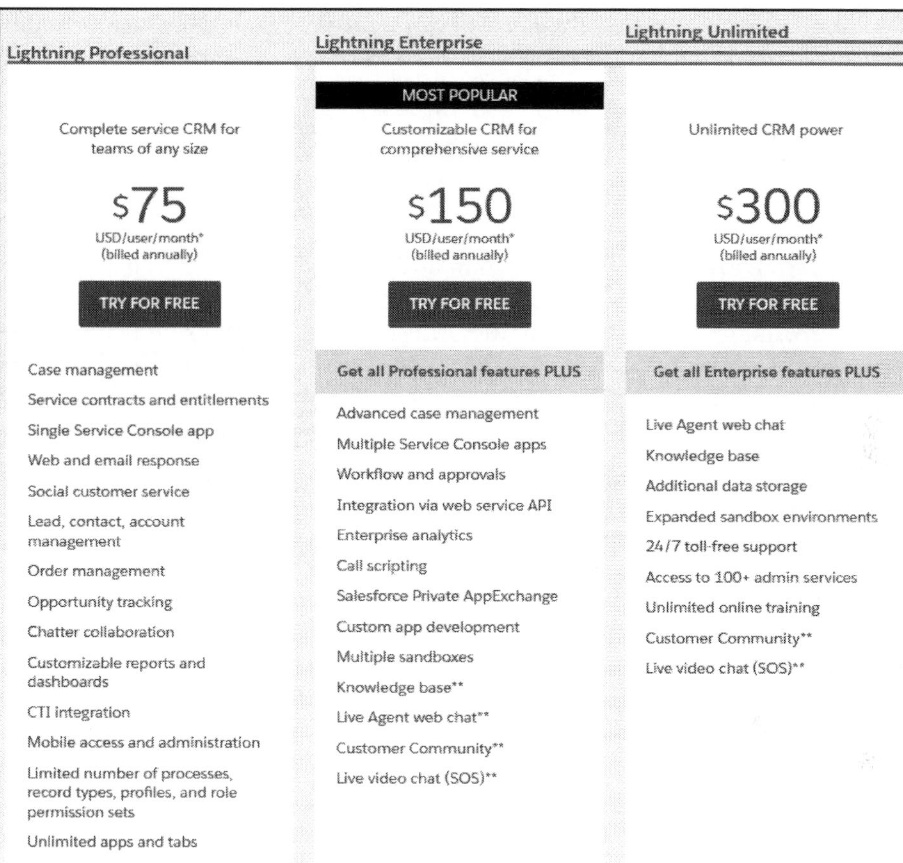

Let's take a closer look at the three Service Cloud Lightning Editions:

- **Lightning Professional**: This edition is for SMEs. It provides CRM functionality for customer support through various channels. It is a perfect fit for small- to mid-sized businesses. It includes features, such as case management, CTI integration, mobile access, solution management, content library, reports, and analytics, along with sales features such as opportunity management and forecasting. After the *Summer'16* release, in this edition, you can create a limited number of processes, record types, roles, profiles, and permission sets. For each Lightning Professional Edition license, organizations have to pay USD 75 per month.

- **Lightning Enterprise**: This edition is for businesses with large and complex business requirements. It includes all the features available in the Professional edition, plus it provides advanced customization capabilities to automate business processes and web service API access for integration with other systems. It also includes Service console, Service contract and entitlement management, workflow, visual workflow, approval process, web chat, offline access, and knowledge base. Organizations get Salesforce Identity feature with this edition. For each Lightning Enterprise Edition license, organizations have to pay USD 150 per month.
- **Lightning Unlimited**: This edition includes all Salesforce.com features for an entire enterprise. It provides all the features of Enterprise Edition and a new level of platform flexibility for managing and sharing all of their information on demand. The key features of Salesforce.com Unlimited edition (in addition to the Enterprise features) are premier support, full mobile access, unlimited custom apps, and increased storage limits. It also includes Work.com, Service Cloud, knowledge base, live agent chat, multiple sandboxes, and unlimited custom app development. For each Lightning Unlimited Edition license, organizations have to pay USD 300 per month.

While purchasing the licenses, organizations have to negotiate with Salesforce to get the maximum number of sandboxes. Salesforce edition prices are subjective to change. Latest information would always available on Salesforce official site. To know more about these license types, please visit the Salesforce website at `https://www.salesforce.com/service-cloud/pricing/`.

Creating a Salesforce developer account

To get started with the given topics in this book, it is recommended to use a Salesforce developer account. Using Salesforce production instance is not essential for practicing. You can use the Salesforce sandbox or developer account to practice on the examples covered in this book.

If you currently do not have your developer account, you can create a new Salesforce developer account. The Salesforce developer account is completely free and can be used to practice newly learned concepts, but you cannot use this for commercial purposes. To create a Salesforce developer account follow these steps:

1. Visit the website `http://developer.force.com/`.
2. Click on the **Sign Up** button.

3. It will open a sign up page; fill it out to create one for you. The signup page will look like the following screenshot:

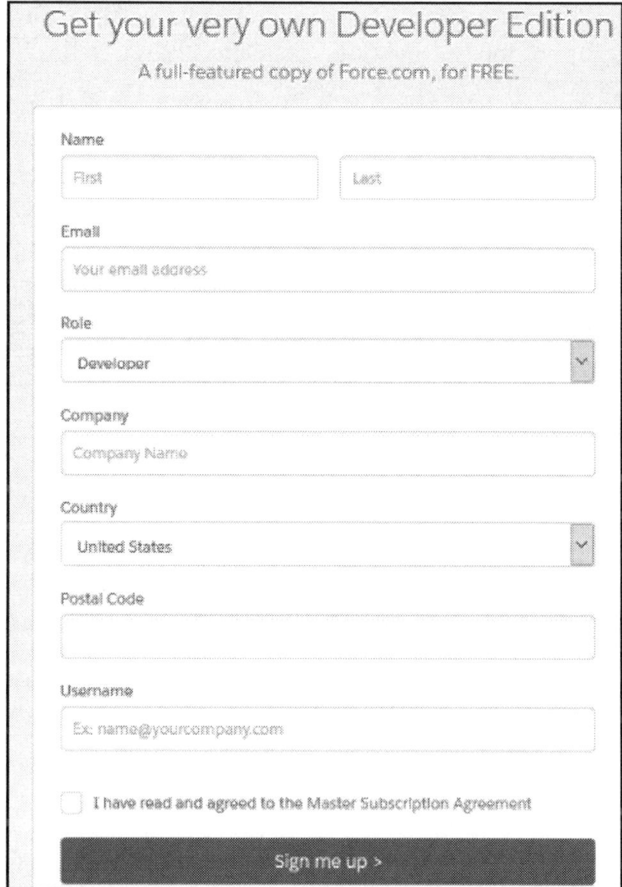

4. Once you register for the developer account, Salesforce.com will send you login details on the e-mail ID you have provided during the registration.

By following the instructions in the e-mail, you are ready to get started with Salesforce.

Enabling the Lightning Experience for users

Once you are ready to roll out the Lightning Experience for your users, navigate to the Lightning Setup page, which is available in Setup, by clicking Lightning Experience. The slider button at the bottom of the Lightning Setup page, shown in the following screenshot, enables Lightning Experience for your organization:

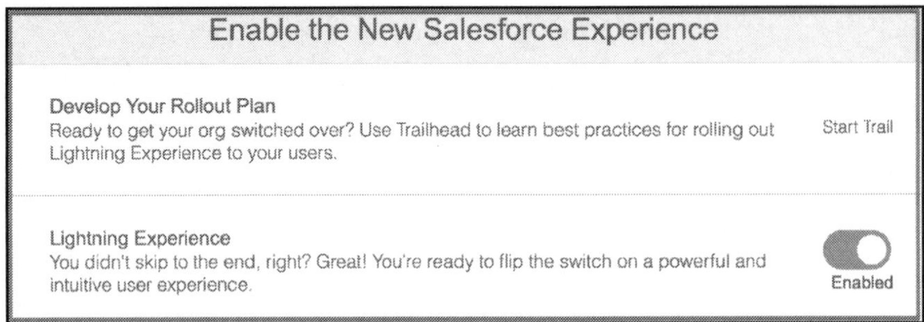

Flip that switch, and Lightning Experience will be enabled for your Salesforce organization. The Lightning Experience is now enabled for all standard profiles by default.

Granting permission to users through Profiles

Depending on the number of users for a rollout, you have to decide how to enable the Lightning Experience for them. If you are planning to do a mass rollout, it is better to update **Profiles**.

A business scenario: *Helina Jolly* is working as a *system administrator* at Universal Containers. She has received a requirement to enable Lightning Experience for a custom profile, `Training User`.

First of all, create a custom profile for the license type, **Salesforce**, and give it the name, `Training User`. To enable the Lightning Experience for a custom profile, follow these instructions:

1. In the Lightning Experience user interface, click on **Gear icon** | **Setup** | **ADMINISTRATION** | **Users** | **Profiles**, and then select the `Training User` profile, as shown in the following screenshot:

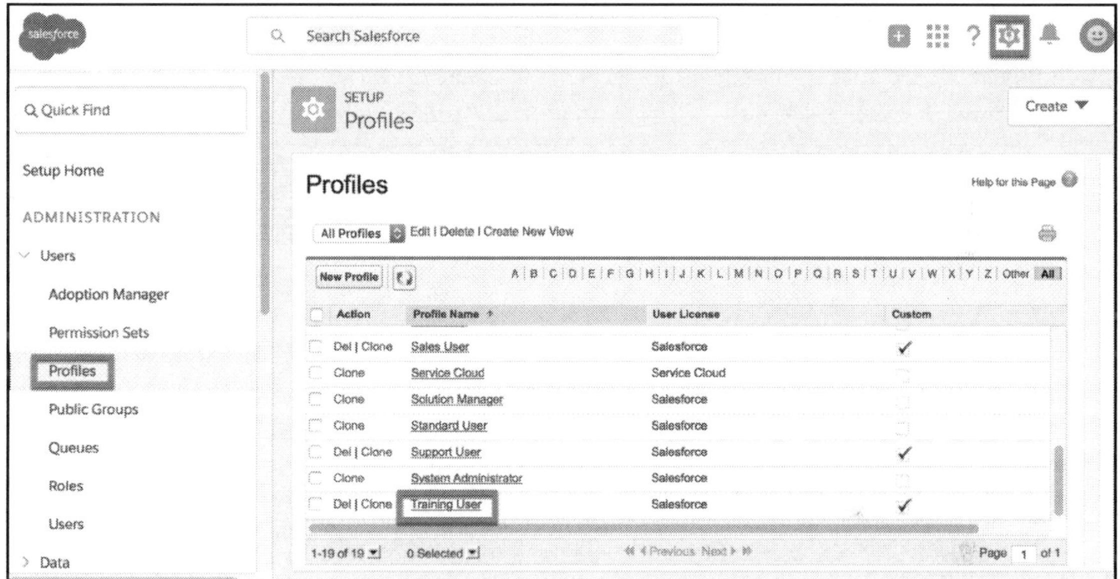

2. Then, navigate to the **System Permission** section, and select the **Lightning Experience User** checkbox.

Granting permission to users through permission sets

If you want to enable the Lightning Experience for a small group of users, or if you are not sure whether you will keep the Lightning Experience on for a group of users, consider using permission sets. Permission sets are mainly a collection of settings and permissions that give the users access to numerous tools and functions within Salesforce. By creating a permission set, you can grant the *Lightning Experience user* permission to the users in your organization.

In this book, we are going to use the new Lightning Experience for step-by-step instructions or screenshots wherever applicable.

Switching between Lightning Experience and Salesforce Classic

If you have enabled Lightning Experience for your users, they can use the *switcher* to switch back and forth between Lightning Experience and Salesforce Classic.

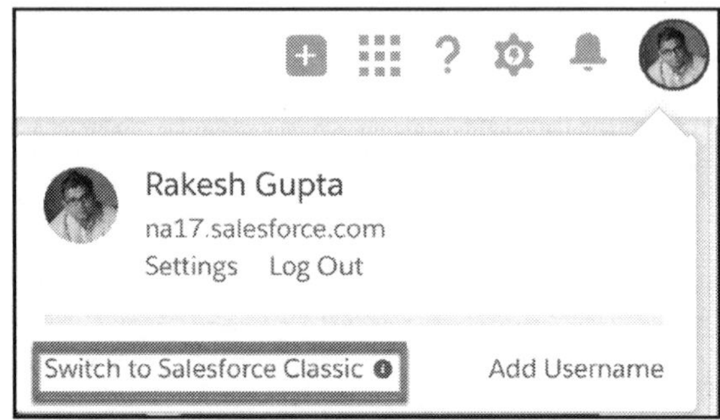

The switcher is very smart. Every time a user switches, it remembers that user experience as their new default preference. So, if a user switches to Lightning Experience, it is now their default user experience until they switch back to Salesforce Classic. If you want to restrict your users to switch back to Salesforce Classic, you have to develop an Apex trigger or process with Flow. When the `UserPreferencesLightningExperiencePreferred` field on the user object is true, then it redirects the user to the Lightning Experience interface.

The Lightning Experience for end users

The Lightning Experience is an entirely new user interface to provide users with new experience in order to help them sell more efficiently. The Lightning Experience takes all the things that users love about Salesforce1 app and combines them with an all-new reimagined responsive desktop experience.

The Lightning Experience navigation menu

In Salesforce Classic, users see their tabs on the top of the screen. In the Lightning Experience, these tabs are also available on top of the screen. Turning the Lightning Experience on will provide users with a set of standard objects predefined by Salesforce. The Lightning Experience screen is represented in the following screenshot:

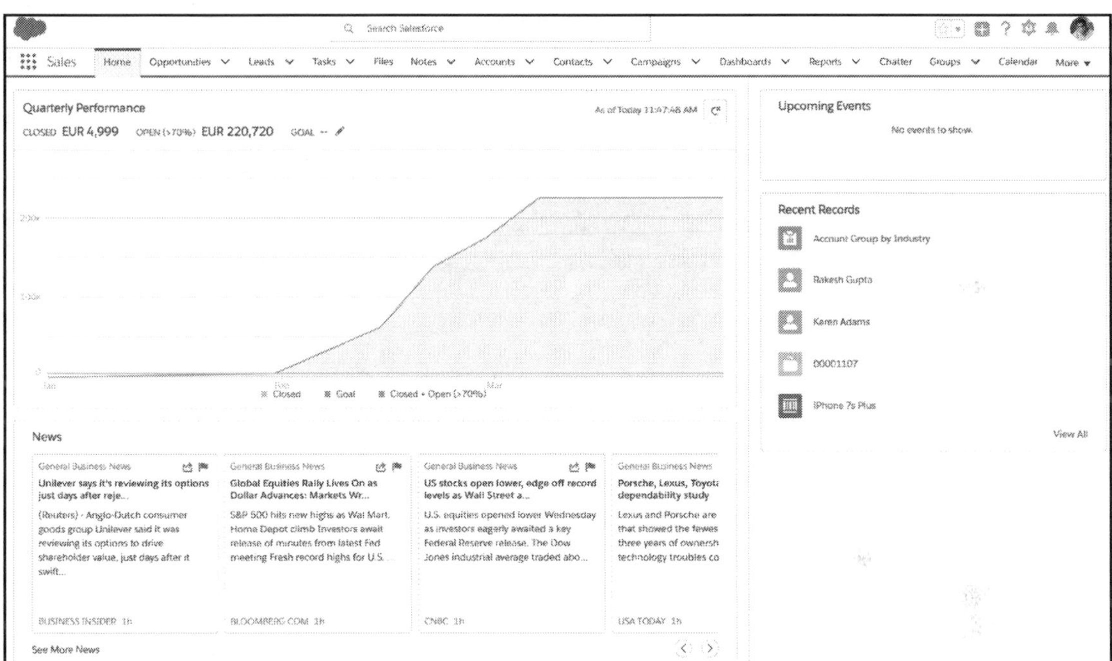

The names that appear in the navigation menu are associated with the objects or the app's tab. Salesforce also allows us to customize the navigation menu to include both standard and custom objects.

The App Launcher in Lightning

In Salesforce Classic, we can switch between apps in one of the two ways, that is, through **App Launcher** or through **Force.com App Menu**. On the other hand, in the Lightning Experience, there is no **Force.com App Menu**. We can find apps by searching for the app name or by using the **App Launcher**, which is shown in the following screenshot:

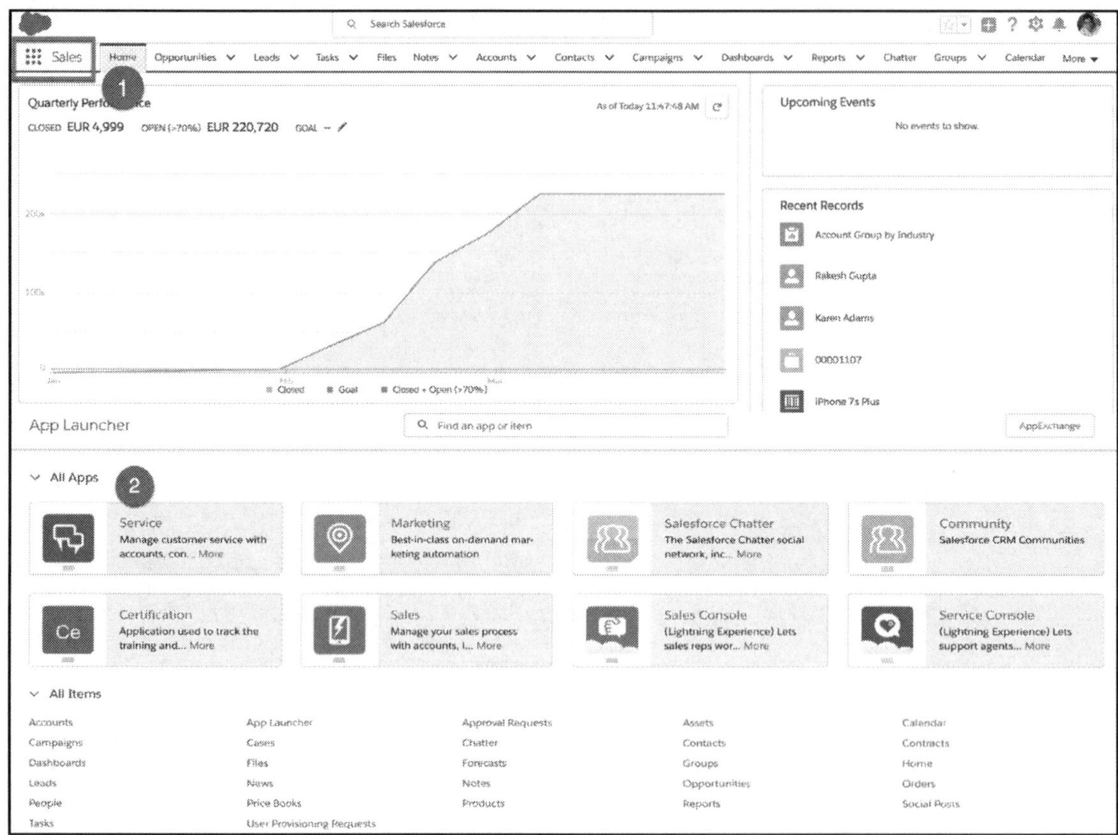

All our custom apps, connected apps, and custom object tabs are available through **App Launcher**. We can personalize the order of the apps on this page by dragging the tiles as per our needs.

The Home page

The Home page displays key components for each user's day. From the **Home** page, your users can manage their day, including viewing their Top deals, quarterly performance summary, and the most relevant tasks. Customize the **Home** page for your users to display the opportunity details so that they can get the most out of the **Home** page. It is presented in the next screenshot:

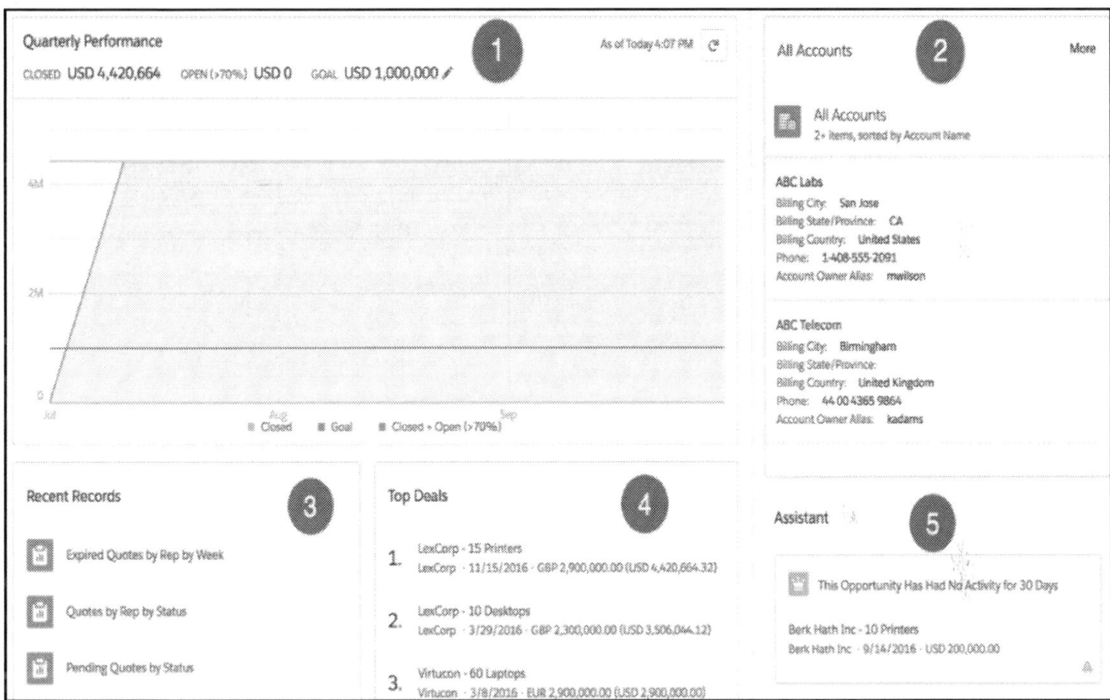

In Salesforce Classic, the **Home** page has a Chatter feed, whereas the Lightning Experience **Home** page doesn't have a Chatter feed. To access the Chatter (the *Feed*) on the Lightning Experience, use navigation menu; it's available under the **Feed** icon. When you want to access Chatter on a record, go to the **Collaborate** tab.

Global search

Global search proficiently finds what you are looking for by breaking your search terms. You can find the global search box at the top of every page in Lightning Experience. When you click on the global search box, you see a drop-down of all your recent items, as shown in the following screenshot:

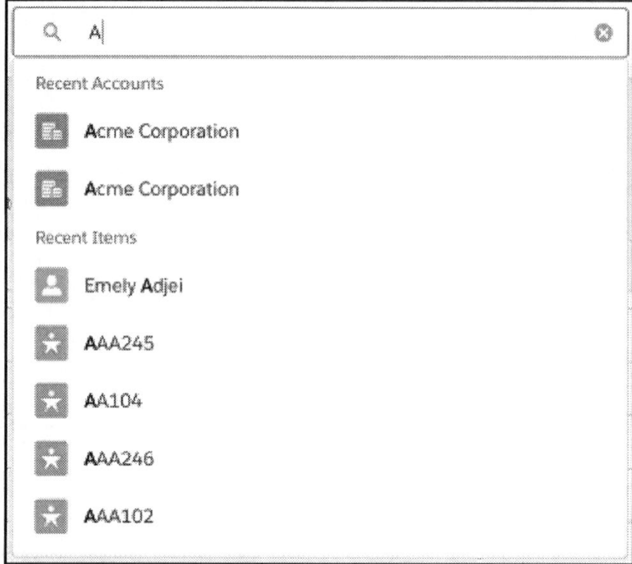

If you click on the global search from an object-specific view, such as from a **Leads** page, the global search looks for **Leads** based on your search string.

Types of objects and fields in Salesforce

Objects are a crucial element in Salesforce as they provide a structure for storing data and are incorporated into the interface, allowing users to interact with the data. It is similar to a database table. Object fields are similar in concept to a database column while records are similar in concept to a database row.

Standard objects

Standard objects are provided by Salesforce as a basic CRM structure. These include account, contact, opportunity, lead, campaign and so on. These are the tables that contain the records in any standard tabs, such as **Accounts**, **Contacts**, **Opportunities**, **Leads**, **Campaigns**, and so on.

Custom objects

In addition to standard objects, Salesforce allows you to create **custom objects** to store data specific to your organization, which is not doable through standard objects. For example, creating a custom object to store employee checking, saving account details to process biweekly salary, and keeping employee account details private so that only the system administrator and employee (who created the record) can access it. You can create reports and dashboards based on the record data in your custom object. Custom objects are usually identified by a `__c` suffix.

Difference between standard and custom objects

Let's have a look at the differences between the standard and custom objects in the following table:

Standard object	Custom object
Can't delete	Can delete
Can't change the Grant Access Using Hierarchies sharing access	Can change the Grant Access Using Hierarchies sharing access
We can't Truncate standard objects	It is possible to Truncate custom objects
It is possible to create custom fields on standard objects	Custom objects contain some standard field, for example, **Name**, **Created by**, **Last modified by** and so on

External objects

External objects are similar to custom objects. They allow us to map the data that's stored outside your Salesforce organization. The following screenshot represents how you can connect external system with Salesforce using the **Salesforce Connect**.

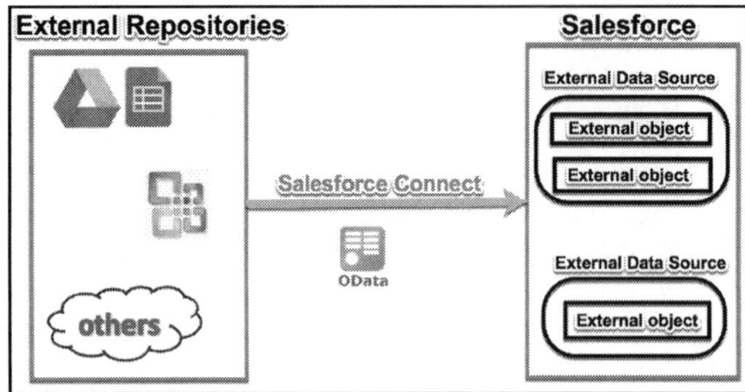

Each external object trusts on an external data source definition such as **Salesforce Connect** or **OData** to connect with the external system's data. Each external object maps to a data table on the external system. Each of the external object's fields maps to a table column on the external system. External objects are usually identified by a `__x` suffix.

Standard fields

Standard fields are predefined fields that are included as standard within the Salesforce application. Standard fields cannot be deleted, but non-required standard fields can be removed from page layouts whenever needed. Both standard and custom objects contain a few common standard fields, for example, `Name`, `CreateDate`, `LastModifiedDate`, and `Owner` fields.

Custom fields

Custom fields are unique to your business needs and not only can they be added and amended, but also deleted. Creating custom fields allows you to store the information that is necessary for your organization. Both standard and custom fields can be customized to include custom help text, which helps users understand how to use the fields. Custom fields are usually identified by a `__c` suffix.

Types of relationship in Salesforce

You can establish relationships between objects in Salesforce. You can associate one object with another. For example, you have an object named `Meetup` (to store information about a meeting), and you want to associate it with another object, `Participant` (to store information about participants for a particular meeting) so that you can associate the `Participant` records with the respective `Meetup` record. These relationship types also determine how they handle record sharing, data deletion capability, and required fields in page layouts. Salesforce provides the following types of relationships that can be established among objects:

- Master-detail relationship
- Lookup relationship
- Self-relationship
- External lookup relationship
- Indirect lookup relationship
- Many-to-many relationship (junction object)
- Hierarchical relationship

Master-detail relationship

It is a strongly coupled relationship among Salesforce objects, which means if a master record gets deleted, then the child records associated with it are also deleted. In this type of relationship, the parent record controls the behavior of the child record regarding visibility and sharing. It means the security setting of a parent object applies to the child object.

For example, if we create a master-detail relationship between the `Meetup` and `Participant` objects, where `Meetup` will act as the parent object and `Participant` will serve as the child object, then if someone deletes a `Meetup` record, all the associated `Participant` records will also get deleted. The following image gives a visual representation of the master-detail relationship between `Meetup` and `Participant`:

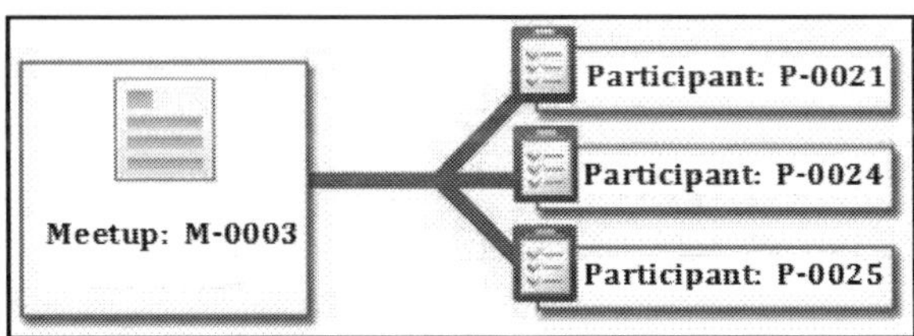

When there is a master-detail relationship between two objects, you can create a unique type of field over the master object, called **Roll-up summary**. A roll-up summary field allows us to calculate values from child records, such as the number of child records linked to a parent record.

For best practice, don't create more than 10,000 child records for a master-detail relationship.

Lookup relationship

It is a loosely coupled relationship among Salesforce objects, which means even if a parent record gets deleted, the child records remain in the system. Here, both the parent and child have their own sharing settings and security controls. The following image gives a visual representation of the lookup relationship between `Meetup` and `Participant` objects and what happen when parent (`Meetup`) record gets deleted:

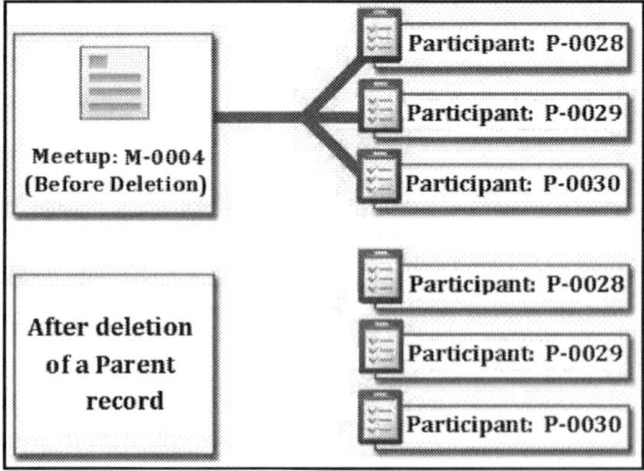

For example, if we create a lookup relationship between the `Meetup` and `Participant` objects, where `Meetup` will act as the parent object and `Participant` will serve as the child object, then if someone deletes a `Meetup` record, all the associated `Participant` records will still exist in the system.

Difference between master-detail and lookup relationships

Let's have a look at the differences between the lookup and master-detail relationships in the following table:

Lookup relationship	Master-detail relationship
Loosely coupled.	Strongly coupled.
Roll-up summary field cannot be created.	Roll-up summary field can be created.
Parent record is not required while creating a child record.	Parent record is always required in order to create a child record.
Lookup fields are not required on the page layout of the detail record.	Master-detail field is always required on the page layout of the detail record.
Standard object record can be on the detail side of a custom object in a lookup relationship.	Standard object record cannot be a child.
By default record ownership of child records is not controlled by the parent.	Parent controls the record ownership of child records. The owner field is not available on the detail record in master-detail relationship queues, sharing rules and manual sharing is not possible for detail records as it requires the owner field.
You can have a child record without a parent.	You cannot have a child record without a parent.
You can have a maximum of 40 lookups on an object.	You can have a maximum of two master details on an object.
No cascade delete.	Cascade delete.

Self-relationship

Self-relationship is another example of a lookup relationship. In Salesforce, we can use lookup relationships to create self-relationship among objects; we can have a maximum of 40 self-lookups. For example, a campaign record can have a **Parent Campaign** record, as shown in the following screenshot:

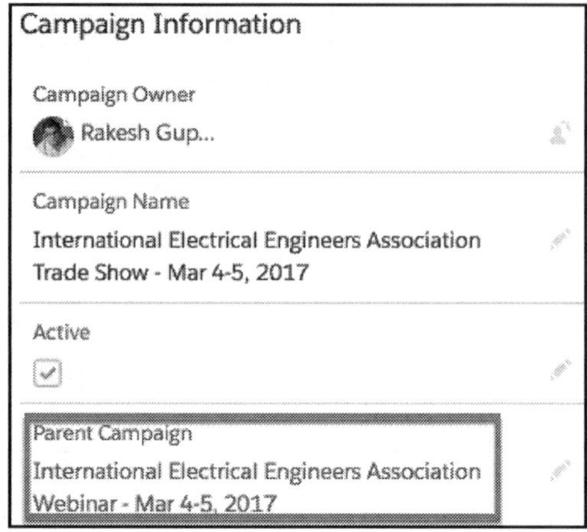

External lookup relationship

We can create two special lookups on an external object apart from the standard lookup relationship. They are external lookup relationship and indirect lookup relationship.

External lookup relationship allows us to link an external object to a parent external object whose data is stored in an external data source. In other words, it allows us to link two external objects.

Indirect lookup relationship

An indirect lookup relationship allows us to link an external object to a standard or custom object. We can only create an indirect lookup to an object with a unique external ID field on the parent object that is used to match the records in this relationship. While creating an indirect lookup relationship field on an external object, we have to specify the child object field and the parent object field to match and associate records in the relationship. For example, we can display a related list of payments from the ERP external record with matching external IDs on the account object.

Many-to-many relationship

The many-to-many relationship in Salesforce allows us to link a child record to multiple parents. For example, a campaign is attached to many leads, and one lead may have more than one campaign. A visual representation of the many-to-many relationship is shown in the following image:

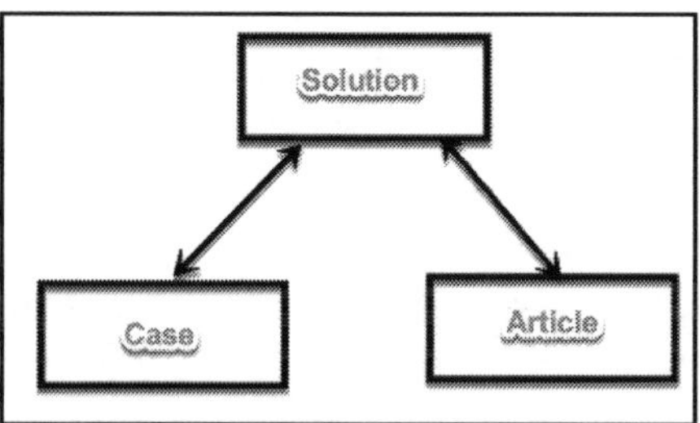

If you have two objects, called **Case** and **Article**, and you want to relate these two objects in such a manner that one case can have multiple articles and one article is linked to many cases, then we have to use the many-to-many relationship. The many-to-many relationship is made with the help of a junction object. In this case, we can create the third object, let's say, **Solution** with two master-detail relationships with **Solution – Case** and **Solution – Article**.

One object can have only two master-detail relationships.

Hierarchical relationship

In Salesforce, only a user object has this type of relationship where we can create a hierarchy of users in the organization. For example, a user can have his manager, and his manager may have senior manager, and so on till the CEO or CIO level. The best example is the manager field on a user object as shown in the following image:

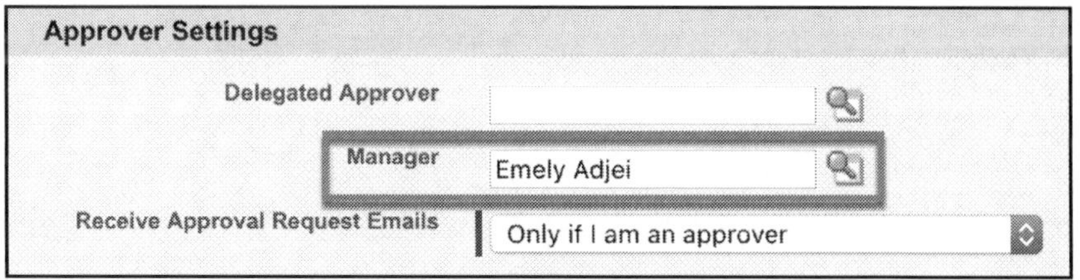

A few points to remember

1. Use permission sets to enable Lightning Experience for a set of users.
2. After *Summer'16* release, we can have 5 active processes on the Lightning Professional edition.
3. It is not possible to change standard objects' and fields' API name.
4. We can add custom fields to standard and custom objects in Salesforce.
5. We can have a maximum of 40 lookup relationships on an object.
6. We can have a maximum of two master-detail relationships on an object.
7. Each Salesforce organization can have up to 100 external objects.
8. When we delete a custom object, it appears in the **Deleted Objects** list for 15 days, from where the system administrator can restore it.
9. Salesforce doesn't allow us to delete a custom field that is used in a roll-up summary field on another object or reference in Apex and Visualforce pages.
10. If a custom object contains more than 100,000 records and you want to delete it, then first delete an appropriate number of records and then delete the object.
11. By default, Lightning Experience is now enabled for all standard profiles.

Test your knowledge

Q1. What types of paid Salesforce editions are available?

1. Lightning Enterprise Edition
2. Lightning Unlimited Edition
3. Lightning Trial Edition
4. Developer Edition

Q2. What are the two ways to get the record ID?

1. Dashboard
2. Report
3. Data Loader
4. Validation Rule

Q3. After how many days is a deleted record permanently removed from the recycle bin?

1. 10
2. 15
3. 30
4. 45

Q4. What is the total number of custom fields we can create in a Lightning Enterprise Edition custom object?

1. 300
2. 500
3. 800
4. Unlimited

Q5. It is possible for a Salesforce object to exist independently of an application.

1. True
2. False

Q6. What is the maximum number of master-detail relationships that can be created on a custom object?

1. 10
2. 40
3. 2
4. 8

Q7. An organization wants to leverage a custom object to track sales orders. The organization wants the ability to relate orders to parent orders in a parent-child relationship. What type of relationship should be used?

1. Master-detail relationship
2. Self-relationship
3. Hierarchical relationship
4. Many-to-many relationship

Summary

In this chapter, we covered the overview of Salesforce Lightning Experience, as well as its comparison with Salesforce Classic. We also covered various Salesforce editions available in the market. We also went through standard, custom and external objects. In the end, we explored the types of relationships in Salesforce, including external lookup relationships and indirect lookup relationships. In the next chapter, we will go through the user management and security setting key concepts. In the meantime, don't forget to enable Lightning Experience in your developer organization.

2

Security Settings in Salesforce

This chapter starts with a high-level overview of company profile settings, followed by an overview of role hierarchy, profiles and **organization-wide default** (**OWD**) in Salesforce, which will help you to brush up the concepts that you will need as an administrator. We will also discuss permission sets, the various ways for an organization to manage users, and the key concepts related to this management. Later, we will go through how you can troubleshoot common business challenges related to record access and field visibility. All these concepts are very important as these are one time setups that will decide how your Salesforce organization will work in accordance with your organization's structure.

The following topics will be covered in this chapter:

- Using OWD to secure your organization's data
- Using the sharing rule to grant record access to users
- Securing record data using field-level security
- Managing profiles and permission sets in Salesforce

Company Information setup

In the last chapter, we went through ways of setting up a developer account. Now it's time to move forward to the next step. Company Information contains all basic information about your company, such as local address, fax number and phone numbers.

A business scenario: *Universal Containers* just brought Salesforce Lightning Unlimited Edition (LUE). *Richard Gall* has been working as the Salesforce administrator for two years, and he knows how to update the company's basic information, such as the company contact information, the default time zone, and the address.

Just to remind you, once the company has purchased the Salesforce organization, the company has to set up the company profile. Under the heading **Setup** (gear icon) | **Setup** | **SETTINGS** | **Company Settings** | **Company Information**, there are various setups available, as shown in the following screenshot:

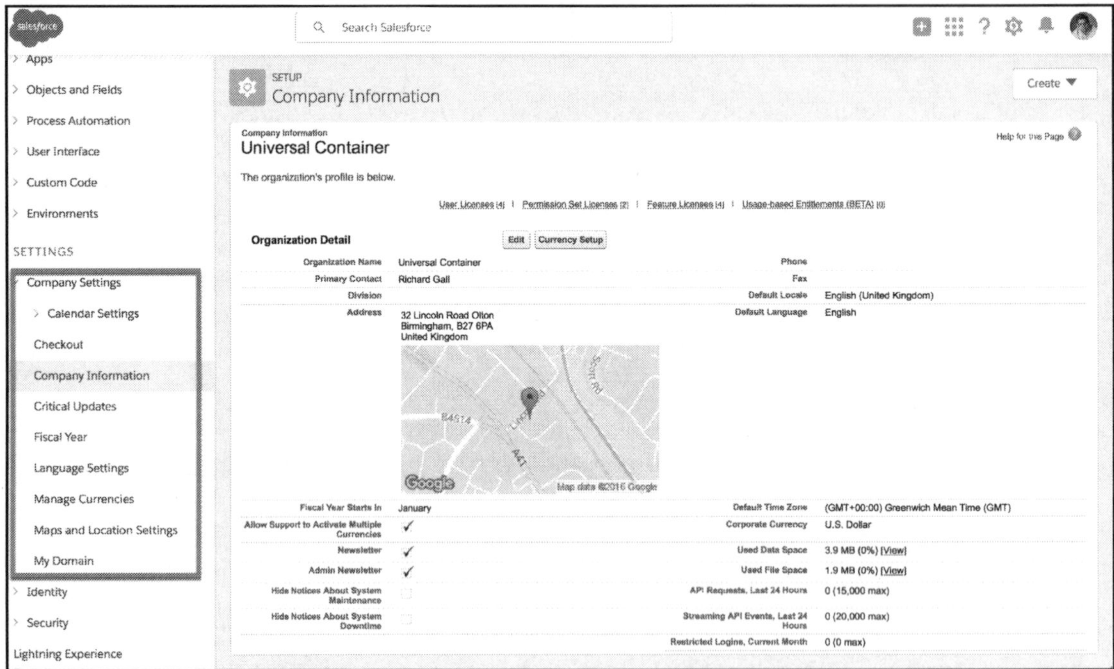

At any time, the system administrator can update the company information in Salesforce. The **Company Information** page contains the company address, company contact details, corporate currency, organization default time zone, language, and locale setting. You can also use it to find details about licenses, such as the licenses available, used, and remaining.

Viewing the licenses

In the **Company Information** page, it also displays all the user licenses, feature licenses permission set licenses, and Usage-based Entitlements (beta) you have purchased for your organization. On the **Company Information** detail page, the user can find the information about these licenses as follows:

- **User license type**: A user license allows a user to use different functionality within Salesforce and determines which profiles and permission sets are available to the user. You may have more than one type of user license in your organization.
- **Permission set license type**: You can assign permission sets to give a user access to certain features. However, sometimes permission sets require users to have a permission set license before they can be allotted the permissions in question.
- **Feature license type**: A feature license allows a user to use an additional Salesforce feature, such as marketing or connect offline.

Depending on the features that are enabled for your organization, you might be able to assign more than one type of feature license to users.

- **Usage-based Entitlements** (beta): Now you can control the number of monthly logins to a Partner Community or the record limit for Data.com list users.

You can check the latest licenses available here, as the license types are subject to change: `https://help.salesforce.com/HTViewHelpDoc?id=users_understanding_license_types.htm&language=en_US`.

Setting up multiple currencies

Let's start with a business scenario: *Richard Gall* is the Salesforce administrator at *Universal Containers*. His company has their footprint across the globe, generating businesses equally from the Americas, Asia and the Pacific, Europe, and the Middle East. Currently, only USD is enabled in his Salesforce organization, so the sales reps are finding it difficult to enter the right amounts in their local currency.

Multi currency is a Salesforce-limited and advanced feature. After enabling, sales reps can enter the amount in the opportunity field in their local currency. Organizations can also use multiple currencies in the forecasts, reports, quotes, and other currency fields. The administrator can set the *corporate currency*, which reflects the currency of the corporate headquarters. The administrator also maintains the list of active currencies and their conversion rates relative to the corporate currency. Now, let's say that *Richard Gall* decides to enable multiple currencies. He contacted Salesforce.com support and has it enabled a few days later in his sandbox.

Before contacting Salesforce, make sure that you have enabled the **Allow Support to Activate Multiple Currencies** setting on the **Company Information** page.

Enabling a single currency

In a single currency organization, you can set the organization-wide currency locale for your company, and your Salesforce users will not be able to set individual currency locales.

Adding a new currency

At any time, the system administrator can add a new currency to the organization. To do so, follow the steps given here:

1. Click on **Setup** (gear icon) | **Setup** | **SETTINGS** | **Company Settings** | **Manage Currencies**.

2. Click on **Add New** to add a new currency. It will redirect you to a new window where you can add new currency for your organization.
3. To do that, you have to select **Currency Type**, **Conversion Rate** (find it from an exchange website), and **Decimal Places**:

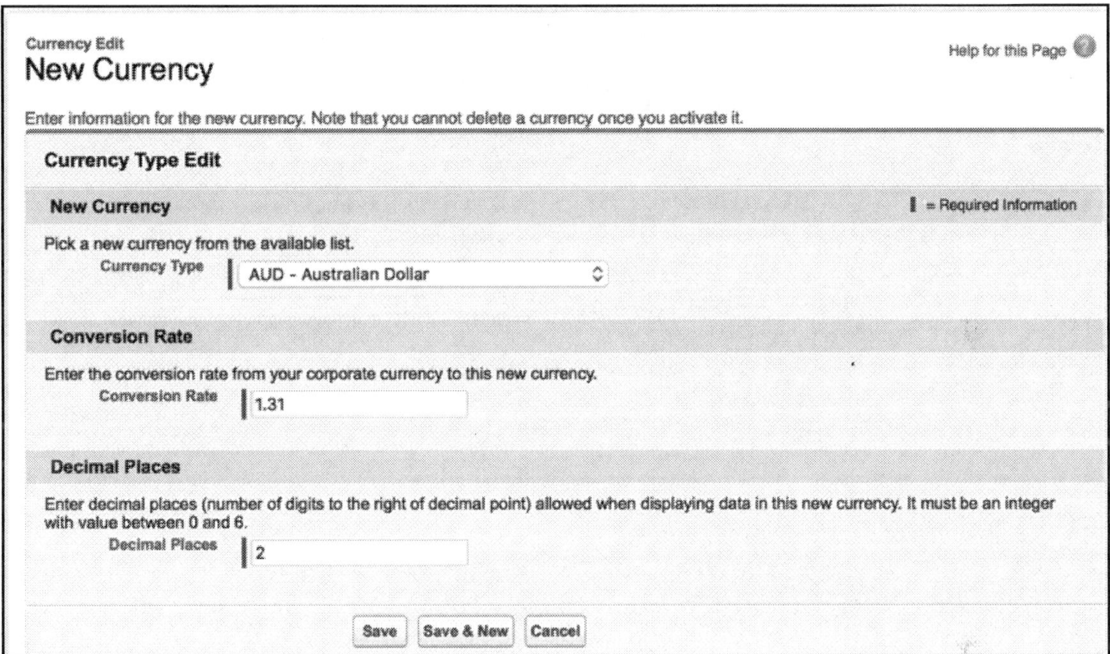

4. Once done, click on **Save**.

Changing corporate currency

At any time, system administrator can change the corporate currency of the organization. To do this, follow the steps given here:

1. Click on **Setup** (gear icon) | **Setup** | **SETTINGS** | **Company Settings** | **Manage Currencies**:

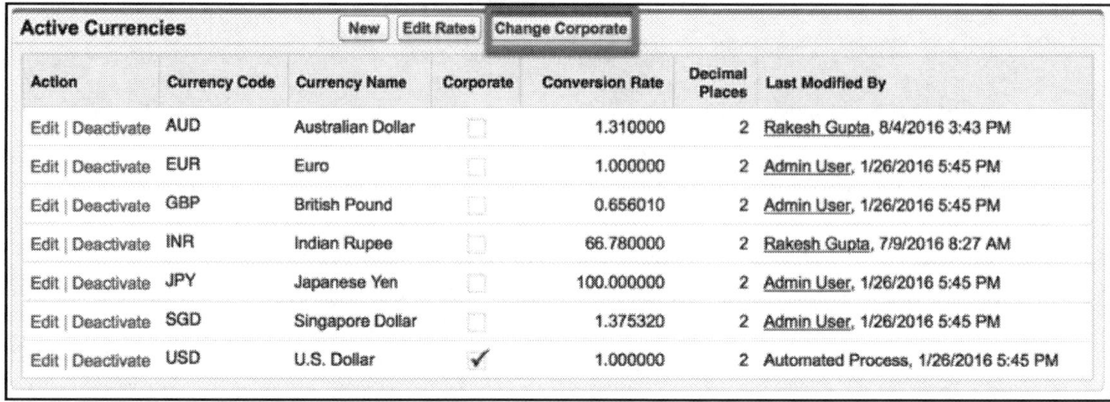

Active Currencies New Edit Rates Change Corporate

Action	Currency Code	Currency Name	Corporate	Conversion Rate	Decimal Places	Last Modified By
Edit | Deactivate	AUD	Australian Dollar	☐	1.310000	2	Rakesh Gupta, 8/4/2016 3:43 PM
Edit | Deactivate	EUR	Euro	☐	1.000000	2	Admin User, 1/26/2016 5:45 PM
Edit | Deactivate	GBP	British Pound	☐	0.656010	2	Admin User, 1/26/2016 5:45 PM
Edit | Deactivate	INR	Indian Rupee	☐	66.780000	2	Rakesh Gupta, 7/9/2016 8:27 AM
Edit | Deactivate	JPY	Japanese Yen	☐	100.000000	2	Admin User, 1/26/2016 5:45 PM
Edit | Deactivate	SGD	Singapore Dollar	☐	1.375320	2	Admin User, 1/26/2016 5:45 PM
Edit | Deactivate	USD	U.S. Dollar	✓	1.000000	2	Automated Process, 1/26/2016 5:45 PM

2. Click on **Change Corporate**.
3. It will redirect you to a new window from where you can select a new **Corporate Currency** for your organization.

The new **Corporate Currency** dropdown shows only those currencies that are currently active for your organization.

We will talk more about how we can use multi currency and its use cases in `Chapter 5`, *Getting More Value from Sales Cloud*.

Updating multi currency value

Once you have enabled multi currency in a Salesforce organization, the next step is to update the currency value either daily or periodically. As you all know, a currency's value changes every minute; it's tough for a system administrator to manage it manually. The following are the ways through which a system administrator can update the currency values in Salesforce:

- Use advanced currency management to update the currency values manually
- Use REST API to update the currency values directly from ERP or third-party websites
- You can also use an AppExchange app such as *S4G* (`https://appexchange.salesforce.com/listingDetail?listingId=a0N300000025GWyEAM`)

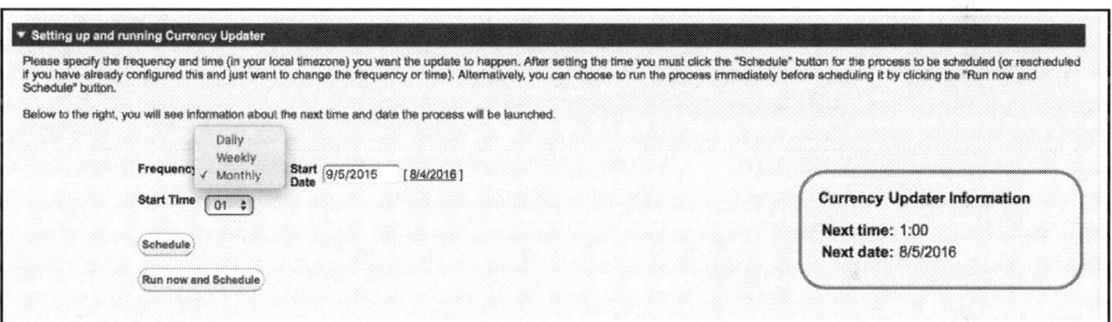

S4G Currency Updater lets you automatically update the exchange rates for your organization's currencies on a periodic basis. You can choose the frequency and time of the day when the update will happen.

Effects of enabling multi currency

Effects of enabling multi currency in your Salesforce organization are as follows:

- It is not possible to disable multi currency once enabled.
- All records have their default currency stamped; this is the currency that you mentioned at the time of enabling it.
- Opportunities, opportunity products, opportunity product schedules, and campaign objects are all fields that are multi currency compatible, which allows you to specify the currency for the record.

- Currency fields display the ISO code before the field value–for example, $10,000 is USD 10,000.
- Once you deactivate supportive currency, it can't be removed from the administrator's currencies list.
- Users can set their own personal default currency, which is known as the **secondary currency**. In the report (while running a report for the user) the primary default currency is shown as the organization's default corporate currency and the user's personal currency is shown as the secondary currency.

The fiscal year and its customization

A fiscal year or financial year is a period used for calculating annual (yearly) financial statements in businesses and other organizations. The system administrator can set the fiscal year for your organization. The fiscal year settings are used to report on the fiscal year timeline.

Salesforce supports two types of fiscal years:

- Standard fiscal year
- Custom fiscal year

Standard fiscal year

Salesforce provides the Gregorian calendar as the standard fiscal year calendar by default. But this is not the same for every organization as some organizations use different calendars and need to change the fiscal year start month. For example, our typical business year starts from 1st April and ends on the 31st March of the next year, which follows the standard fiscal year. Standard fiscal years can start on the first day of any month. Additionally, they can be defined whether the fiscal year is based on the start or the end of the selected month.

To set up the standard fiscal year for your organization, take the following steps:

1. Click on the **Setup** (gear icon) | **Setup** | **SETTINGS** | **Company Settings** | **Fiscal Year**.
2. Select the **Standard Fiscal Year** option.
3. Select the start month for the fiscal year.
4. Choose whether the fiscal year is defined based on the start or end of the month:

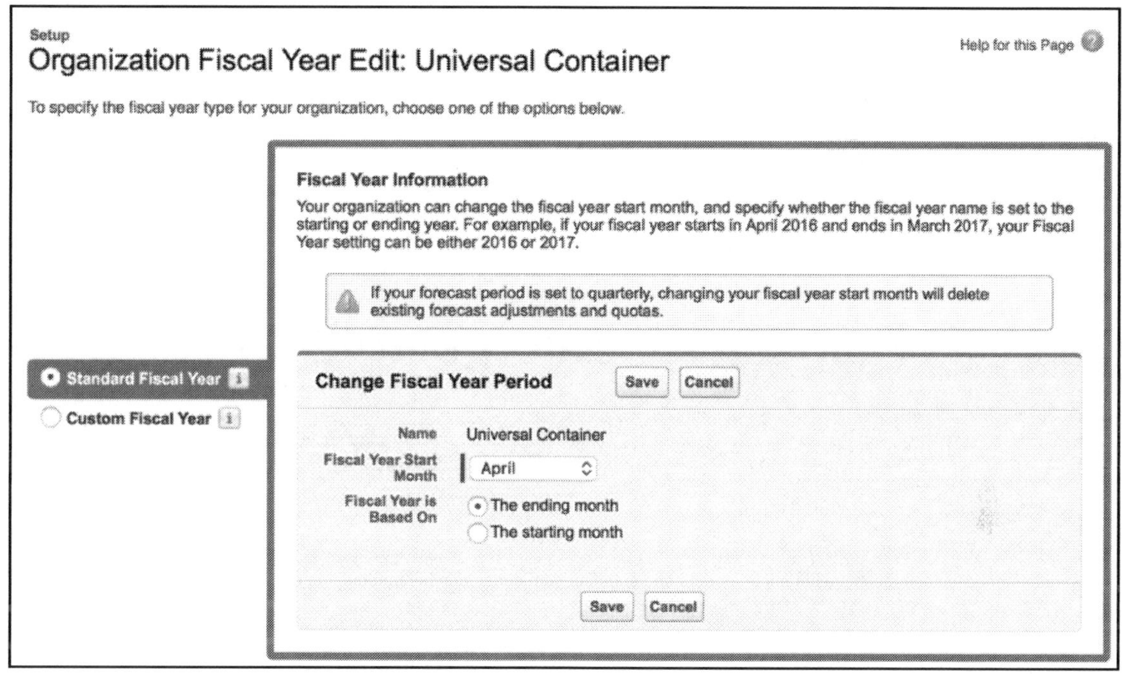

5. You could also select **Apply to All Forecasts and Quotas** if you want to apply the new fiscal year settings to your existing forecasts and quotas. This option may or may not be available depending on your forecast settings.
6. Click **Save**.

Custom fiscal year

The custom fiscal year is used when the standard fiscal year does not meet the organization's requirements. To use the custom fiscal year, the system administrator has to enable it. A complex fiscal year structure can be achieved using the custom fiscal year option. Enabling custom fiscal years does not automatically define them. You must define all of your company's custom fiscal years so that they fit your company's calendar.

To set up the custom fiscal year for your organization, take the following steps:

1. Click **Setup** (gear icon) | **Setup** | **SETTINGS** | **Company Settings** | **Fiscal Year**.
2. Select the **Custom Fiscal Year** option.
3. Select the checkbox, next to the statement **Yes, I understand the implications the custom fiscal year feature has on my organization and I want to enable it.**

4. Click **Enable Custom Fiscal Years**.
5. Click **OK**.

Enabling custom fiscal years is not reversible. After enabling custom fiscal years, you cannot revert to standard fiscal years.

Secure organization data using OWD

Organization-wide default is also known as OWD. This is the base-level sharing and setting of objects in any organization. By using this, you can secure your data so that other users can't access data to which they haven't been allowed access. The following diagram shows the basic record security in Salesforce. In this, OWD plays a key role:

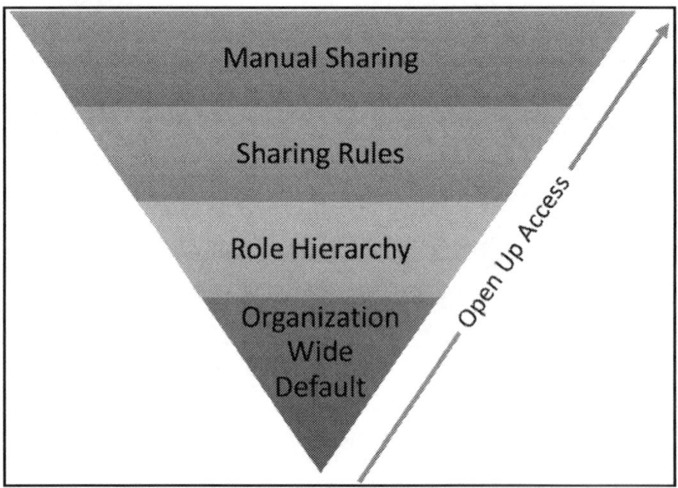

It's a base-level object setting in the organization, and you can't restrict the access below this. We will now discuss OWD in Salesforce.

A business scenario: *Alok Sinfal* is the system administrator at *Universal Containers*. As per the business requirement, he wants to set the security setting for the lead object so that the user who has created or owns the lead records, as well as users that are higher in the role hierarchy, can access the records.

Before thinking about any solution, you have to think about the OWD because it is the base-level setting to restrict object-level access in Salesforce. To achieve this, the system administrator has to set the OWD for **Lead** object to **Private**.

Setting up OWD

Use the following steps to change or update the organization-wide default setting for your organization:

1. Click **Setup** (gear icon) | **Setup** | **SETTINGS** | **Security** | **Sharing Settings** and then click **Edit** in the **Organization-Wide Sharing Defaults Edit** area.
2. From the **Default Internal Access** dropdown, select the default access for each object you want to use:

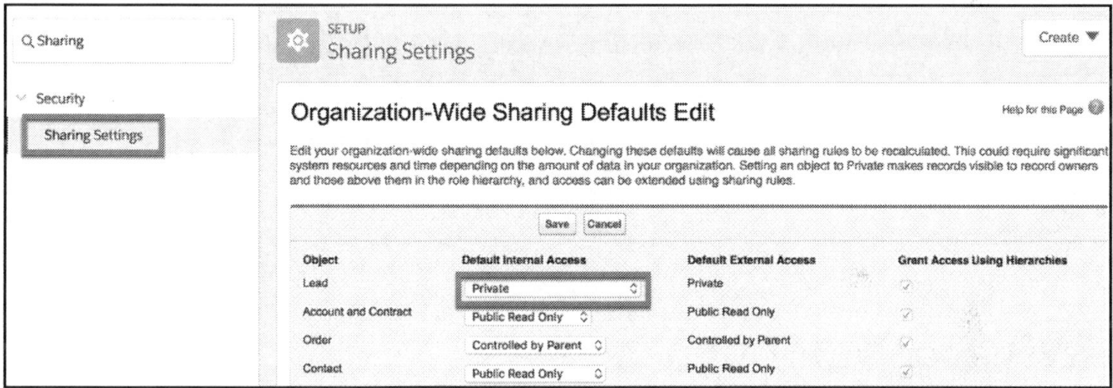

3. For the **Default Internal Access** option, select **Private** access for the **Lead** object. By default, it grants access to users who are at a higher position in the role hierarchy by selecting **Grant Access Using Hierarchy**. For standard objects, it is automatically selected and for custom objects you have the option to select it.
4. Click **Save**.

The following table depicts the various types of organization-wide access and their description:

OWD Access	Description
Private	Only the owner of the records and the user above in the role hierarchy are able to access and report on the records.
Public Read Only	All users can view the records, but only the owners and the users above in the role hierarchy can edit them.
Public Read/Write	All users can view, edit, and report on all records.
Public Read/Write/Transfer	All users can view, edit, transfer, and report on all records. This is only available for case and lead objects.
Controlled by Parent	This says that access to the child object's records is controlled by the parent.
Public Full Access	This is available for campaigns. In this, all users can view, edit, transfer, and report on all records.

If you are changing the default access, such as from **Public Read Only** to **Public Read/Write**, your changes will take effect after the recalculation is run.

OWD access for objects

A new Salesforce organization comes with predefined organization-wide default access settings for standard objects. Later on, you can change it by following the path **Setup** (gear icon) | **Setup** | **SETTINGS** | **Security** | **Sharing Settings**. The following table describes the default access to standard objects:

Object	Default Access
Account	Public Read/Write
Activity	Private
Asset	Public Read/Write
Campaign	Public Full Access
Case	Public Read/Write Transfer
Contact	Controlled by Parent

Contract	Public Read/Write
Custom Object	Public Read/Write
Lead	Public Read/Write Transfer
Opportunity	Public Read Only
Users	Public Read Only and Private for external users

Now it's your turn. *Alok Sinfal* is working as system administrator at *Universal Containers*. Apart from their sales management, they are also using Salesforce to process employee salaries, using the custom object `Bank Detail`, to save their employees' preferred bank account details. *Alok Sinfal* has received a request from his manager *Brigette Hyacinth* to change the security and settings for `Bank Detail` object so that only users who created the record for the `Bank Detail` object can access it, no one else can have the power to view, edit, or delete it.

When you select the **Grant Access Using Hierarchy** field, it provides access to people who are above in the role hierarchy.

Role hierarchy

Salesforce allows us to control the records access and organization reports using *role*. In other words, you can use it to control record-level access in Salesforce. It describes how roles connect to each other. It may or may not be exactly akin to your organization hierarchy. A *role* can have one, more than one, or even no users assigned to it. It is best practice to ensure that every user is assigned a role when they are first added to the system.

Users who are higher in the role hierarchy will be able to see the records of people below them. Users who share the same the role or who are at the same level (for example, the VP of Sales and the VP of Marketing) cannot access each other's records:

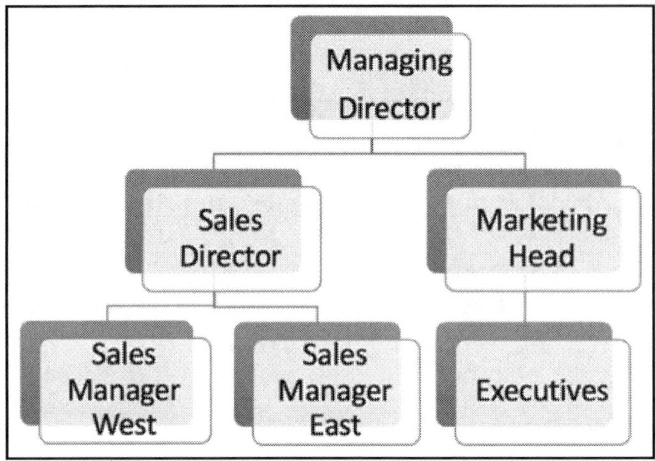

In the preceding image, the **Managing Director** can see all the organization records, as they are at the top of the role hierarchy. At the same time the **Sales Director** and **Marketing Head** can't see each other's records even though both are at the same level. While the **Sales Director** can access the **Sales Manager West** and **Sales Manager East** records, the **Marketing Head** can access the **Executives** records. The **Sales Manager West**, **Sales Manager**, and the **Executives** can see only their records as these roles are lower in the role hierarchy. Users at any role level can view, edit, and report on all the data owned by or shared with users below them in the role hierarchy.

In the preceding example, it is assumed that the OWD is **Private** for objects. To learn more about role hierarchy, please visit `https://developer.salesforce.com/trailhead/en/data_security/data_security_roles`.

Sharing rule

To open record-level access for groups of users, role, or role and subordinates outside of the OWD, you can use the sharing rule. The sharing rule is used to open up access; you can't restrict the access using the sharing rule. Salesforce has the following types of sharing rules:

- **Criteria-based sharing rule**: If you want to share the records based on the field values in the record, then you have to use a criteria-based sharing rule. For example, let's say you use a lead object to better manage prospects. A criteria-based sharing rule could share all lead records in which the **Country** field is set to `India` with all sales reps from APAC. You can have a maximum of 50 criteria-based sharing rules per object.
- **Owner-based sharing rule**: If you want to share the records based on the owner of a record, then you have to use an owner-based sharing rule. For example, let's say you use an account object to better manage customers. An owner-based sharing rule could share all account records in which the `owner` belongs to a public group `APAC` with another public group `EMEA`.
- **Manual sharing**: When the OWD is set to **Private** or **Public Read Only** for any object, then a **Sharing** button will be enabled in the record detail page, using which the record owner, or users who are at a higher position in the role hierarchy, can share records with other users. Visibility of the buttons can be controlled with help of page layout.
- **Apex managed sharing**: If you have a very complex business requirement, and you want to share the record access with users for a few hours or days, then you can use Apex-managed sharing. You can either use Apex or Flow with Process Builder to handle such scenarios. To access the sharing object programmatically, you must use the share object associated with the standard or custom object with which you want to share.

Criteria-based sharing rule

A business scenario: *Alok Sinfal* is working as system administrator in *Universal Containers*. His manager *Brigette Hyacinth* wants every user in the organization to be able to view the lead records, but only a group of users (that is, a public group: **Global Sales**) can edit it if the lead **Country** field is set to `India`.

Perform the following steps to solve this requirement:

1. First of all, change the **Lead** object **Organization-Wide Sharing Defaults Edits** to **Public Read Only** by following the path **Setup** (gear icon) | **Setup** | **SETTINGS** | **Security** | **Sharing Settings**. This way, all users from the organization can view the lead records:

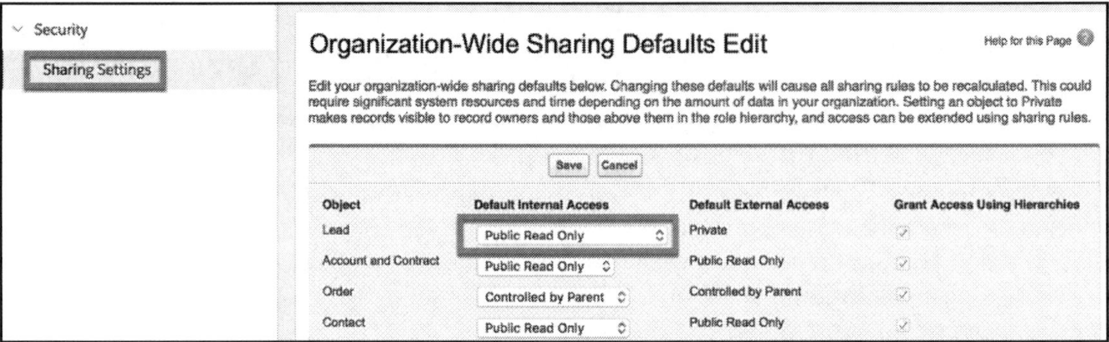

2. Now create a public group **Global Sales** and add users as per the business requirement.
3. The next step is to create a sharing rule by following the path **Setup** (gear icon) | **Setup** | **SETTINGS** | **Security** | **Sharing Settings** and navigating to the **Lead Sharing Rules** list:

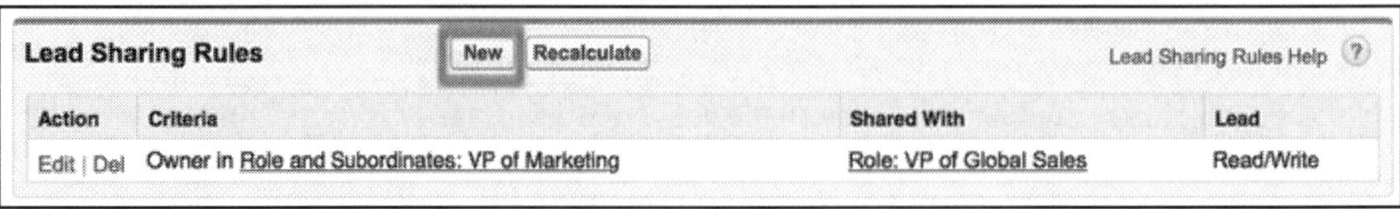

4. Click on **New**, and it will redirect you to a new window where you have to enter the **Label**, **Rule Name**, and **Description** (always write a description so that other administrators or developers know why this rule was created).
5. Then for the **Rule Type**, select **Based on criteria**. For the criteria by which records are to be shared, create a criteria such as **Country** equals `India`.
6. Then select the public group with whom you want to share the records, in this case select **Global Sales**

7. The final step is to choose the level of access for the users. For the preceding business requirement, select **Read/Write** from the dropdown.

   When you have reached the end, your screen should look like the following screenshot:

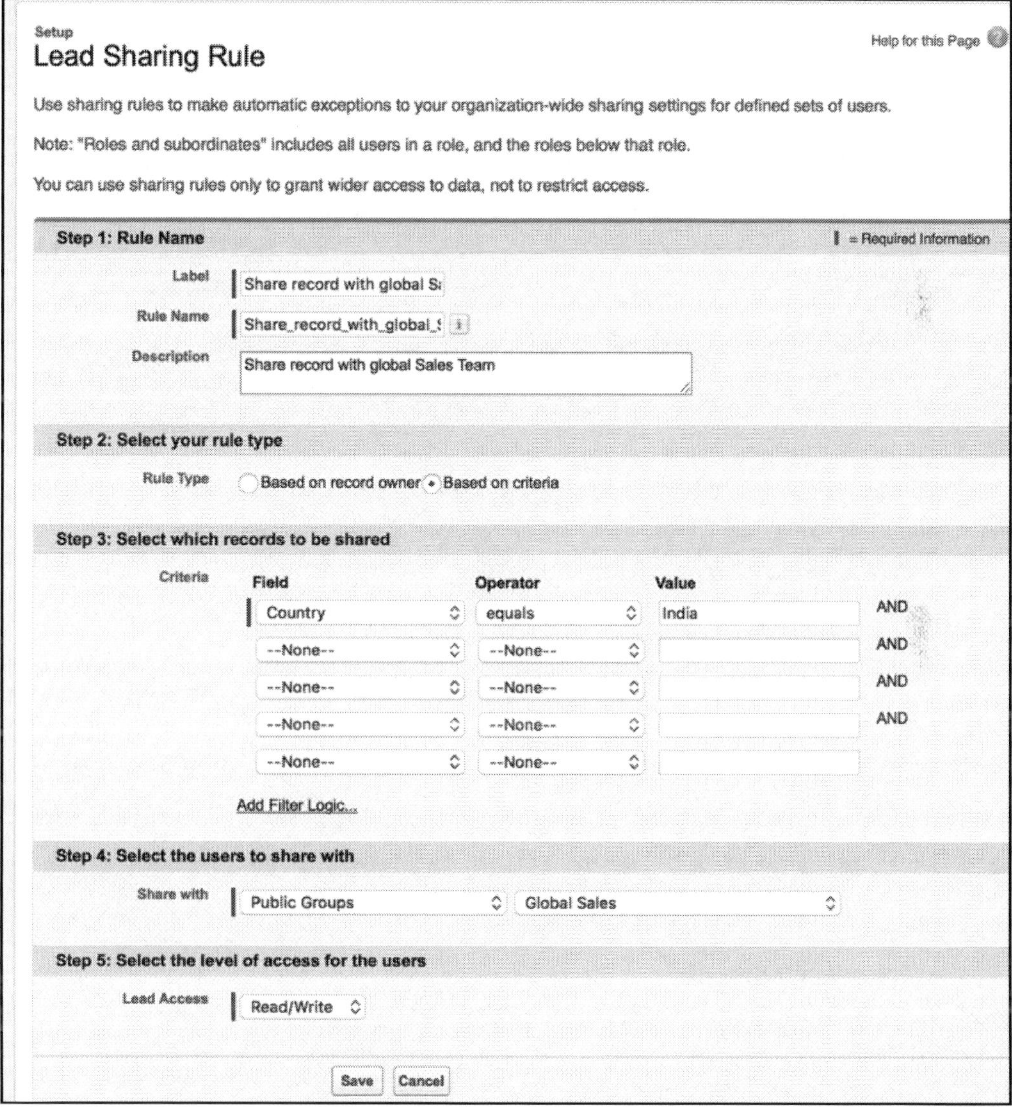

8. Once you are done, click **Save**.

Manual sharing

When the OWD is set to **Private** or **Public Read Only** for any object, then a **Sharing** button will be enabled in the record detail page. From here, the record owner or users who are at a higher position in the role hierarchy can share records with other users. Currently, Lightning Experience doesn't support the manual sharing feature, so if you want to use manual sharing then switch back to Salesforce Classic:

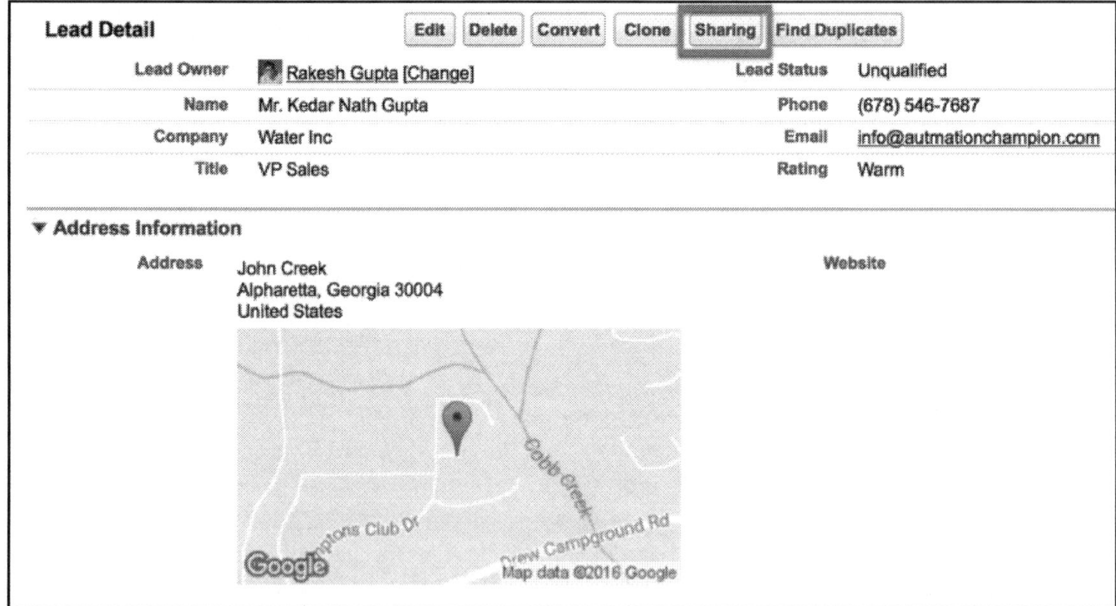

To manually share the record, click on the **Sharing** button and it will redirect you to a new window. Then click on the **Add** button and you are ready to share records with the following:

- Public groups
- Users
- Roles
- Roles and subordinates
- Personal groups
- Manager groups
- Manager subordinate groups

The final step is to select the access type. Once you have done this, click **Save**. It will look like the following screenshot:

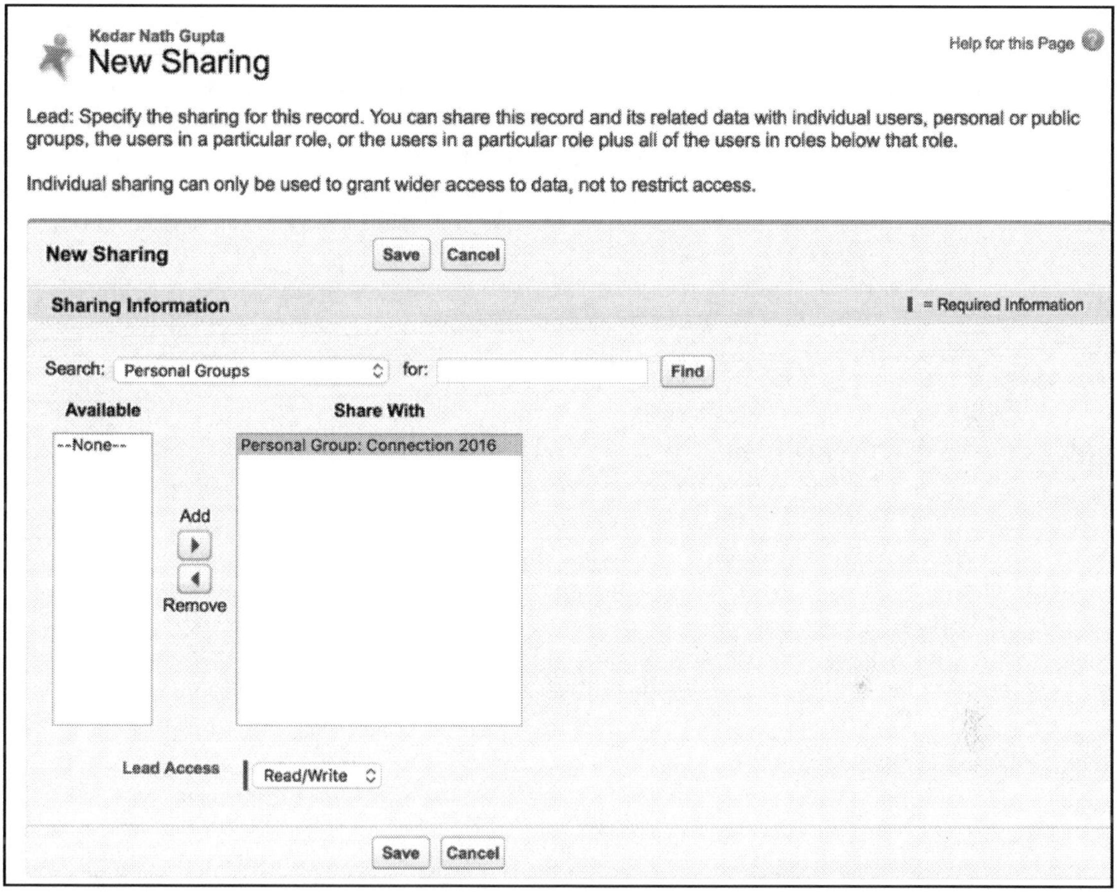

Kedar Nath Gupta
New Sharing
Help for this Page

Lead: Specify the sharing for this record. You can share this record and its related data with individual users, personal or public groups, the users in a particular role, or the users in a particular role plus all of the users in roles below that role.

Individual sharing can only be used to grant wider access to data, not to restrict access.

New Sharing Save Cancel

Sharing Information = Required Information

Search: Personal Groups for: Find

Available: --None--

Add / Remove

Share With: Personal Group: Connection 2016

Lead Access: Read/Write

Save Cancel

The **Lead** and **Case Sharing** buttons will be enabled when OWD is set to **Private**, **Public Read Only**, and **Public Read/Writ**e.

Apex managed sharing

When all other sharing rules can't fulfill your requirements, then you can use the Apex sharing method to share records. Using the Apex managed sharing rule, you can be able to handle complex sharing. For example, say you want to share the case record access with a field support worker for a few hours or days; in this scenario, you can use Apex managed sharing. You can either use Apex or Flow with Process Builder to handle such scenarios. To access the sharing object programmatically, you must use the share object associated with the standard or custom object for which you want to share. We will talk more about how we can use Flow and Process Builder to create Apex managed sharing in `Chapter 8`, *Automating Complex Business Processes*.

Defer sharing calculations

If you are changing the organization-wide access for an object, such as from **Public Read Only** to **Public Read/Write**, your changes take effect after the recalculation is run, and recalculation may take one minute to several hours depending on whether customization happens in your Salesforce organization. The same thing happens if you change the user role; on the backend, Salesforce will run all sharing rules. For each update, it has to recalculate all the access rights and sharing rules, and if a user has lots of accounts and other records, then it will take a long time. It means that if the recalculation runs in the background, then you are not allowed to create a new sharing rule or modify any security settings (such as the organization-side default or the sharing rule) in Salesforce:

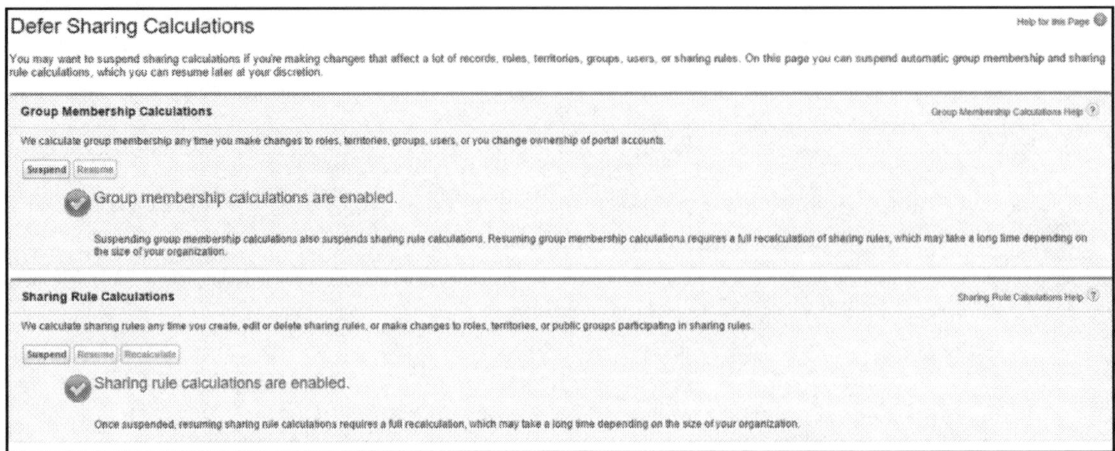

If you want to overcome such a scenario, then you have to enable one limited feature by raising a support ticket called **Defer Sharing Calculations**. If you have an object that utilizes sharing and has a large volume of records (such as more than three million leads), and you need to make a bulk change (such as a periodical realignment requiring a hierarchy change), then there is a limited feature that can be enabled by Salesforce support to defer automatic sharing calculations. By default, every single change to the role hierarchy, groups, sharing rules, territory hierarchy, user roles, team membership, or ownership of records can initiate automatic sharing calculations. When a bulk change is made, it causes many automatic sharing recalculations to begin. By suspending these temporarily, you can make the change and then have the sharing calculations happen all at once. Enable this feature when you need to suspend sharing calculations during maintenance windows to have a minimal impact on users.

Profiles

Profiles are a way to customize the overall experience of a Salesforce user. Profiles are used to decide the data security by granting object-level permissions and field-level security that decides which fields need to be shown to which specific set of users. Profiles have certain rules or settings that we can set in order to grant or restrict a set of user permissions. The role decides record-level access in Salesforce and the profile decides what users can see in those records, as well as which actions the user can perform.

Different types of profiles

There are two types of profile in Salesforce:

- **Standard**: Profiles which come with standard CRM when you purchase a new Salesforce organization. You cannot delete these profiles.
- **Custom**: Custom profiles are profiles that we create by cloning the existing Salesforce standard profiles.

The major difference between both the profiles lies in their applicable permissions and settings; administrative permissions, general user permissions, object-level permissions, and the **Password Never Expires** setting can't be applied to the standard profile. You can only delete a custom profile when users are not assigned to it.

The following is list of a few important standard profiles available in Salesforce:

Profile	Description
System Administrator	System administrators have full access to Salesforce. They are allowed to configure and customize the application.
Standard Platform User	These users are allowed to use custom apps developed by the organization or installed from AppExchange and the main functionality of the platform.
Standard Platform One App User	Users with this profile can access one custom app developed in your organization or one installed from AppExchange. The custom app is limited to five tabs. In addition, they can use core platform functionality such as accounts, contacts, reports, dashboards, and custom tabs.
Standard User	Users with this profile are allowed to create and edit most major types of record, run reports, and view the organization's setup. They can view, but not manage, campaigns. They can also create, but not review, solutions. They can edit personal quotas and override forecasts.
Partner User	Users are only allowed to log in from a partner portal.
Marketing User	Users can manage campaigns, import leads, create letterheads, create HTML e-mail templates, manage public documents, and update the campaign history via the import wizards. They can also act as a standard user.
Contract Manager	Users are allowed to create, edit, activate, and approve contracts. This profile can also delete contracts as long as they are not activated. They can edit personal quotas and override forecasts.
Chatter Only User	Only allowed to log in to Chatter. Allowed access to all standard Chatter features: people, profiles, groups, and files. Additionally, they can view Salesforce accounts and contacts, use Salesforce CRM content, ideas, and answers, and modify up to 10 custom objects.
Chatter Free User	Only allowed to log in to Chatter. Can access all standard Chatter features: people, profiles, groups, and files. Only available with the Chatter Free user license.
Chatter External User	Allowed to only log in to Chatter and access groups they've been invited to. They are allowed to interact with members of only those groups. Only available with the Chatter external user license.
Site.com Only User	Can only log in to the Site.com app.

High-Volume Customer Portal And Authenticated Website (both user licenses are high-volume portal users)	Can log in only from a customer portal.
Solution Manager	Users with this profile are allowed to review and publish solutions. They can also act as a standard user.
Read Only	Users with this profile can view all records, but cannot edit them.

It is always best practice to create a new profile by cloning it from a **Read Only** profile, because a read only profile comes with minimum permissions and it's easy to add or remove such permission.

Permission sets

Salesforce allows you assign only one profile to a user, but sometimes it's necessary to assign more than one profile to users based on your business requirements. Through the permission set, you can grant a group of settings and permissions to your users that allows them to access various apps and functions, in addition to the profile. The settings available in these permission sets are similar to those in profiles, but they extend the user's functional access without changing their profiles.

A business scenario: *Eric Cordell* is working as *Sales Manager West* at Universal *Containers*. As per the initial business requirement, *Sales Manager West* can only access the opportunity records for an account that belongs to North America. Over the past few years, Eric helped Universal Containers to increase their sales pipeline from $15 million to $40 million. Now Sales Director *Merint Mathew* wants to grant all opportunities access (either edit or delete) to *Eric Cordell*, so he can manage it and generate more revenue.

To solve the preceding business requirement, you have the following options:

1. Create a new profile that is a combination of the *Sales Manager West* profile and **Modify all** permissions on opportunity objects (not a recommended solution, as it is very hard to manage).
2. Using the sharing rule, you can only grant **Read** or **Read/Write** permission, not delete.
3. Use permission set to grant **Modify all** permission on opportunity objects (recommended solution). In future, you can assign the same permission set to other users who have different profile.

Settings available under permission sets

Use permission sets to grant the following access to users:

- **Assigned apps**: Select the apps whose access you want to grant to users.
- **Object settings**: You can grant the following permissions to users:
    - Tab settings
    - Record type settings
    - Object permissions
    - Field-level permissions
- **App permissions**: Select the app-specific permission you want to grant to users.
- **Apex class and Visualforce page access**: This defines which Apex classes and Visualforce pages users can access.
- **Service providers**: Use this only if you've enabled Salesforce as an identity provider.
- **Custom permission**: Using this you can grant permission to access custom processes and apps to users.
- **System permissions**: Here you can define permissions to perform actions that apply across apps, such as **Password Never Expires**.

Creating a permission set

Perform the following steps to create a new permission set:

1. Click **Setup** (gear icon) | **Setup** | **ADMINISTRATION** | **Users** | **Permission Sets** and then click on the **New** button, as shown in the following screenshot:

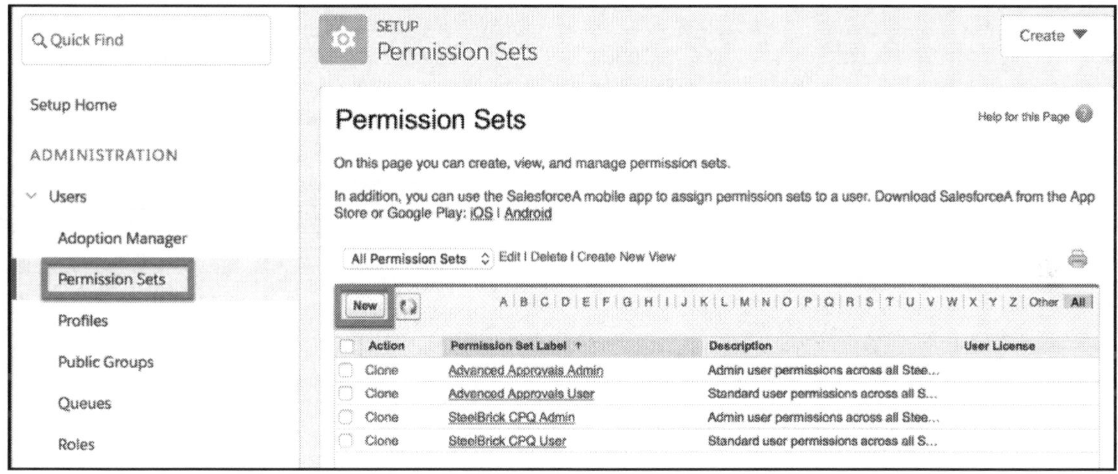

2. It will redirect you to a new screen from where you can create a new permission set. To create a permission set, enter the **Label, API Name**, and **Description**, and select **User License** from the dropdown:

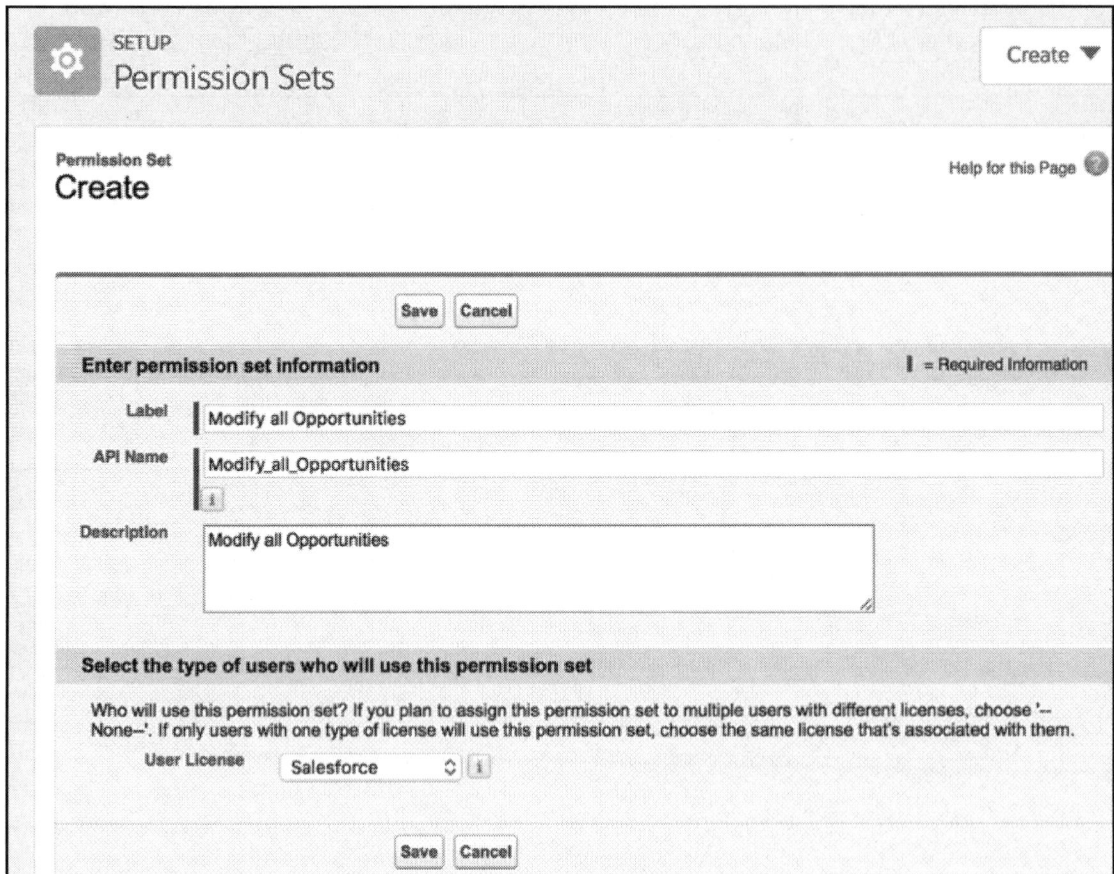

3. Once you are done, click **Save**.

If you are planning to assign the permission set to all users who have the same user license type, it is best practice to associate that user license with the permission set. But if you are planning to assign the permission set to users who currently have different licenses (or might have different licenses in the future), it is probably best to create a permission set without a **User License** type.

Field-level security

Until now, we have talked about record-level access; it refers to governing which records are accessible by users, including the OWD and sharing rule. Now we will go a step further and discuss how we can hide key fields from a group of users. Data is very important for any organization; it may contain highly sensitive information, such as bank account details. Salesforce allows you to use field-level security to make fields hidden or read only for a specific profile. There are three ways to set field-level security in Salesforce:

- From an object field
- From a profile
- Field accessibility

From an object field

A business scenario: *Alok Sinfal* is working as *system administrator* at *Universal Containers*. His manager *Brigette Hyacinth* wants to set the **Rating** field on the **Lead** object to be read-only for all users because they have a process created to auto-set the rating for lead objects based on a few fields.

Perform the following steps to solve the preceding business requirement:

1. Click on **Setup** (gear icon) | **Setup** | **PLATFORM TOOLS** | **Objects and Fields** | **Object Manager** and then click on the **Lead** object.
2. Now navigate to the **Fields & Relationships** section, and click on the **Rating** field.

3. The next step is to click on the **Set Field-Level Security** button, as shown in the following screenshot. It will redirect you to a new page where you can set the field-level security:

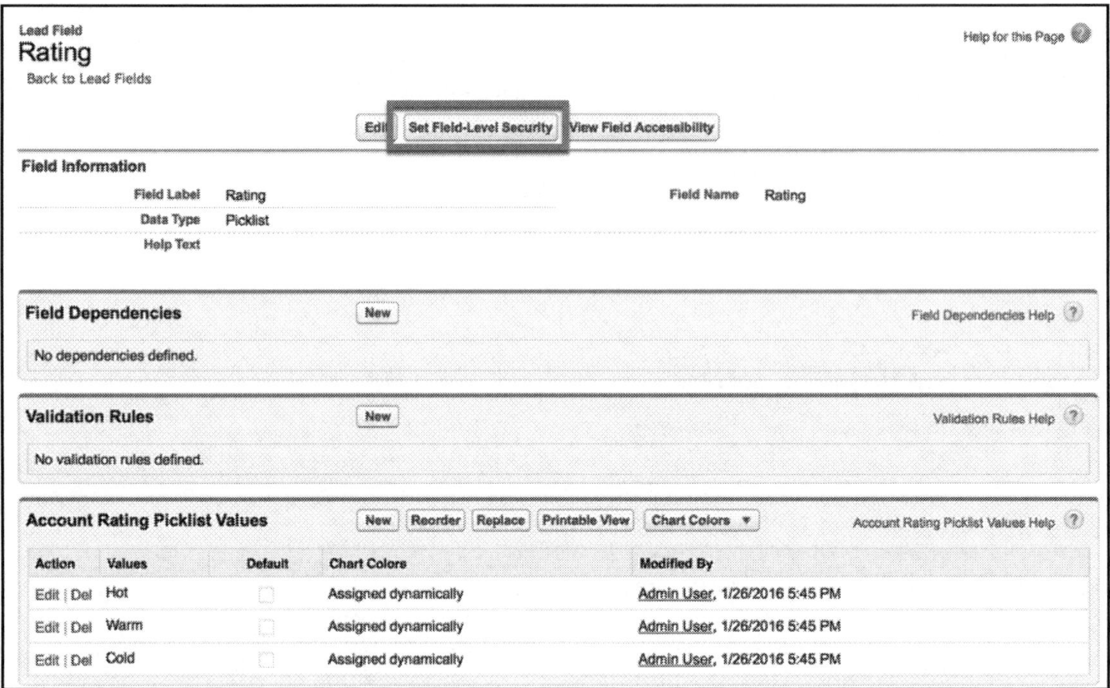

4. Select **Visible** and **Read-Only** for all profiles other than that of the **System Administrator**. For **System Administrator**, select only **Visible**, as shown in the following screenshot:

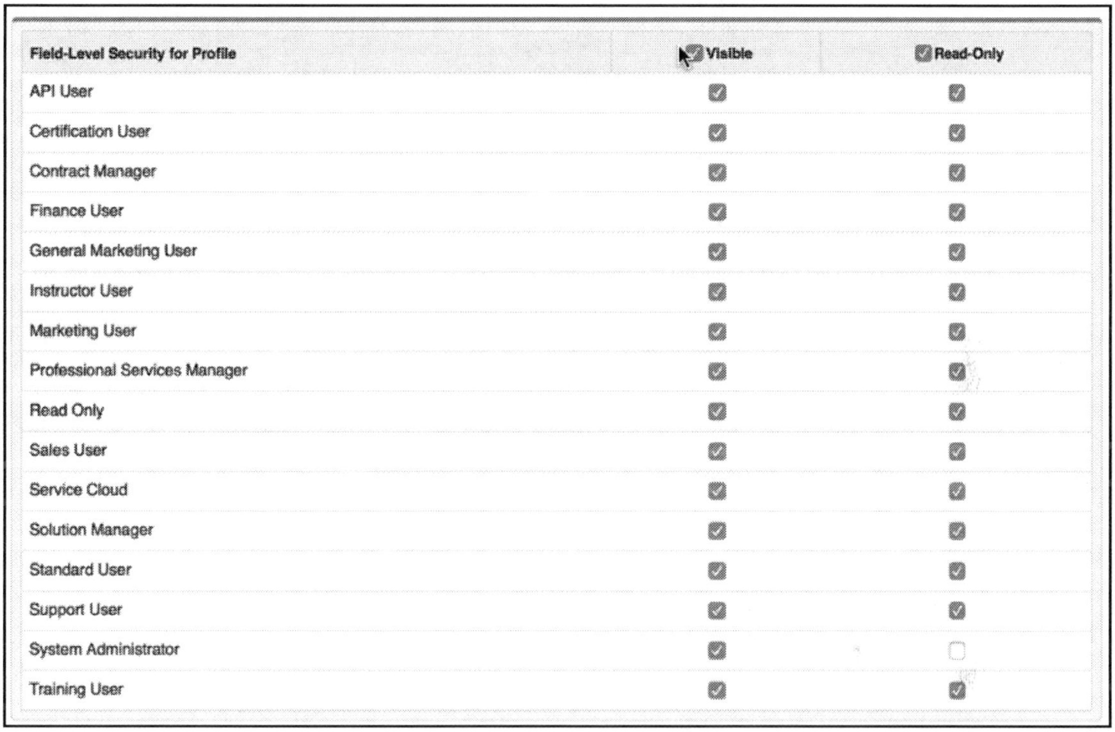

Field-Level Security for Profile	☑ Visible	☑ Read-Only
API User	☑	☑
Certification User	☑	☑
Contract Manager	☑	☑
Finance User	☑	☑
General Marketing User	☑	☑
Instructor User	☑	☑
Marketing User	☑	☑
Professional Services Manager	☑	☑
Read Only	☑	☑
Sales User	☑	☑
Service Cloud	☑	☑
Solution Manager	☑	☑
Standard User	☑	☑
Support User	☑	☑
System Administrator	☑	☐
Training User	☑	☑

5. Once you are done, click on **Save.**

Through profile

The field-level setting is also available on the profile. Perform the following steps to solve the preceding business requirement using profile settings:

1. Click on **Setup** (gear icon) | **Setup** | **ADMINISTRATION** | **Users** | **Profiles**, then click on the **System Administrator** profile.
2. Under the **Apps** section, click on **Object Settings**, and then select the **Lead** object.

3. The next step is to click on **Edit** and navigate to the **Field Permission** section, as shown in the following screenshot:

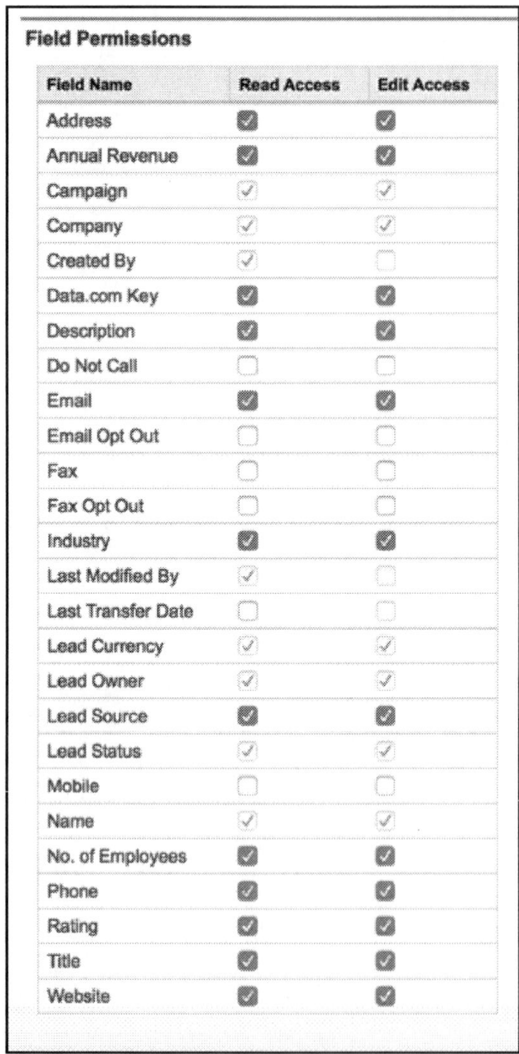

Field Permissions

Field Name	Read Access	Edit Access
Address	☑	☑
Annual Revenue	☑	☑
Campaign	☑	☑
Company	☑	☑
Created By	☑	☐
Data.com Key	☑	☑
Description	☑	☑
Do Not Call	☐	☐
Email	☑	☑
Email Opt Out	☐	☐
Fax	☐	☐
Fax Opt Out	☐	☐
Industry	☑	☑
Last Modified By	☑	☐
Last Transfer Date	☐	☐
Lead Currency	☑	☑
Lead Owner	☑	☑
Lead Source	☑	☑
Lead Status	☑	☑
Mobile	☐	☐
Name	☑	☑
No. of Employees	☑	☑
Phone	☑	☑
Rating	☑	☑
Title	☑	☑
Website	☑	☑

From here you can set the **Field-Level Security** for **Lead** object fields.

Field accessibility

We can achieve a similar outcome by using **Field Accessibility** option. Perform the following steps to solve the preceding business requirement using **Field Accessibility**:

1. Click on **Setup** (gear icon) | **Setup** | **SETTINGS** | **Security** | **Field Accessibility**.
2. Click on the **Lead** object. It will redirect you to a new page where you can select **View by Fields** or **View by Profiles**.
3. For the preceding business requirement, select **View by Fields** and then select the field **Rating.**
4. Click on the **Editable** link as shown in the following screenshot:

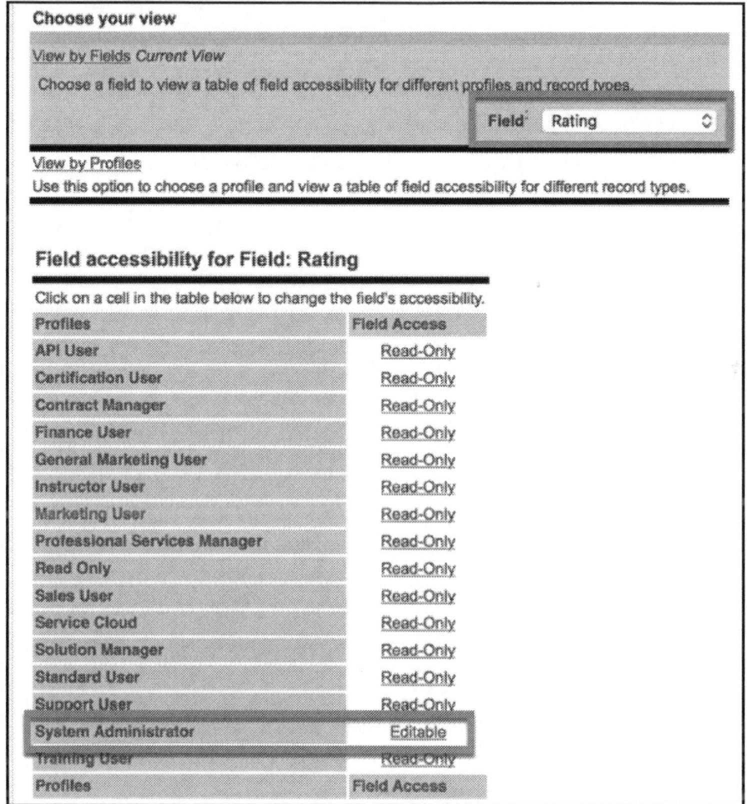

5. It will open the **Lead Settings for Lead Field** page, where you can edit the field-level security. Once done, click **Save**.

Viewing Setup and Audit Trail

Salesforce keeps an Audit Trail of configuration changes made in the **Setup** section. Audit Trail helps the organization administration track recent setup changes. This is very helpful if there are multiple administrators for an organization.

A business scenario: *Alok Sinfal* is working as *system administrator* at *Universal Containers*. He has just received an e-mail from business user *Nishant Nagre*, who says that someone has recently reset his password (because Nishant has received a password reset e-mail from Salesforce). If Alok Sinfal wants to track who did this, then he has to use **Setup** and **Audit Trail** in Salesforce. Only the system administrator or a user with **View Setup and Configuration** permissions can use this feature. To access the **Audit Trail**, click on **Setup** (gear icon) | **Setup** | **SETTINGS** | **Security** | **View Setup Audit Trail**.

Audit Trail key concepts

You can check **Audit Trail** for the following types of changes:

- **Administration**: It will track various administration changes, such as changes in company information, multiple currencies, users, e-mail address, profile, roles, record types, creating e-mail footers, domain names, and many others.
- **Customization**: These changes are related to changes to the interface, forecast, contract, ideas, field tracking in feeds, support-related settings, process setups, and changes to groups.
- **Security and sharing**: These are related to security settings and sharing, such as password policy changes, session setting changes, changes in SAML settings, and so forth.
- **Data management**: These changes are related to the mass deletion of records, data export requests, the mass transfer of records and import wizard usage, changes in analytic snapshots, and so on.
- **Development**: This change is related to Apex classes, triggers, and Visualforce. Changes can include modifications to triggers, classes or Visualforce, remote site access setup, and Force.com sites setup.
- **Various setups**: Various setup changes, such as the creation of an API, usage metering notifications, territories usage, workflow and approvals settings, AppExchange package installation/uninstallation, and the creation and deletion of workflow actions are tracked.

- **Using the application**: These changes are related to changes to the account team and opportunity team selling settings, Google App services, and the enabling and disabling of partner and customer portal users.

If you want to learn more about the types of changes that **Audit Trail** history can track go to this link: `https://help.salesforce.com/htviewhelpdoc?id=admin_monitorsetup.htm&siteLang=en_US`

A few points to remember

1. If you want to change the fiscal year start month, and your company follows the Gregorian calendar year, then use standard fiscal years
2. It is not possible to disable custom fiscal years once enabled. Enabling custom fiscal years has impacts on your reports, forecasts, quotas, and other date-sensitive material.
3. Once multiple currencies are enabled for your organization, it is not possible to disable them.
4. The **Sharing** button may appear on an account detail page even though your sharing model for accounts is **Public Read/Write**, if your sharing model for related opportunities is **Public Read Only**.
5. By default, Salesforce uses hierarchies, for example the *role* or *territory* hierarchy, to automatically grant records access to users above the record owner in the hierarchy.
6. It is not possible to include high-volume portal users in sharing rules because they don't have roles and can't be in public groups.
7. The sharing rule is always used to open up the access. By
8. It is not possible to delete standard profiles in Salesforce.
9. If you select the **Read-Only** checkbox under object **Field-Level Security**, then the visible checkbox will automatically get selected.
10. You can see the last 20 entries under **Setup Audit Trail**. If you wish, you can download the last six months' data for your organization.
11. Using permission set, we can only open up permission and cannot restrict them.

Test your knowledge

Q1. Who are the two types of users that can grant sharing privileges on a given record?

1. Record Owner
2. Group Members
3. Queue Members
4. Anyone higher in the role hierarchy

Q2. Which of the following tools assists in auditing EXCEPT?

1. Reports
2. Field history
3. Page layout
4. Setup Audit Trail

Q3. How many days of audit history can you download?

1. 20
2. 90
3. 180
4. 365

Q4. When creating a sharing rule, you can share the data with which of the following entities?

1. Public groups
2. Users
3. Roles
4. Roles and subordinates
5. Queues

Q5. What settings can you configure on a profile?

1. Revoke sharing permissions
2. Enable record types
3. Enable read, create, edit, and delete on objects
4. Specify language

Q6. An organization wants to create a field to store manager data on the user object. What type of relationship should be used?

1. Master-detail
2. Hierarchical
3. Lookup
4. Many-to-many

Q7. Which of the following is true about a junction object?

1. A custom object that has two master-detail relationships
2. A custom object that has two lookup relationships
3. A standard object that has two master-detail relationships
4. A standard object that has a master-detail relationship

Q8. A business user is complaining that the lead e-mail field is no longer on the page layout. What should you check?

1. Field history tracking
2. System log
3. Field audit
4. Setup Audit Trail

Q9. How can Eric Cordell become the owner of a lead record he did not create?

1. By accepting the record from a queue
2. By being above the current owner of the record in the role hierarchy
3. By already being a record owner
4. By having someone share the record with him
5. By having Modify All Data permission

Q10. A sales user has been asked to assist with an upcoming major sales project that he will need additional permissions for. Since other users share the same profile, how would you grant access to him without granting access to other sales users?

1. Permission set
2. Sharing rule
3. Role hierarchy
4. Field accessibility

Summary

In this chapter, we discussed the company profile and its various settings. Then we moved ahead and discussed organization-wide access, followed by the sharing and setting options available in Salesforce. We also learned the customization guidelines that we need to set up our organization's role hierarchy in Salesforce. We also covered the profiles needed to restrict user access to certain features available in Salesforce. We discussed how to use permission sets to grant permission to a set of users. In the end, we discussed Audit Trail and its key concepts. In the next chapter, we will go through territory management in Salesforce.

3
Territory Management

This chapter starts with a high-level overview of Territory Management. We will also discuss how to enable Enterprise Territory Management, and look at the key concepts related to it. Later, we will go through how to define a territory model and assign users to it. All these concepts are very important to consider as Territory Management is a one-time setup, and these concepts will dictate how your Salesforce organization will work in accordance with your organization's territory structure. The following topics will be covered in this chapter:

- Introduction to Territory Management
- Difference between role hierarchy and territory hierarchy
- Difference between Territory Management and Enterprise Territory Management
- Enterprise Territory Management key concepts
- Configuration of Enterprise Territory Management

Introduction to Territory Management

Territory Management is an account-sharing model that grants access to accounts based on the attributes of the accounts. It empowers your company to edifice your Salesforce data and business users the same way you manage your sales territories:

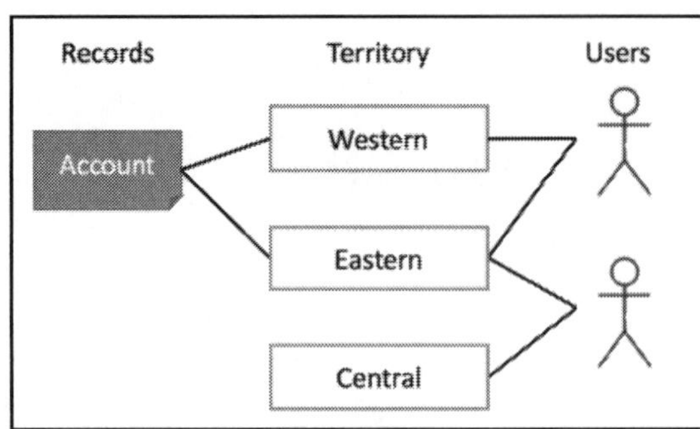

A territory is a collection of the account records and business users where the users have minimum read access to the accounts, irrespective of who owns the account records. By enabling territory settings, users can get read, read/write, or owner-like access to the accounts in that territory. Both users and accounts can exist in multiple territories. Salesforce allows you to add accounts manually to territories or define account assignment rules that assign accounts to territories for you. It also makes it possible to control users' access to the opportunities and cases related to the accounts in the territory, irrespective of who owns the records.

Salesforce's original Territory Management feature allowed you to grant users access to accounts based on specific criteria, such as zip code, industry, type, or a custom field. Enterprise Territory Management builds on top of the original feature by introducing territory types, territory models, and territory model states.

Difference between role hierarchy and territory hierarchy

Territory Management works in parallel with other sharing functionalities. You have to manage both the role hierarchy and the territory hierarchy. The following is a list of a few key differences between the role hierarchy and the territory hierarchy:

Role hierarchy	**Territory hierarchy**
A user has a one role.	A user can be part of multiple territories.
An account is owned by a single user.	An account can be belonged to multiple territories.
An account is accessible by the owner and users above in the role hierarchy.	An account is accessible by all users in the territories to which it is assigned, as well as those above them in the territory hierarchy.
Role hierarchy affects sharing settings for all standard and custom objects in Salesforce.	Territory Management only affects the sharing settings of accounts and the standard objects that have a master-detail relationship to accounts.

The differences mentioned in the preceding table apply to the original Territory Management feature, and not to Enterprise Territory Management.

Difference between Territory Management and Enterprise Territory Management

The following is a list of a few key differences between Territory Management and Enterprise Territory Management:

Territory Management	**Enterprise Territory Management**
Available in organizations that were created prior to *Winter'15*.	Available by default in organizations that were created in *Winter'15* or after.
An administrator can set up the territory access for accounts, contacts, cases, and opportunities.	An administrator can set up the territory access level for accounts. Users are automatically granted access to associated contacts, cases, and opportunities.

If only one territory is common to both the account and opportunity owner, Salesforce automatically assigns the opportunity to the territory in common.	Uses the filter-based **Opportunity Territory Assignment** rule to assign opportunities to a territory.
Customizable forecasting must be enabled. Forecasts are derived from territory hierarchy, not forecast hierarchy.	Can be used with collaborative forecasts. Forecasts are derived from forecast hierarchy, not territory hierarchy.

In this book, we will cover Enterprise Territory Management.

Enterprise Territory Management key concepts

Now we will explore the features and related concepts that make Enterprise Territory Management easy for you. Understanding these concepts will help you design your territories more effectively:

- **Territory type**: Territory types help you to manage your territories by key characteristics significant to your company. Every territory you create must belong to a territory type. Territory types are used for organizing and creating territories only.
- **Territory**: A territory contains the groups of accounts and the users who work with those accounts.
- **Territory type priority**: This feature will help you choose the correct territory type for territories you create or edit. By default, there are no priorities defined, so you have to create your own priority system. For example, 001 may indicate that a territory type is the highest priority or the lowest.
- **Territory model**: This represents a complete Territory Management system for your organization. It also includes a hierarchy and a list view of parent and child territories.
- **Territory hierarchy**: It shows a model's territory structure. Start from the hierarchy to create, edit, and delete territories; run assignment rules for territories.

- **Territory model states**: A territory model state shows whether a territory is in the **Planning** stage, **Active** stage, or **Archived**. Your organization can have only one active territory model at a time. The territory model's life cycle states are as follows:
    - **Planning**: This is the default state for every new territory model. It allows you to preview a model's territory hierarchy before deploying it.
    - **Active**: This is the state of a territory model after you activate it and all processing has completed.
    - **Archived**: This is the state of a territory model after you archive it and all processing has completed.

Configuring Enterprise Territory Management

You can use Enterprise Territory Management to manage and maintain your sales territories in Salesforce. First, create territory types, build a model, and then finally add and test your account assignment rules. When you're done with your model, activate it, and then assign users and accounts.

Enabling Enterprise Territory Management

Following the *Winter '15* release, Enterprise Territory Management is ready to be enabled by Salesforce administrators in new organizations. Organizations that were created before the *Winter '15* release need to call Salesforce support to enable the feature. It is not possible to enable Enterprise Territory Management in existing organizations that have customizable forecasting enabled.

Enterprise Territory Management is available in Salesforce Classic only. To enable Enterprise Territory Management, follow the steps given as follows:

1. In the Salesforce Classic view, click on **Setup | Administer | Manage Territories | Settings**, and then click on the **Enable Enterprise Territory Management** button, as shown in the following screenshot:

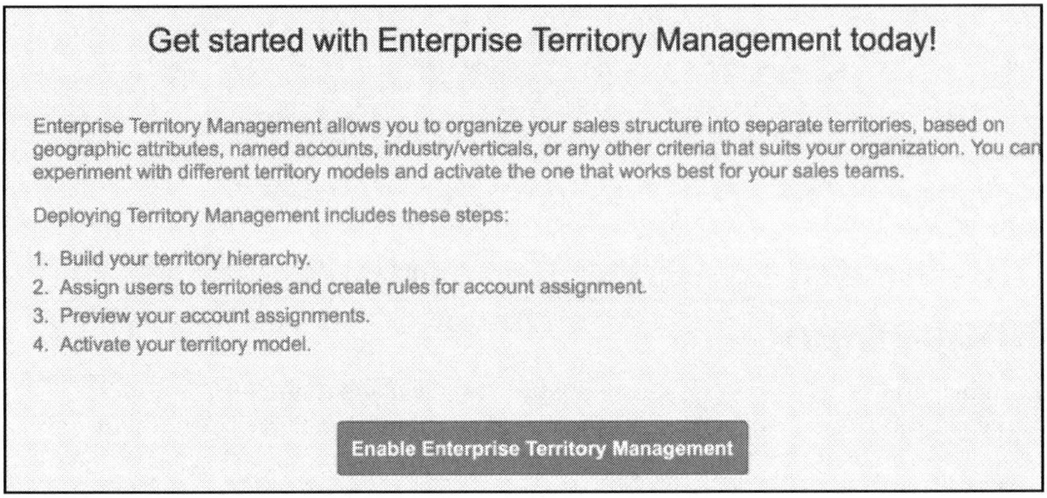

Get started with Enterprise Territory Management today!

Enterprise Territory Management allows you to organize your sales structure into separate territories, based on geographic attributes, named accounts, industry/verticals, or any other criteria that suits your organization. You can experiment with different territory models and activate the one that works best for your sales teams.

Deploying Territory Management includes these steps:

1. Build your territory hierarchy.
2. Assign users to territories and create rules for account assignment.
3. Preview your account assignments.
4. Activate your territory model.

Enable Enterprise Territory Management

2. The next step is to define the **default user access** for records associated with the sales territories you set up. Select the default access levels you want for accounts, opportunities, and cases. Depending on your organization-wide default settings, you may have to select the access level for contacts as well:

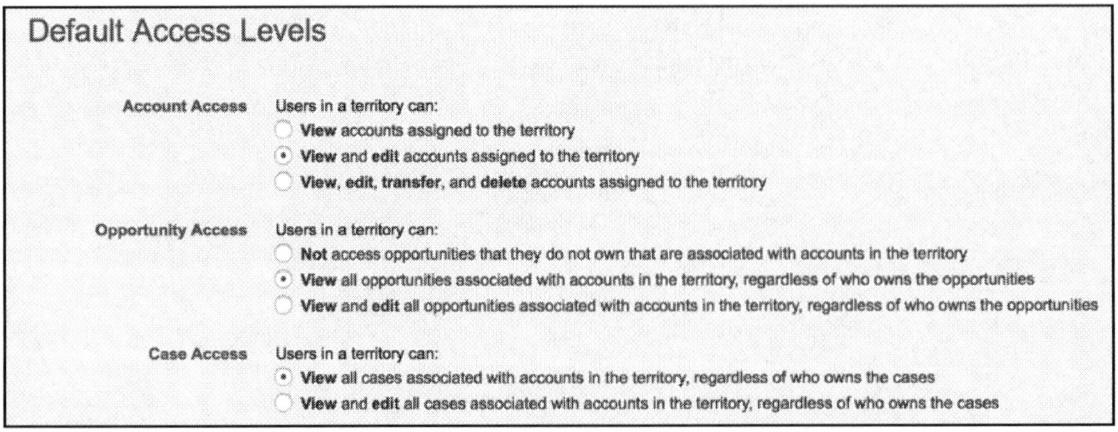

Default Access Levels

Account Access Users in a territory can:
- **View** accounts assigned to the territory
- **View** and **edit** accounts assigned to the territory
- **View, edit, transfer,** and **delete** accounts assigned to the territory

Opportunity Access Users in a territory can:
- **Not** access opportunities that they do not own that are associated with accounts in the territory
- **View** all opportunities associated with accounts in the territory, regardless of who owns the opportunities
- **View** and **edit** all opportunities associated with accounts in the territory, regardless of who owns the opportunities

Case Access Users in a territory can:
- **View** all cases associated with accounts in the territory, regardless of who owns the cases
- **View** and **edit** all cases associated with accounts in the territory, regardless of who owns the cases

3. The final step is to enable and configure the filter-based assignments of territories to opportunities. Select **Enable Filter-Based Opportunity Territory Assignment**, if you are planning to use the Apex code Salesforce provides the create Apex class first and enter the class name `OppTerrAssignDefaultLogicFilter`. Select **Run filter-based opportunity territory assignment job when opportunities are created**, if you want to run the opportunity territory assignment rule when opportunities are created:

Opportunity Territory Assignment

Assignment Filter ☑ Enable Filter-Based Opportunity Territory Assignment
Apex Class Name: OppTerrAssignDefaultLogicFilter
☑ Run filter-based opportunity territory assignment job when opportunities are created

4. Once done, click on **Save**.

You can find the Apex code provided by Salesforce at the following URL: `https://developer.salesforce.com/docs/atlas.en-us.apexcode.meta/apexcode/apex_interface_TerritoryMgmt_OpportunityTerritory2AssignmentFilter.htm`

Building a territory model

A territory model organizes all the elements of your organization's Territory Management in one place, including a territory hierarchy, account assignments, and user assignments. Keep your model in the **Planning** state until you build your hierarchy, define assignment rules for territories, add users to territories, and run your rules to see the resulting account assignments.

Creating territory types

Territory types help you categorize and define different territories. Creating territory types is the first step in building your territory model in Salesforce. To create the territory types, follow the steps given as follows:

1. Click on **Setup** | **Administer** | **Manage Territories** | **Territory Types**.

2. Click on the **New Territory Type** button; it will redirect you to the new territory type page.
3. Enter the **Label** as `Direct Accounts`; you can also add a **Description**. Make sure that you specify a territory type priority:

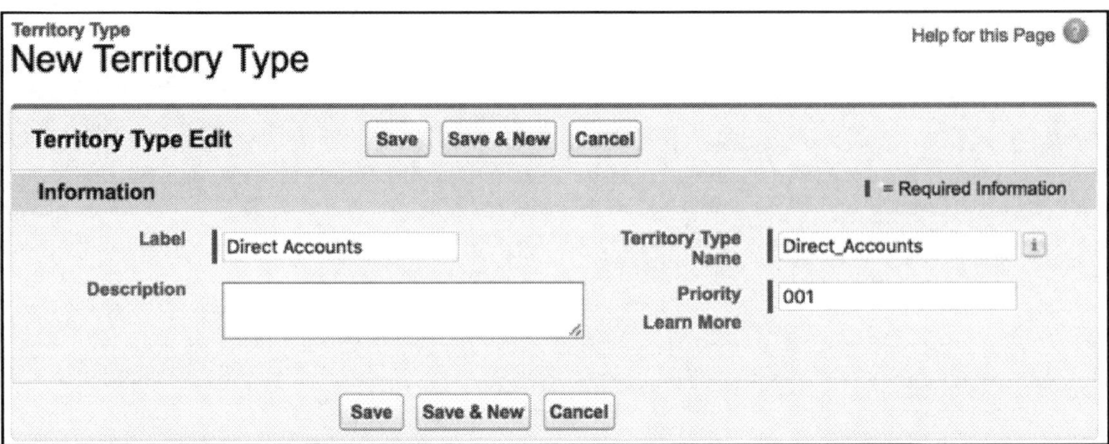

4. Once done, click on **Save**.

Creating a territory model record

The first step in building your territory model is creating the record that connects the elements, such as territories, user assignments, and account assignments. When you create a territory model record, Salesforce generates a territory hierarchy for it. To create the territory model record, follow the steps given as follows:

1. Click on **Setup** | **Administer** | **Manage Territories** | **Territory Models**.
2. Click on the **New Territory Model** button; it will redirect you to the new territory type page.
3. Enter the **Label** as `Worldwide Sales`; you can also add a **Description**:

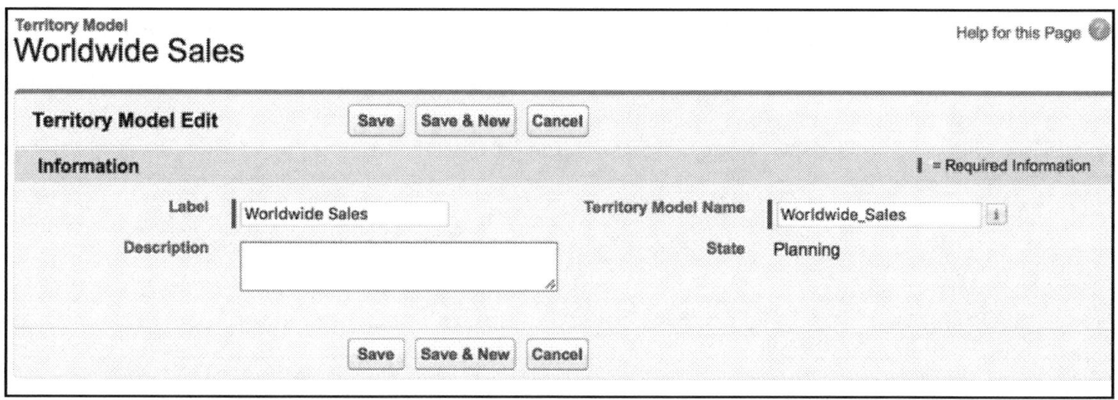

4. Once done, click on **Save**.

Defining the territory hierarchy

You should create a territory hierarchy as you build your organization's territory model. When you create a territory, it appears on the model's territory hierarchy. To create the territory hierarchy, follow the steps given as follows:

1. Click on **Setup** | **Administer** | **Manage Territories** | **Territory Models**.
2. Open the territory model **Worldwide Sales** and then click on the **View Hierarchy** button to create or edit an existing territory hierarchy:

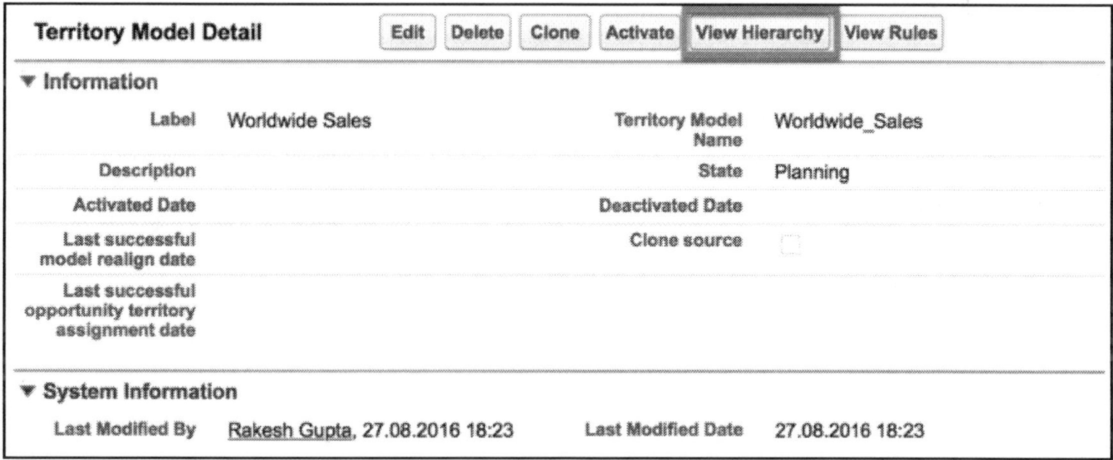

3. To create a top-level territory, hover over the territory model **Worldwide Sales** and click **Create Territory**:

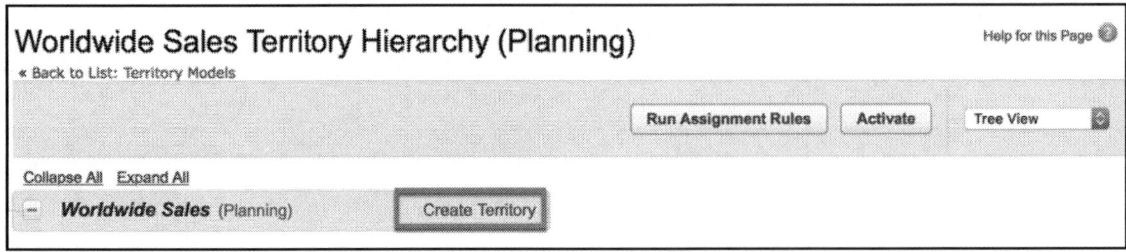

To create a child territory from an existing territory, hover over the territory name and click **Create Territory**.

4. On the **New Territory** page, enter the **Label** as `EMEA`, and choose a **Territory Type** as `Direct Accounts`; you can also add **Description**. Finally, define the territory users' access level for accounts, opportunities, and cases as the **default user access** for those records:

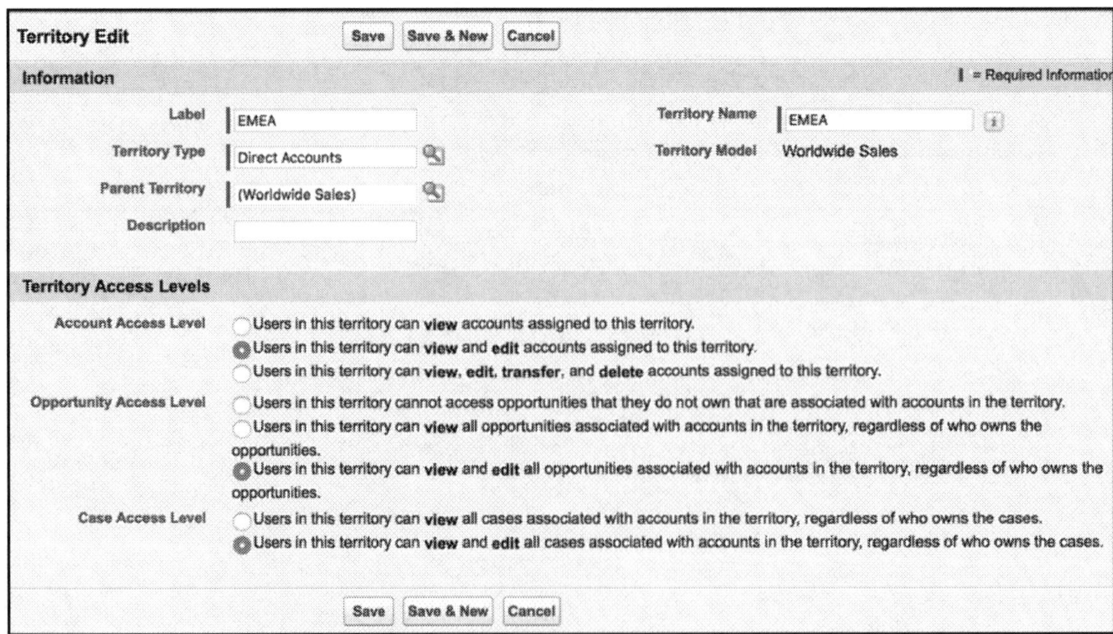

5. Once done, click on **Save**.

Likewise, define the complete territory hierarchy in a way similar to the following screenshot:

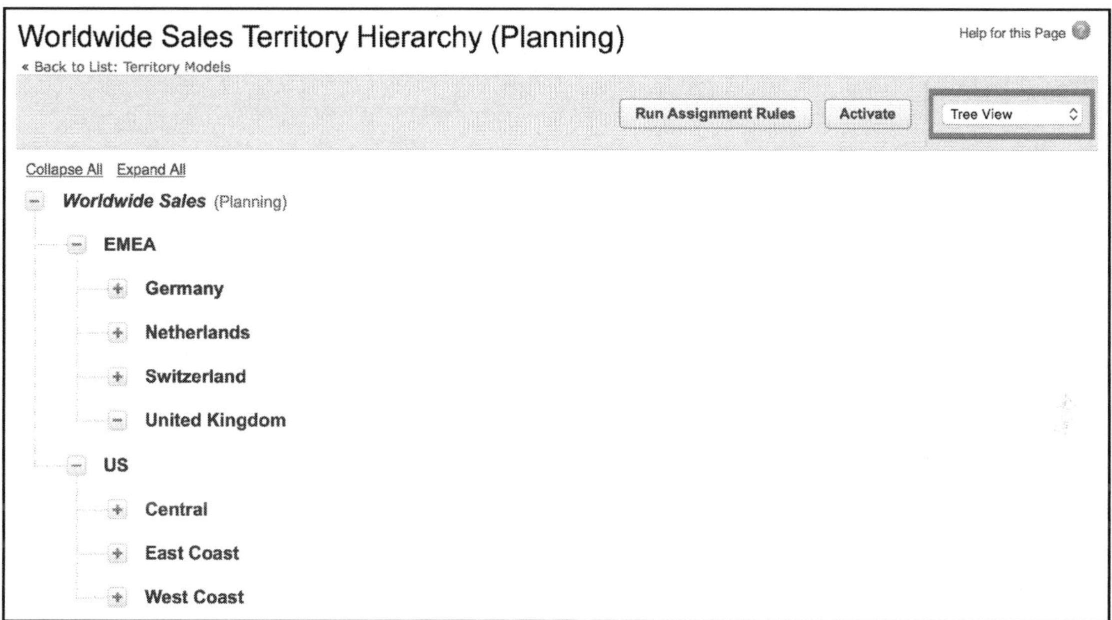

You can select the **Tree View** from the dropdown to show the model's territory hierarchy.

Creating a territory account assignments rule

You can assign accounts to territories either by using assignment rules that assign them automatically, or by adding them manually. Rules can be configured to apply to both parent territories and their descendants. Manual assignments apply only to the territory where they are made. Before you activate your territories' account assignments rule, make sure that you preview them by running assignment rules and related reports while the model is in a **Planning** state. When you are fully satisfied with your planned account assignments, change it to an **Active** state. Then, run the assignment rules again so that your territories include affected accounts that were created or updated during the activation process.

Assignment rules to assign accounts to territories

An assignment rule allows you to automatically assign new or edited accounts to territories. The rule identifies one or more criteria used to define that territory, and assigns accounts with those criteria to a specified territory automatically. If your territory is in a **Planning** state, running rules lets you preview account assignments. If your territory is in an **Active** state when you run the rules, accounts are assigned to territories according to your rules.

Consider a business scenario wherein, *David Guzman* is working as *system administrator* at Universal Containers. His manager *Brigette Hyacinth* wants to auto-assign an account to *West Coast* territory for the account's where billing state is California.

Perform the following steps to solve the preceding business requirement:

1. Click on **Setup** | **Administer** | **Manage Territories** | **Territory Models**.
2. Open the territory model **Worldwide Sales** and then click on the **West Coast** territory hierarchy.
3. Navigate to the **Assignment Rules Assigned to This Territory** related list and click on **New**.
4. Enter the **Rule Name** as `Billing State California`. For the criteria, select **Account: Billing State/Province** contains `California`.
5. If you want the rule to also apply to the current territory's descendants, select the **Apply to child territories** checkbox. For the current business scenario, don't select this checkbox. If you also want the rule to run automatically whenever a user creates or edits an account, select the **Active** checkbox:

Object Territory Assignment Rule Edit

Step 1: Enter the name of this rule

= Required Information

Rule Name: Billing State California

Unique Name: Billing_State_California

Step 2: Enter the selection criteria for this rule

Base your rule on object characteristics such as:

- Industry
- Annual revenue
- Number of employees
- Region

Field	Operator	Value	
Account: Billing State/Province	contains	California	AND
--None--	--None--		AND
--None--	--None--		AND
--None--	--None--		AND
--None--	--None--		

Add Filter Logic...

Step 3 (optional): Apply to child territories

Apply to child territories: Applies the rule to **West Coast** territory and its descendants

Step 4 (optional): Set as active

Active ✓

Learn More

Save | Save & New | Cancel

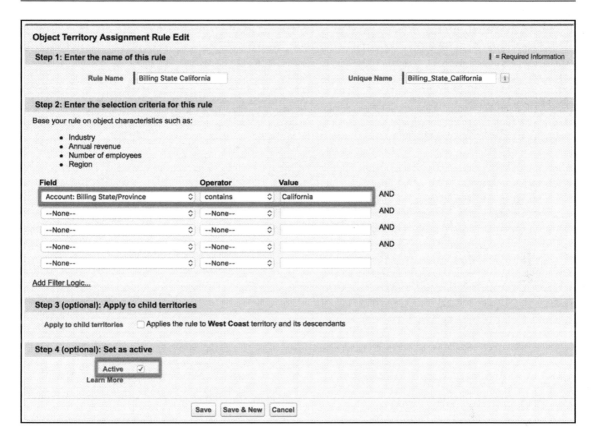

6. Once done, click on **Save**.
7. If you want to test the territory assignment rule for existing accounts, then click on **Run Rules**:

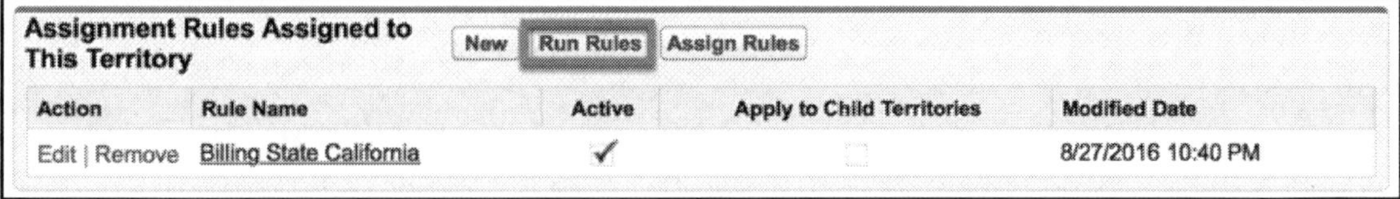

You'll receive an e-mail when the process is complete. Now, open an existing account where the billing state is California and check the **Assigned Territories** related list, as shown in the following screenshot:

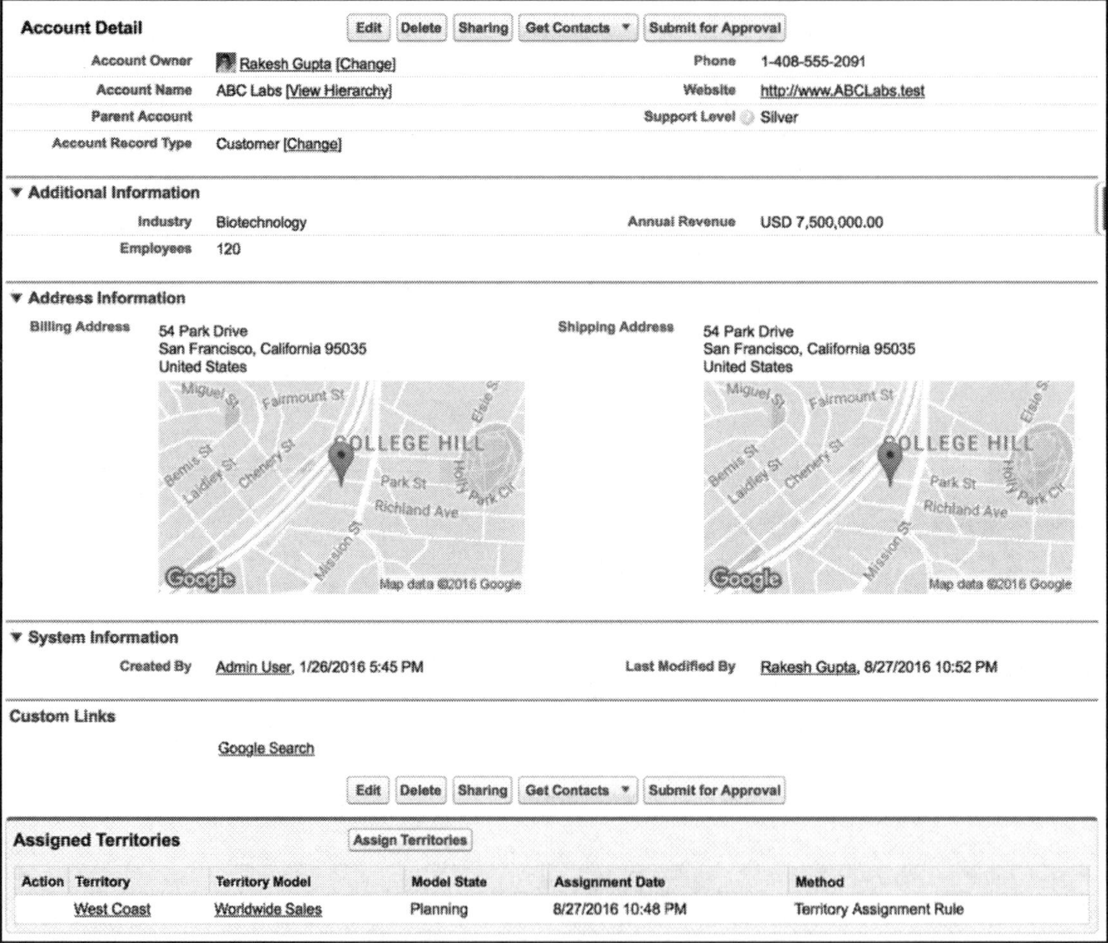

Make sure to add the **Assigned Territories** related list to the account page layouts.

Manually assigning accounts to a territory

Accounts that are not assigned to territories by assignment rules can be assigned manually to one or more than one territory at a time. Manual assignment is useful for accounts that have unique characteristics, and which, therefore, can't be assigned by rules. To manually assign accounts to a territory, follow the steps given as follows:

1. Click on **Setup** | **Administer** | **Manage Territories** | **Territory Models**.
2. Open the territory model **Worldwide Sales**, click on the **View Hierarchy** button, and then open **West Coast** territory hierarchy.
3. Navigate to the **Manually Assigned Accounts** related list and click on **Add Accounts** to see a list of your organization's accounts:

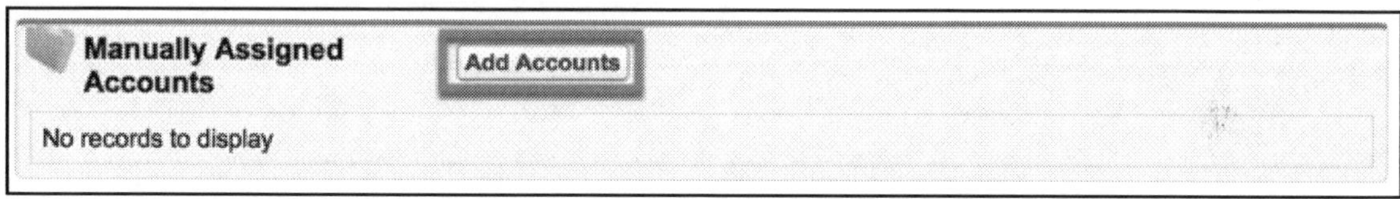

4. In the **Available** related list, select the checkbox for each account you want to assign. Each selected account appears in the **Selected** related list:

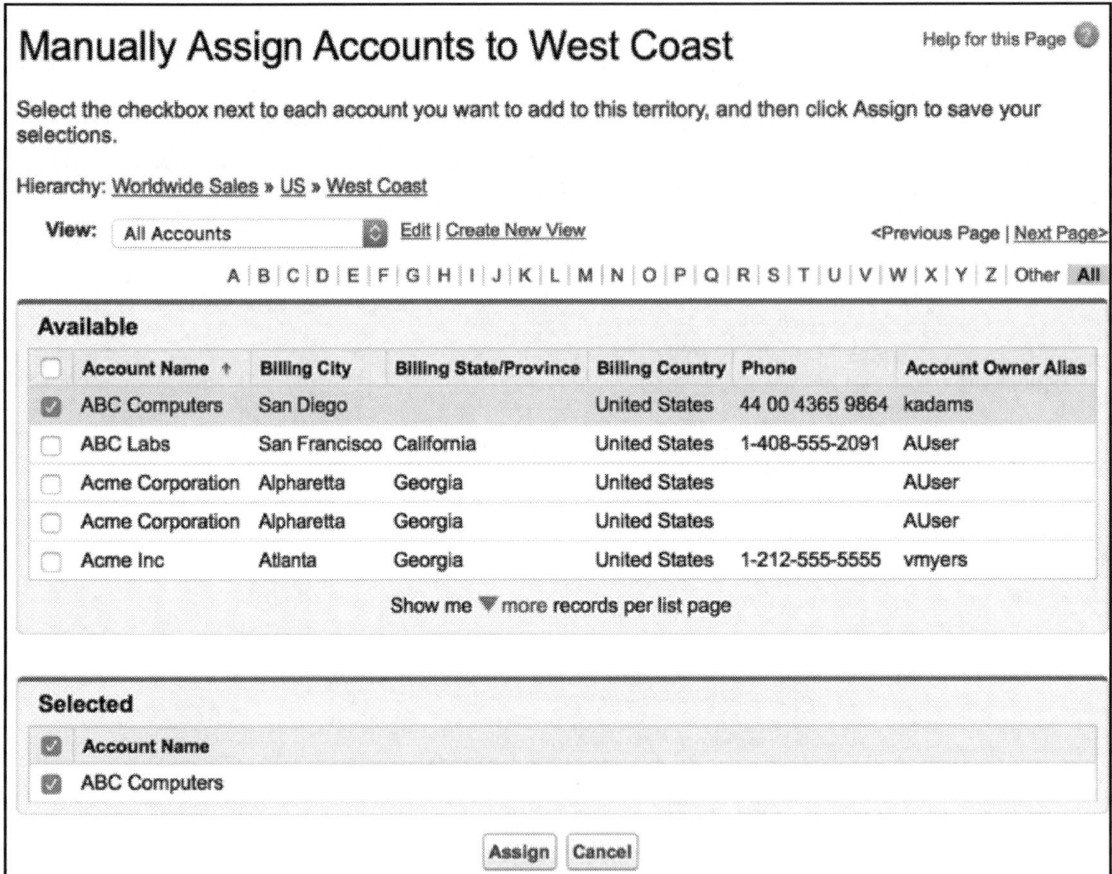

5. Once done, click on **Assign**. Now check the **Manually Assigned Accounts** related list and it will display the account you have assigned to the **West Coast** territory:

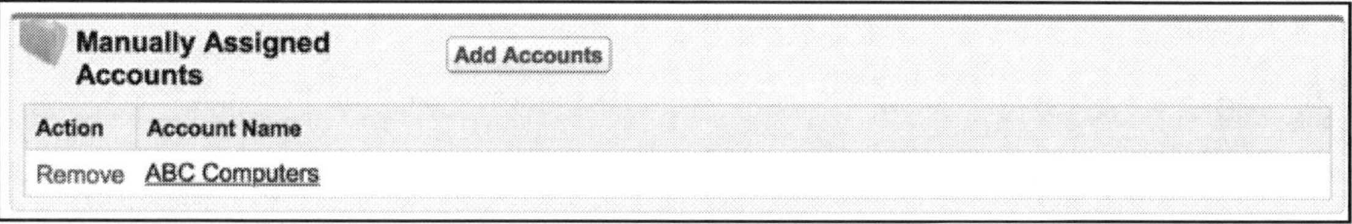

Likewise, you can create assignment rules for other territories and manually assign account records to them.

Manually assigning an account to one or more territories

This feature allows us to assign an account to one or more territories directly from the account record. Only territories that are in a **Planning** or an **Active** state can be assigned to accounts. To manually assign accounts to one or more territories, follow the steps given as follows:

1. Open the account you want to assign territories to.
2. From the account detail page, navigate to the **Assigned Territories** related list and then click on the **Assign Territories** button:

3. It will display a list of your organization's territories. Now select the territories that you want to assign to the account. In the **Available** related list, select the checkbox for each territory you want to assign. Each selected territory appears in the **Selected** related list:

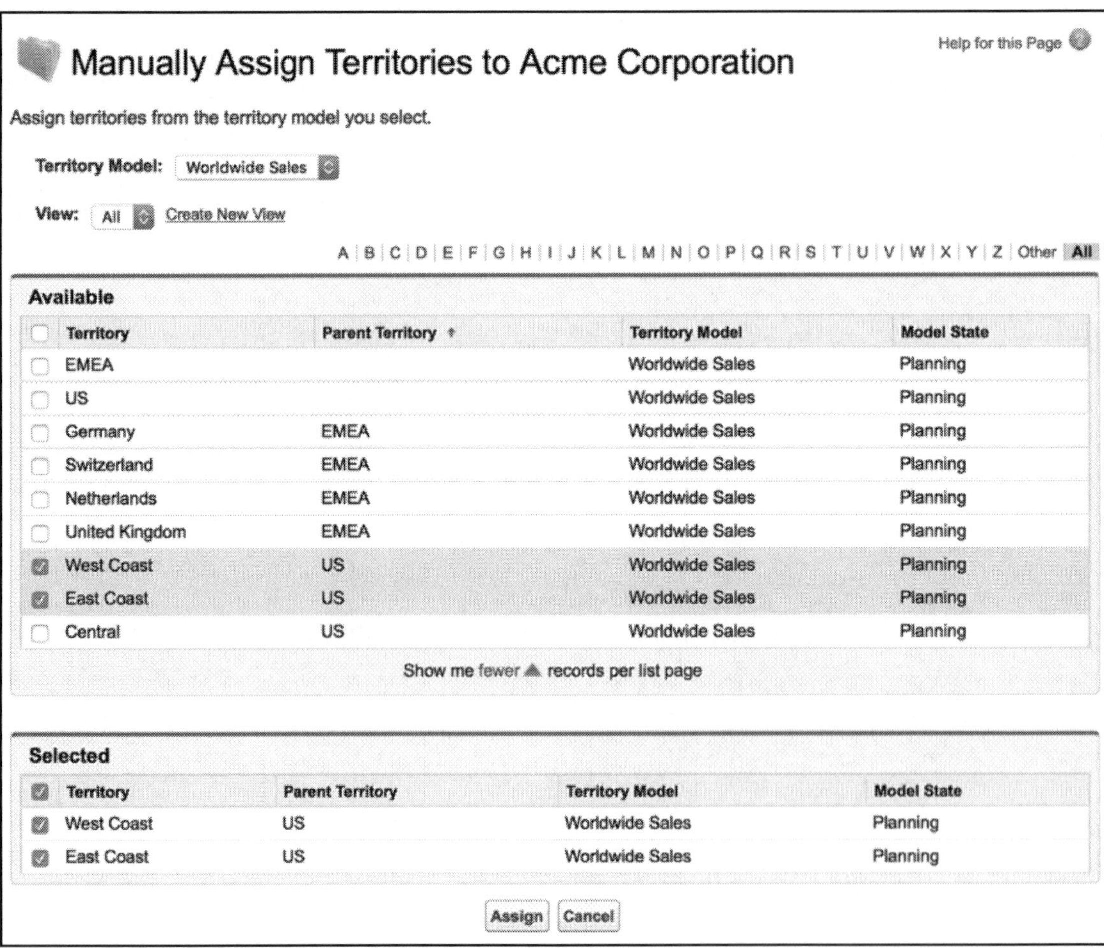

4. Once done, click on **Assign**. Now go back to the account detail page and check the **Assigned Territories** related list:

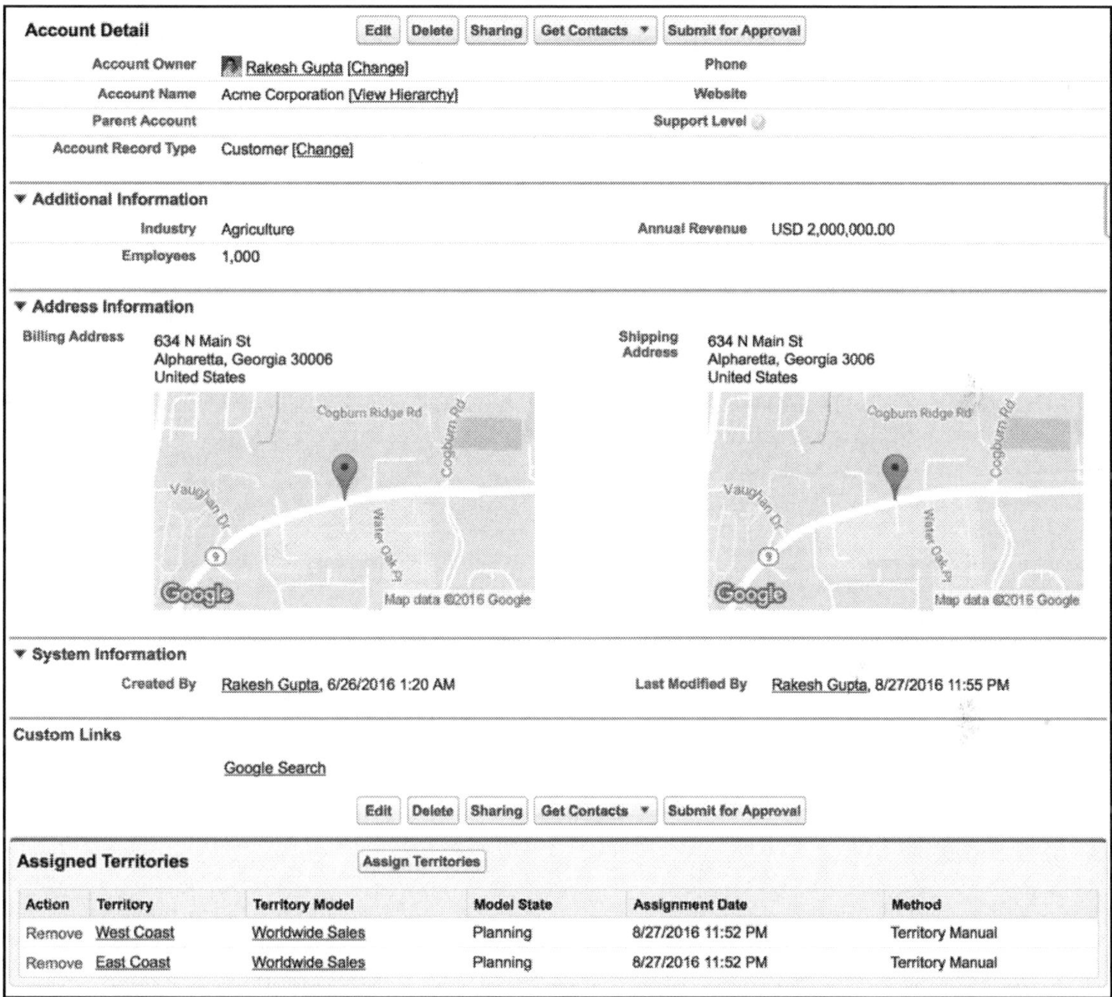

Make sure to verify your selection.

Assigning users to territories

Make sure to assign users to the territories. This way, they will gain the accounts' access to sell products and services. You can assign users to territories that belong to models in an **Active** or a **Planning** state. To assign users to territories, follow the steps given as follows:

1. Click on **Setup** | **Administer** | **Manage Territories** | **Territory Models**.
2. Open the territory model **Worldwide Sales**, click on the **View Hierarchy** button, and then open the **West Coast** territory hierarchy.
3. Navigate to the **Assigned Users** related list and click on **Manage Users** to see a list of your organization's users. Select or search for the users you want to add:

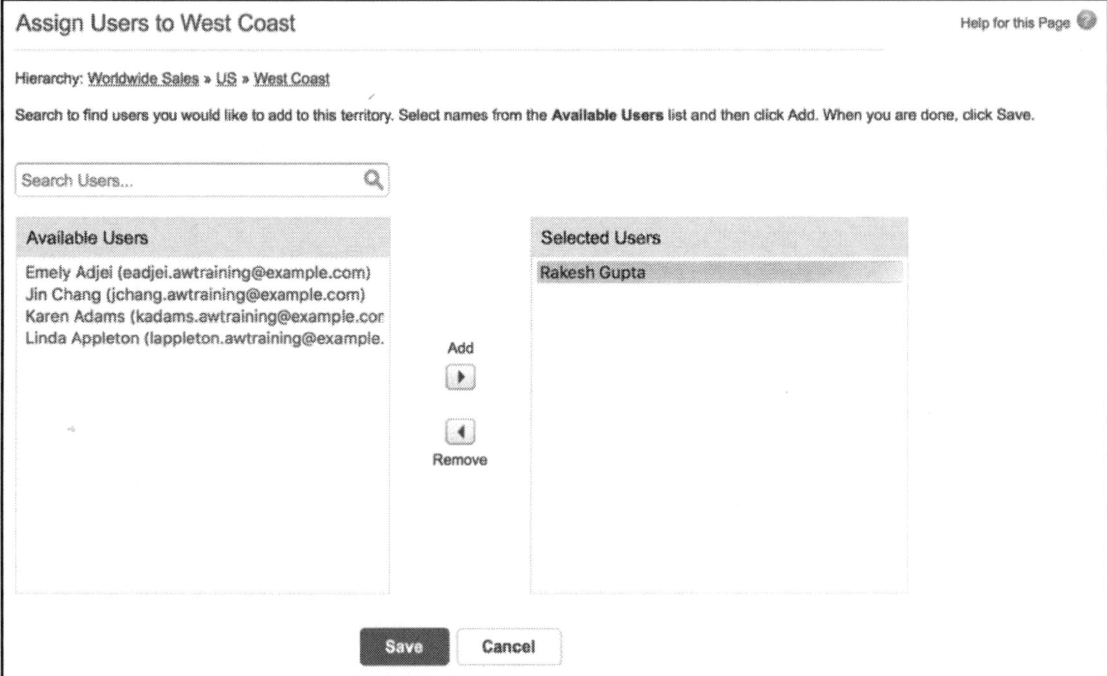

4. Once done, click on **Save**.

Using Chatter to collaborate with territory models

Salesforce allows you to enable Chatter on the **Territory Model** object to collaborate on model development directly within model records. Your team can collaborate and get notifications when any changes happen to the territory model. To enable Chatter on **Territory Model** object, follow the steps given as follows:

1. Click on **Setup** | **Build** | **Customize** | **Chatter** | **Feed Tracking**.
2. Select the **Territory Model** object and enable **Feed Tracking** option for it. Then select the territory model fields you want to track.
3. Once you are done, click on **Save**:

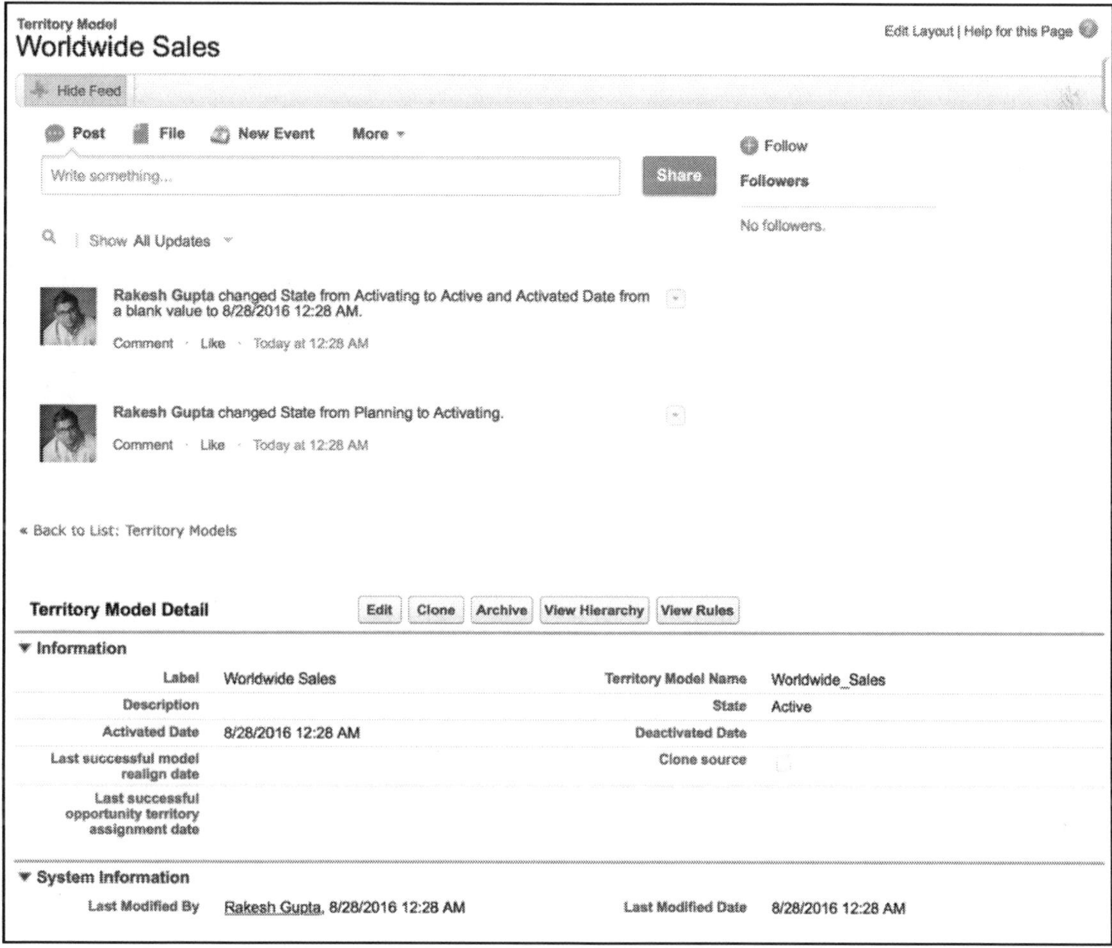

To verify the changes, navigate to **Setup** | **Administer** | **Manage Territories** | **Territory Models** and open the **Worldwide Sales** territory model.

Activating a territory model

When you are done with your testing, and are satisfied with the structure of the territory model and its territory account assignments, then the next step is to activate it. To activate a territory model, follow the steps given as follows:

1. Click on **Setup** | **Administer** | **Manage Territories** | **Territory Models**.
2. Open the territory model **Worldwide Sales**:

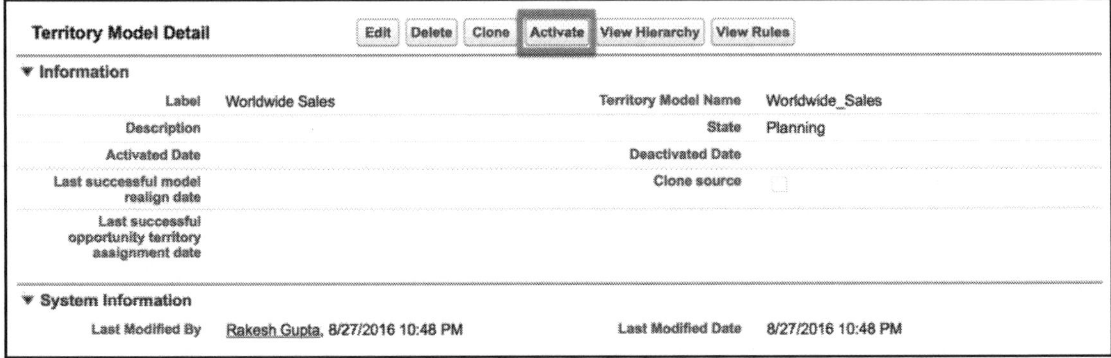

3. Once done, click on **Activate**.

Running the Opportunity Territory Assignment filter

The **Opportunity Territory Assignment** filter automatically assigns territories to opportunities based on the filter logic in the Apex class. To run it, follow the steps given as follows:

1. Click on **Setup** | **Administer** | **Manage Territories** | **Territory Models**.
2. Open the **View Hierarchy** for the **Worldwide Sales** territory model.
3. Click on **Run Opportunity Filter** to initiate the job that applies the filter:

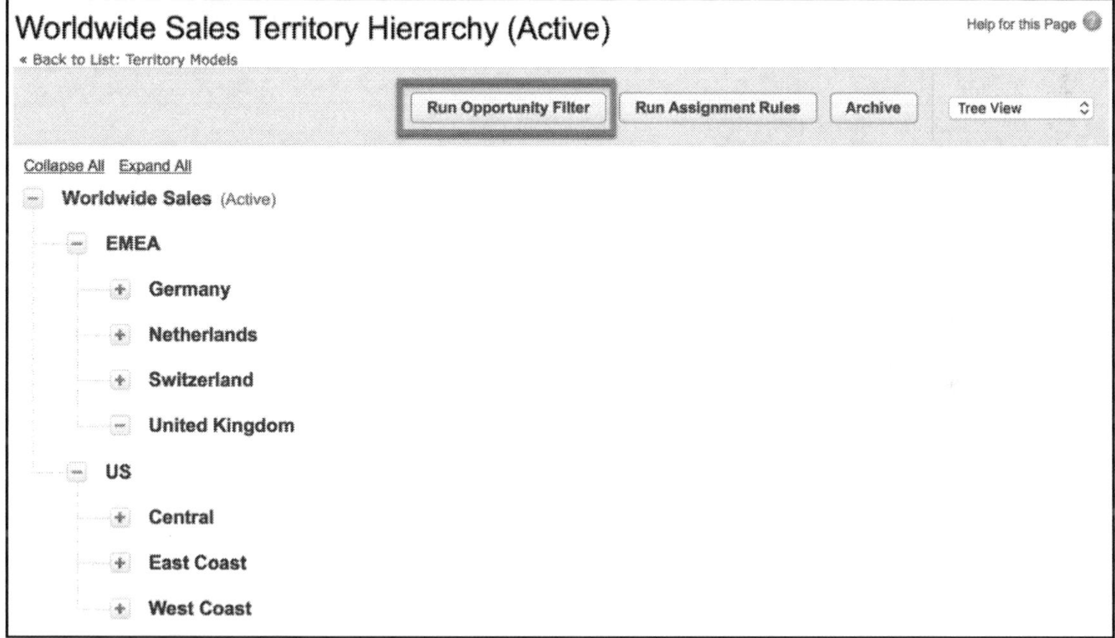

4. The next step is to select the options for which you want to run the opportunity territory filter.

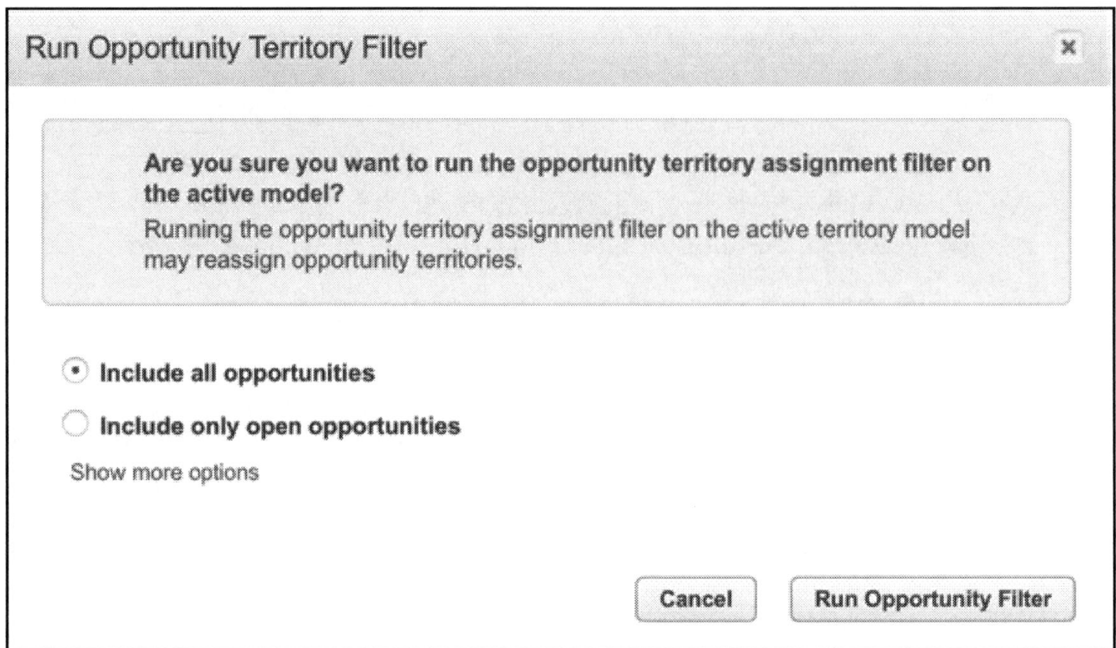

5. Once done, click on **Save**. You'll receive an e-mail when the job is complete.

To verify this, open an opportunity and check the **Territory** field. Make sure to add **Territory** and **Exclude from the territory assignment filter logic** fields on the opportunity page layouts:

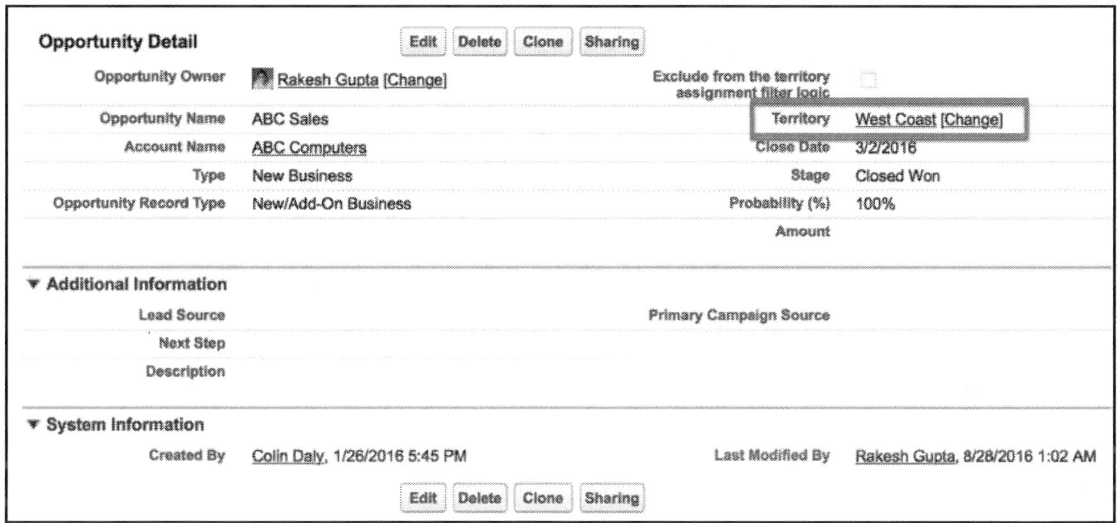

Manually excluding an opportunity from filter-based territory assignment

It is possible to exclude an opportunity from filter-based territory assignment via the API or manually. To do this, open the opportunity record that you want to exclude, and then select the **Exclude from the territory assignment filter logic**. Once you are done, click on **Save**.

A few points to remember

1. As of the *Winter'17* release, Enterprise Territory Management is available in Salesforce Classic only.
2. Each territory can have up to 15 assignment rules.
3. Only one model can be in the **Active** state at one time in your organization.
4. If you disable Enterprise Territory Management, your users will lose the record access that was based on territory assignment.
5. By default, each territory model can have up to 1,000 territories.

6. As of *Winter'17* release, Enterprise Territory Management components cannot be included in packages or change sets.

Test your knowledge

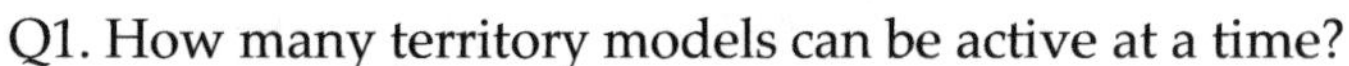

Q1. How many territory models can be active at a time?

1. 1
2. 2
3. 3
4. 4

Q2. How many assignment rules can each territory have?

1. 20
2. 15
3. 10
4. 25

Q3. When creating a sharing rule, you can share the data with which of the following entities?

1. Public Groups
2. Users
3. Roles
4. Roles and Subordinates
5. Queues

Summary

In this chapter, we started with an overview of Territory Management. Then we moved ahead and discussed the difference between Territory Management and Enterprise Territory Management. We also learned how to configure Enterprise Territory Management for your Salesforce organization. We also covered how to run opportunity filter-based territory assignment. At the end, we discussed a way to enable Chatter for a territory model. In the next chapter, we will go through the Salesforce customization options.

4
Extending Salesforce with Custom Objects and Applications

In the previous chapters, we had discussed about the various concepts of data security and data sharing in Salesforce. We discussed about an organization-wide default, sharing settings, territory management, and field level security in Salesforce. We also discussed about standard and custom objects and fields. In this chapter, we will describe in detail how we can customize the user interfaces, such as objects, fields, and page layouts. In addition to this, we will look at the methods to configure and customize the application to suit the way your company information can be best represented. We will also cover, the way you can establish relationships between objects, create formula fields, and so on. Finally, we will see the key features to improve the data quality in Salesforce. The following topics will be covered in this chapter:

- Creating custom objects
- Creating custom fields
- Creating custom tabs
- Creating Lightning apps
- Creating Lightning record pages
- Improving the data quality

Creating custom objects

Salesforce comes with several standard objects according to the CRM structure, but if your requirement is not satisfied by using them, you could go ahead and create custom objects. For example, creating a custom object to store employee checking or saving account details to process the biweekly salary and keep the employee account details private, so only the system administrator can access it. Custom objects are usually identified by a `__c` suffix:

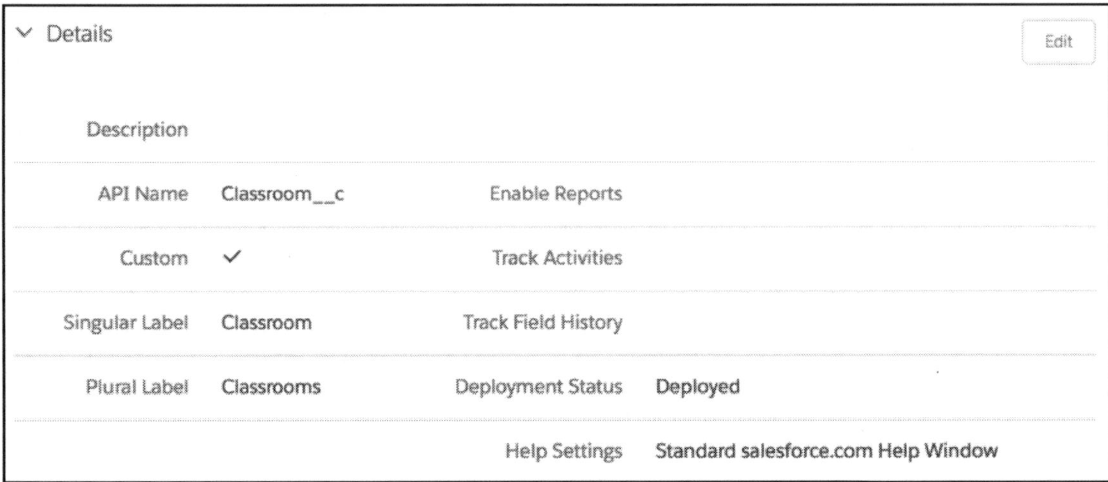

Objects are a crucial element in Salesforce, as they provide a structure for storing data and are incorporated into the interface, allowing users to interact with the data. It is similar to a database table. Object fields are similar in concept to a database column. Records are similar in concept to a database row. The following diagram represents the steps for creating a custom object and configuring it as per your business requirements:

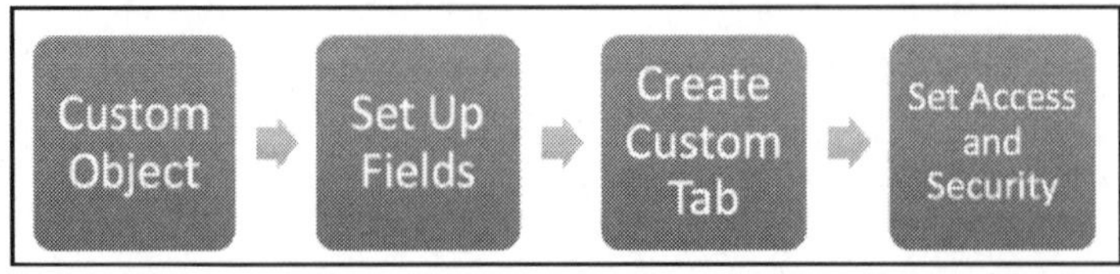

We will now be developing a sample *Registration Management* app for Universal Containers to better manage their upcoming events.

A business scenario: *David Guzman* works as a System Administrator at *Universal Containers*. His manager, *Brigette Hyacinth*, would like to create a custom object to save the registration details. Universal Containers is planning to integrate the registration form with the payment gateway to process the registration fee. We will be building the following database model throughout the book from now on:

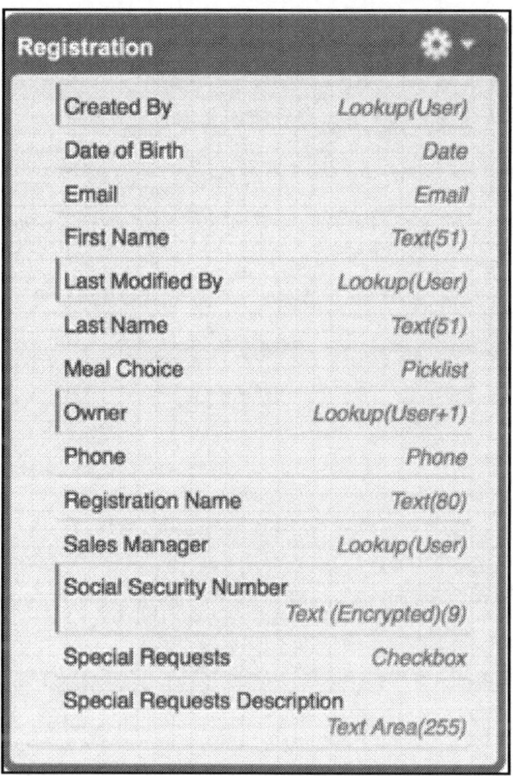

To create the `registration` object, follow these steps:

1. Click on **Setup** (gear icon) | **Setup** | **PLATFORM TOOLS** | **Objects and Fields** | **Object Manager**. Object manager is a single place to manage your organization, both standard and custom objects.

2. To create a new object, select **Create** | **Custom Object**:

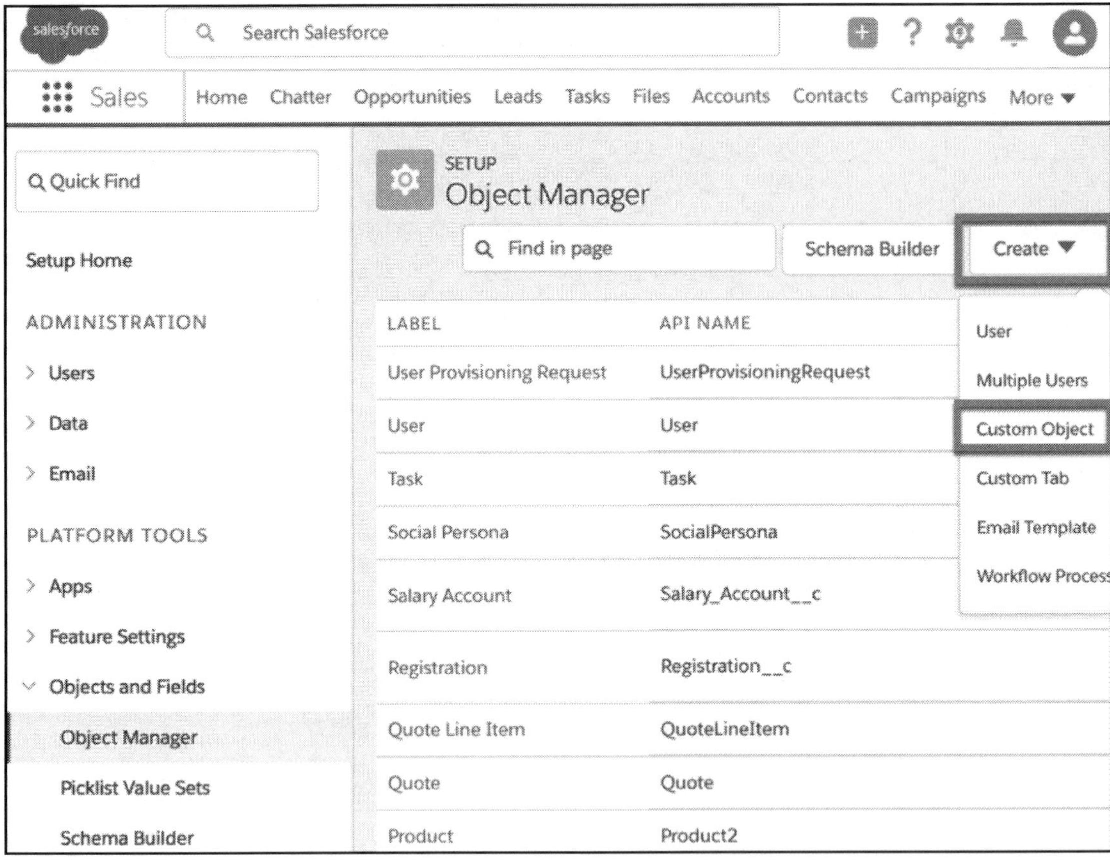

3. Enter all the details as mentioned in the following to create a new object:
    1. **Label**: This is the label of the object definition. This label is used on page layouts and reports. Here, we used **Registration** as the label of this object.
    2. **Plural Label**: The plural label is used in Salesforce object tabs. In this case, we have used **Registrations** as the plural label.
    3. **Start with vowel sound**: Check if the label starts with a vowel sound, in which case, it should be preceded by *an* instead of *a*.
    4. **Object Name**: This is nothing but the API name of the object that you have to use when you use it anywhere in a formula or Apex code. For custom objects, Salesforce automatically appends `__c` with the object name. Finally, even the object name will look like `Registration__c`.
    5. **Description**: Always use a meaningful name, so other developers can easily understand why this object has been created.
    6. **Context-Sensitive Help Setting**: Salesforce provides a standard help page for all custom objects; if you want to overwrite it for a custom object, then select the **Open a window using a Visualforce** page option.
    7. **Content Name**: Here, you can select the Visualforce page that you want to open when users click on the help link.
    8. **Enter Record Name Label and Format**: The **Record Name** appears in page layouts, for example, related list and search results. The **Record Name** field is always referred as name while referenced via the API:
        1. **Record Name**: Under the **Enter Record Name Label and Format** section, enter **Registration Name** as the **Record Name**.

2. Data Type: Select **Text** as **Data Type**:

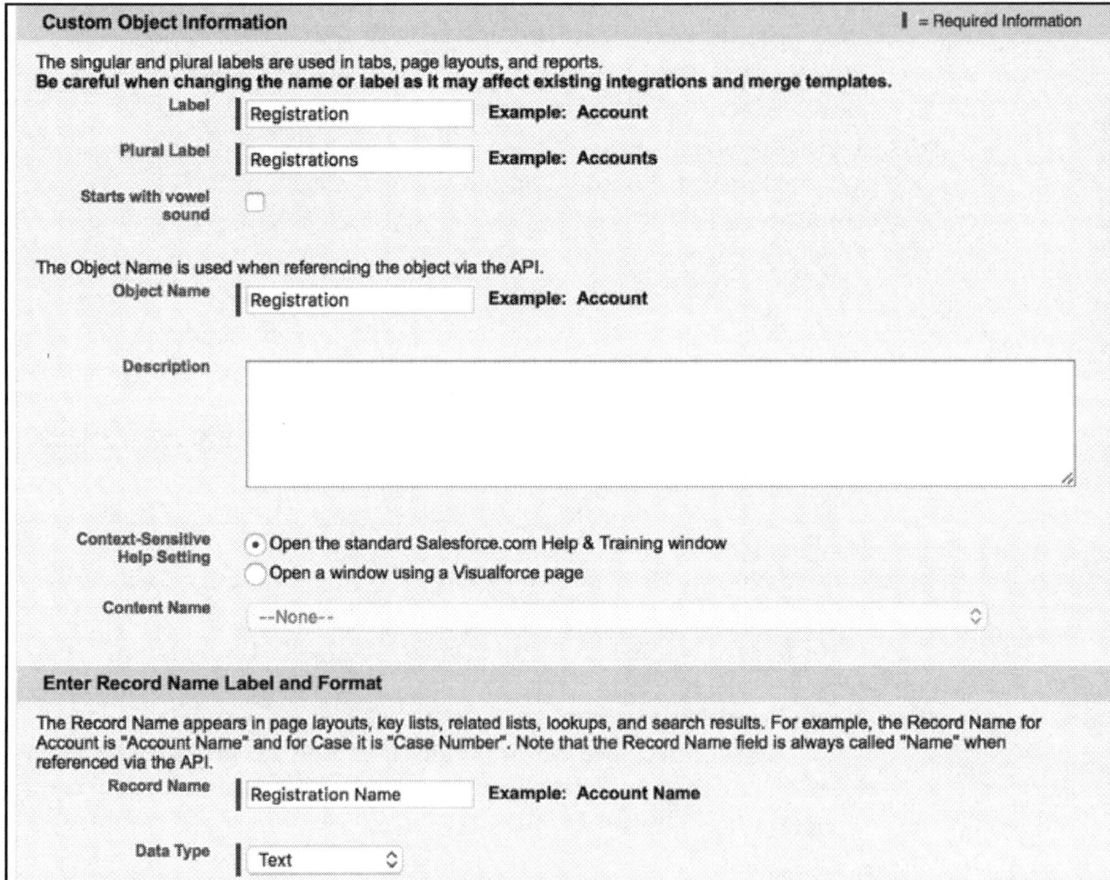

There are a few optional features available; select them as per your business needs:

1. **Allow Reports**: This option will allow you to create reports on a `Registration` object. If the option is not selected, then you can't create a report on the said object.
2. **Allow Activities**: This feature allows users to add tasks and events on registration records.

    3. **Track Field History**: Participant's e-mail address field is very important, and if you want to track any changes happening on this field, then you should select the **Track Field History** option first. Once this checkbox is selected, it will capture all old and new values for a field under the object history related list.
    4. **Allow in Chatter Groups**: Here, you have an option to select, if you want to allow your users to add the object records to Chatter groups.
    5. **Object classification**: When the following settings are enabled, the object is categorized as an Enterprise Application object. If these settings are disabled, the object is categorized as a Light Application object:
        1. Allow Sharing
        2. Allow Bulk API Access
        3. Allow Streaming API Access
    6. **Deployment Status**: This option is used to deploy a specific object for business users. When **In development** stage only system administrator can access these objects.
    7. **Search Status**: By default, you can search the records of standard objects from global search. For a custom object you, have an option to enable or disable these settings as per data criticality.

4. Once you are done, click on **Save**. It will redirect you to the `registration` object detail page. The next step is to navigate to the **Fields & Relationships** section, and you can easily identify that a few fields are already created by Salesforce. These fields, **Created By** and **Last Modified By,** are referred to as audit fields:

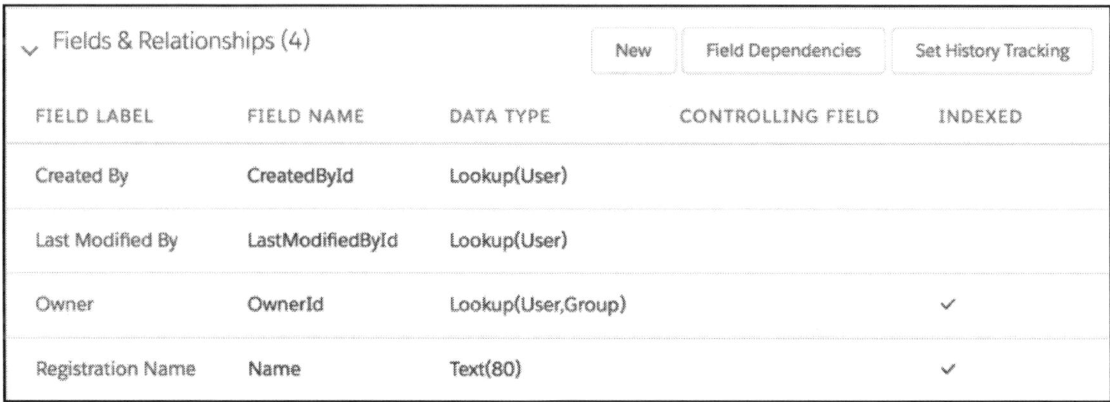

Fields & Relationships (4)

New | Field Dependencies | Set History Tracking

FIELD LABEL	FIELD NAME	DATA TYPE	CONTROLLING FIELD	INDEXED
Created By	CreatedById	Lookup(User)		
Last Modified By	LastModifiedById	Lookup(User)		
Owner	OwnerId	Lookup(User,Group)		✓
Registration Name	Name	Text(80)		✓

In a similar manner, you can create other custom objects.

Creating custom fields

Custom fields are unique to your business needs and can not only be added and amended, but also deleted. Creating custom fields allows you to store the necessary information for your organization. Both standard and custom fields can be customized to include the custom help text that helps users understand how to use the field. Custom fields are usually identified by a `__c` suffix.

A business scenario: *David Guzman* is working as a System Administrator at *Universal Containers*. His manager, *Brigette Hyacinth*, would like him to create a custom field to save all participants' social security numbers, but at the same time, he doesn't want to share the field value with every sales rep as the social security number is confidential information.

To create a custom field on a `registration` object, follow these steps:

1. Click on **Setup** (gear icon) | **Setup** | **PLATFORM TOOLS** | **Objects and Fields** | **Object Manager**.
2. To find the `registration` object, enter the first few characters of its label or name in the find in page box:

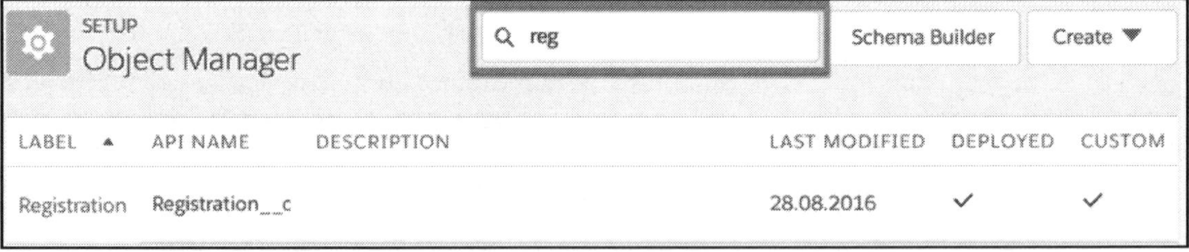

Click on the object label, which, in this scenario, is **Registration**.

3. The next step is to navigate to the **Fields & Relationships** section and click on the **New** button. It will redirect you to a new page where you have to select the data type. For the current business scenario, select **Text (Encrypted)** and then click on the **Next**.
4. It will open a window for you, where you have to enter the following details:
    1. **Field Label**: Enter the label for the custom field. In this case, enter the social security number as **Field Label**.
    2. **Length**: Enter the field length; in this case, enter `9`.
    3. **Field Name**: This will be autopopulated, based on the **Field Label**.

4. **Description**: Write some meaningful text, so other developers/administrators can easily understand why this custom field has been created.
5. **Help Text**: Write some meaningful help text, so whenever users hover on this field, they will easily understand what they have to enter in this field.
6. **Required**: You can make this field required by using this option. Best practice is to use a validation rule to make a field required. Don't select this checkbox.
7. **Mask Type**: For the mask type, select the social security number.
8. **Mask Character**: For the mask character, select **X**.

It will look like the following screenshot:

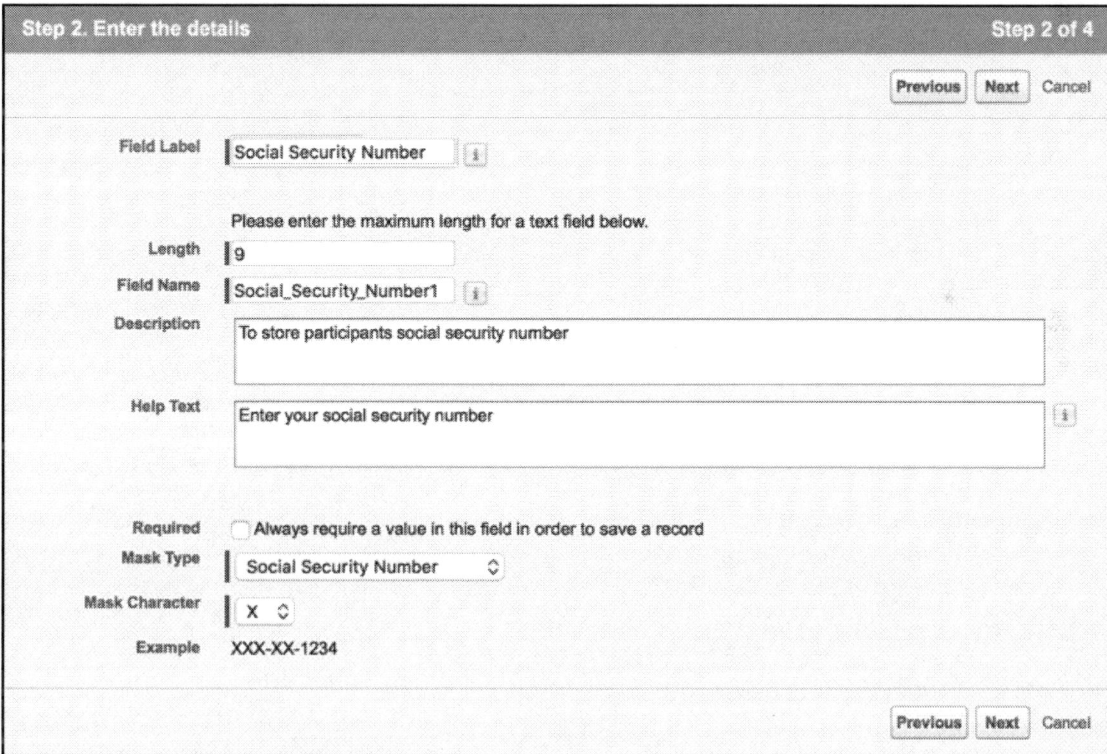

Click on **Next**, once you are done.

5. The next step is to **Establish field level visibility** and add fields to the page layout.
6. Once you are done, click on **Save**.

Use a permission set to grant users access to encrypted files. In a similar manner, create a few custom fields that are marked in numbers on the `registration` object:

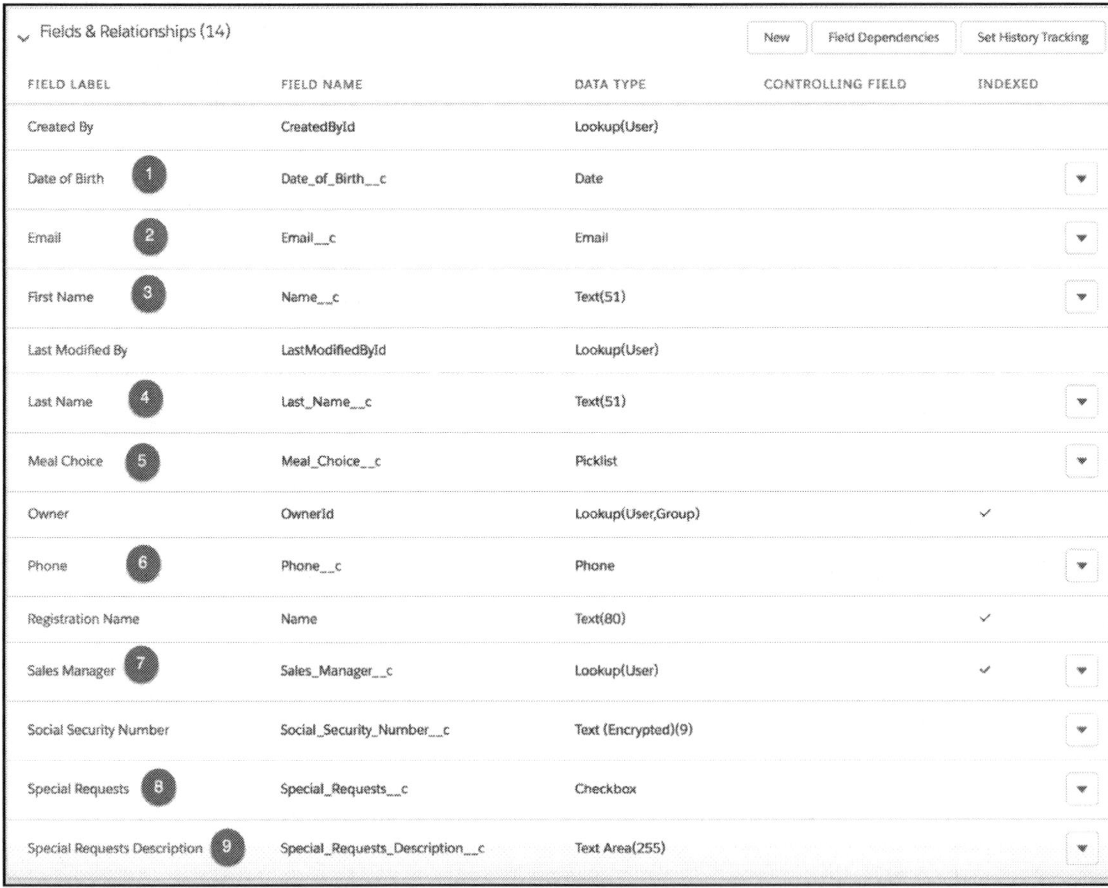

Fields & Relationships (14) — New | Field Dependencies | Set History Tracking

FIELD LABEL	FIELD NAME	DATA TYPE	CONTROLLING FIELD	INDEXED
Created By	CreatedById	Lookup(User)		
Date of Birth (1)	Date_of_Birth__c	Date		
Email (2)	Email__c	Email		
First Name (3)	Name__c	Text(51)		
Last Modified By	LastModifiedById	Lookup(User)		
Last Name (4)	Last_Name__c	Text(51)		
Meal Choice (5)	Meal_Choice__c	Picklist		
Owner	OwnerId	Lookup(User,Group)		✓
Phone (6)	Phone__c	Phone		
Registration Name	Name	Text(80)		✓
Sales Manager (7)	Sales_Manager__c	Lookup(User)		✓
Social Security Number	Social_Security_Number__c	Text (Encrypted)(9)		
Special Requests (8)	Special_Requests__c	Checkbox		
Special Requests Description (9)	Special_Requests_Description__c	Text Area(255)		

For picklist **Meal Choice**, use **Chicken, Fish**, and **Vegetarian** as the values.

Creating custom tabs

To create or view records related to the objects, you have to associate a tab with it. In Salesforce, tabs are ways to create, manage, edit, and delete records. Custom objects and tabs have a one-to-one relationship; it means that you can't associate one object with more than one tab. The following types of tab exist in Salesforce:

- **Custom Object Tabs**: This type of tab is used to associate a custom object
- **Web Tabs**: This type of tab is used to display any external web-based application or web page in a tab
- **Visualforce Tabs**: This type of tab is used to associate a Visualforce page
- **Lightning Page Tabs**: This type of tab is used to associate a Lightning page

A business scenario: *David Guzman* has created the custom object registration and all the necessary fields. Now he wants to create a few records to test it out.

To fulfill the preceding requirement, we have to associate a `registration` object with a tab. To create a tab for a `registration` object, follow these steps:

1. Click on **Setup** (gear icon) | **Setup** | **PLATFORM TOOLS** | **User Interface** | **Tabs**.
2. Navigate to the **Custom Object Tabs** section and click on the **New** button.

3. Select the **Registration** object from a list of objects and then select a **Tab Style** by clicking on the magnifying glass icon. In this case, select **Form** as **Tab Style**. Optionally, you can enter the description:

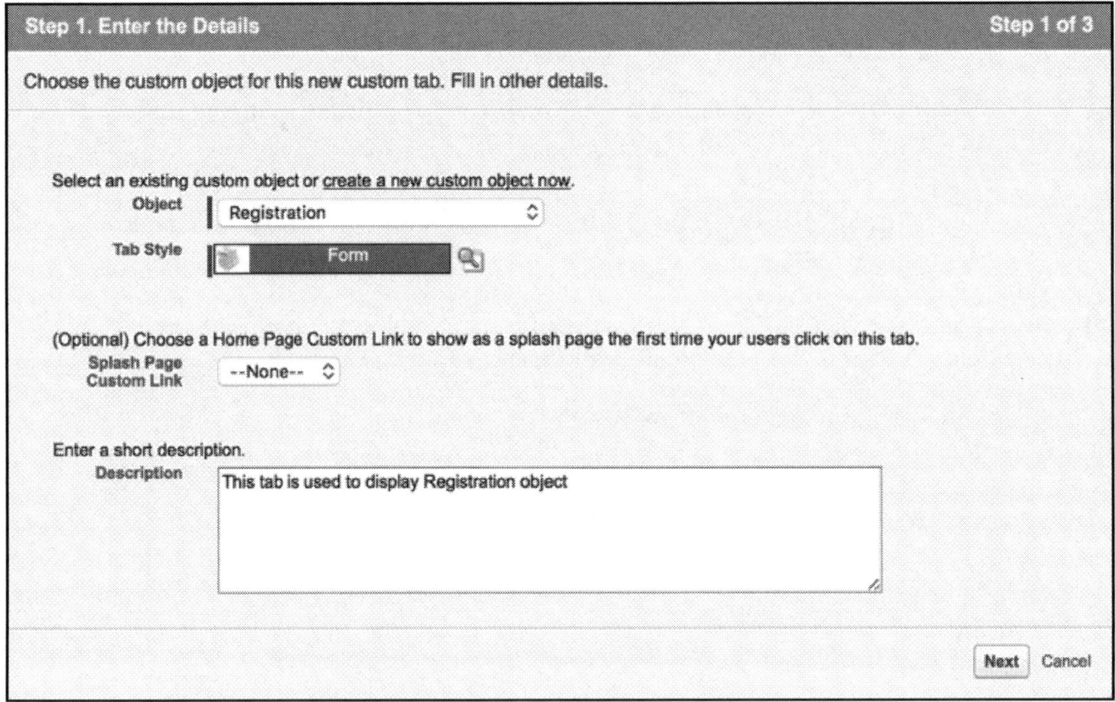

4. On the next screen, keep the default values for all the profiles and again click on **Next**.
5. Finally, you can choose for which app you want to add this tab; don't select any app right now. We will create a custom app in the next section of this chapter:

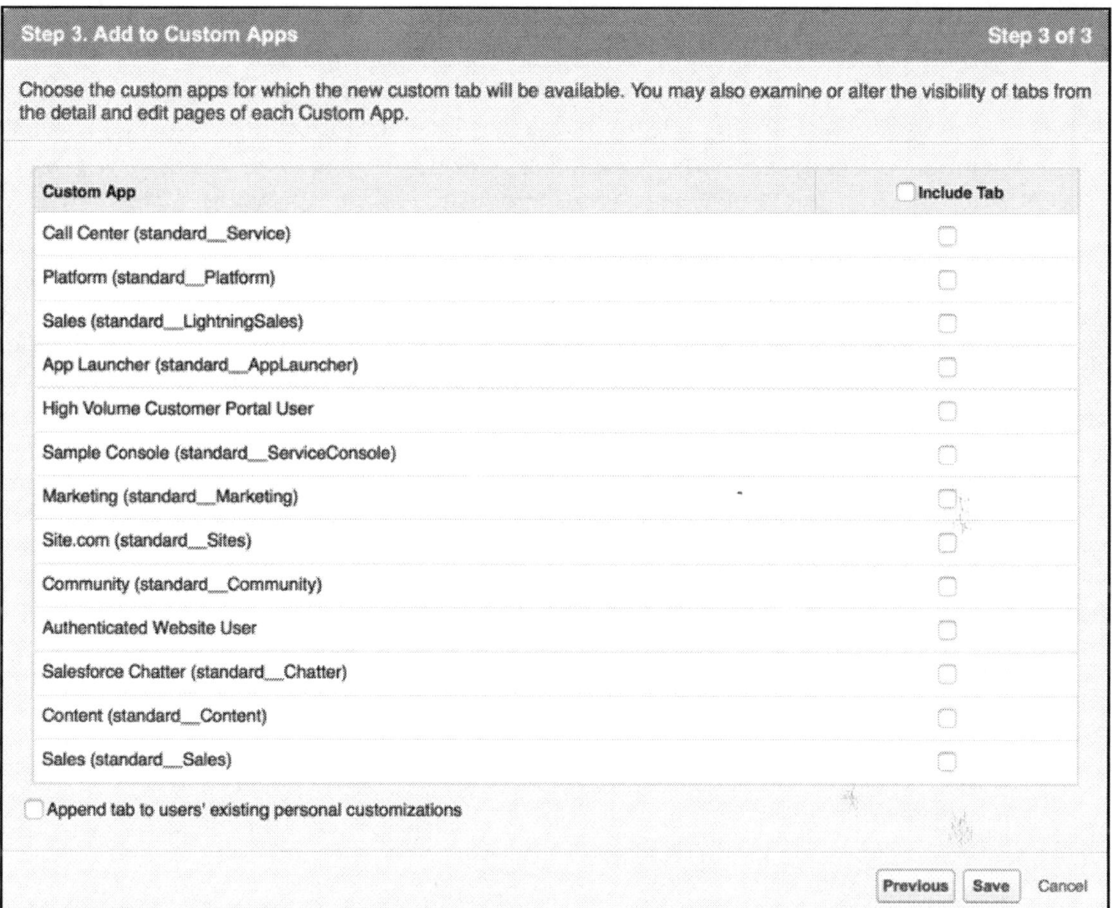

6. Once you are done, click on **Save**.

Creating Lightning apps

In Salesforce, app is a combination of tabs, processes, and services associated with a business function. The next goal is to create a custom app for our registration management. To do so, follow these steps:

1. Click on **Setup** (gear icon) | **Setup** | **PLATFORM TOOLS** | **Apps** | **App Manager**.

2. Click on the **New Lightning App** button. It will redirect you to a new screen where you have to enter app details and branding information:
    1. **App Name**: App name will appear in the navigation bar, so users can easily identify the app name they are currently using. In this case, enter **Registration Management** as **App Name**.
    2. **Developer Name**: This will be autopopulated, based on **App Name**.
    3. **Description**: Write some meaningful text, so other developers/administrators can easily understand why this custom app has been created.
    4. **App Branding**: You can also add an image to your custom app. The file size of a custom app image must be smaller than 5 MB.

    Once you are done, click on **Next**:

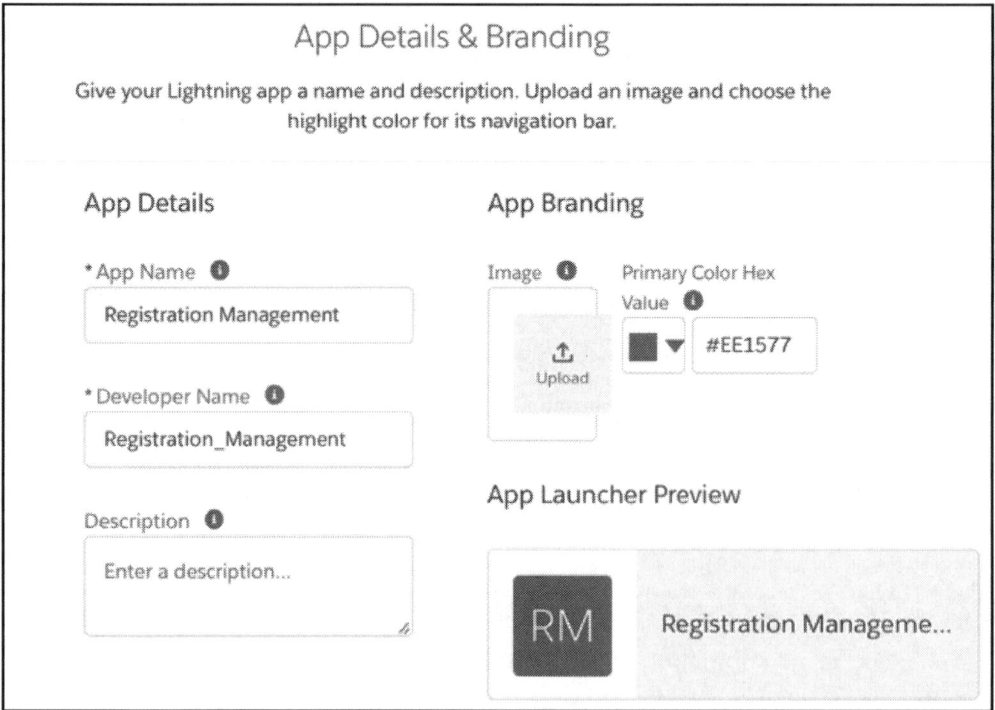

3. Optionally, you can enable a utility bar that will allow users instance access to productivity tools, for example, **CTI Softphone**:

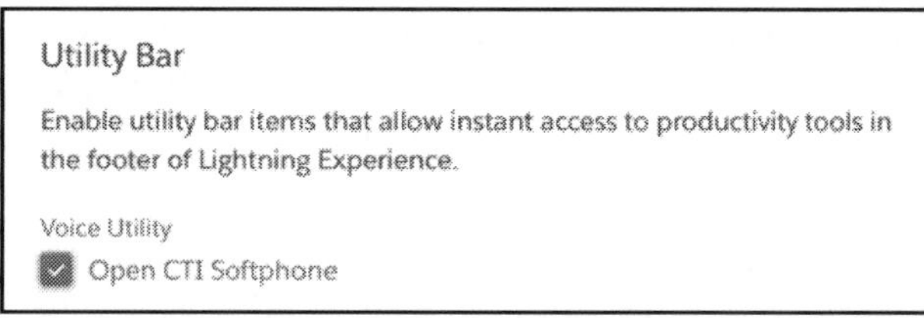

Computer Telephony Integration (**CTI**) is a common name for any technology that allows interactions on a telephone and a computer to be integrated.

Once you are done, click on **Next**.

4. The next step is to add tabs into your app. To do so, move the tabs from the **Available Items** tabs pane to the **Selected Items** tabs pane, as shown in the following screenshot:

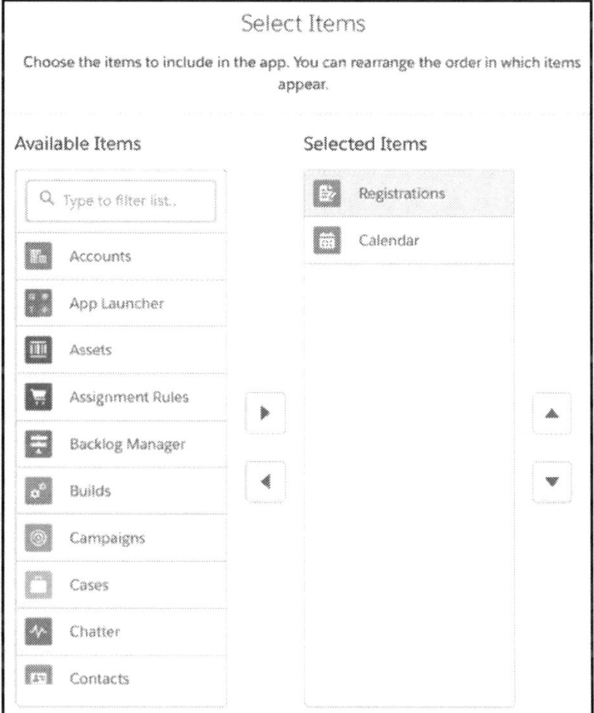

Once you are done, click on **Next**.

5. The final step is to assign the app to user profiles so that the users can access it. To do so, move the profiles from the **Available Profiles** pane to the **Selected Profiles** pane.
6. Once you are done, click on **Save & Finish**.
7. To access the app, navigate to **App Launcher** and select **Registration Management app**, as shown in the following screenshot:

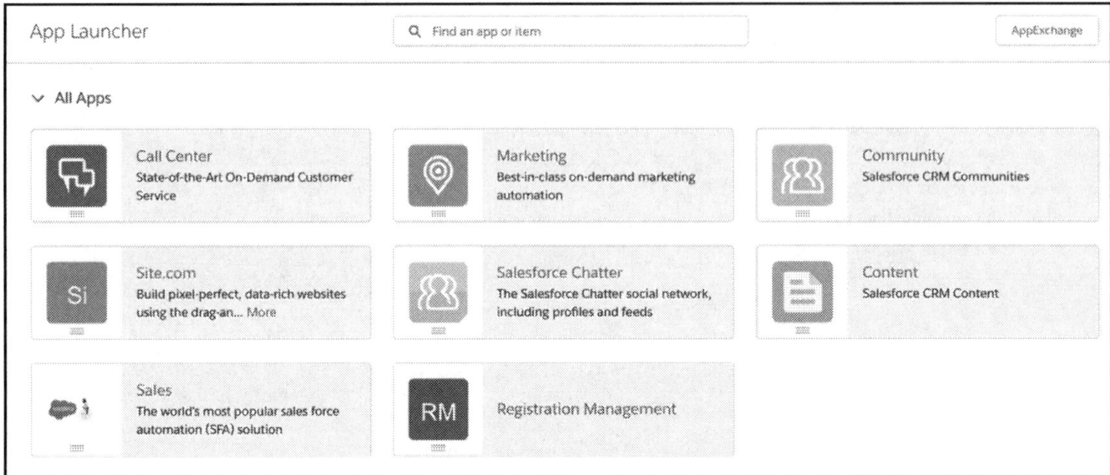

After *Winter'17* release, tabs are organized in a horizontal bar instead of a vertical line, as shown in the following screenshot:

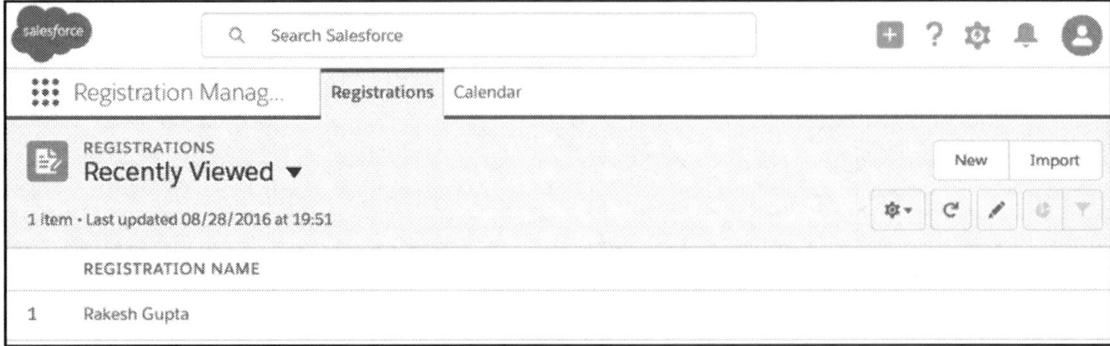

Lightning apps aren't available in Salesforce Classic.

Creating Lightning record pages

Now you can give your users a customized view for each object's records, using the Lightning App Builder. The Lightning App Builder allows you to add, remove, or reorder components on a Lightning record page. To create Lightning record pages for a `registration` object, follow these steps:

1. Click on **Setup** (gear icon) | **Setup** | **PLATFORM TOOLS** | **Objects and Fields** | **Object Manager**.
2. To find the `registration` object, enter the first few characters of its label or name in the find in page box.
3. The next step is to navigate to the **Lightning Record Pages** section and click on the **New** button:

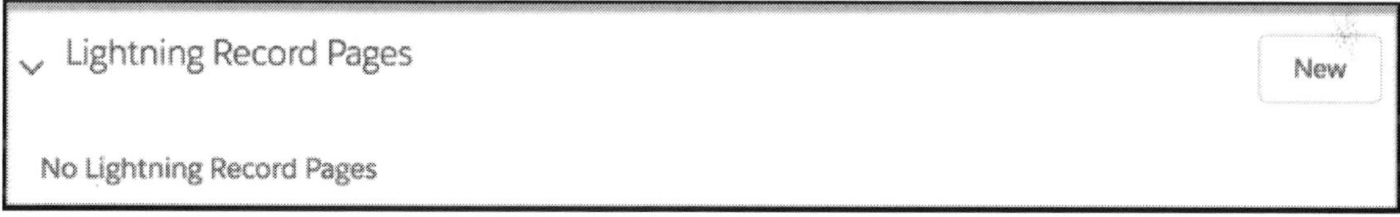

It will redirect you to a new page where you have to select the Lightning page type. For the current business scenario, select **Record Page**, as shown in the following screenshot:

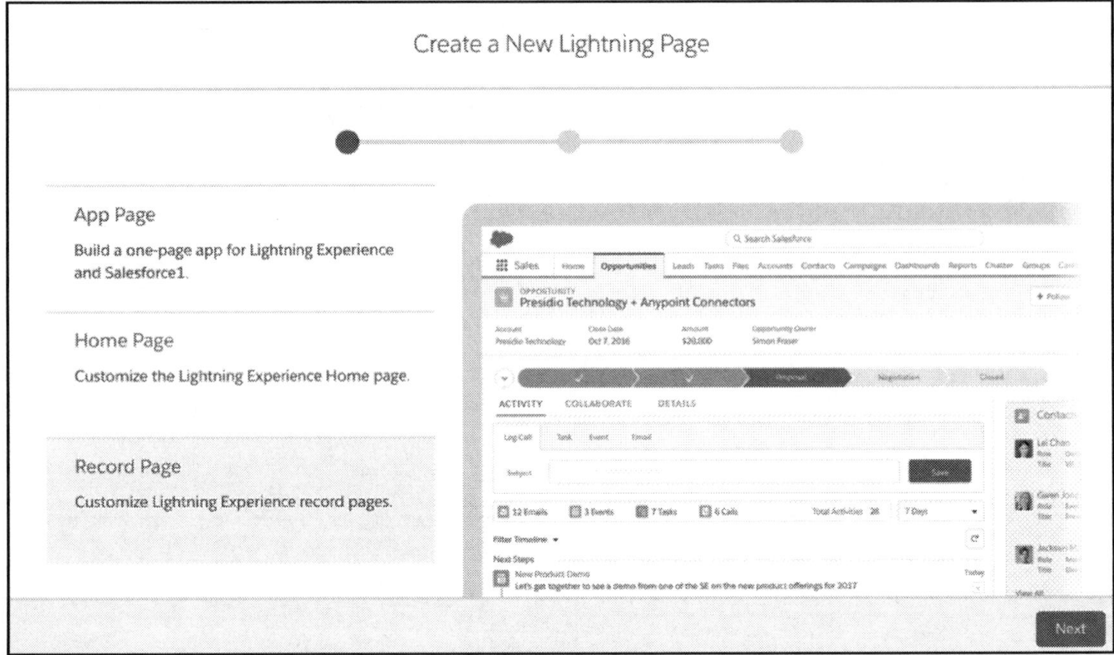

Once you are done, click on **Next**.

4. The next step is to select a page template. For the current business scenario, select the **Header and Two Columns** template, as shown in the following screenshot:

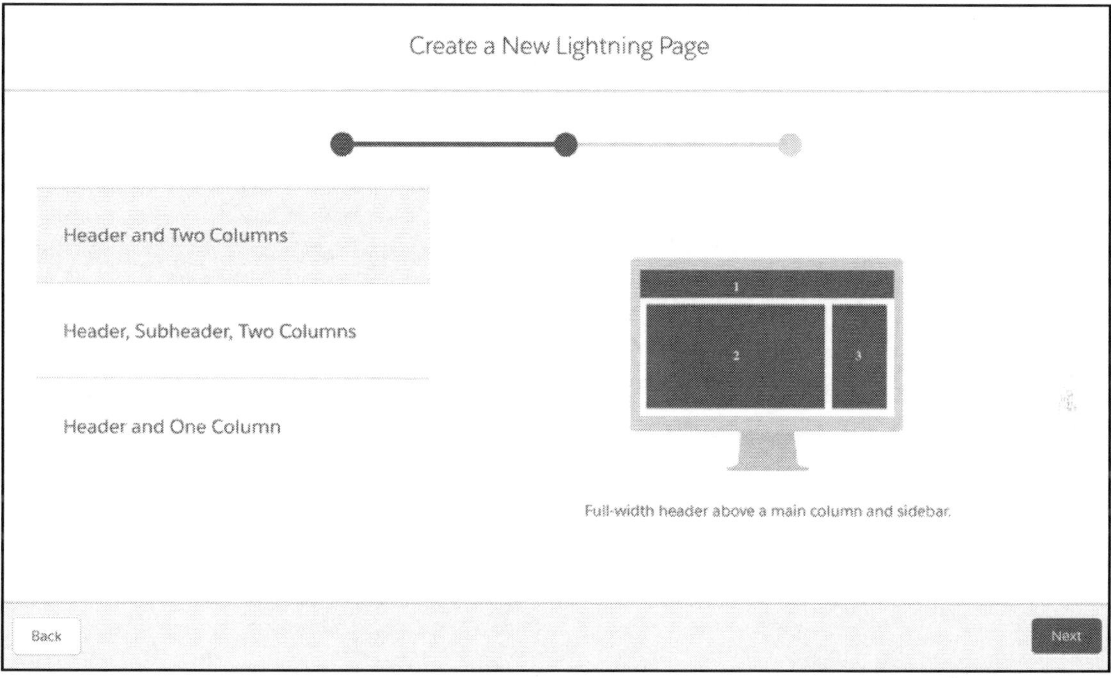

Once you are done, click on **Next**.

5. On the next screen, enter **Label** as `Registration Lightning page`, and for **Object**, select **Registration**, as shown in the following screenshot:

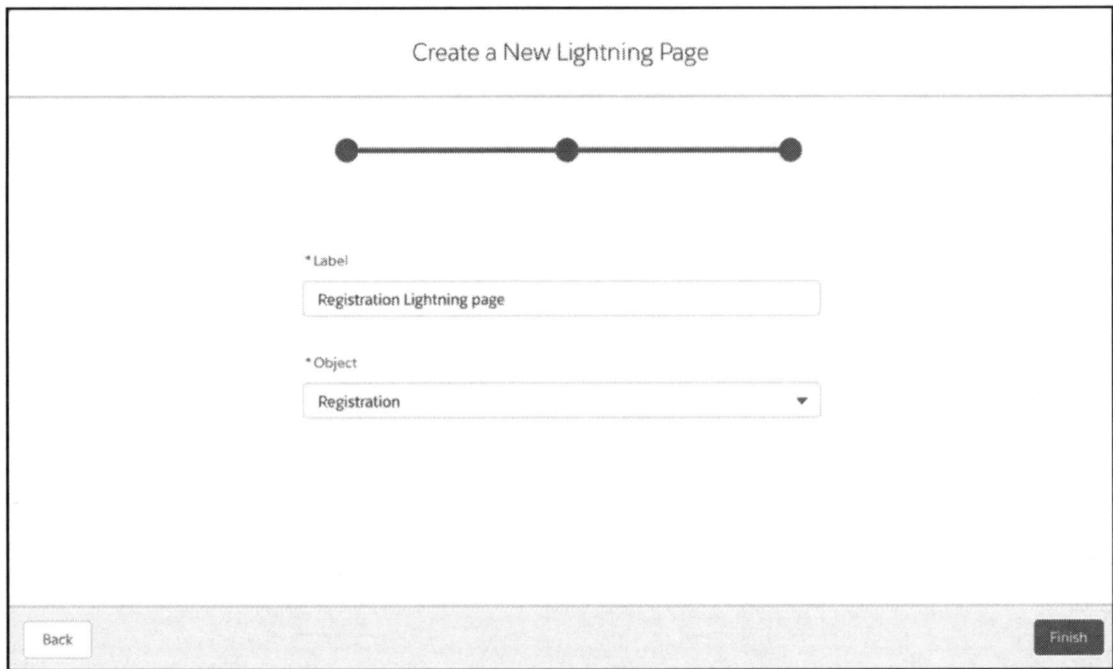

Once you are done, click on **Finish**.

6. In the Lightning App Builder, add, edit, or remove components to customize the page's layout:

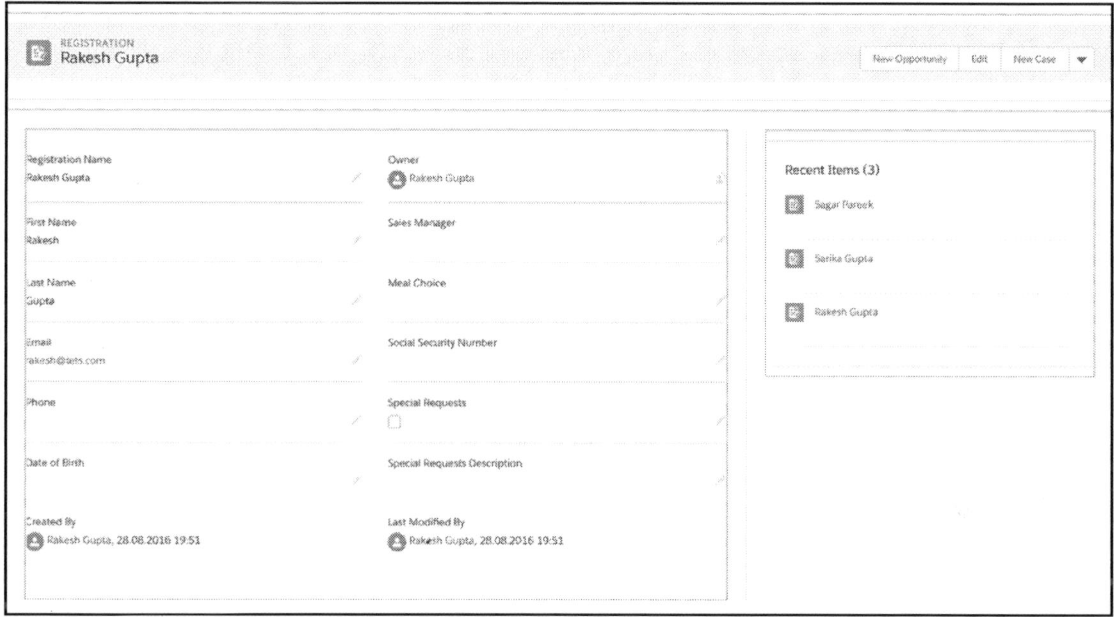

7. Once you are done, click on **Save**. It will open a pop-up, that will allow you to activate the page on clicking the **Activate** button, as shown in the following screenshot:

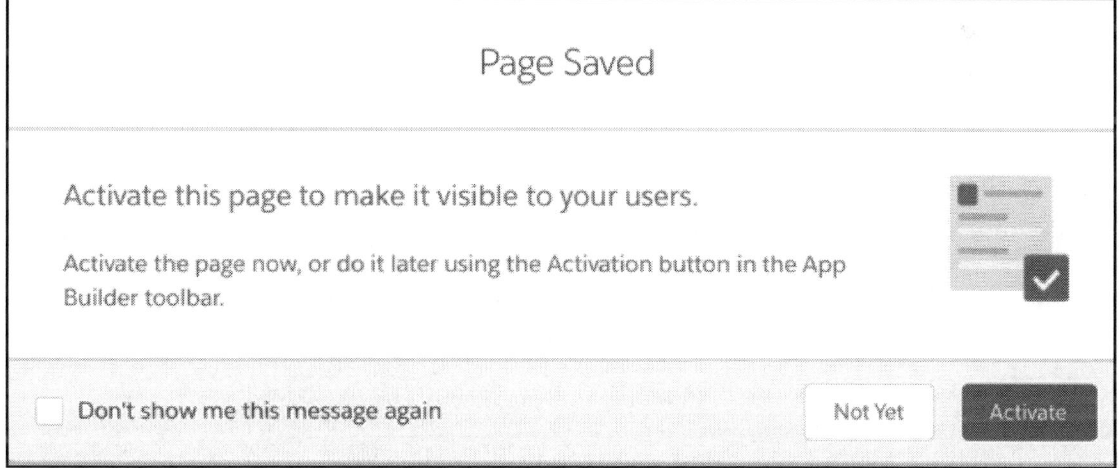

8. The next step is to assign the page as the default record page, or you can assign it to specific apps, as per your requirement. For the current situation, select **Assign this page as the default record page**, as shown in the following screenshot:

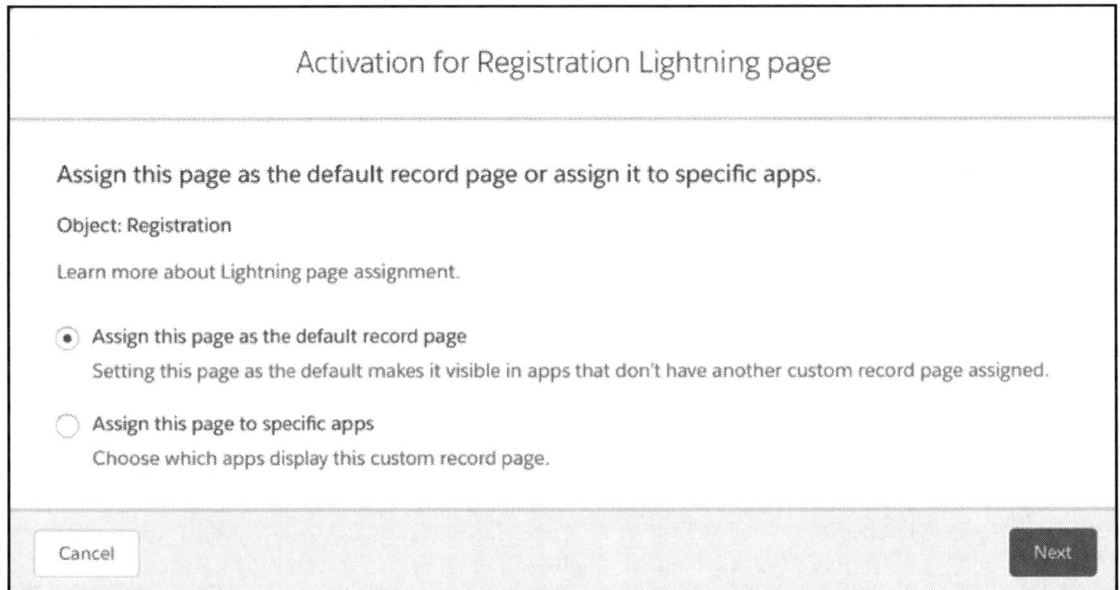

Once you are done, click on **Next**.

9. On the final screen, review the settings and click on **Save**.

Improving the data quality

In order to make your data valid and healthy when entered by the user, it is very important that you must impose some constraints over the values being entered by the user in the system so that the user must not enter any junk values or values that don't meet your business requirement. To enforce data quality, you can use the following option:

1. **Validation rules**: Use a validation rule to conditionally require fields. You can also ensure proper data format, for example, ZIP code must be of five digits or the date of birth must be greater than 01/01/1990.

2. **Unique fields**: Use a unique field to make a record unique, based on some fields. For example, in the `registration` object, make the e-mail field unique so that you don't have two records with the same e-mail address:

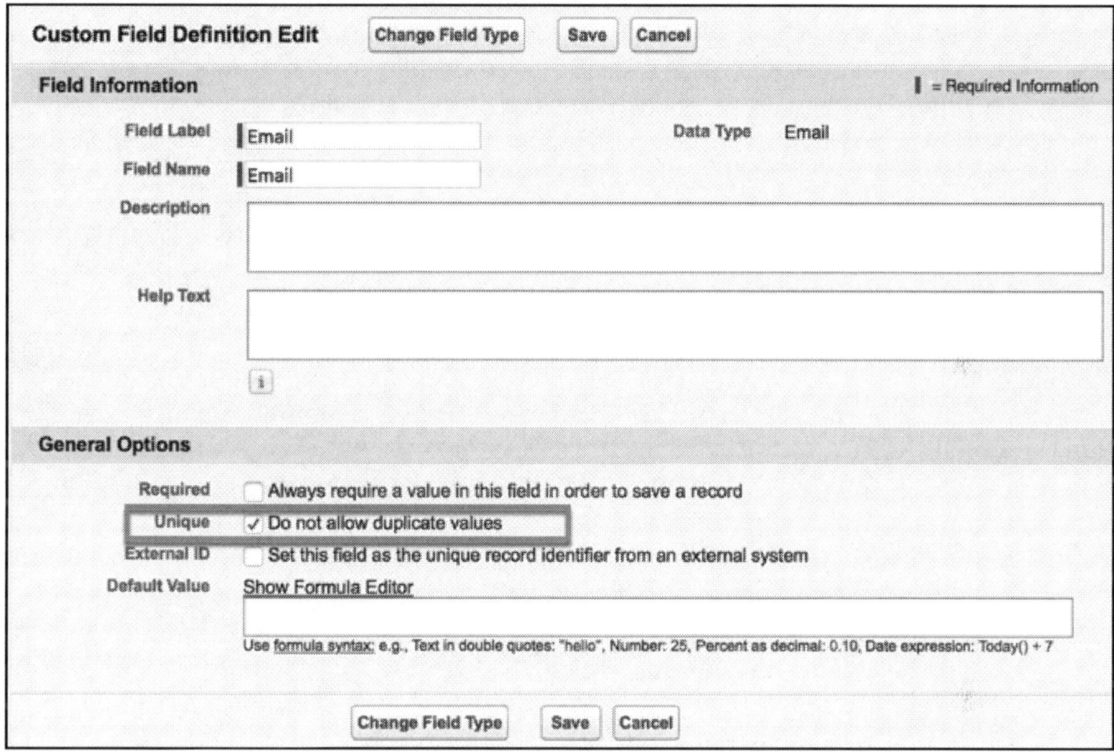

3. **Picklist and dependent picklist fields**: Use picklist and dependent fields to force users to enter a permission value.
4. **Custom lookup fields and lookup filters**: Use lookup fields and lookup filters to select a subset of records from another object to enforce data consistency.
5. **Record types and page layout**: Use record types and page layout to display only the relevant fields to users.
6. **Process builder record updates**: Use the process builder record update action to automatically update the value of a field and reduce the need for manual entry.

Preventing duplicate records with Duplicate Management

You can use out-of-the-box **Duplicate Management** feature to control when and whether users can create duplicate records in Salesforce. It is fully customizable and allows you to create reports on duplicates that users save. Duplicate Management is part of Data.com, but it doesn't require Data.com license. This feature is only available for the account, contact, lead, and custom objects.

Creating matching rule

Matching rules are used to identify how two records are compared and recognized as duplicates. Each matching rule is built up of multiple criteria on different fields.

A business scenario: *David Guzman* has created the custom object registration and all the necessary fields. Now, he has received a requirement from his senior management to not allow any employees to create duplicate records if records already exist with the same e-mail address. They also want to prompt a list of duplicate records to employees at runtime.

To create a matching rule on the `registration` object, follow these steps:

1. Click on **Setup** (gear icon) | **Setup** | **PLATFORM TOOLS** | **Feature Settings** | **Data.com** | **Matching Rules**.
2. To create a new matching rule, click on **New Rule**.
3. The next step is to select the object on which matching rule will apply. In this case, select the **Registration** object.
4. Enter all the details as mentioned here to define the new matching rule:
    1. **Rule Name**: This is the rule name of the matching rule. Enter `Registration Matching Rule` as the **Rule Name**.
    2. **Unique Name**: This will be autopopulated, based on the rule name.
    3. **Description**: Write some meaningful text, so other developers/administrators can easily understand why this matching rule was created.
    4. **Matching Criteria**: To define matching criteria for a field type, select **Email** and for **Matching Method**, select **Exact**:

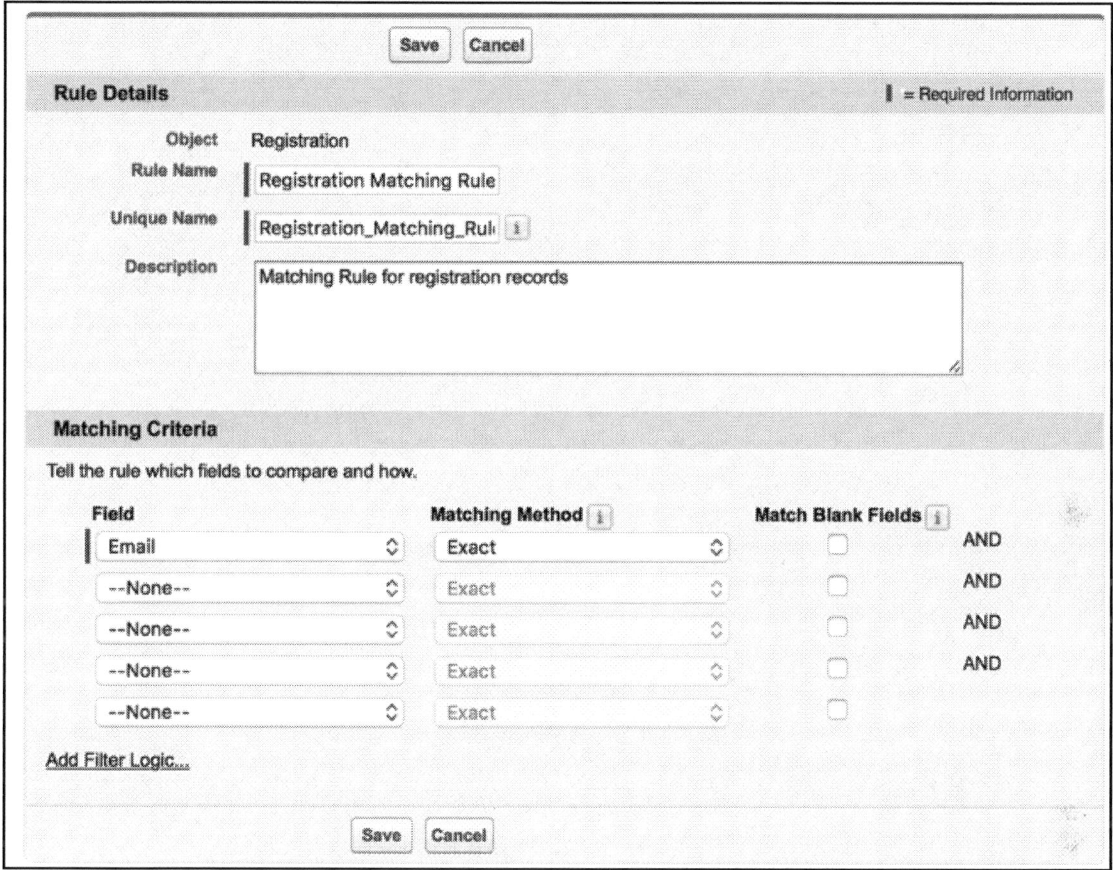

5. Once you are done, click on **Save**.
6. Then **Activate** the rule.

Creating a duplicate rule

You can use duplicate rules to define what happens when a user tries to create duplicate records in Salesforce. Duplicate rules and matching rules work together. For example, a field updates work with the Workflow Rule. Create duplicate rules to run matching rule, follow the steps given as follows:

1. Click on **Setup** (gear icon) | **Setup** | **PLATFORM TOOLS** | **Feature Settings** | **Data.com** | **Duplicate Rules**.

2. To create a new duplicate rule, click on **New Rule** and then select the object on which the duplicate rule will apply. In this case, select the **Registration** object.
3. Enter all the details as mentioned in the following to define the new matching rule:
    1. **Rule Name**: This is the rule name of the duplicate rule. Enter `Registration Duplicate Rule` as the **Rule Name**.
    2. **Description**: Write some meaningful text, so other developers/administrators can easily understand why this duplicate rule was created.
    3. **Record-Level Security**: Select how you want duplicate rules to identify duplicate records: whether within complete records of a `registration` object or only within the records that the current user has access to. Select the **Bypass sharing rules** option.
    4. **Actions**: Now select what will happen when a user tries to create or edit a duplicate record:
        1. **Action on Create**: Select the block option.
        2. **Action on Edit**: Select the block option.
        3. **Alert Text**: Change the alert message as you want.
    5. **Matching Rules**: The final step is defining how duplicate records are identified:
        1. **Compare Registrations with**: Select the **Registration** object.
        2. **Matching Rule**: Now, select which matching rules will determine how records are identified as duplicates. Select **Registration Matching Rule**.

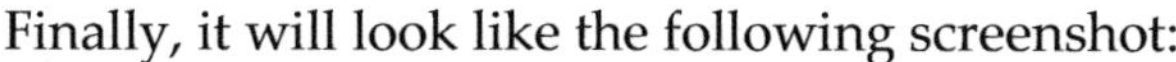

Finally, it will look like the following screenshot:

Rule Details

Rule Name: Registration Duplicate Rule
Description: Duplicate Rule for registration
Object: Registration
Record-Level Security: Enforce sharing rules / Bypass sharing rules

Actions

Specify what happens when a user tries to save a duplicate record.

Action On Create: Block
Action On Edit: Block
Alert Text: You're creating a duplicate record. We recommend you use an existing record instead.

Matching Rules

Define how duplicate records are identified.

Compare Registrations With: Registrations
Matching Rule: Registration Matching Rule
Matching Criteria: Registration: Email EXACT MatchBlank = FALSE
Field Mapping: Mapping Selected

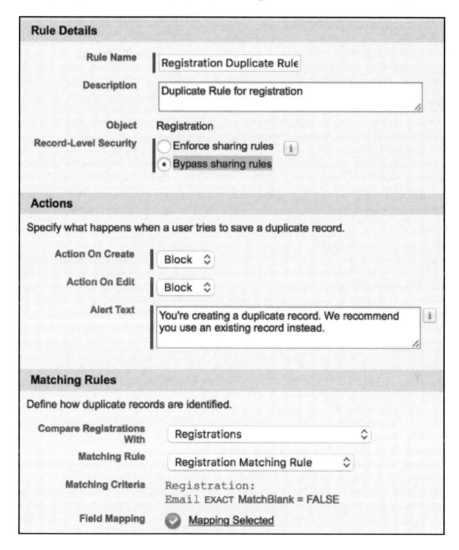

4. Once you are done, click on **Save**.
5. Then **Activate** the rule.

Now onwards, if a user tries to create a duplicate record (based on e-mail address) for a `registration` object, then he will get a **Duplicate Block** pop-up, as shown in the following screenshot:

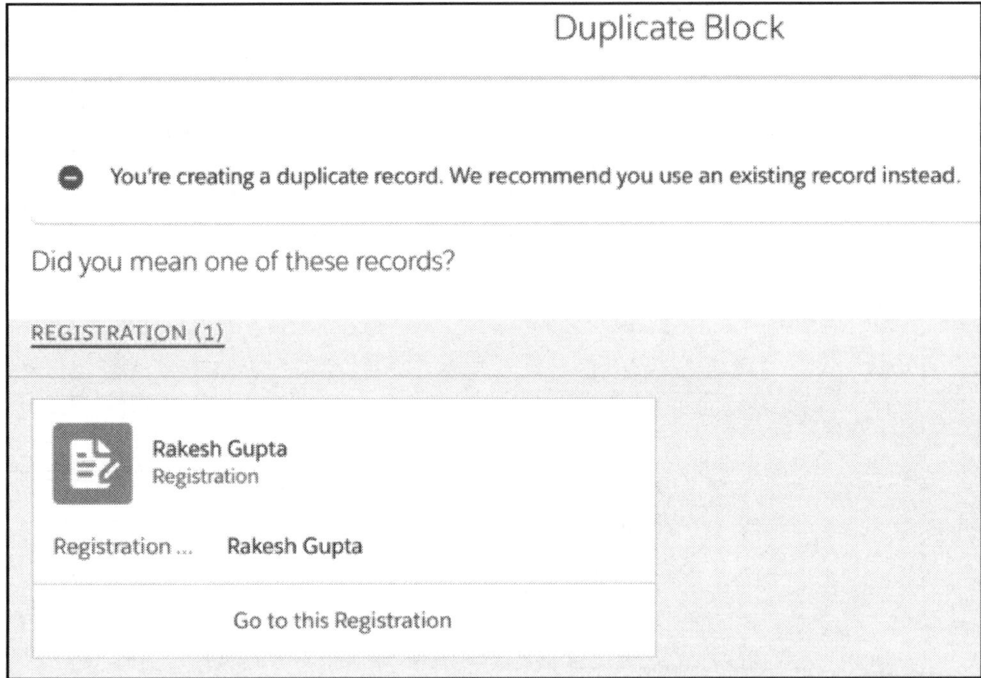

A few points to remember

1. Lightning apps aren't available in Salesforce Classic.
2. Field help text is now available in Salesforce Lighting Experience.
3. You can create 40 lookup relationships on an object.
4. You can have a maximum of 26 roll-up summary fields on a master object in the case of a master-detail relationship.
5. A validation rule is the best way to make a field required.
6. You can have a maximum of five active lookup filters per object.
7. After the *Winter'17* release, inline editing is now available in Lightning Experience.

Test your knowledge

Q1. When you want to share a specific record with a user, which of the following sharing models will you use?

1. Sharing rule
2. Role hierarchies
3. Organization-wide default
4. Territory management

Q2. How many lookup relationships are allowed on an object?

1. 20
2. 15
3. 25
4. 40

Q3. How do you autopopulate the city picklist values based on the state selected?

1. Dependent Picklist
2. Validation Rules
3. Workflows
4. Duplicate Rule

Q4. What are the different custom tabs that you can create?

1. Web Tab
2. Apex Tab
3. Visualforce Tab
4. Custom Object Tab
5. Standard Object Tab

Q5. In a master-detail relationship, the fields of the parent object need to be displayed in the child object. How you will accomplish it?

1. Cross-object formula field
2. Workflow rule
3. Validation rule
4. Assignment rule

Summary

In this chapter, we started with an overview of custom objects. Then, we moved ahead and discussed how to create custom fields and how to associate custom objects with tabs. You also learned how to configure Lightning record pages for your Salesforce object. In the end, we discussed how to avoid duplicate data in Salesforce. In the next chapter, we will go through the Salesforce Sales Cloud and its key concepts, including collaborative forecasting.

5

Getting More Value from Sales Cloud

In the previous chapters, we discussed the basic concepts of objects and fields. We also talked about the different types of relationships in Salesforce. We have gone through the process for setting up Lightning apps, Lightning record pages, validation rules, and duplicate management in Salesforce. In this chapter, we will describe Sales Cloud features in detail, such as account management, opportunity management, quote management, and so on. In addition to this, we will also look at the way of setting up forecasting in your Salesforce org. The following topics will be covered in this chapter:

- Account management
- Contact management
- Manage products and price books
- Opportunity management
- Quote management
- Collaborative forecasting

Sales Cloud is a product designed to automate business sales processes. By implementing Sales Cloud, you can boost your sales reps' productivity by allowing them to manage customers in a faster and simpler way. It includes all Sales Cloud features, for example, campaign, lead, account, contact, opportunity, quote, report, and dashboard. Sales Cloud can help an organization to close a deal faster using an inbuilt functionality called Einstein.

Sales Cloud helps you to maintain a robust sales pipeline, from quotation to contract management, on the cloud. The productivity accomplished by implementing Sales Cloud in your organization will allow your sales reps to focus on managing good relationships with the existing customers and will help them bring new business as well. Your sales team will work more competently while your marketing executives are provided with the actual information for making more informed and quicker business decisions.

Sales Cloud also helps align the marketing team, inside sales team, and sales team, so they can work together in an organized manner to win more deals, bring new customers, and retain existing customers. There are some advantages of implementing Sales Cloud. They are as follows:

- Improve lead conversation rate
- Close more deals with the help of Einstein
- Align territories and quotas to business strategy
- Get a 360-degree view of your customer
- Standardized quoting and contracting management capability
- Accelerate productivity with Salesforce1 mobile app
- Automate business processes by using Process Builder and approval processes
- Make insightful decisions with the help of reports and dashboards

Customer life cycle starts from campaign (company branding or product awareness) and completes with closing a deal successfully to win customer loyalty, as shown in the following diagram:

In Salesforce words, it starts from creating a campaign. Through the campaign, an organization may get leads, and once those leads are ready to buy some products from you, then convert those leads into accounts, contacts, or, optionally, opportunities. Once you win those opportunities, the next step is to deliver the orders.

Campaign management

A campaign is an awareness or branding program that a company runs to promote its products or business. An organization can run campaigns through various channels, for example, seminar, trade show, advertisement, banner, billboards, and e-mail blast. Through a campaign, an organization can generate prospects (a person or another organization who is interested in your product or business).

Salesforce allows the marketing team to capture their campaign plan, manage, track, and execute it within Salesforce. It is very easy to capture new prospects directly from your corporate website's **Contact Us** form into Salesforce or capture prospects from **GoToWebinar** register attendees for an event to Salesforce. Then, you can associate those prospects to campaign to track in the future to see how successful the marketing effort was. The marketing team can also send a mass e-mail to prospects, that too within Salesforce.

Steps to executing an outstanding marketing campaign

The success of a campaign does not depend on the size of your business or the marketing trends in your industry. The success of a campaign is measured through various parameters, such as demand generation, high-quality sales-ready leads, and profit in the end. To make a campaign successful, you have to focus on a few areas. The following diagram shows a consistent and proactive lead generation approach through a successful campaign.

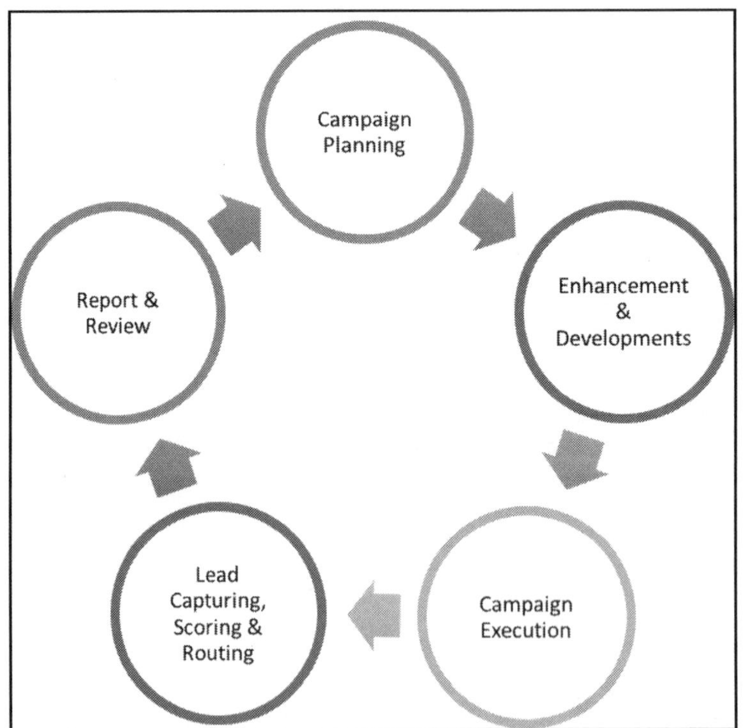

The following are some tips on running successful marketing campaigns:

1. Start with the planning of your campaign, for example, the modes of campaign, budget, campaign owner, expectations, and so on. You can't just pull off a marketing campaign overnight. Create your detailed campaign strategy by including the following questions as you start to create your campaign strategy:
    - Who is your target audience?
    - What is your campaign end goal?
    - Which social media, print media, webinar, or advertisement are the best fit for your campaign?
    - What's your team member's role in running this campaign?
    - How do you measure success?
2. The next step is to enhance and add some value to your campaign. As you are aware that several campaigns are running these days on social media or print media, people need a reason to listen and participate in your campaign. For example, for a better outcome, you can add some perks of winning the prize and so on.
3. Then run your campaign through the various channels. Make sure you use SEO to target key audiences.
4. Once you start getting the prospects, before passing it to the sales team, ensure that these prospects are qualified prospects. To do so, you can implement scoring and grading to a lead object. As soon as prospects cross the MQL score, assign it to the sales team for further nurturing.
5. At last, run the report and check the business profits and new active customer summary.

Creating a new campaign

Before creating a new campaign, make sure that the user has **Marketing User** checkbox selected on their user record. Perform the following steps to create a new campaign:

1. Make sure that you have selected the **Sales** app.

2. Click on the **Campaign** Tab and then click on the **New** button. Now, create a new campaign, as shown in the following screenshot:

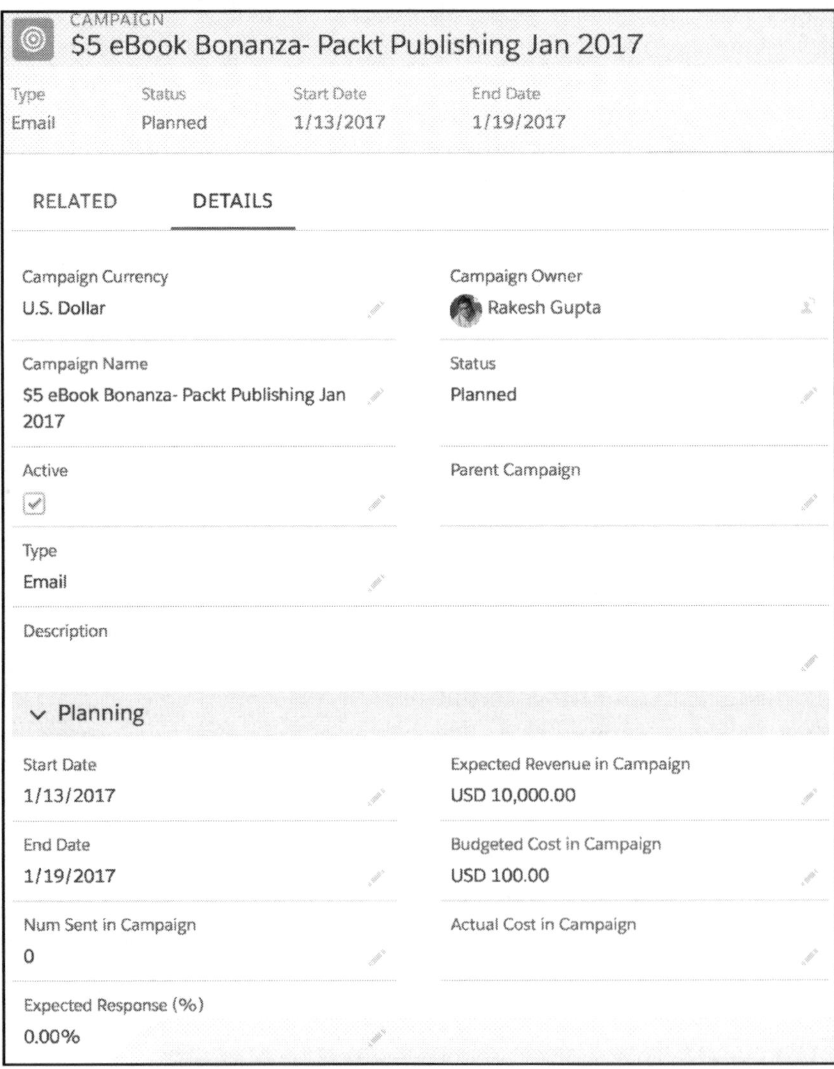

3. Once you are done, click on the **Save** button.

Lead management

Lead represents prospects that are interested in purchasing your product or someone who is interested in doing business with your organization. A campaign is one way to generate leads for your organization. Salesforce provides numerous ways to capture leads from different sources, for example, scan business cards and save the information in Salesforce as a lead, or through web-to-lead, and so on. You can easily access leads through any device, such as mobile, tablet, or workstation. If you want to increase inside sales productivity by assigning qualified leads to them, follow these best practices:

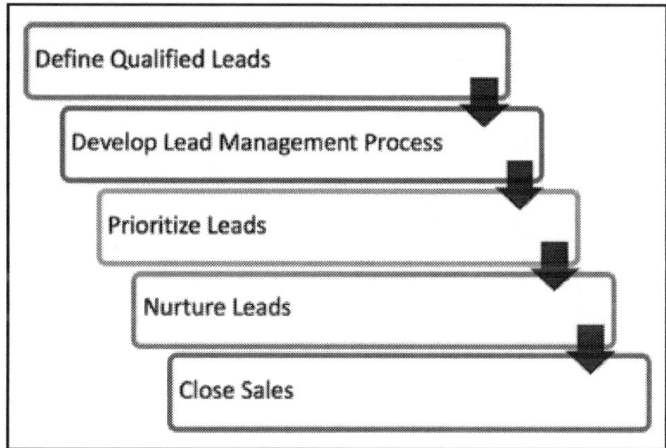

Follow these best practices to build a strong funnel of marketing qualified leads:

1. Before you start managing a qualified lead, you have to define it. A qualified marketing lead is nothing but a person or an organization who has shown interest in buying your product or doing business with your organization and passed a set of lead qualifications criteria in order to progress further down the funnel. To better manage leads, you can use middleware systems such as Pardot or Eloqua. The following sample questions will help you to identify qualified leads:
    - Does the person or company have enough money to afford your product or service?
    - Can the person make a buying decision?
    - Does the person or company have a specific timeframe to buy a product or service?

2. Once you have qualified the lead, the next step is developing the sales process for your inside sales team to work on leads throughout the sales life cycle.
3. The next step is to develop a plan to prioritize leads, then assign them to sales reps. It is crucial to assign the right lead at the right time to your sales team for better results.
4. Nurturing is the key step to converting a cold call into a hot call. Remember that not all leads are ready to buy your product or service right away. For example, the prospect doesn't have money at the current time, but a future event will make it a lead after a few months. Lead nurturing is nothing but building a relationship and establishing a trust with the prospects over time through consistent messaging. It allows sales reps to send highly targeted messages to prospects, based on the information provided by them.
5. Once the prospects are ready to buy a product or service, then pass it to the sales team and close the deal successfully.

Creating a new lead

Before creating a new lead, make sure that the user has appropriate permissions on their profile. Perform the following steps to create a new lead:

1. Make sure that you have selected the **Sales** app.
2. Click on the **Lead** tab and then click on the **New** button. Now create a new lead, as shown in the following screenshot:

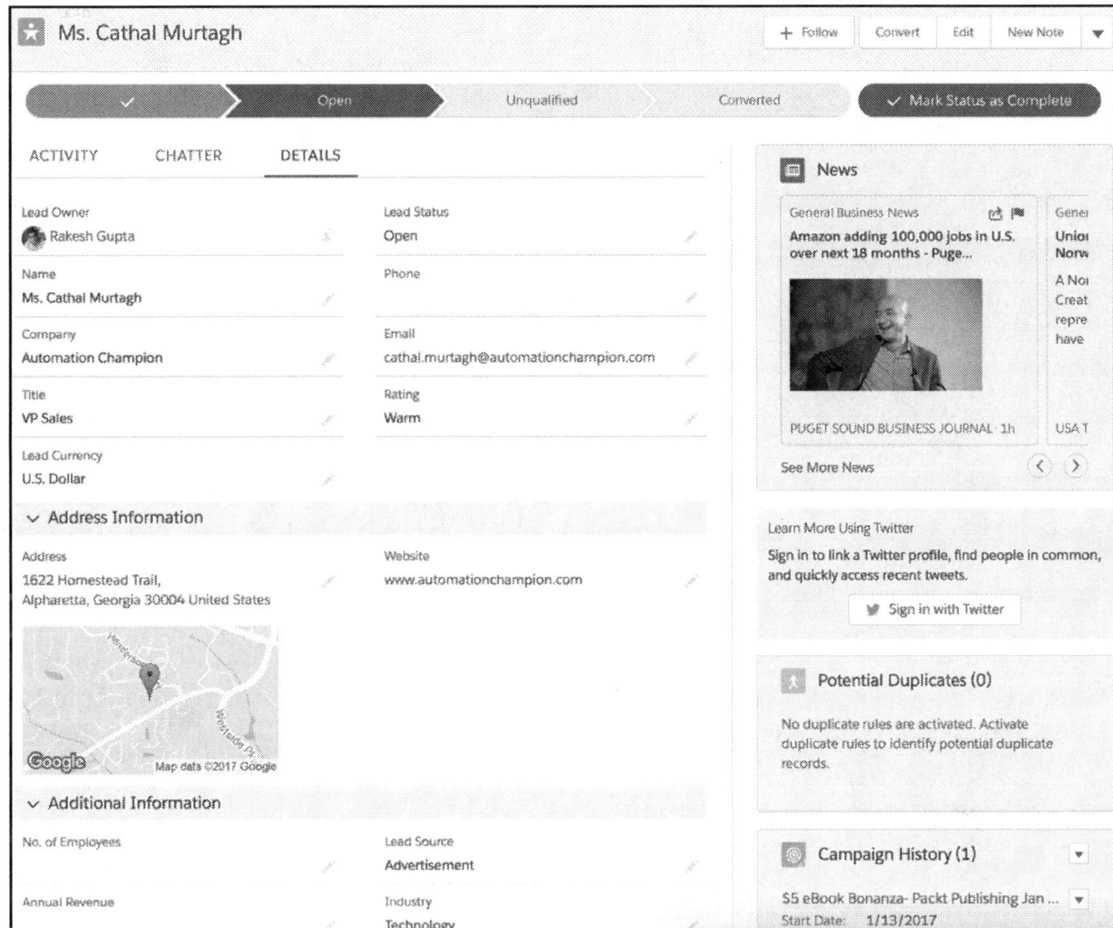

Converting a lead

Once you are ready to convert a lead, click on the **Convert** button. Lead conversion will create an account, contact, and optionally, an opportunity in Salesforce. Opportunities that are created by lead conversion default value for required field like opportunity **Close Date** is set to the **last day of the current quarter** and **Stage** will set to the first value of opportunity stage picklist. During lead conversion, the opportunity **Amount** field on opportunity remains blank. To convert a lead, click on the **Convert** button available on the lead detail page.

If a person account is enabled for your organization, than the company name on the lead is no more a required field. If a lead with an empty company name converts, it will create a person account (not business account and contact).

Account management

An account can represent your customer, partner, or competitor. A customer account allows you to store your customer data, so you can have a 360-degree view of your customer. Whereas, a partner account helps you to better manage your partner by allowing them limited access to your Salesforce using the Partner community. A competitor account allows you to manage your competitor offerings, rates, and service industries.

As per a Gartner report, 65% of a company's business comes from existing customers and it costs them five times more to attract a new customer than to keep an existing one satisfied. This indicates the importance of maintaining a good relationship with existing customers and, at the same time, follow-up with focused customer engagement to grow the relationship and increase revenue growth on an ongoing basis.

The different types of accounts in Salesforce are as follows:

- **Business account (B2B)**: When you sell a product or offering to another organization, such a business is called **business-to-business selling**. Use the business (business-to-business) account to store your customer (organization) information in Salesforce. By default, the business account is enabled for every Salesforce organization. For example, Salesforce.com Inc. sells its product to other organizations.
- **Person account (B2C)**: When you sell a product or service to an individual, it is called **business-to-person selling**. Use the person (business-to-person) account to store customer (individual) information in Salesforce. To enable a person account in your Salesforce org, you must raise a support case with Salesforce. For example, MetLife is an insurance firm selling their products to an individual as well as organizations.

Creating a new business account

You can create a new business account by using a user interface, or you can also import it from another organization by using the import wizard and data loader. Perform the following steps to create a new account:

1. Go to the **Lead** tab, then open **Cathal Murtagh** lead.
2. Now, click on the **Convert** button available on top of the page to convert the lead.
3. The new account will look like the following screenshot:

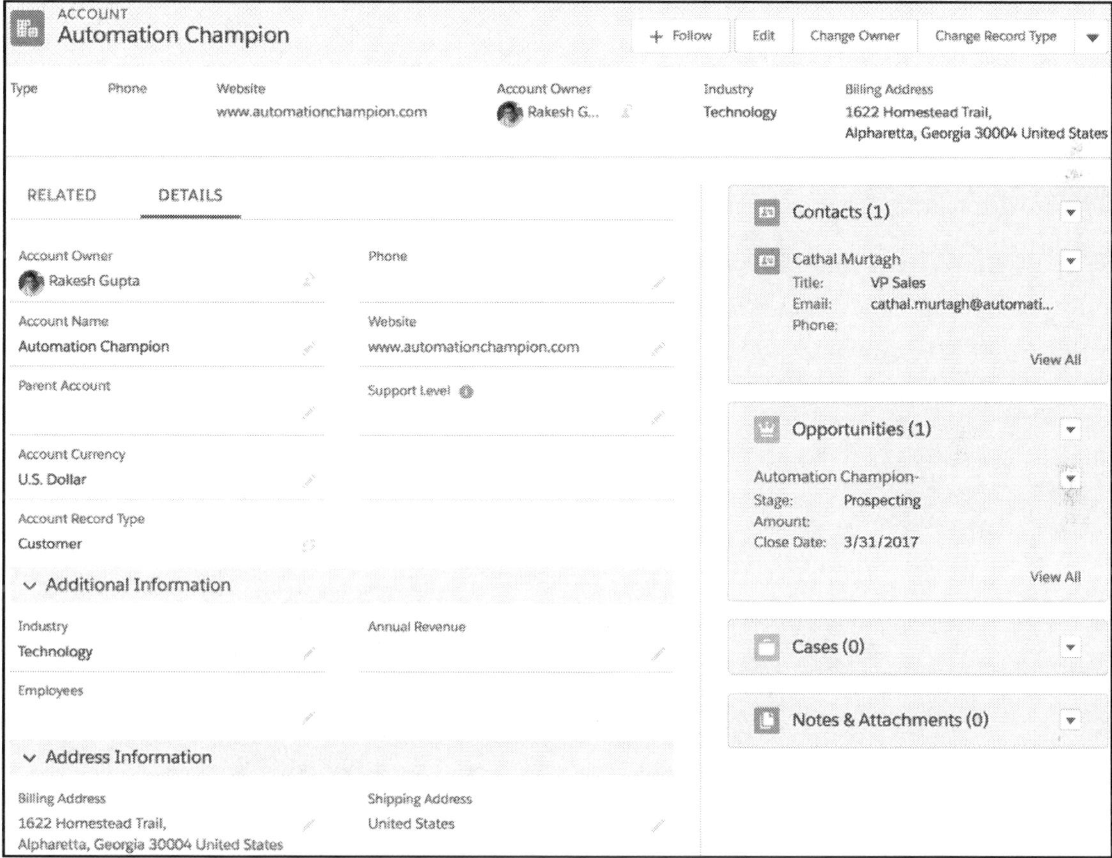

Make sure that you have created an account, a contact, and an opportunity, as shown in the preceding screenshot.

Contact management

Contact is a way to maintain the information about key decision makers, buyers, and key influential people for an account in Salesforce. The sales and marketing people often need it as they should visit the customer site and give a demo to them about products or services to finalize the deal. You can store contact information, such as first name, last name, account name, billing address or shipping address, contact number, and e-mail address.

You can create a contact in Salesforce by using the user interface, or you can import it from another organization by using the import wizard and data loader.

Understanding account and contact relationships

One account may have more than one contact and one contact may be associated with multiple accounts. For example, say, your company is currently selling a product to two sites of Automation Champion, USA and India. You have two accounts for Automation Champion in your Salesforce. For the USA account, *Cathal Murtagh* is the decision maker, and for the India account, she is the executive sponsor. To associate one contact with multiple accounts, we can use the contact to multiple accounts feature.

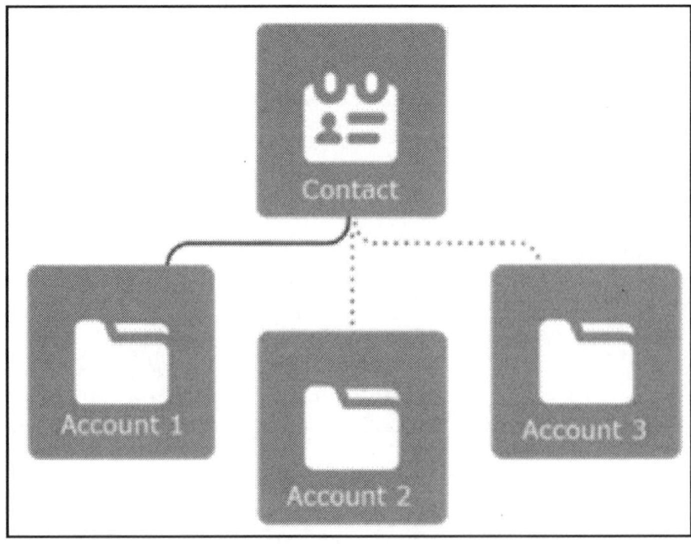

Before proceeding ahead, create a new account for **Automation Champion – India**, as shown in the following screenshot:

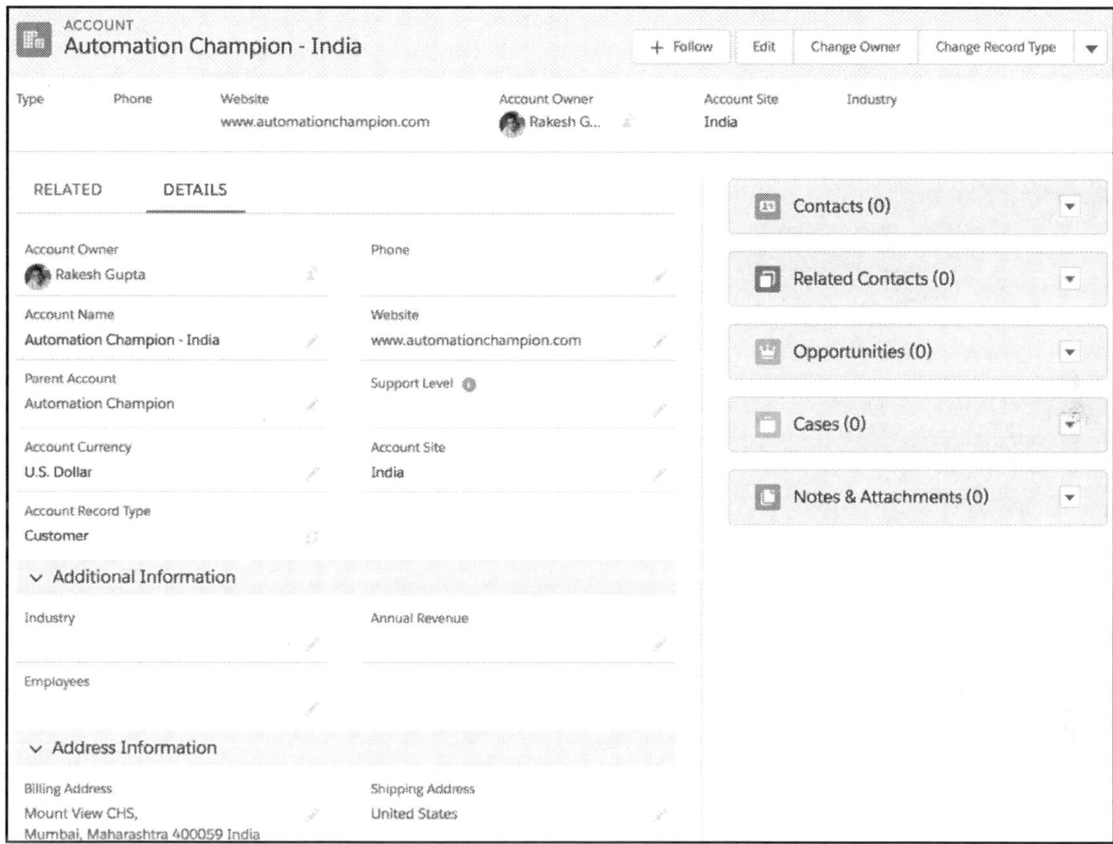

Make sure to set the correct name for the account and site, as shown in the preceding screenshot, to eliminate any confusion.

Contact to multiple accounts

A business scenario: currently, *Cathal Murtagh* is the decision maker for **Automation Champion – USA** account. As Universal Containers has set up a new account for Automation Champion, the India business wants to list *Cathal Murtagh* as executive sponsor for the India account, without creating a duplicate contact.

Perform the following instructions to set up a contact to multiple accounts:

1. Click on **Setup** (gear icon) | **Setup** | **PLATFORM TOOLS** | **Feature Settings** | **Sales** | **Account Settings**.
2. Click on the **Edit** button and then navigate to **Contacts to Multiple Accounts Settings** and select the **Allow users to relate a contact to multiple accounts** checkbox, as shown in the following screenshot:

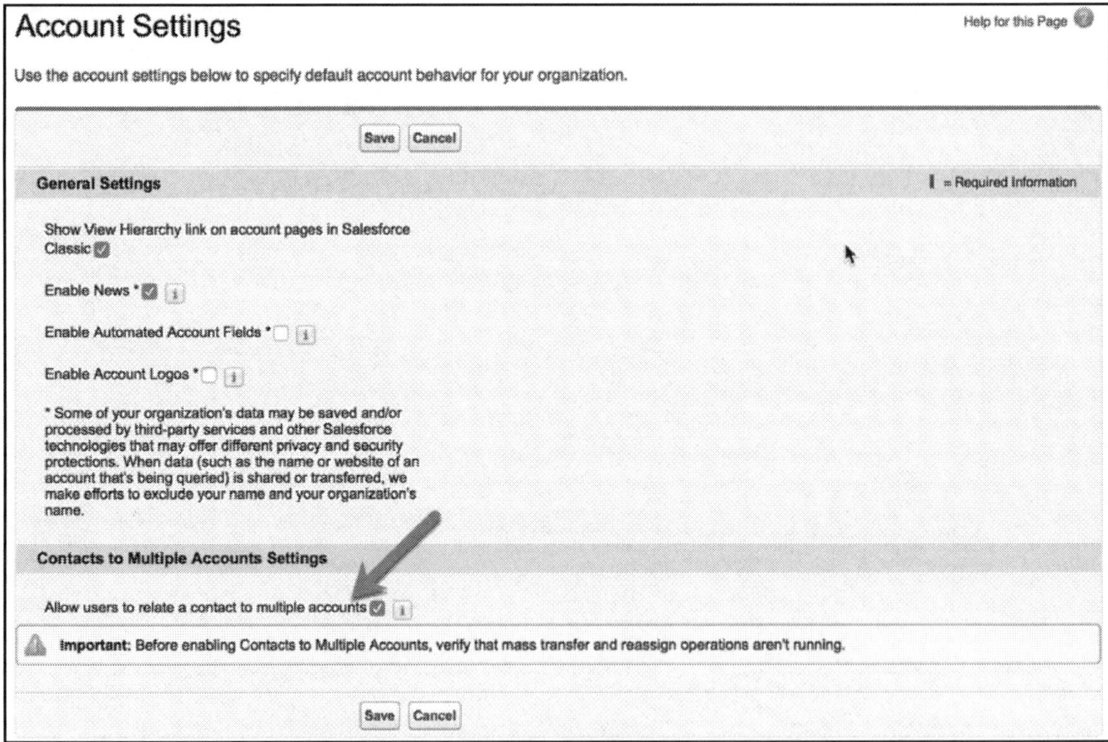

3. Once you are done, click on the **Save** button.

4. The next steps are to add the **Related Contacts** related list to the account page layouts:
    1. Click on **Setup** (gear icon) | **Setup** | **PLATFORM TOOLS** | **Objects and Fields** | **Object Manager** | **Account** | **Page Layout**, then select the appropriate page layouts.
    2. Then, select **Related Lists** section.
    3. Drag **Related Contacts** onto the page layout, as the related contacts related list automatically includes all the direct contacts.
    4. Once you are done, click on the **Save** button.
5. Like what you just did in step 4, take it as a reference; now, add the **Related Accounts** related list to the contact page layouts.
6. Now, open the **Automation Champion – India** account, navigate to **Related Contacts** related list, and then select **Add Relationship** from the drop-down menu, as shown in the following screenshot:

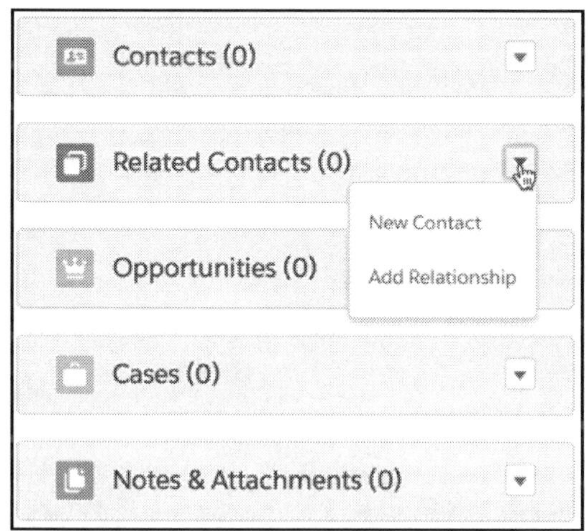

7. The next step is to create an account contact relationship for **Cathal Murtagh** as **Executive Sponsor** for the **Automation Champion – India** account, as shown in the following screenshot:

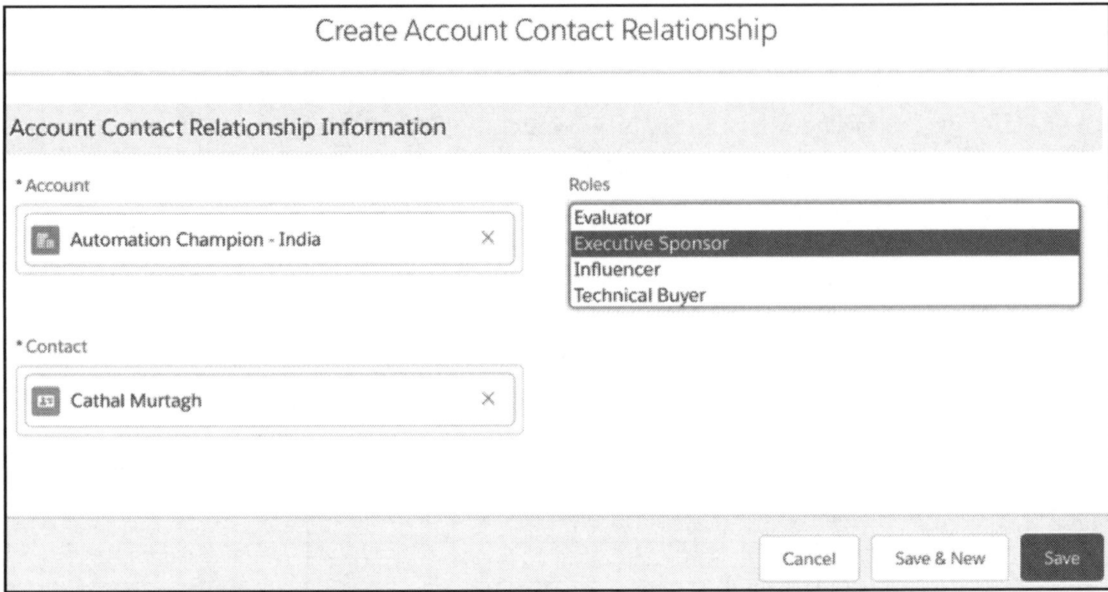

8. Once you are done, click on the **Save** button.

This is how you can associate one contact with multiple accounts without creating duplicate contact records in the database.

Managing product and price books

Products are the backbone of any system. Products are the physical products or services that you sell to customers. Your sales reps can use the products to generate sales quotes, marketing campaigns, contracts, or orders. Your service reps might also use products to create customer service cases. When you see the detail page of an opportunity, quote, order or service contract, the opportunity product related list, or the quote line items, the related list displays the linked products for that record.

Once you have listed all the products in Salesforce, then you can associate it with multiple price books with different prices. Price books are used for selling products at different prices based on the geography and business year, or based on the agreement with a customer:

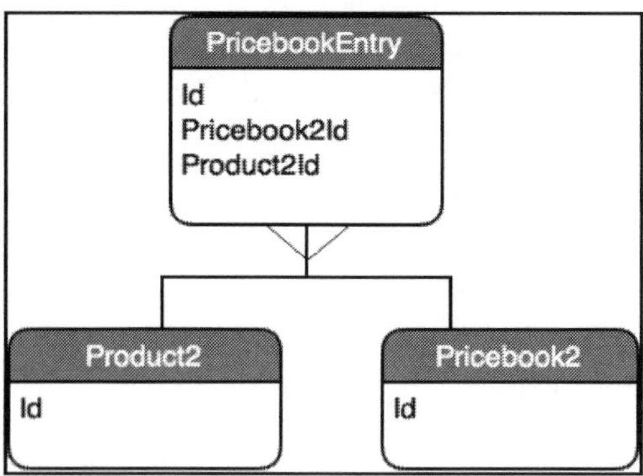

PricebookEntry is a junction object that has an associate product in a price book. It means you can add one product to multiple price books. There are two main prices in price books. One is the standard price and the other is the list price:

- Standard prices are the prices fixed by the manufacturer of the product and which cannot be changed.
- List price is the selling price of a product for a price book. The sales reps may sell the same product with different prices to customers, based on the geography.

Creating a product

A business scenario: *David Guzman* is working as a *System Administrator* at Universal Containers. His manager, *Brigette Hyacinth*, asked him to create a new product with the following details:

- Product Name: Learning Salesforce Visual Workflow
- Product Code: 9781785289835
- Active: True
- Product Currency: U.S. Dollar
- Product Description: Learning Salesforce Visual Workflow – Printed book

Perform the following instructions to create a new product:

1. Make sure that you have selected the **Sales** app.
2. Click on the **Product** tab, and then click on the **New** button. Now, create a new product, as shown in the following screenshot:

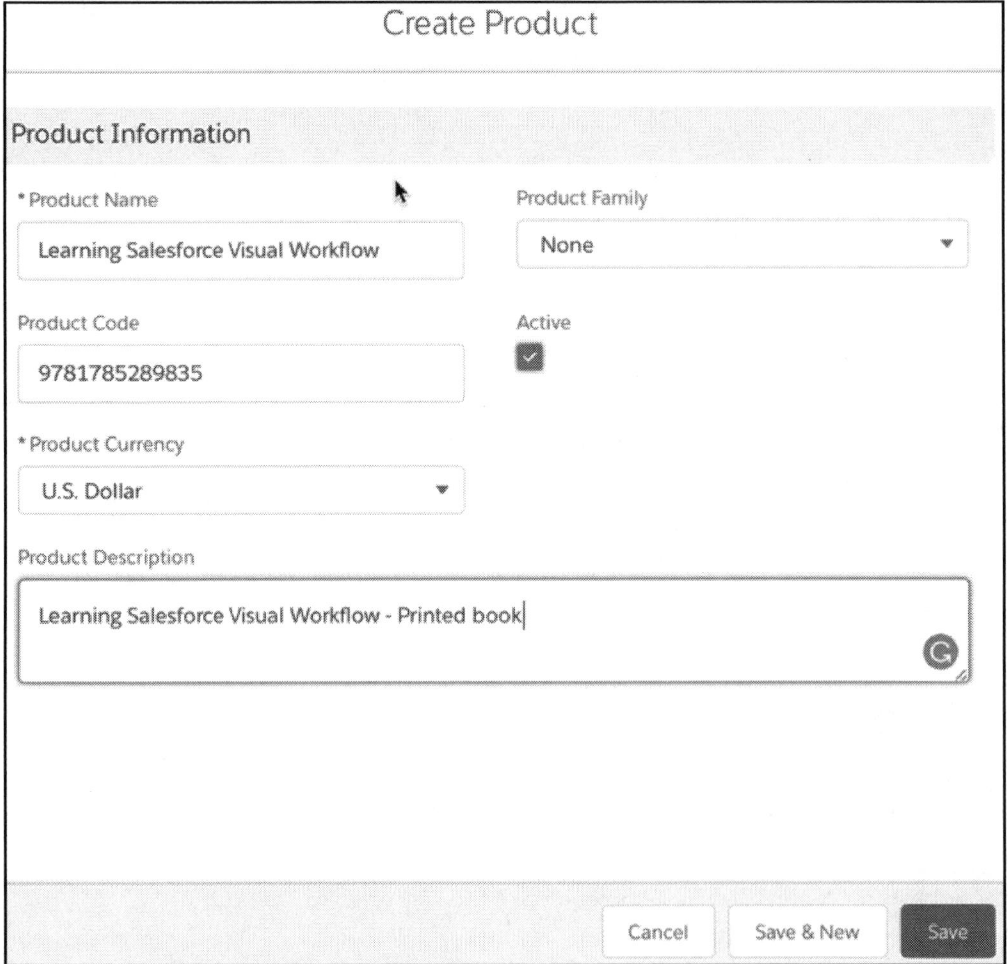

3. Once you are done, click on the **Save** button.

Perform the preceding steps (1 to 3) to enter as many products into Salesforce as you want. If you want to add a product to the custom price books, then it must be active.

Adding standard price to a product

Once you have entered the products in Salesforce, the next step is to add a standard price to it. Standard prices are prices fixed by the manufacturer of the product and which cannot be changed.

A business scenario: *David Guzman* is working as a *System Administrator* at Universal Containers. As per the preceding business requirement, *David Guzman* has already created a product in Salesforce. Now, his manager, *Brigette Hyacinth,* asked him to enter a standard price for this product, which is $32.00.

Perform the following instructions to add the standard price to a product:

1. Make sure that you have selected the **Sales** app.
2. Click on the **Product** tab, and then open the **Learning Salesforce Visual Workflow** product.
3. From the details page, navigate to the **RELATED** list. Now, click on the **Add Standard Price** button available under the **Price Books** related list, as shown in the following screenshot:

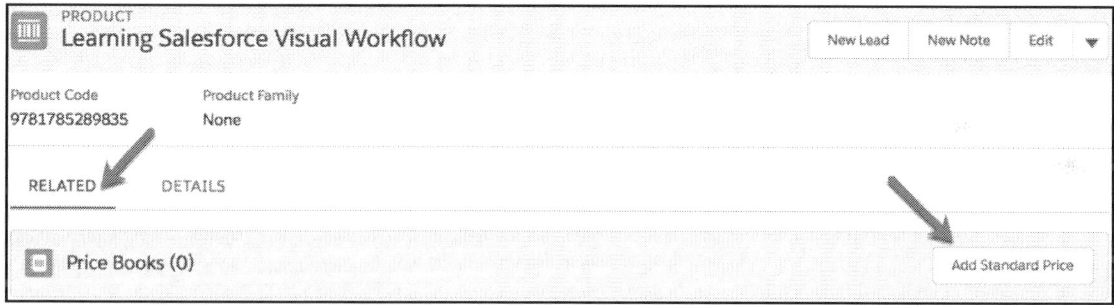

4. It will open a popup. Now, enter the standard price, that is, `$32.00` into the **List Price** box, as shown in the following screenshot:

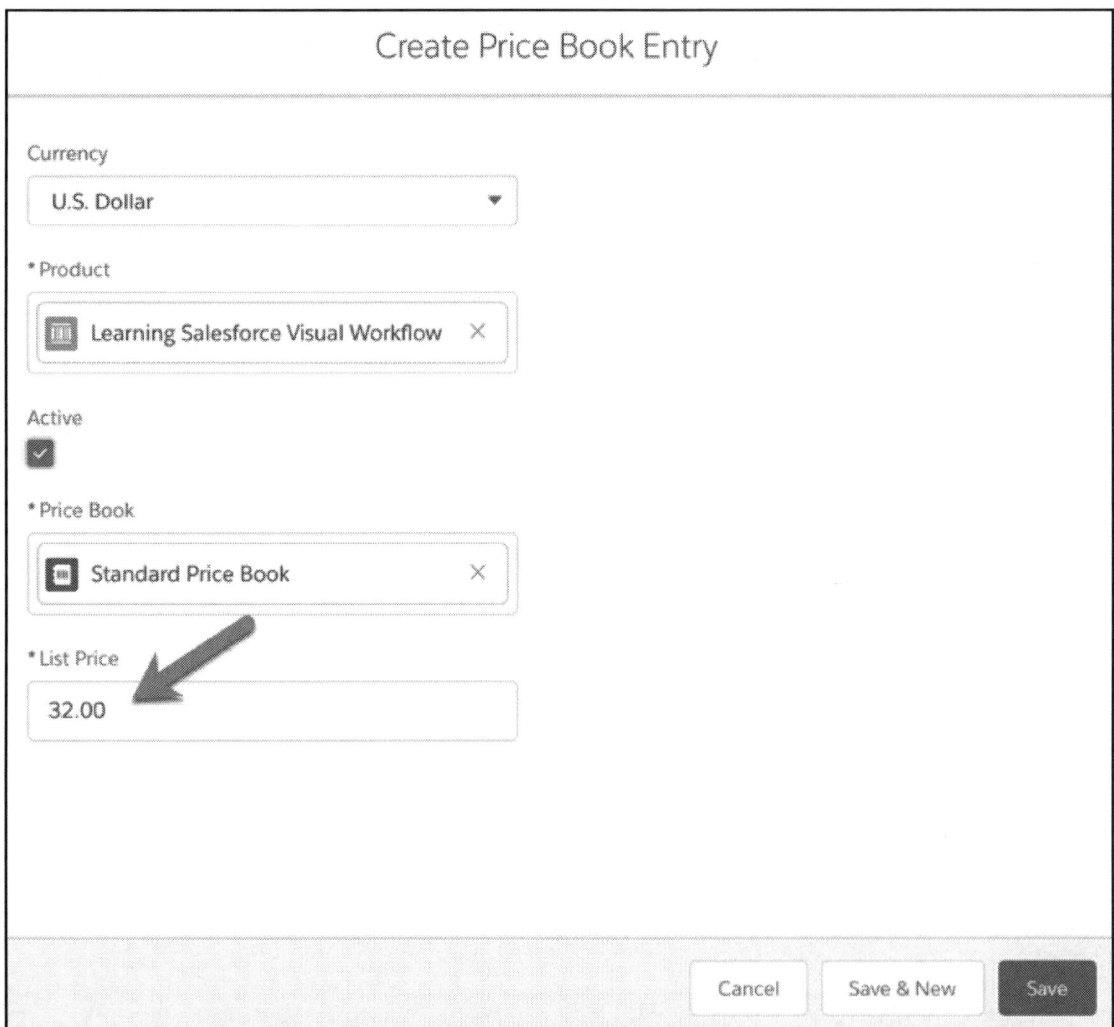

5. Once you are done, click on the **Save** button.

This is how you can associate a product to a standard price. One product can have only one standard price. **Standard Price Book** is by default available in all instances of Salesforce.

Creating a price book

Price book is a catalog in which the regular selling prices of an item are listed. Price books are used for selling products at different prices based on the geography and business year, or based on the agreement with a customer. Two types of price books exist in Salesforce:

- **Standard price book** is a price book that contains all products and their standard prices.
- **Custom price book** allows us to offer products to distinctive groups of customers at different list prices.

A business scenario: *David Guzman* is working as a *System Administrator* at Universal Containers. Universal Containers has their customers in USA, Europe, and India.

His manager, *Brigette Hyacinth*, asked him to create three separate price books for each region.

Perform the following instructions to create a new price book:

1. Make sure that you have selected the **Sales** app.
2. Click on the **Price Book** tab, and then click on the **New** button. Now create a new Price Book for India, as shown in the following screenshot:

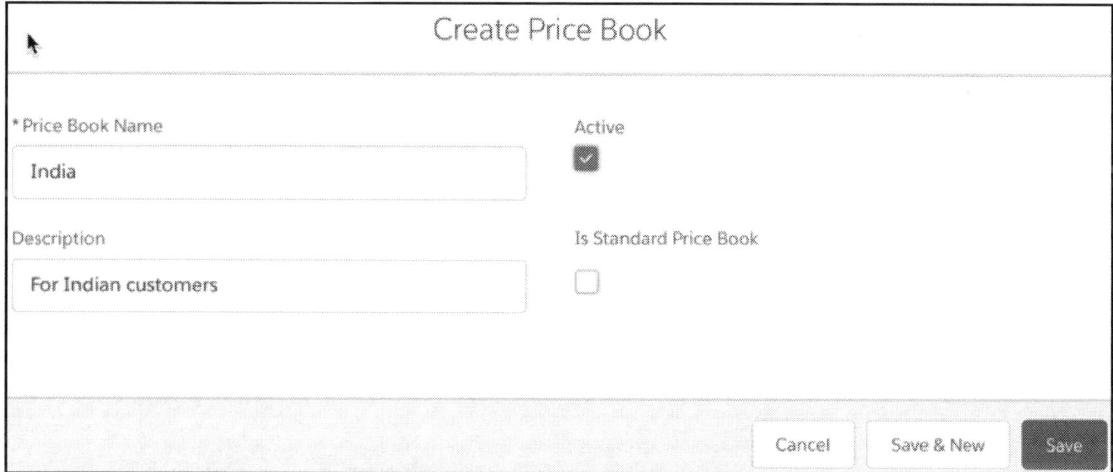

3. Once you are done, click on the **Save** button.
4. Repeat steps 1 to 3 to create a price book for USA and Europe.

By default, the organization-wide sharing for a price book is **Use**. It means that users who have read access on the product and price book object will be able to select any active price book. Use the organization-wide sharing setting to control the price book visibility to **View Only** or **No Access**. Then, use the **Share** button to allow access to a price book based on the role, specific users, and so on. For example, you want to share a price book with users, based on their geographic location.

Associating a product with a price book

Once you have defined the products and price books, the next step is to associate both of them, using the price book entry object. You can either associate a product with a price book through the product page or from the price book page.

A business scenario: *David Guzman* is working as a *System Administrator* at Universal Containers. As per the preceding business requirements, *David Guzman* has already created a product and different price books. Now, his manager, *Brigette Hyacinth*, asked him to associate the product, *Learning Salesforce Visual Workflow*, to a custom price book USA with **List Price**, that is, $49.99.

Perform the following instructions to add the standard price to a product:

1. Make sure that you have selected the **Sales** app.
2. Click on the **Product** tab, and then open the **Learning Salesforce Visual Workflow** product.
3. From the details page, navigate to the **RELATED** list. Now, click on the **Add to Price Book** button available under the **Price Books** related list, as shown in the following screenshot:

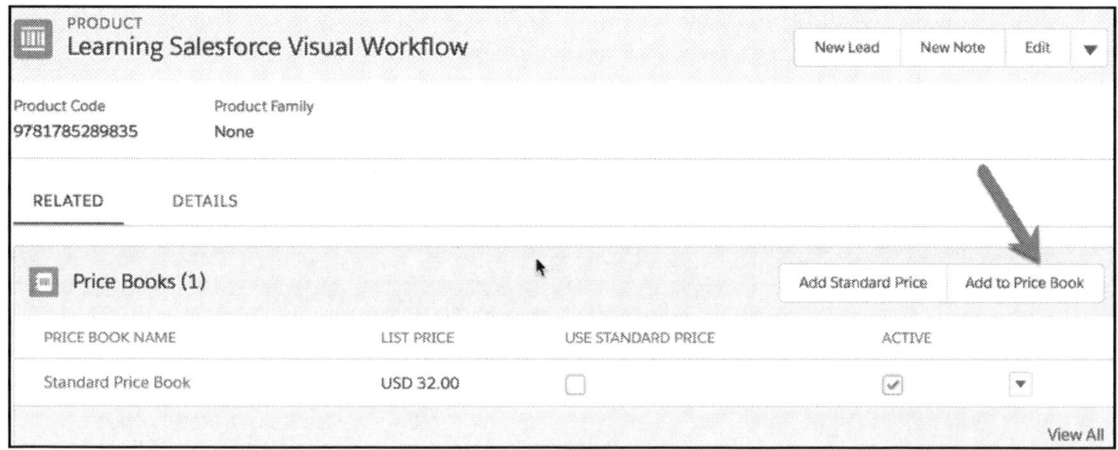

4. It will open a popup where you have to select **Price Book** and **Currency**. Select **USA** for **Price Book** and **USD** for **Currency**, as shown in the following screenshot:

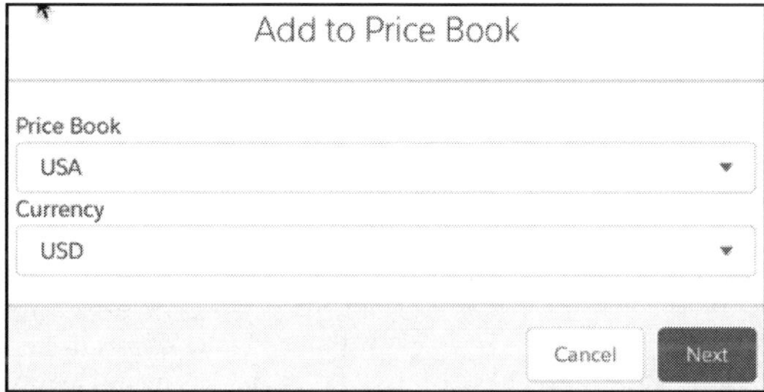

5. Once you are done, click on the **Next** button.

6. On the next screen, you can see that **List Price** is automatically populated from the standard price. Change the **List Price** from `32.00` to `49.99`:

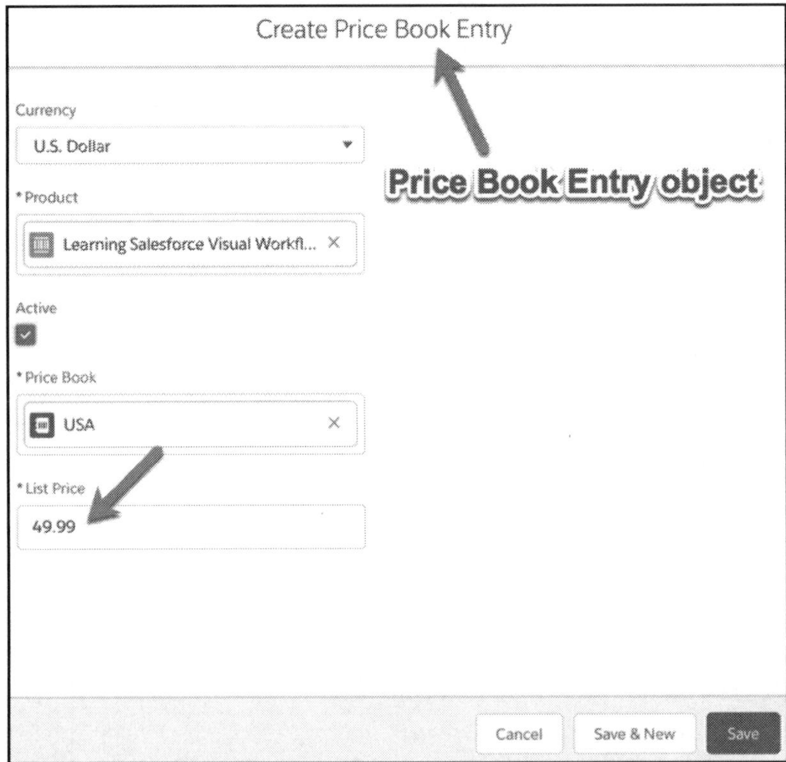

The association happens between the products, and the price book object is stored in the **Price Book** entry object, as shown in the preceding screenshot

7. Once you are done, click on the **Save** button.

Repeat steps 1 to 7 to add products to other price books. You can also use the data loader to add products to multiple price books in bulk.

Opportunity management

An opportunity is a revenue-generating event. Adding deals to Salesforce will help you build a strong pipeline and help the organization in forecasting. An opportunity is also called as deal.

Opportunity – standard fields

Numerous standard fields exist on an opportunity object. Out of them, a few are very important, and they are mentioned in the following table:

Field label	Data type	Description
Account Name	Lookup (Account)	This field is used to associate an account with an opportunity.
Amount	Currency(16, 2)	This field is used to store the amount of the opportunity.
Close Date	Date	This field is to store the probable deal closing date.
Stage	Picklist	This field is used to capture the status of an opportunity. The values available under this picklist are: • **Prospecting** • **Qualification** • **Needs Analysis** • **Value Proposition** • **Id. Decision Makers** • **Closed Won** • **Closed Lost** • **Negotiation/Review** • **Proposal/Price Quote** • **Perception Analysis**
Probability (%)	Percent(3, 0)	This field auto-populates, based on the Stage you selected. It is possible to change the probability (%) any time by editing the opportunity records.
Opportunity Name	Text(120)	This field is used to store the opportunity name. You can enter a maximum of 120 characters.

Creating a new opportunity

You can create a new opportunity by using the user interface, or you can also import it from another organization by using data loader. As we have already created an opportunity from lead conversion, now the next step is to open it. Perform the following steps to open the opportunity that is created from lead conversion:

1. Go to the **Opportunity** tab and open the **Automation Champion-** opportunity. – indicates that the opportunity is created from lead conversion.
2. Now click on the **DETAILS** section; it will look like the following screenshot:

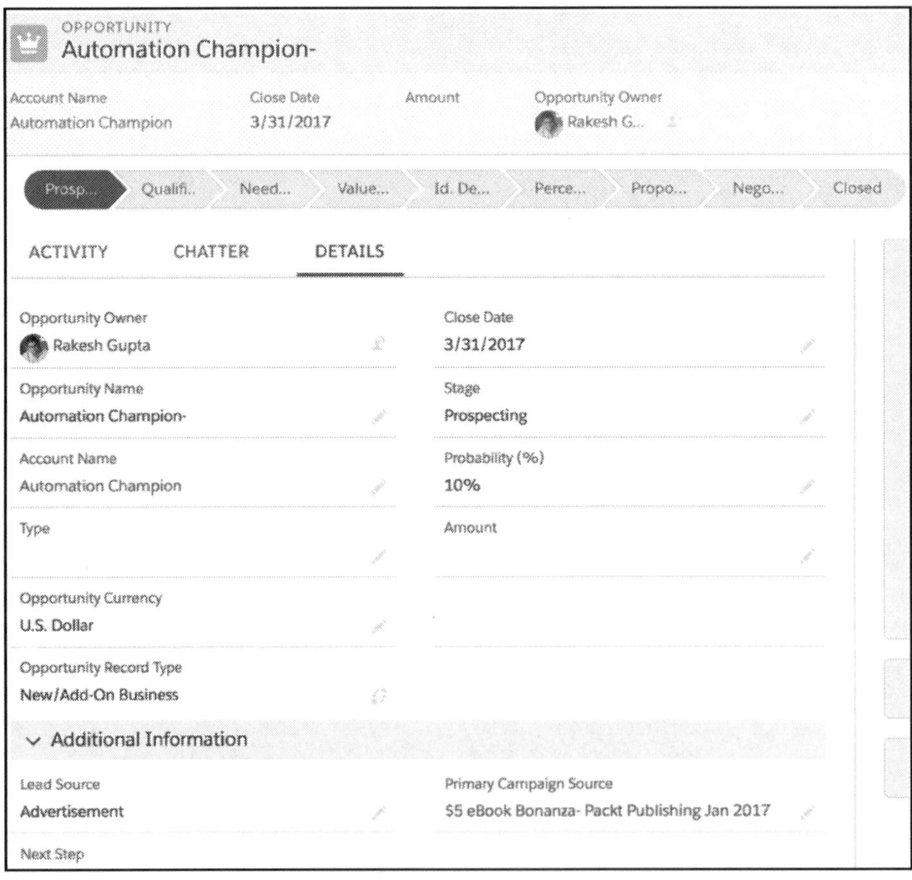

Look at **Close Date** and **Stage** carefully. Remember that when the opportunity is created from lead conversation, the **Close Date** opportunity is set to **last date of current quarter** and **Stage** is set **first value of stage** picklist.

Adding products to an opportunity

Salesforce allows you to add products to an opportunity, in order to track what's selling and in what number, by adding the products to opportunities. To add products to an opportunity, first, you must add the price book to it. You can select products from one price book only, so be careful while selecting a price book. Products in opportunity are stored in the opportunity product (API Name `OpporunityLineItem`) object, as shown in the following screenshot:

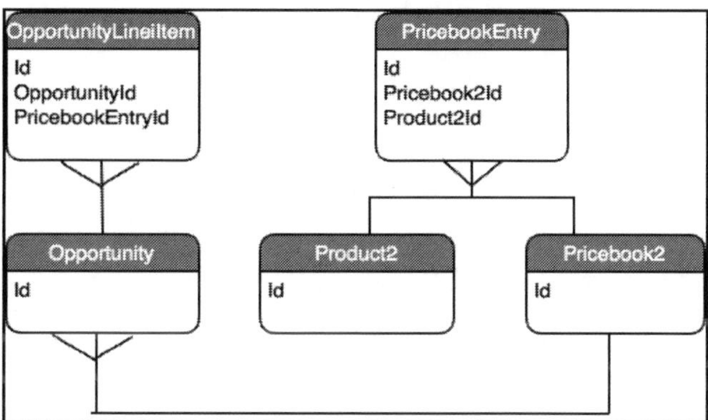

A business scenario: *David Guzman* is working as the *System Administrator* at Universal Containers. He wants to add 100 as the quantity of the product, *Learning Salesforce Visual Workflow* from the *USA* price book to the **Automation Champion-** opportunity.

Perform the following steps to solve the preceding business requirement:

1. Go to the **Opportunity** tab, and open the **Automation Champion-** opportunity. – indicates that the opportunity is created from lead conversion.
2. From the **Products** related list, select **Choose Price Book** option, as shown in the following screenshot:

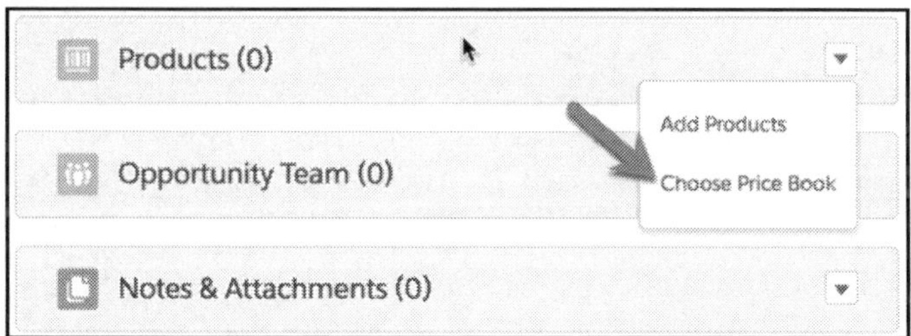

3. It will open a popup that allows you to select the price book. In this case, select the **USA** price book.
4. Once you are done, click on the **Save** button.
5. The next step is to add products from the USA price book to opportunity. To add this, from the **Products** related list, select the **Add Products** option.
6. Click on the **Plus** icon to add products; utilize the search box option to find a product. After product selection, it will look like the following screenshot:

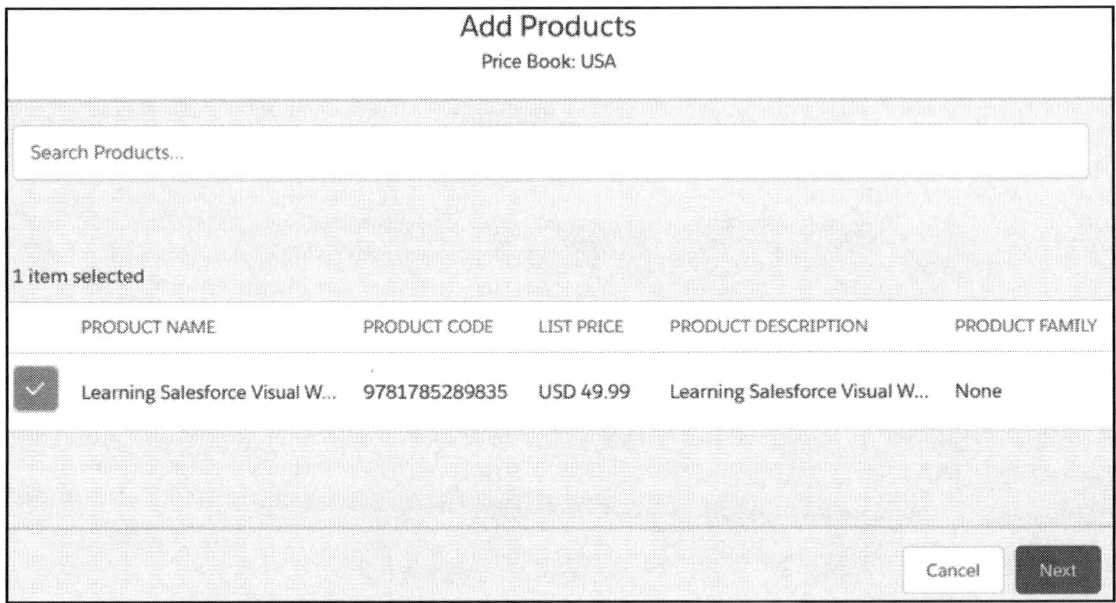

You can select as many products as you want to add into an opportunity.

7. Once you are done with the selection of products, click on the **Next** button.
8. Now enter the attributes for each product, such as quantity, sales price, or discount. Fields may vary based on the customization done by the administrator. The sales price is the final price paid by the customer at the time the items or services are sold. The sales price defaults to the list price of a selected product in the price book. Depending on user permissions, they can change this value. In this scenario, enter the **Quantity** as `100`, as shown in the following screenshot:

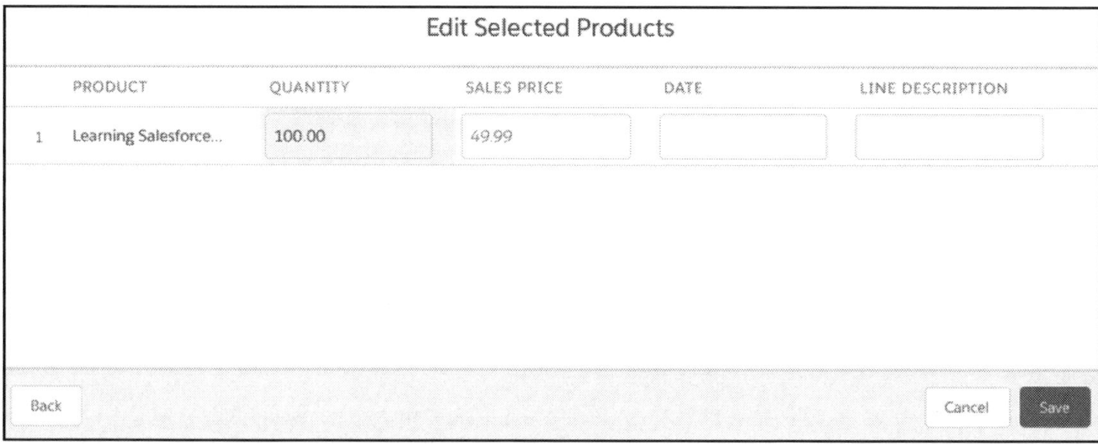

9. Once you are done, click on the **Save** button.

Establishing schedules on opportunity products

A product schedule is an estimate of recurring future income from a product associated with an opportunity. The product schedule is linked with the product that is on the opportunity rather than directly with the opportunity itself. There are two types of product schedules:

- **Quantity schedule**: In simple words, it means your organization fulfills the customer purchased products over time. For example, you have purchased the 1-year subscription of a magazine for $144 on January 1, 2017. The magazine publisher has started the shipment of the fulfillment of that product over time, which means you will get an e-copy of the magazine on the last day of every month that runs throughout the year. This is called quantity schedule.
- **Revenue schedule**: Suppose, someone has bought a car worth $15,000 at payments of $750 for 20 months. It means that on the opportunity level, it will show they have sold a $15,000 product, but they are billed month by month. It means at the end of 20 months, they will get the complete amount, not in the first month. This is the revenue schedule.

Enabling product schedules

System administrators can enable product schedule settings that allow users to create schedules for each product on opportunities. The product schedule feature is not available in Lightning Experience as of the *Spring'17* release. To enable this feature, use the switcher to go to the Salesforce Classic view.

A business scenario: *David Guzman* is working as a *System Administrator* at Universal Containers. He has received a requirement from his manager, *Brigette Hyacinth,* to enable quantity schedule for all products.

Perform the following steps to solve the preceding business requirement:

1. In the Salesforce Classic view, click on **Setup** | **Build** | **Customize** | **Products** | **Product Schedule Settings**.
2. Enable both **Quantity Schedules** by selecting the **Scheduling Enabled** and **Enable quantity scheduling for all products** checkboxes, as shown in the following screenshot:

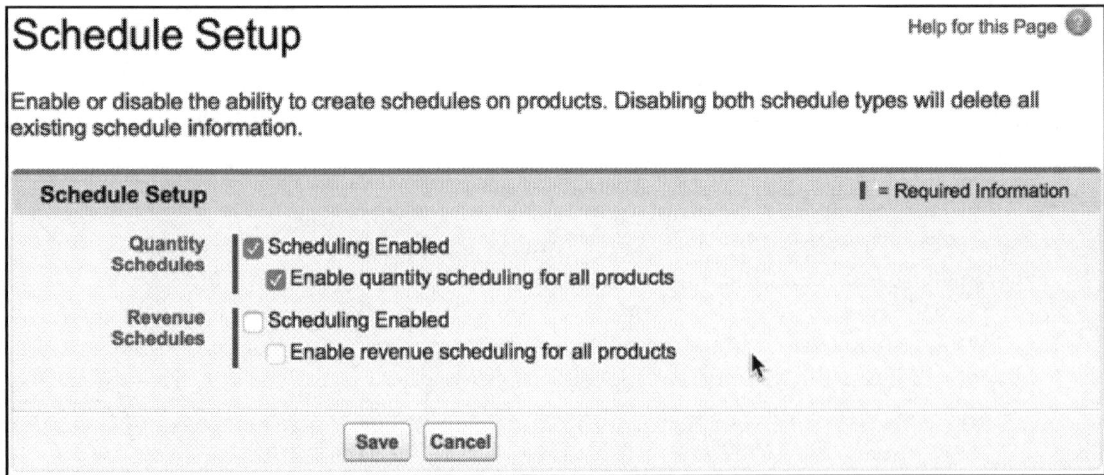

3. Once you are done, click on the **Save** button.

Inserting opportunity product schedules

Once the product schedules are enabled, you can utilize them while adding products to an opportunity.

A business scenario: *David Guzman* is working as a *System Administrator* at Universal Containers. He has added 100 as the quantity of the product, *Learning Salesforce Visual Workflow*, from the *USA* price book to **Automation Champion-** opportunity. As per the contract signed by Universal Containers with their customers, they are going to fulfill this order in four installments. His manager, *Brigette Hyacinth*, asked him to create a product schedule for this. For the starting date (delivery date of first installment), use January 31, 2017.

Perform the following steps to solve the preceding business requirement:

1. In the Salesforce Classic view, click on **Opportunity** tab, and open the **Automation Champion-** opportunity. – indicates that the opportunity is created from lead conversion.
2. Navigate to the **Products** related list, and click on the product name, that is, **Learning Salesforce Visual Workflow**. It will look like the following screenshot:

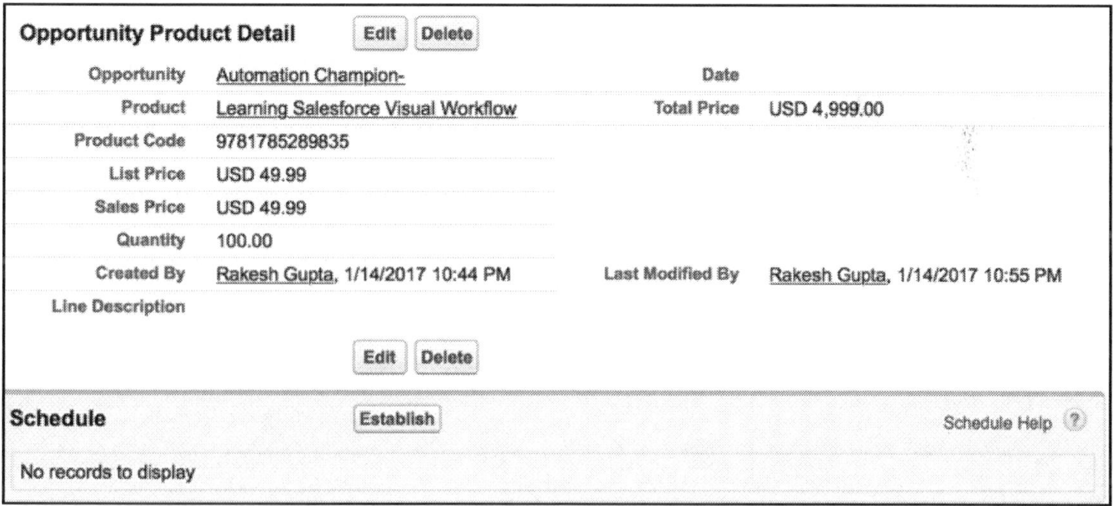

3. From the **Schedule** related list, click on the **Establish** button.
4. It will redirect you to a new window from where you can create the quantity schedule for a selected product. In this scenario, for **Start Date**, enter `1/31/2017`, for **Schedule Type**, select **Divide Amount into multiple installments**, for **Installment Period**, select **Monthly**, and for **Number of Instalments**, enter `4`. It will look like the following screenshot:

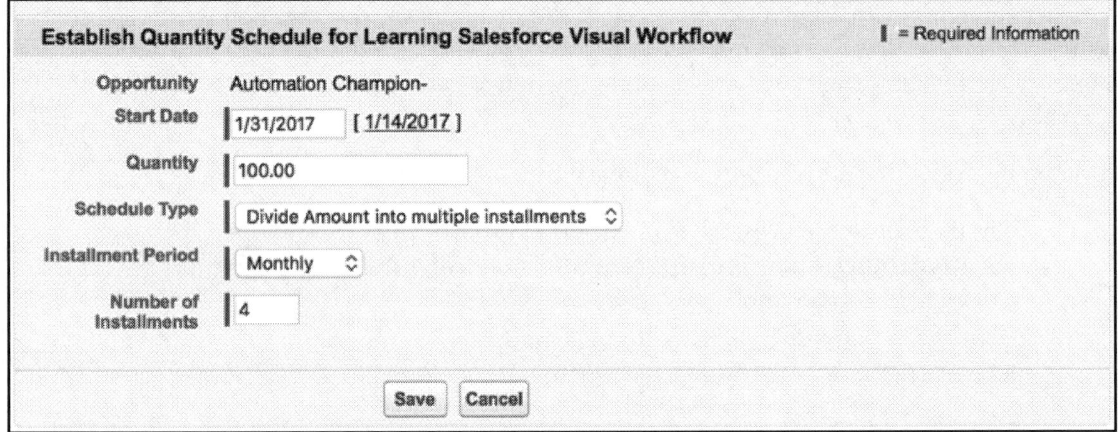

For **Schedule Type**, the picklist has two values, which are as follows:

1. **Divide amount into multiple installments**: Use this option when you want to divide the quantity of products equally for each installment.
2. **Repeat amount for each installment**: Use this option when you want to repeat the original quantity (#100) for each installment.

5. Once you are done, click on the **Save** button.

6. It will redirect you to another screen from where you can verify the scheduled delivery date for each installment, **Quantity**, and add a comment for each installment. It will look like the following screenshot:

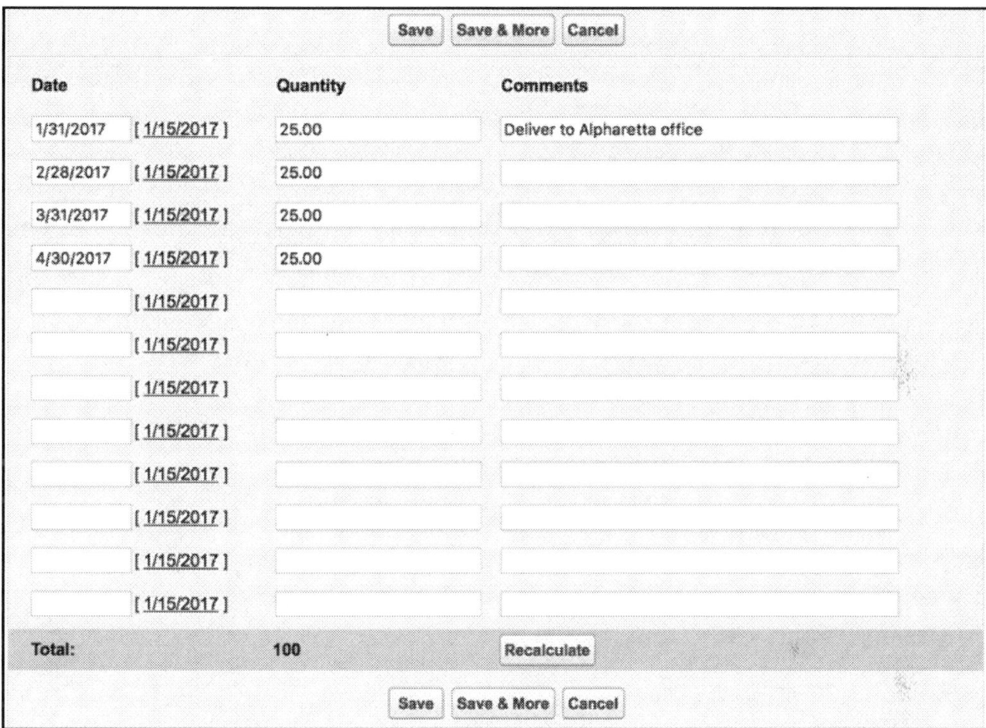

7. Once you are done, click on the **Save** button.

Likewise, you can enable the revenue schedule in your organization.

Quote management

A quote is fundamentally a record displaying projected prices for any product or service. When you add a product into an opportunity, it will automatically link your quote with the product and allow you to generate and e-mail the quote PDF to the customers. You can have multiple quotes linked to an opportunity, but only one of them can be synced with the opportunity. Only the products associated with that quote and opportunity are synchronized with each other.

Quote-to-cash life cycle

Quotation is a very important part for any business. You can either use AppExchange apps to automate quote-to-cash processes or use the traditional manual method for it. The following diagram shows the standard quote-to-cash process:

Quote-to-cash represents end-to-end business processes on the sell side either product or service configuration.

1. **Pricing**: It starts from product pricing, that is, how much discount the sales team is planning to offer. Do you have any special promotional rates for new customers?
2. **Quote**: Then, the next step is to create a quote, make sure that the approved discounts or business rules are properly applied.
3. **Negotiation and Approval**: This can be one of the hardest steps to finalise a deal and is the main reason for deal declaration. Before sending a contract to your customer, make sure that you have received customer approval.
4. **Contract**: This is the step where you must send a contract to the customer with a detailed explanation of each term.
5. **Order**: For better order management and shipping, use an AppExchange package, such as the UPS shipping app, which allows you to raise a shipping request, retune request, RMAs, and tracking.
6. **Payment**: The last step is to get the payment from customer. You must set up a system in place to handle the inflow of cash from customers and send receipts to them.

Enabling quotes

By default, quotes are not enabled, but the system administrator can perform the following steps in Lightning Experience to enable it:

1. Click on **Setup** (gear icon) | **Setup** | **PLATFORM TOOLS** | **Feature Settings** | **Sales** | **Quotes** | **Quotes Settings**.

2. Click on the **Enable** button, as shown in the following screenshot:

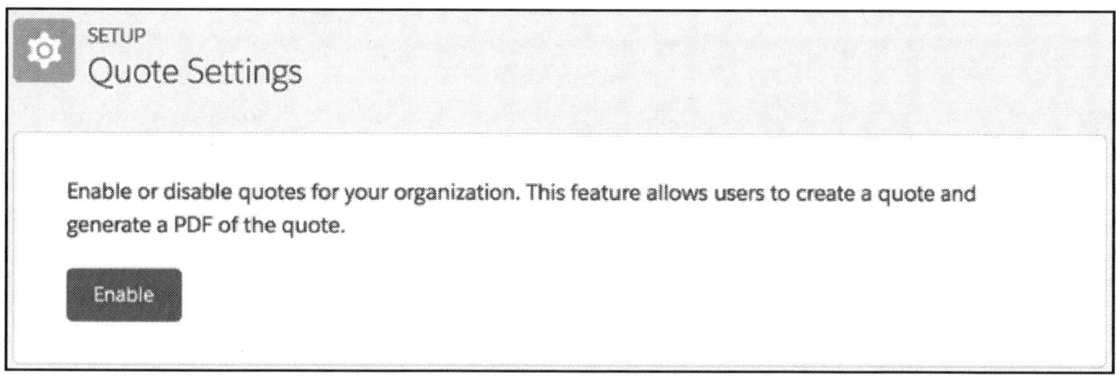

3. On the next screen, make sure to add a quote to the related list to **opportunity page layouts**.
4. Once you are done, click on the **Save** button.

Creating a new quote

Creating a quote means that you are presenting your customers the prices of the products and services that you offer. You can create multiple quotes to an opportunity to show different combinations of products, quantities, and discounts so that the customers can compare the prices.

You can create a new quote from an opportunity using the Classic or Lightning Experience user interface, or you can also import it from another organization by using the data loader. Perform the following steps to create a new quote:

1. In Salesforce Lightning Experience, click on the **Opportunity** tab and open the **Automation Champion-** opportunity.
2. Navigate to the **Quotes** related list, and click on the **New Quote** button. The quote will autopopulate the **Subtotal**, **Discount**, **Total Price**, and **Grand Total** field values from the opportunity.

3. Complete the fields, for example, enter **Expiration Date**, **Quote Name**, and so on. It will look like the following screenshot:

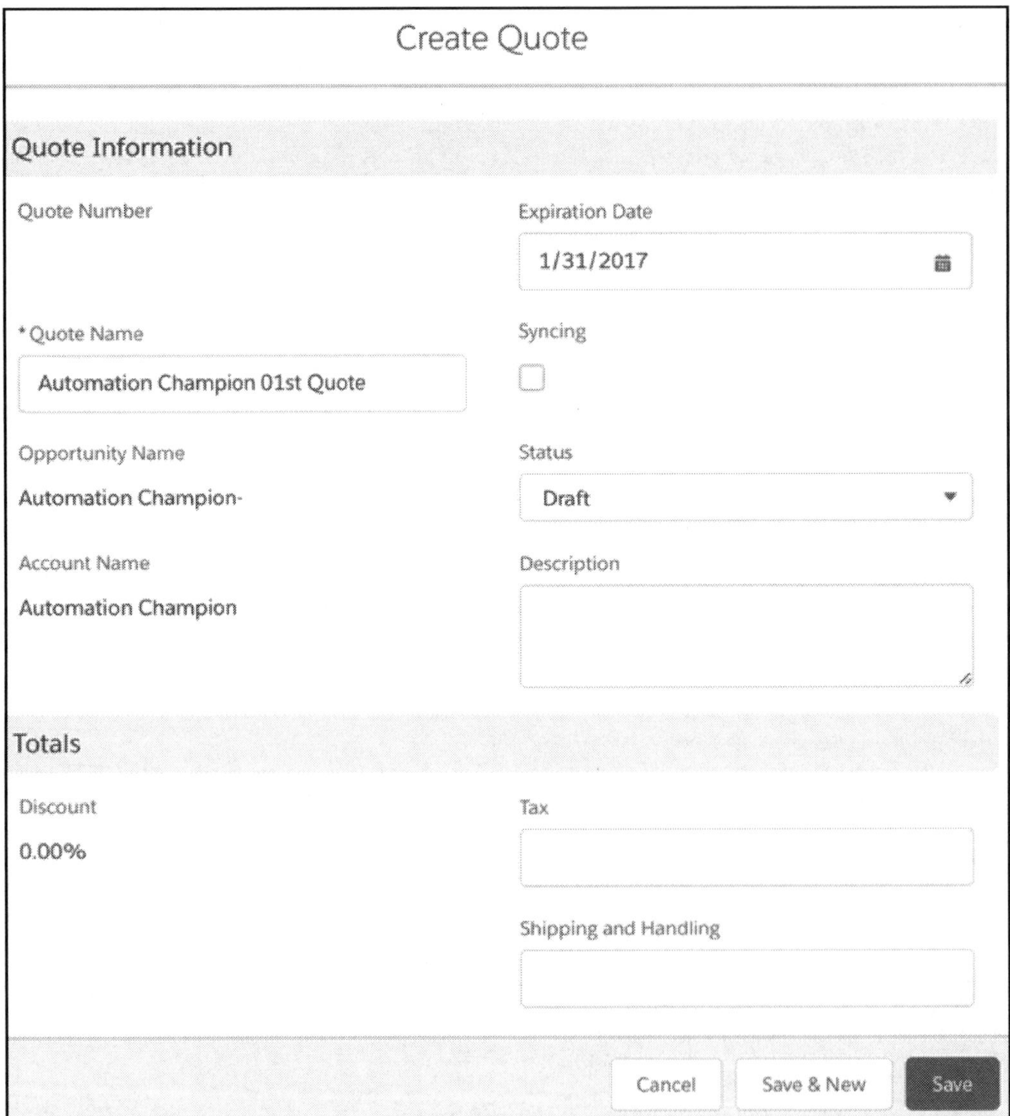

4. Once you are done, click on the **Save** button.

If you look at the quote related list carefully, you can find that the products from the opportunity are copied to the quote as a quote line item related list:

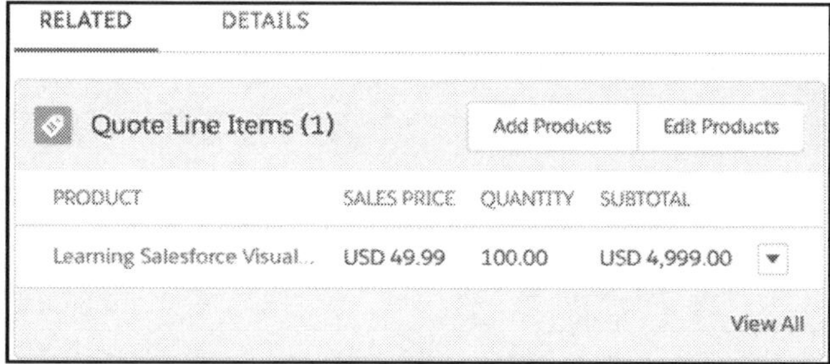

The **Grand Total** field is recalculated based on the taxes and shipping information that you have entered. It is also possible to add line items to the quote directly. To do so, use the **Quote Line Items** related list available on the quote page.

Generating a quote PDF

To send a quotation to your customer, you can generate a quote in a PDF form by using the standard template. To create a quote in the PDF format, perform the following instructions:

1. On the **Quote** detail page, click on the **Create PDF** button to generate a quote PDF.
2. Navigate to the **Quotes** related list, then click on the **New Quote** button.
3. You can save the quote PDF by clicking on the **Save to Quote** button. The PDF name is a combination of **Quote Name** and a version number, for example, `Automation Champion 01st Quote_V1`.

E-mail quotation to customer

It is also possible to send a copy of the quote PDF to the customer for approval, directly from Salesforce.

A business scenario: *Daniel Beardmore* is working as a *Sales rep* at Universal Containers. He has just created a quote and a quote PDF for **Automation Champion-** opportunity. Now he wants to e-mail the quote PDF to the customer, *Cathal Murtagh*.

To send a quote PDF to a customer, perform the following instructions:

1. On the quote detail page, click on the **Email Quote** button to send a copy of the quote PDF to the customer.
2. It will open an e-mail task with the quote PDF attached to it.
3. Enter the customer's **email address**, a **subject**, and **body** text:

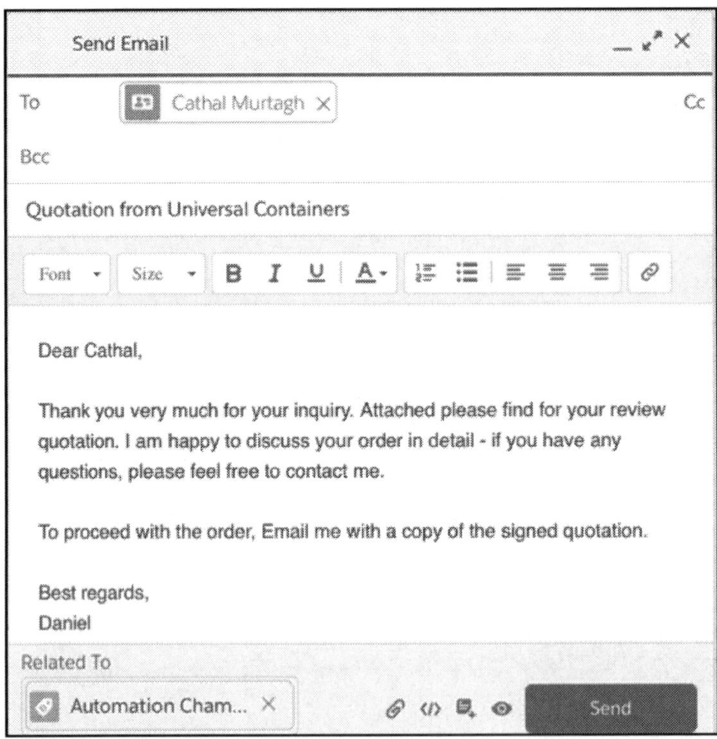

4. Once you are done, click on the **Send** button.

Syncing a quote with an opportunity

In the end, once the quote gets approved by the customer, sync a quote to the opportunity that it was created from. This way, updates to one record are always reflected in the other. To sync a quote with the opportunity, perform the following instructions:

1. Open the **Quote** that you want to sync, then click on the **Start Sync** button to start the syncing process.

2. It will open a popup with the detailed information. Read it carefully. Once you are done, click on the **Continue** button.

Finally, update the opportunity **Stage** to **Closed Won**

Collaborative forecasts

Forecasting is a process of making an estimation of the future, based on the existing and historical data, and most commonly, by the analysis of trends. It plays a major part in the financial planning of company business. It also measures your company growth and success. Forecasts in Salesforce provide an actual insight to tracking the sales effort and help an organization to modify the sales processes and monitor the sales pipeline. It also provides a complete picture of the organization's sales pipeline as well as the individual efforts of the sales team. Collaborative forecasting is the process of gathering and merging the information from different sources inside and outside the organization in order to come up with a single unified statement. In other words, collaborative forecast allows a sales team to generate accurate forecasts and track quota attainment.

On the forecast page, the amounts are totals and subtotals of the opportunities in the four different forecast categories, which are, **Pipeline**, **Best Case**, **Commit**, and **Closed**. Forecasts can be built on opportunities, opportunity splits, or product families. You can use up to four different types of forecasts, depending on the business necessities.

Enabling collaborative forecasts

System administrators can enable collaborative forecasts that allow users to see their future revenue and quota. The collaborative forecast feature is not available in Lightning Experience as of the *Spring'17* release. To enable this feature, use the switcher to go to the Salesforce Classic view.

A business scenario: *David Guzman* is working as a *System Administrator* at Universal Containers. He has received a requirement from his manager, *Brigette Hyacinth*, to enable collaborative forecasts.

Perform the following steps to solve the preceding business requirement:

1. In the Salesforce Classic view, click on **Setup** | **Build** | **Customize** | **Forecasts** | **Forecasts Settings**.

2. Select the **Enable Forecasts** checkbox. Once enabled, the forecasts setting page should look like the following screenshot:

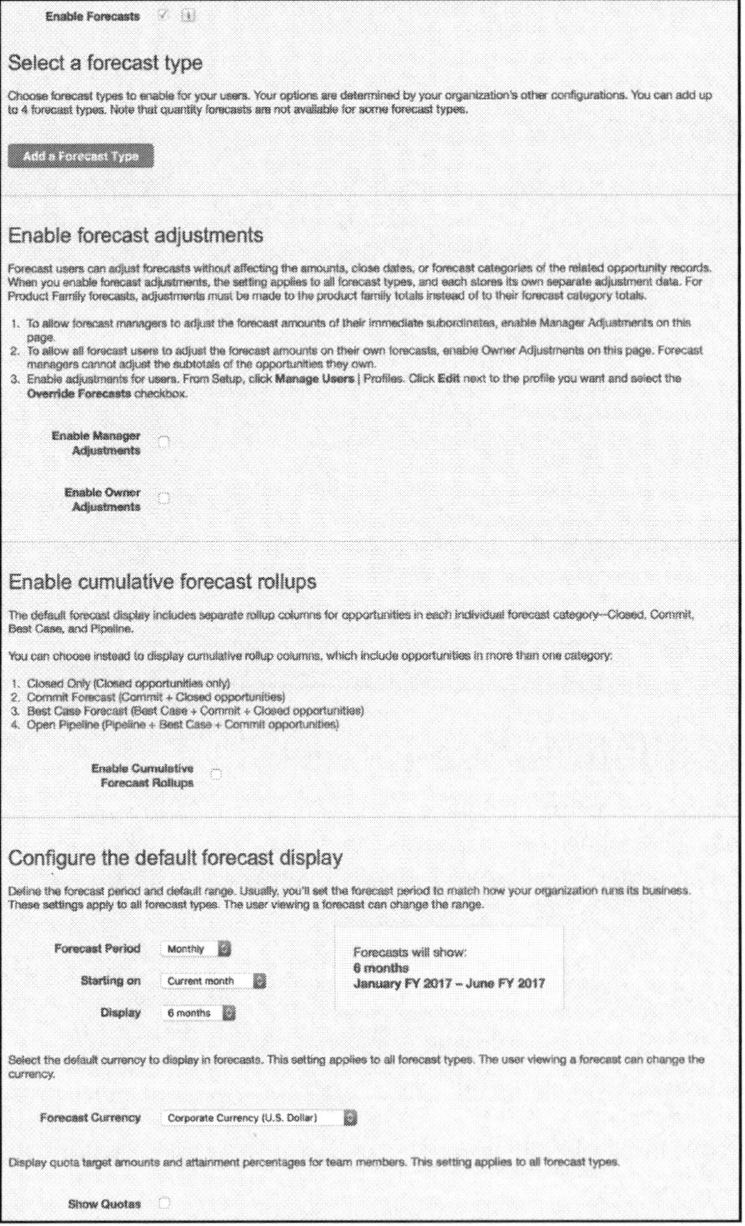

3. Once you are done, click on the **Save** button.
4. The next step is to set the **Forecasts** tab visibility for the right profiles. Navigate to the respective profile and set the **Forecasts** tab visibility to **Default On**.

Enabling a forecasts type

Different types of forecasts exist in Salesforce, but you can choose up to four types of forecasts to use. They are as follows:

Forecasts type	**What the Rollup is based on**
Opportunity – Revenue	Rollup is based on opportunity **Amount** field.
Opportunity – Quantity	Rollup is based on opportunity **Quantity** field.
Product Families – Revenue	Rollup is based on opportunity **Amount** field. Forecast amounts are separated by product family. To use a **Product Family** forecast, use opportunity **Products and Product Families**.
Product Families – Quantity	Rollup is based on opportunity **Quantity** field. Forecast amounts are separated by a product family. To use a **Product Family** forecast, use opportunity **Products and Product Families**.
Opportunity Splits – Revenue	Rollup is based on opportunity **Amount** field and each sales team member's split percentage. To use opportunity splits forecasts, enable **Opportunity Teams**, **Opportunity Splits**, and **Revenue Split** type.
Overlay Splits – Quantity	Rollup is based on opportunity **Amount** field and each overlay sales team member's split percentage. To use opportunity splits forecasts, enable **Opportunity Teams**, **Opportunity Splits**, and **Overlay Split** type.
Custom Opportunity Currency Field – Revenue	Rollup is based on the **Amount** in the custom opportunity currency field that you define. To use custom opportunity currency field forecasts, **Opportunity Teams** and **Opportunity Splits** must be enabled. Enable a custom split type for the field.
Expected Revenue – Revenue	Roll up is based on the **Amount** in the opportunity **Expected Revenue** field. To forecast on the **Expected Revenue** field, enable **Opportunity Teams** and **Opportunity Splits**. Enable a custom split type for the field.

If you want to forecast on the **Amount** field of opportunities, then use the **Opportunity Revenue** forecast. In case you want forecasts on the **Quantity** field of opportunities, then use the opportunity quantity forecast.

A business scenario: *David Guzman* is working as a *System Administrator* at Universal Containers. He has received a requirement from his manager, *Brigette Hyacinth*, to enable the **Opportunity Revenue** and **Opportunity Quantity** forecast types.

Perform the following steps to solve the preceding business requirement:

1. Navigate to **Setup** | **Build** | **Customize** | **Forecasts** | **Forecasts Settings**.
2. Click on the **Add a Forecast Type** button. From the **Forecast Type** drop-down menu, choose the data source to use for the forecast, that is **Opportunities**.
3. The next step is to choose **Forecast Measurement** to use. For now, select **Revenue**.
4. The last step is to select the columns that you want to display in the related opportunities list on the forecasts page for the forecast type. Finally, it will look like the following screenshot:

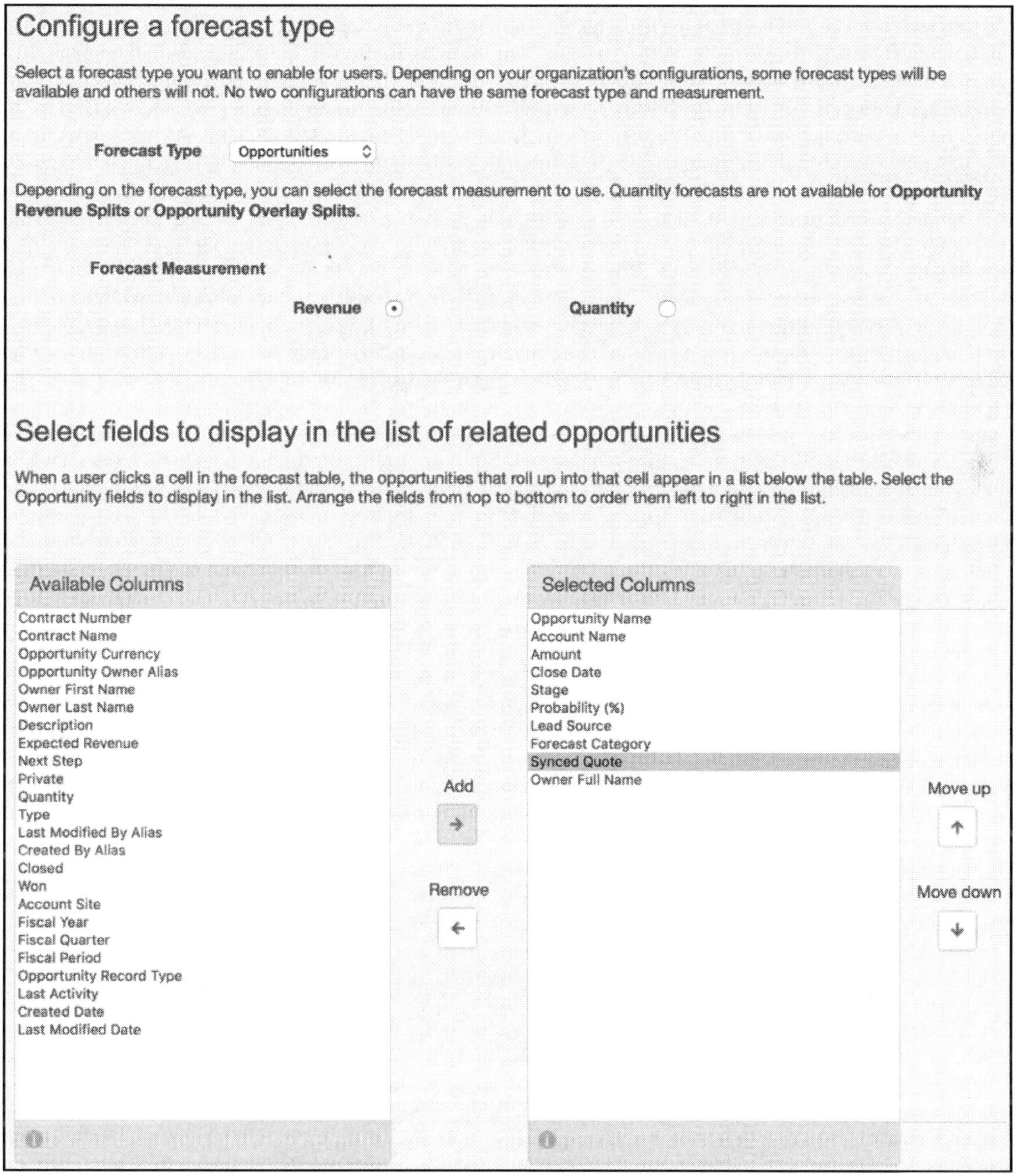

Configure a forecast type

Select a forecast type you want to enable for users. Depending on your organization's configurations, some forecast types will be available and others will not. No two configurations can have the same forecast type and measurement.

Forecast Type Opportunities

Depending on the forecast type, you can select the forecast measurement to use. Quantity forecasts are not available for **Opportunity Revenue Splits** or **Opportunity Overlay Splits**.

Forecast Measurement

Revenue **Quantity**

Select fields to display in the list of related opportunities

When a user clicks a cell in the forecast table, the opportunities that roll up into that cell appear in a list below the table. Select the Opportunity fields to display in the list. Arrange the fields from top to bottom to order them left to right in the list.

Available Columns
Contract Number
Contract Name
Opportunity Currency
Opportunity Owner Alias
Owner First Name
Owner Last Name
Description
Expected Revenue
Next Step
Private
Quantity
Type
Last Modified By Alias
Created By Alias
Closed
Won
Account Site
Fiscal Year
Fiscal Quarter
Fiscal Period
Opportunity Record Type
Last Activity
Created Date
Last Modified Date

Add

Remove

Selected Columns
Opportunity Name
Account Name
Amount
Close Date
Stage
Probability (%)
Lead Source
Forecast Category
Synced Quote
Owner Full Name

Move up

Move down

5. Once you are done, click on the **OK** button.
6. Repeat steps 1 to 5 to add the **Opportunity Quantity** forecast type.

Defining collaborative forecasts date range

Now, you must set up the date range to use for collaborative forecasts. The range you define here is used as the default for the rollup table on the **Forecasts** tab. The collaborative forecasts rollup table can display forecast amounts for each month, quarter, and a range of months or quarters. Perform the following steps to make any changes in the forecast date range:

1. Navigate to **Setup** | **Build** | **Customize** | **Forecasts** | **Forecasts Settings**.
2. Navigate to the **Configure the default forecast display** section and then select the forecast starting month, number of months to display, and the forecast period. Select **Monthly** for **Forecast Period**, **Current month** for **Starting on**, and **6 months** for **Display**, as shown in the following screenshot:

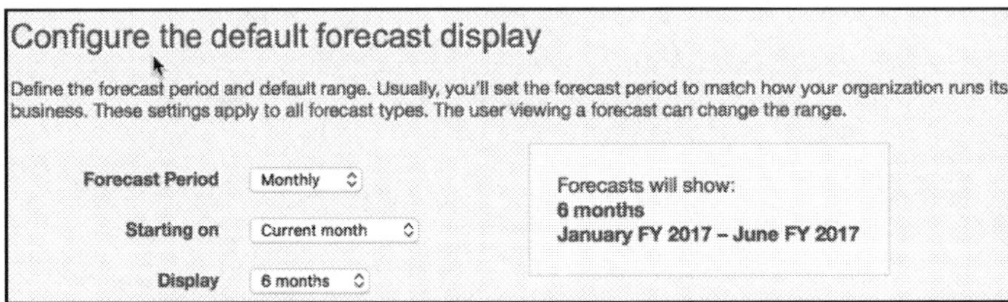

3. Once you are done, Click on the **Save** button.

Enabling collaborative forecasts users

Now you must enable the forecast capability to every user who needs it. By enabling each user, you can manage a granular control over the access even though you might have different users using the same profile.

A business scenario: *David Guzman* is working as a *System Administrator* at Universal Containers. He has received a requirement from his manager, *Brigette Hyacinth,* to grant the forecast capability to a sales rep, *Daniel Beardmore.*

Perform the following steps to solve the preceding business requirement:

1. Navigate to **Setup** | **Administer** | **Manage Users** | **Users**.
2. For the user whom you want to grant the forecasting capability, click on **Edit**. In this scenario, **Edit** user **Daniel Beardmore.** You can also use your user account to enable the forecasting capability for yourself.

3. Navigate to the **General Information** section and select the **Allow Forecasting** checkbox.
4. Once you are done, click on the **Save** button.

Understanding the collaborative forecasts hierarchy

The forecast hierarchy is automatically generated based on your role hierarchy setup in Salesforce. The forecast hierarchy is built on the role hierarchy and specifies which users are forecast managers. Remember that when you enable a user as a forecast user, and if they have a role defined on their user record, they're automatically added to the forecast hierarchy:

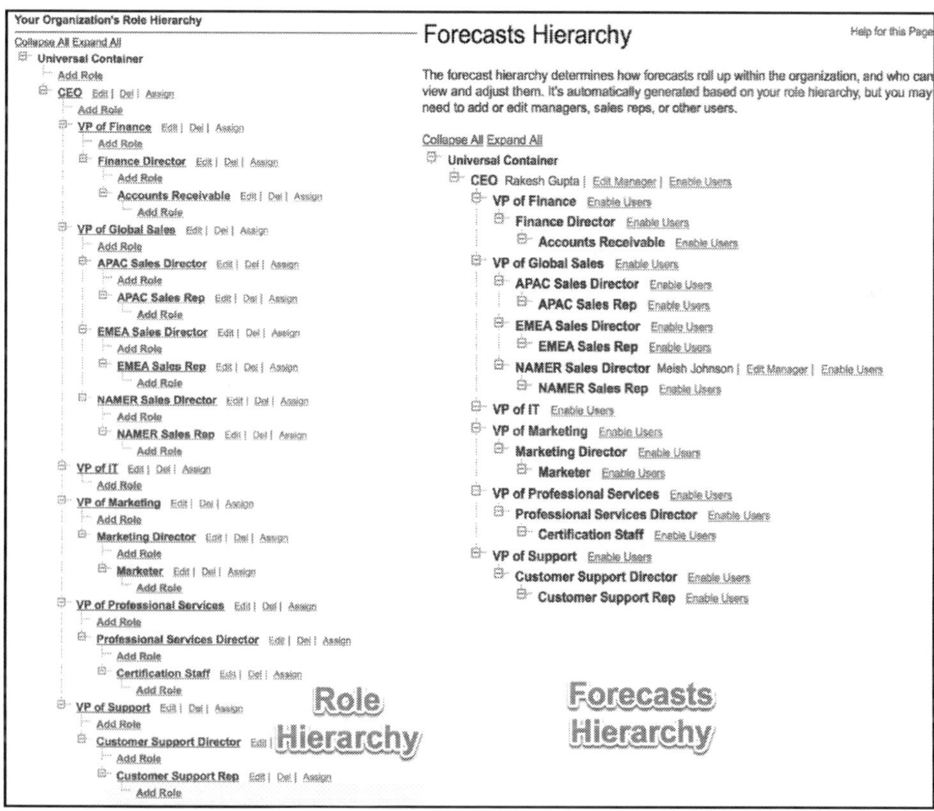

The preceding screenshot displays the **Role Hierarchy** and **Forecasts Hierarchy** side-by-side. You can also enable forecast users directly from the forecast hierarchy page. However, it is not possible to customize the forecast hierarchy as it is directly created from role hierarchy. Let's take an example, you have enabled forecasts for the following users:

- One user in the **NAMER Sales Director** role, that is, **Meish Johnson**.
- One user in the **NAMER Sales Rep** role (**Daniel Beardmore**); he reports to the **NAMER Sales Director**.

Even though the **NAMER Sales Rep** role might report to the **NAMER Sales Director** in the role hierarchy, the user in the **NAMER Sales Rep** role won't automatically report to the **NAMER Sales Director** in the forecast hierarchy. You must enable a user in the forecast hierarchy to act as the forecast manager, for them to be able to view their subordinates' forecasts, as shown in the preceding screenshot marked in blue, that is, **Meish Johnson**. Only one user at each level in the forecast hierarchy acts as a manager at one time.

Enabling adjustments

An adjustment shows the forecast managers' decision about the total amount that they expect from forecast opportunities to generate in at the close of the forecast period. Sometimes, the forecast managers need to modify their subordinates' forecast. For example, they know that some sales reps have the potential to bring in more business for the organization. It is also possible for sales reps to adjust their own forecasts if he thinks that the opportunity amounts are unpretentious or overstated. To enable the adjustment for the forecast managers or Salesforce, perform the following instructions:

1. Navigate to the **Enable forecast adjustments** section and then select the following options as per your need:
2. Navigate to **Setup** | **Build** | **Customize** | **Forecasts** | **Forecasts Settings**.
    - **Enable Manager Adjustments** when you want to allow forecast managers to adjust their subordinate forecast amount.
    - **Enable Owner Adjustments** when you want to allow forecast managers and sales reps to adjust their own forecast amount.

Select both the options, as shown in the following screenshot:

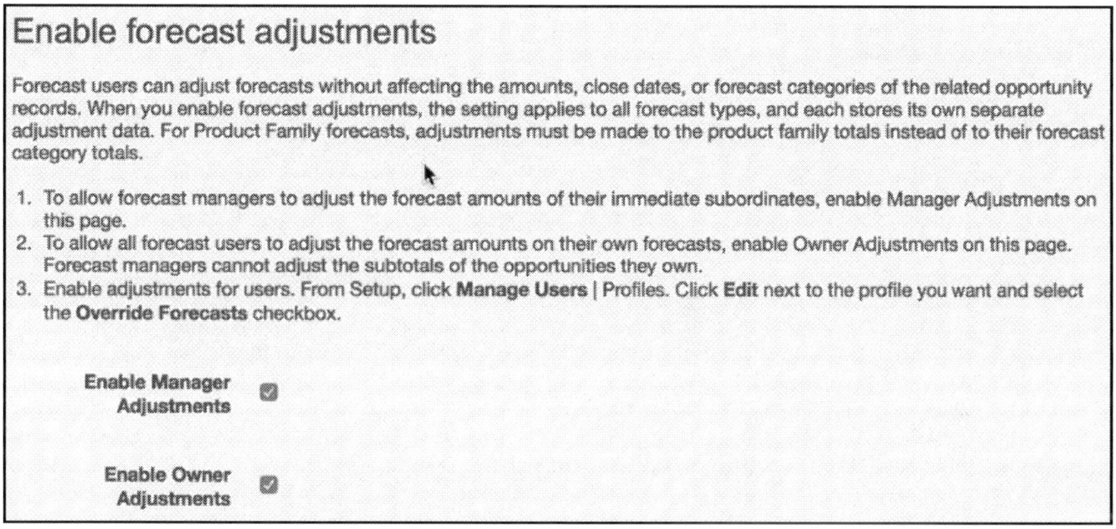

Enable forecast adjustments

Forecast users can adjust forecasts without affecting the amounts, close dates, or forecast categories of the related opportunity records. When you enable forecast adjustments, the setting applies to all forecast types, and each stores its own separate adjustment data. For Product Family forecasts, adjustments must be made to the product family totals instead of to their forecast category totals.

1. To allow forecast managers to adjust the forecast amounts of their immediate subordinates, enable Manager Adjustments on this page.
2. To allow all forecast users to adjust the forecast amounts on their own forecasts, enable Owner Adjustments on this page. Forecast managers cannot adjust the subtotals of the opportunities they own.
3. Enable adjustments for users. From Setup, click **Manage Users** | Profiles. Click **Edit** next to the profile you want and select the **Override Forecasts** checkbox.

Enable Manager Adjustments ☑

Enable Owner Adjustments ☑

3. Once you are done, click on the **Save** button.
4. Adjustments are enabled on an organizational level. The next step is to grant the adjustment permission to the right profiles. Navigate to **Setup** | **Administer** | **Manage Users** | **Profiles**. For the profile that you want to grant the adjustment permission to, click on the **Edit** button.
5. Navigate to the **App Permission** section and select the **Override Forecasts** checkbox.
6. Once you are done, click on the **Save** button.

The following forecast page displays an adjustment of $12,000 to the original amount of $0:

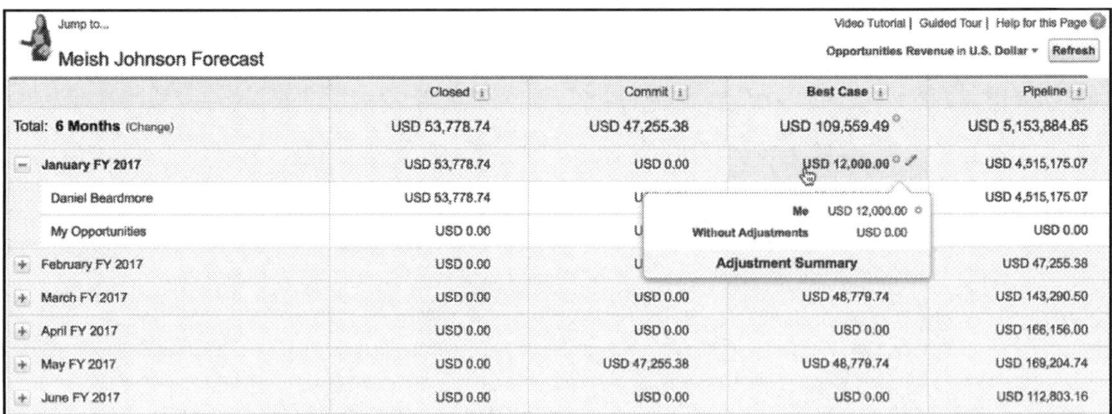

An adjustment doesn't change the original total rollup amount; it just adds a layer of detail. Users must maintain separate adjustments for each forecast type if multiple types of forecasts are enabled.

Enabling quotas

You can allow your users to use quotas to know what revenue he must bring in a month or a quarter. A quota is nothing but a monthly or quarterly sales goal that is assigned to a user. A manager's quota is a combination of the amount that the manager and the team are expected to bring together. If the system administrator has enabled forecast quotas, then the quota data appears on the **Forecasts** tab. A new column quota amount will display, which contains the quota amount for each month and a row that contains the percentage attained for each month in a forecast rollup:

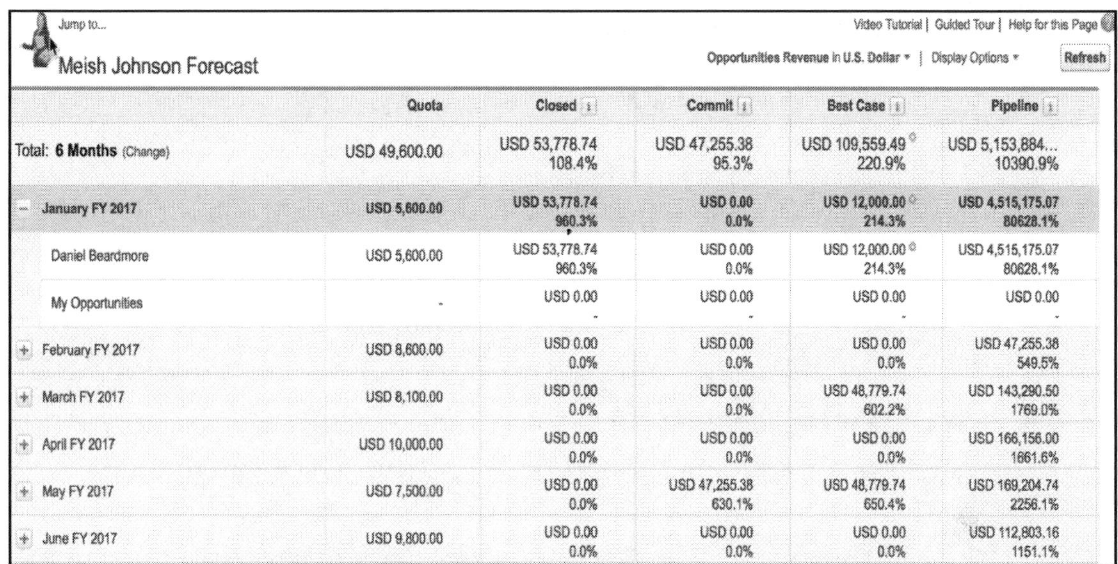

	Quota	Closed	Commit	Best Case	Pipeline
Total: 6 Months (Change)	USD 49,600.00	USD 53,778.74 108.4%	USD 47,255.38 95.3%	USD 109,559.49 220.9%	USD 5,153,884... 10390.9%
– January FY 2017	USD 5,600.00	USD 53,778.74 960.3%	USD 0.00 0.0%	USD 12,000.00 214.3%	USD 4,515,175.07 80628.1%
Daniel Beardmore	USD 5,600.00	USD 53,778.74 960.3%	USD 0.00 0.0%	USD 12,000.00 214.3%	USD 4,515,175.07 80628.1%
My Opportunities	-	USD 0.00 -	USD 0.00 -	USD 0.00 -	USD 0.00 -
+ February FY 2017	USD 8,600.00	USD 0.00 0.0%	USD 0.00 0.0%	USD 0.00 0.0%	USD 47,255.38 549.5%
+ March FY 2017	USD 8,100.00	USD 0.00 0.0%	USD 0.00 0.0%	USD 48,779.74 602.2%	USD 143,290.50 1769.0%
+ April FY 2017	USD 10,000.00	USD 0.00 0.0%	USD 0.00 0.0%	USD 0.00 0.0%	USD 166,156.00 1661.6%
+ May FY 2017	USD 7,500.00	USD 0.00 0.0%	USD 47,255.38 630.1%	USD 48,779.74 650.4%	USD 169,204.74 2256.1%
+ June FY 2017	USD 9,800.00	USD 0.00 0.0%	USD 0.00 0.0%	USD 0.00 0.0%	USD 112,803.16 1151.1%

To enable quotas in your Salesforce org, perform the following instructions:

1. Navigate to **Setup** | **Build** | **Customize** | **Forecasts** | **Forecasts Settings**.
2. Navigate to the **Configure the default forecast display** section and then select the **Show Quotas** checkbox.
3. Once you are done, click on the **Save** button.

A few points to remember

1. If you want to look at the relationships between contacts and accounts, create a custom report type.
2. Custom price books must be active in order to add their products to opportunities or quotes
3. While creating an opportunity, you can select products only from a single price book.
4. When a product or a price book is deleted, all the related price book entries are also deleted.
5. The price books cannot be deleted if they are associated with the approval process or have a pending workflow action.
6. The **Forecasting** tab is hidden by default in Developer Edition org.

7. Use the data loader or API to upload quotas for your users if you are using collaborative forecast.
8. Customizable forecasting allows you to enter quotas via the user details page.
9. The maximum number of records the recycle bin can store is 25 times your Salesforce storage capacity in MBs.
10. By default, you can capture up to 500 web-to-leads per day from your website. To increase the limit, you may reach out to Salesforce support.
11. A campaign member is a lead or a contact record.

Test your knowledge

Q1. Which of the following are true about opportunity pipeline and forecast reporting except?

1. Pipeline reports may include omitted opportunities from the forecast.
2. Forecasts may be overridden.
3. Pipeline reports may be overridden.
4. Opportunity stages may be used to determine the forecast category of an opportunity.

Q2. What feature license needs to be granted to a user to enable forecast capability for them?

1. Allow override forecast.
2. Allow forecasting.
3. Marketing user.
4. Enable forecast tab visibility to Default On.

Q3. Universal Containers would like to associate one contact with more than one account. What solution should you recommend to meet this requirement?

1. Add the contacts to the partner related list on the second account.
2. Clone the contact record and add to the second account.
3. Associate the contact to the other account using the lookup field.
4. Enable contact to multiple account setting.

Q4. The sales rep at Universal Containers won a sales deal and updated the opportunity stage to Closed Won. What impact will this change have on the opportunity in the Forecast?

1. It will be associated with the Closed Won forecast category and contribute to the forecast once approved by the manager.
2. It will be associated with the Closed Won forecast category and will automatically contribute to the forecast.
3. It will be associated with the Closed Won forecast category and will need to be added by the sales rep.
4. It will be associated with the Closed Won forecast category and will need to be committed by the sales rep.

Q5. Universal Containers is migrating data from a legacy system into Salesforce. The company needs to migrate lead, contact, and opportunity data from its legacy system, and they also want to report on historical lead conversion for both legacy and newly created data. What is the recommended order for data migration?

1. User, Account, Contact, Opportunity, Lead.
2. User, Opportunity, Account, Contact, Lead.
3. User, Contact, Account, Lead, Opportunity.
4. User, Lead, Opportunity, Account, Contact.

Summary

In this chapter, we started with an explanation of the sales life cycle. Then, we moved ahead with campaign management and discussed an outstanding way to execute campaigns. We also discussed lead management, account management, and contact management. We also covered how you can associate one contact with multiple accounts and key concepts such as product, price book, and price book entry. You also leaned how to create and manage quotes. In the end, we discussed collaborative forecasting and quota management. In the next chapter, we will go through the Salesforce Service Cloud and its key concepts, including knowledge and entitlement management.

6

Increasing Service Agent Productivity by Using Service Cloud

In the previous chapters, we have discussed about Salesforce Sales Cloud. Sales Cloud is a product designed to automate business sales processes. By implementing Sales Cloud, you can boost your sales reps' productivity by allowing them to manage customers in a faster and simpler way. In this chapter, we will describe Service Cloud features in detail, such as case management, knowledge management, and entitlement management. In addition to this, we will also look at the way of setting up escalation rules in Salesforce. The following topics will be covered in this chapter:

- Case management
- Escalation rule
- Entitlement management
- Knowledge management
- Live agent

Service Cloud is a product designed to automate support processes. By implementing Service Cloud, you can boost your support reps' productivity by allowing them to manage customers in a faster and simpler way, and it also helps reduce the organization's expenses in support. It includes all Service Cloud features, for example, *account*, *contact*, *case*, *article management*, *knowledge*, *entitlement*, *live agent*, *report*, and *dashboard*. Service Cloud can help an organization to reduce the number of support cases open over time by providing self-service to their customers and by implementing communities.

Service Cloud allows an organization to provide various support channels for their customers so that they reach out to them if support is required. Service Cloud helps you maintain a self-service portal, enforce entitlement on new cases, and live chat features to customers–everything on the cloud. The productivity accomplished by implementing Service Cloud in your organization will allow your support reps to close a case faster and maintain good relationships with the existing customers. Quality customer support is crucial to a successful business. When customers get adequate and quality customer support from an organization, they tend to share it on their social network, which leads to direct publicity and increases the reputation of an organization.

A common business challenge in the customer support world is incomplete, outdated, or incorrect information. This is frustrating to customers as well as customer support agents; it can happen because earlier customer contacts with the company are not shared with all support agents, customer history is not shared with support agents, or because of leaving the current or previous customer support agent completely out of the loop. By implementing Service Cloud, you can automatically share customer information across the departments. It is enormously easy to enter and update customer information by support agent, and by putting validation rules, you can ensure that the data entered in Salesforce is correct and accurate.

Service Cloud also helps to align support teams, field service teams, and social customer service team, so they can work together in an organized manner to provide quick support to their customers and close cases faster. There are some advantages of implementing Service Cloud. They are as follows:

- Improve lead conversation rate
- Reduce operational support costs by implementing self-service
- Close cases faster and keep your customers happy
- Personalize customer service by implanting live messages
- Implement different customer support channels traditional to social media to CTI integration
- Analyze how your customer support team works in real time with the help of reports and dashboards
- Utilize performance metrics to understand how to help the customer support team perform even better
- Utilize omni-channel to assign cases to the most knowledgeable agent for each inquiry

Customer life cycle starts from the campaign (company branding or product awareness) and the first stage is completed with closing a deal successfully. The second stage starts with educating the customer and providing them full support to utilize your product or service.

The following diagram represents the customer life cycle chain:

In Salesforce words, it starts from creating a campaign. Through a campaign, an organization may get leads; once those leads are ready to buy some products, convert those leads into accounts, contacts optionally opportunities. Once you have won the opportunities, the next step is to deliver the orders. After this, customer support starts. It means that you grant portal access to them so that they can reach out to support if required, and that you educate your customers so that they can take full advantage of your products or services.

Case management

In the real world, customer support has become a vital part of the organization's business process. For all types of product and service industries, customer support is an important activity. In general, support (case) tickets are used to capture customer comments on various types of problems that start after purchasing a product or service. Occasionally, customers can ask important feature requests using support platform, and that may be beneficial when developing future product enhancements.

Best practices to streamline customer support

Managing support cases can get cruel. Whenever you think you are done with it, another one is waiting for you in the queue. There are a few support cases that nobody wants to accept because it is too difficult. Moving stray tickets from one department to another department can easily cross the proper resolution times. In the end, you will be flooded with increasing support ticket numbers, and your customer gets angry because their cases are not resolved yet. To avoid this, you need to get organized and follow best practices to improve customer support handling:

- **Quick response to new cases**: Make sure that the first response time is under 30 minutes. Even though a support rep does not have an immediate resolution to the customer's issue, it is good to let them know that you are taking care of their problems. To implement this, use entitlement and escalation rules.
- **Pay attention to case status**: Many times, cases get lost or customers don't get a resolution because of incorrectly assigned case statuses. Selecting the right case ticket status is critical to successful case resolution. For example, it is just like dispatching a product to a customer: if you use an incorrect address, the product won't reach the customer.
- **Don't bounce a support case between departments**: It is very hard to get a quicker case resolution if you bounce it from one department to another department. It is a very typical scenario: a support rep sending a case to the technical team to fix a bug, and then the technical team sending the ticket back to get more information. It is better to create a case team and provide necessary access to the team so that they can manage a case better.
- **Handle old cases first**: When accepting cases from a queue, ask your support reps to accept the old cases first instead of accepting an easy one.
- **Don't leave cases unfinished**: A support case remains unsolved for customers unless and until they get a satisfactory resolution. Don't leave your customers in the dark.
- **Post case closure survey**: It is very important to send a survey to the customers to gather their feedback in order to improve support service.

Creating a new case

Before creating a new case, first understand the various channels you can offer to your customer to reach out to support if they have any issue with a product or service:

- Create a case manually
- Create a case via **Email-to-Case**

- Create a case through **Web-to-Case**
- Create a case from a social media post on the company's Facebook page or Twitter
- Reach out to the call center to raise a case
- Create a case through SMS using APIs or with the help of the AppExchange app

Perform the following steps to create a new case:

1. Make sure that you have selected the **Service** app.
2. Click on the **Cases** tab, and then click on the **New** button. Now, create a new case for an `Automation Champion` account, as shown in the following screenshot:

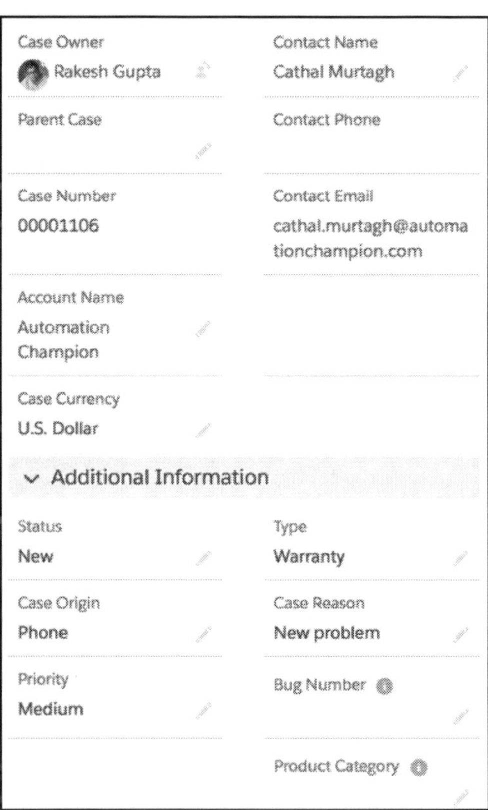

Email-to-Case

The **Email-to-Case** provides another channel to the customer, so that they can reach out to the support team by sending an e-mail to a pre-defined e-mail address.

A business scenario: *David Guzman* is working as *System Administrator* at Universal Containers. He has received a requirement from higher management to enable **Email-to-Case** for the customers of Universal Containers; therefore, customers can create a case by sending an e-mail instead of calling support center. It will also help Universal Container to cut down call center running costs.

Salesforce offers two types of **Email-to-Case** settings; they are **Email-to-Case** and **On-Demand Email-to-Case**. In both the options, if the customer responds to an existing case, then it will attach the e-mail to that existing case only. This means that it is not going to create a new case every time; the decision of creating a new case or adding a comment to an existing case will depend on `Case_Thread ID`. When creating a custom e-mail template for a case, make sure to add `Case_Thread ID` in the subject or the body of the e-mail. Before going ahead, let's understand the difference between **Email-to-Case** and **On-Demand Email-to-Case**:

Email-to-Case	**On-Demand Email-to-Case**
It requires downloading and installing an **Email-to-Case** agent behind your company firewall	It doesn't need you to install any additional software other than enabling it
It helps you to keep the e-mail traffic within the company firewall	It doesn't keep the e-mail traffic within the company firewall
It is a good option if you want to allow your customer to send e-mails with an attachment size greater than 25 MB	It is a good option if you don't want to allow your customers to send e-mails with an attachment size greater than 25 MB.
It requires at least one account that supports the UMAP protocol	It works with any type of e-mail client

Perform the following steps to solve the preceding business requirement:

1. Click on **Setup** (gear icon) | **Setup** | **PLATFORM TOOLS** | **Feature Settings** | **Service** | **Email-to-Case**.
2. Click on **Edit** button and enable the **On-Demand Email-to-Case** setting, as shown in the following screenshot:

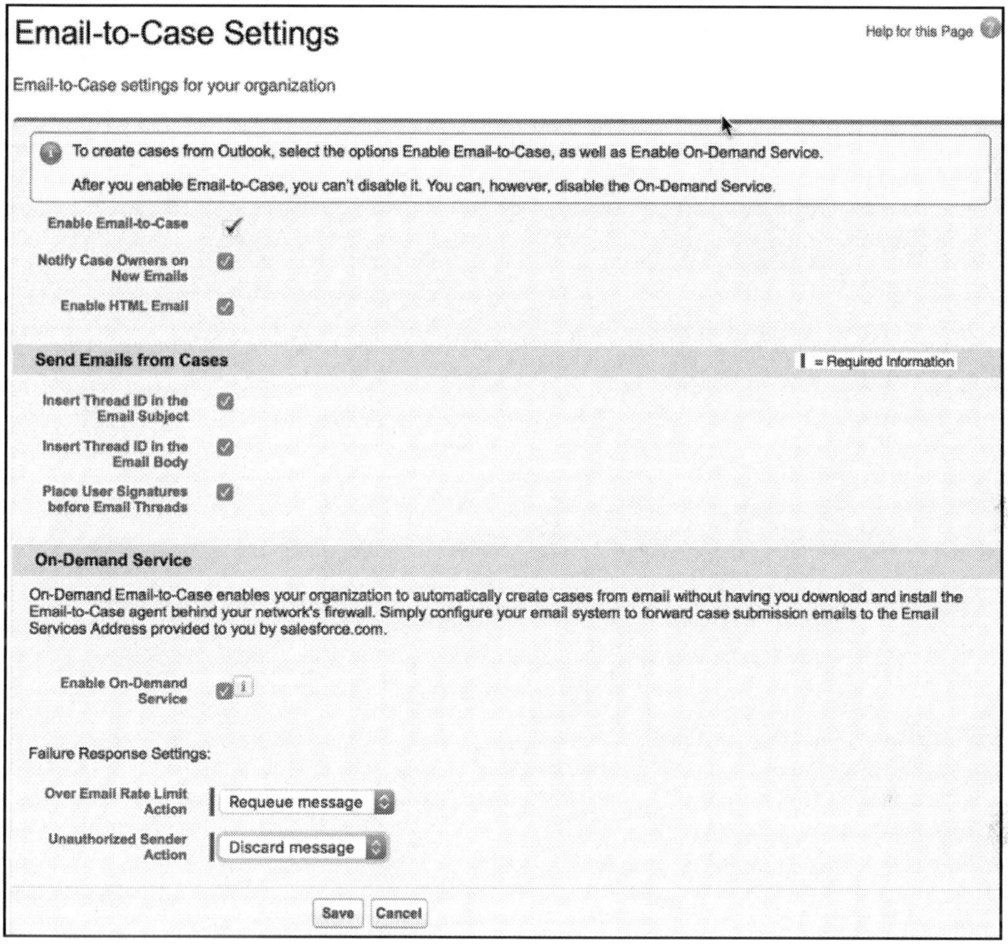

3. Once you are done, click on the **Save** button.
4. Now, the next step is to set up a routing e-mail address to which the customer will send an e-mail in order to create a case. To do so, click on **Setup** (gear icon) | **Setup** | **PLATFORM TOOLS** | **Feature Settings** | **Service** | **Email-to-Case**. Navigate to the **Routing Addresses** related list and click on the **New** button, as shown in the following screenshot:

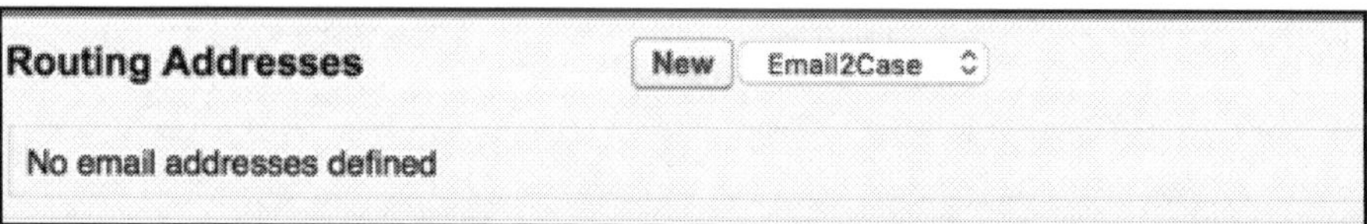

5. The next step is to provide the required information, for example, **Routing Name**, **Email Address**, and set **Case Priority** and **Case Origin**. Optionally, it allows you to create a task for new cases:

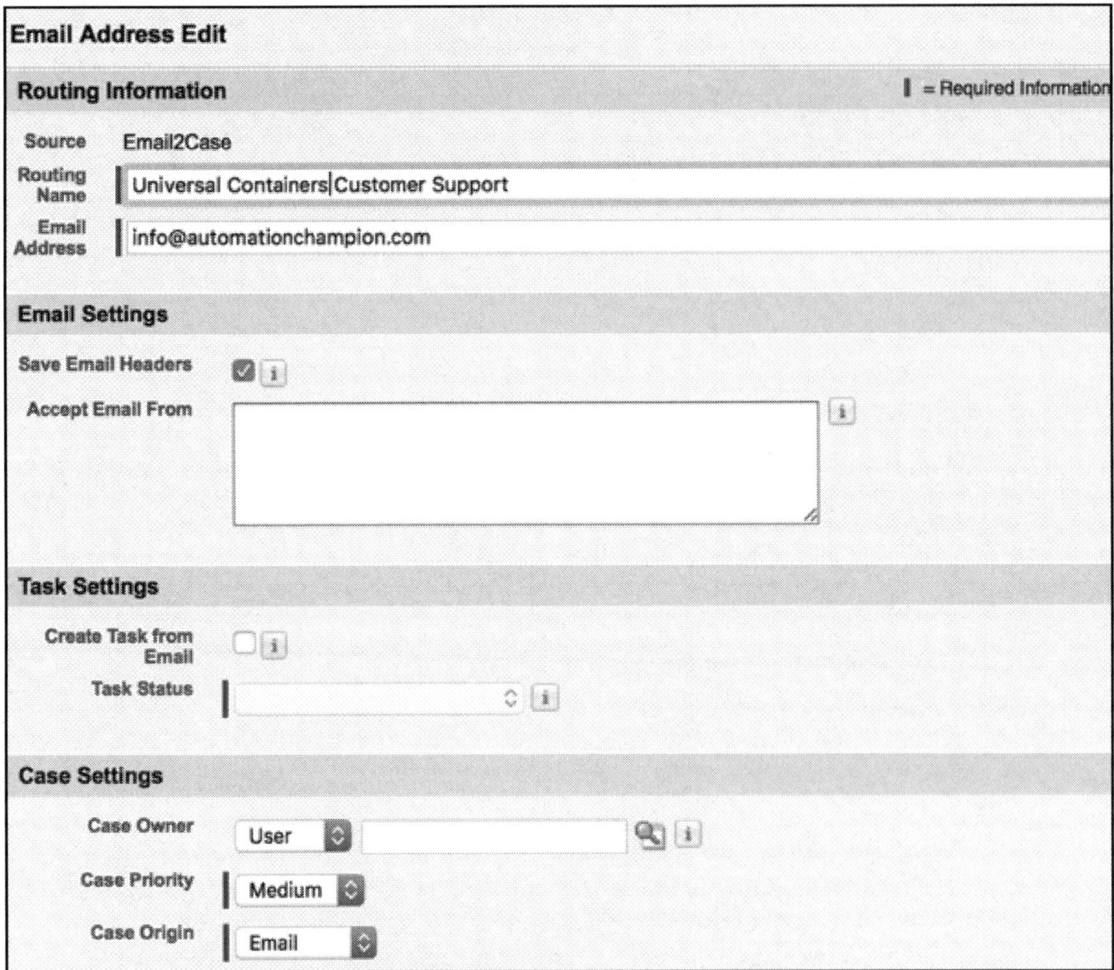

6. The owner of the e-mail mentioned in the **Email Address** field will receive an e-mail notification with the verification link. Once it is verified, you can share **Email Services Address** with your customers.

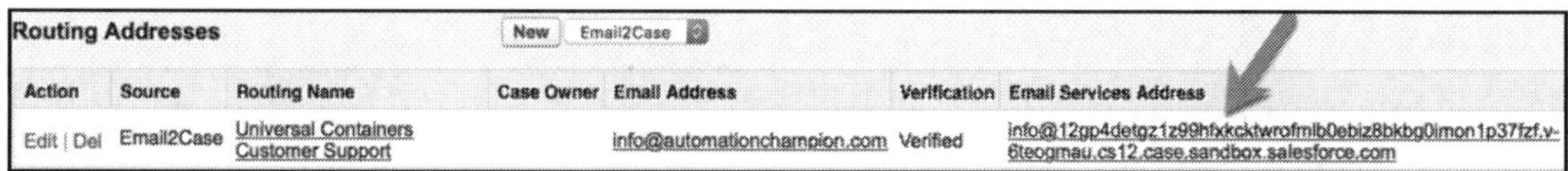

Routing Addresses New Email2Case

Action	Source	Routing Name	Case Owner	Email Address	Verification	Email Services Address
Edit | Del	Email2Case	Universal Containers Customer Support		info@automationchampion.com	Verified	info@12gp4detgz1z99hfxkcktwrofmlb0ebiz8bkbg0imon1p37fzf.v-6teogmau.cs12.case.sandbox.salesforce.com

From the next time, whenever the customer wants to raise a case, they must send an e-mail to the e-mail service address.

7. If you want to use the e-mail address specified in the **Email-to-Case** routing information, that is, `info@automationchampion.com` instead of using a long e-mail services address, then an extra step is required. Open the e-mail client for the aforementioned e-mail address and add a forwarding address:

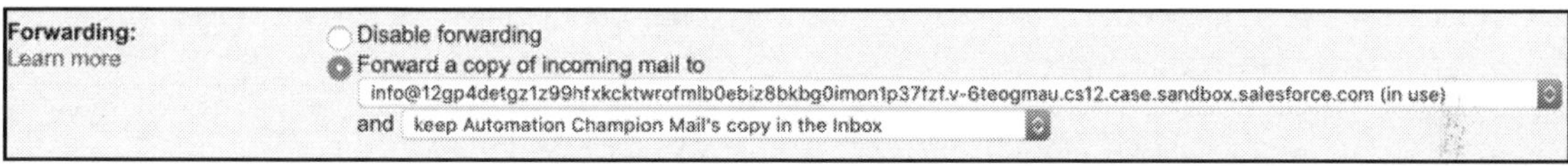

Once the forwarding setting is done as shown in the preceding screenshot, you are ready to share the e-mail address specified in the **Email-to-Case** routing information with customers.

Escalation rule

It may happen a few times that the support rep does not resolve a case on the specified time, as assigned. The **Case Escalation** feature allows us to configure a rule by which the case can be escalated to another user or queue. In other words, its escalation rule is a way of reassigning a case to another user or queue and notifying individuals when a case is not closed in the specified time frame. The benefits of using an escalation rule are as follows:

- It allows an organization to ensure that cases should not remain open forever. For example, if a case is not resolved after 72 hours of its creation, then it is reassigned to a *Tier II* queue.
- It helps the organization to prioritize key customer cases. For example, escalating Silver customer cases after 24 hours of case creation if it is still open.
- It also helps an organization to ensure better customer service.

The following diagram shows how an escalation rule is structured in Salesforce:

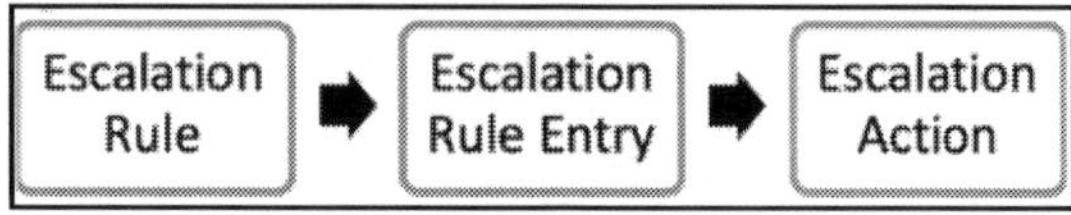

Three are three steps to define an escalation rule, mentioned as follows:

1. Define an escalation rule. Keep in mind that only one escalation rule will be active at a time.
2. The next step is to define the entry criteria for the escalation rule, for example, whether the state equals GA or CA.
3. The final step is to define the escalation action for each escalation rule entry criteria. You can have multiple actions defined for each escalation entry criteria.

Before proceeding ahead, create a custom drop-down field, **Support Level**, on the account object; the values for the drop-down fields are **Silver**, **Gold**, and **Platinum**. Also, create a queue for the case object with the name, `Tier I`. Define a business hour for USA-EST, as per the following screenshot:

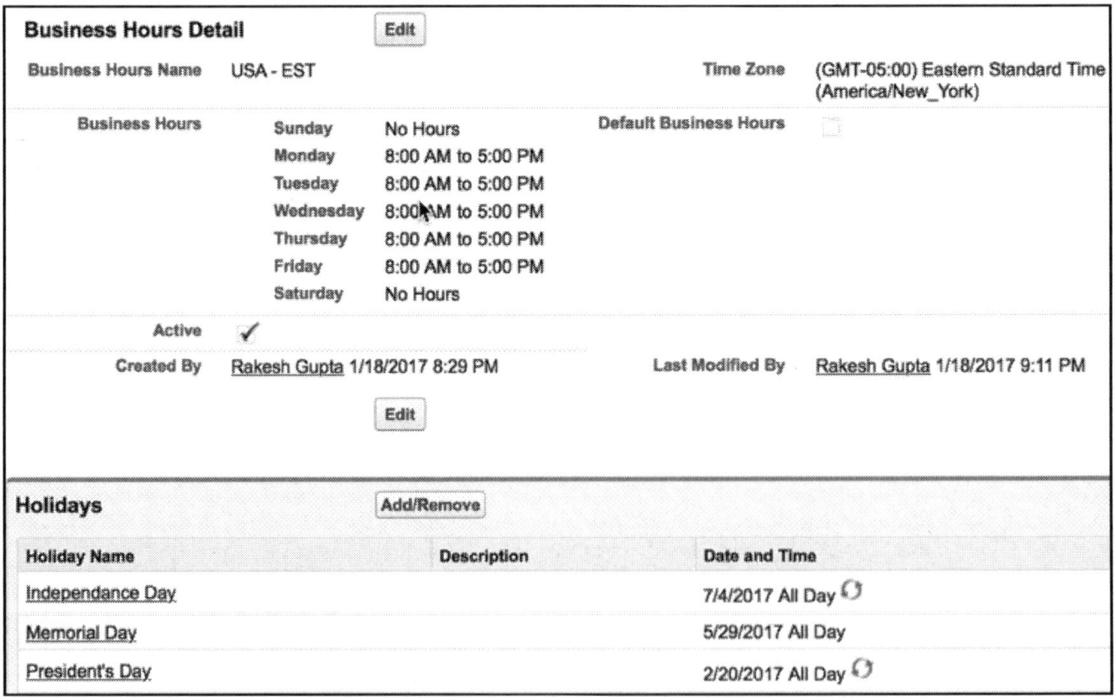

Business Hours Detail Edit

Business Hours Name	USA - EST	Time Zone	(GMT-05:00) Eastern Standard Time (America/New_York)
Business Hours	Sunday No Hours Monday 8:00 AM to 5:00 PM Tuesday 8:00 AM to 5:00 PM Wednesday 8:00 AM to 5:00 PM Thursday 8:00 AM to 5:00 PM Friday 8:00 AM to 5:00 PM Saturday No Hours	Default Business Hours	
Active	✓		
Created By	Rakesh Gupta 1/18/2017 8:29 PM	Last Modified By	Rakesh Gupta 1/18/2017 9:11 PM

Edit

Holidays Add/Remove

Holiday Name	Description	Date and Time
Independance Day		7/4/2017 All Day
Memorial Day		5/29/2017 All Day
President's Day		2/20/2017 All Day

A business scenario: *David Guzman* is working as a *System Administrator* at Universal Containers. The day before, his manager, *Brigette Hyacinth*, had a meeting with the higher management to ensure that all the future cases will close on time. After the discussion, *Brigette Hyacinth* asked *David Guzman* to implement an escalation rule in Salesforce based on the following table:

Support Level	Escalation At	Assign To	Business Hours	Notify to User
Platinum	24 hours	Tier I (Queue)	Allow call center agents to choose	Robert Tan, VP of Support
Gold	32 hours	Tier I (Queue)	Allow call center agents to choose	Adam Busby, Customer Support Director
Silver	48 hours	Tier I (Queue)	Allow call center agents to choose	Adam Busby, Customer Support Director

Perform the following steps to solve the preceding business requirement:

1. Click on **Setup** (gear icon) | **Setup** | **PLATFORM TOOLS** | **Feature Settings** | **Service** | **Escalation Rule**:
    1. To define the escalation rule, click on the **New** button, enter the rule name as `Case Escalation Rule` and make sure to select the **Active** checkbox.
    2. Once you are done, click on the **Save** button.
2. The next step is to define the **Escalation Rule** entry criteria. To define the escalation rule entry criteria, click on **Escalation Rule** to open it.

It will look like the following screenshot:

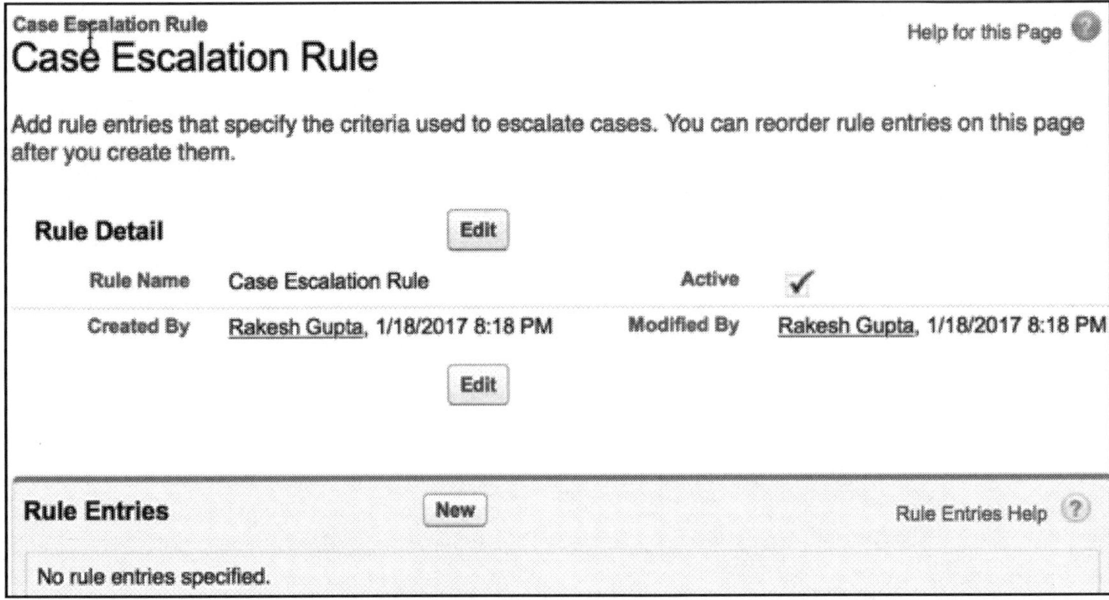

1. Then, navigate to the **Rule Entries** section and click on the **New** button:
    1. Enter `1` for **Sort Order**
    2. For the criteria, select **Account: Support Level** equals **Platinum**

In the end, it will look like the following screenshot:

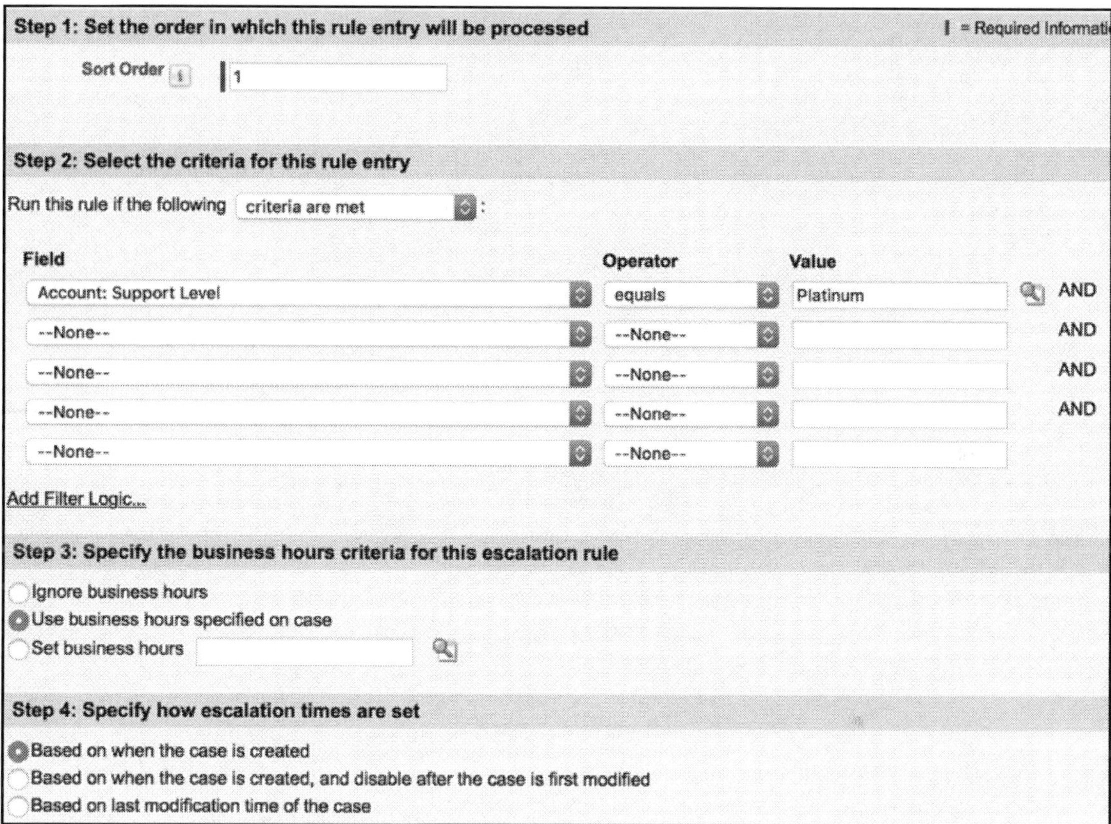

2. Once you are done, click on the **Save** button.
3. Repeat the steps 2.1 and 2.2 to add the rule criteria for **Silver** and **Gold**.

3. The third and the last step is to define the escalation actions. To define the escalation action, click on the **Edit** link available in front of the **Rule Entries**, as shown in the following screenshot:

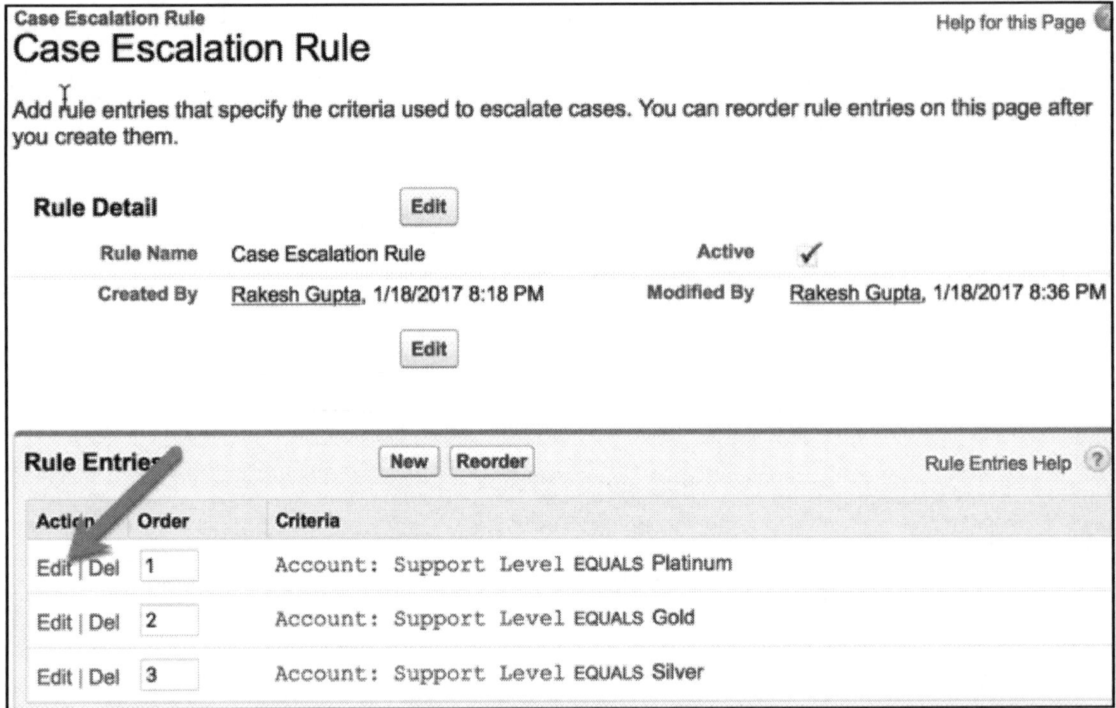

1. Navigate to the **Escalation Actions** related list and click on the **New** button.
2. Enter the details as follows:

    1. Enter `24` for **Age Over**.
    2. For **Auto-reassign cases to** select **Tier I** queue and select standard out-of-the box e-mail template **SUPPORT: Case escalation notification (SAMPLE)** for **Notification Template**
    3. Select **Robert Tan** for **Notify this user** and select standard out-of-the box e-mail template **SUPPORT: Case escalation notification (SAMPLE)** for **Notification Template**
    4. Make sure to select **Notify Case Owner** checkbox.

Finally, it will look like the following screenshot:

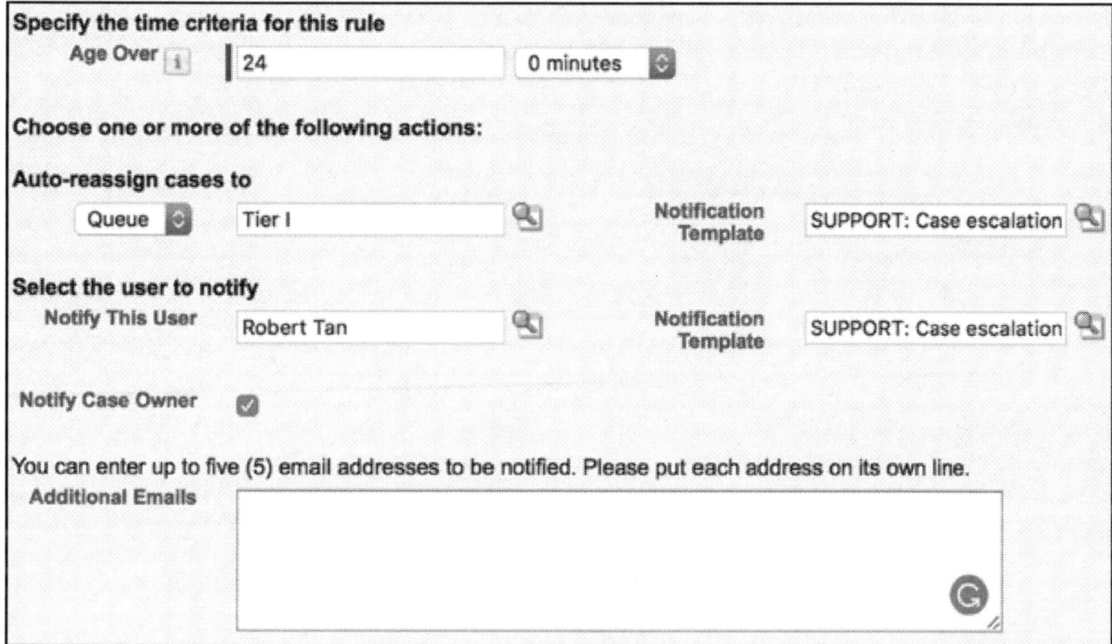

3. Once you are done, click on the **Save** button.
4. Repeat the steps 3.1, 3.2, and 3.3 to define the escalation action for **Rule Entries Silver** and **Gold**.

Remember that, by default, the field-level security of the **Business Hours** field on the case object is hidden; make sure to grant permission on the respective profiles. Make sure to add the **Business Hours** and **Escalated** fields on the case page layouts.

Mentoring case escalations

Before going ahead and checking the escalation status for the case, make sure to update the **Automation Champion Account's Support** level to **Gold**. Create a new support case for the **Automation Champion** account and select the business hour **USA – EST**, as shown in the following screenshot:

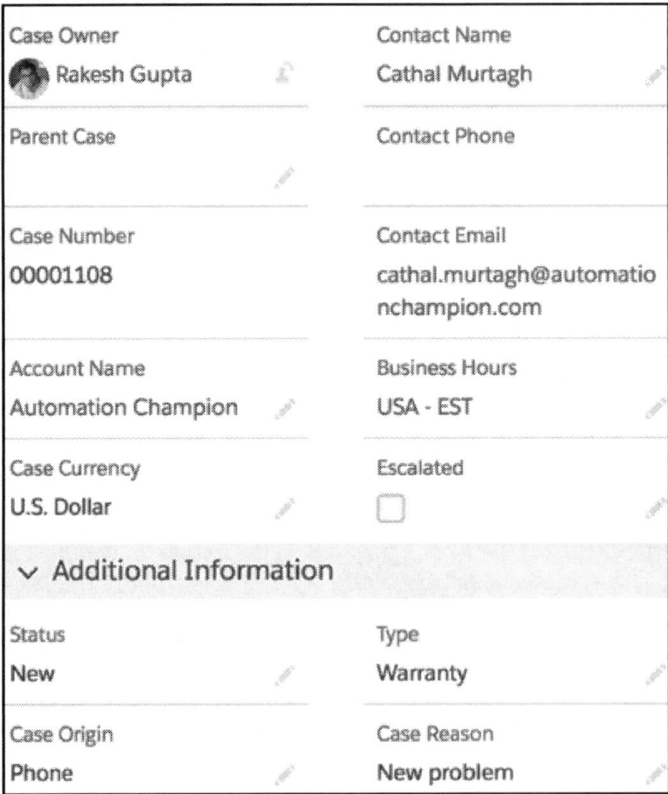

Perform the following steps to check the case escalation rule; it is very helpful in the case of troubleshooting escalation actions:

1. Click on **Setup** (gear icon) | **Setup** | **PLATFORM TOOLS** | **Environments** | **Monitoring** | **Case Escalations**.
2. Click on the **Search** button:

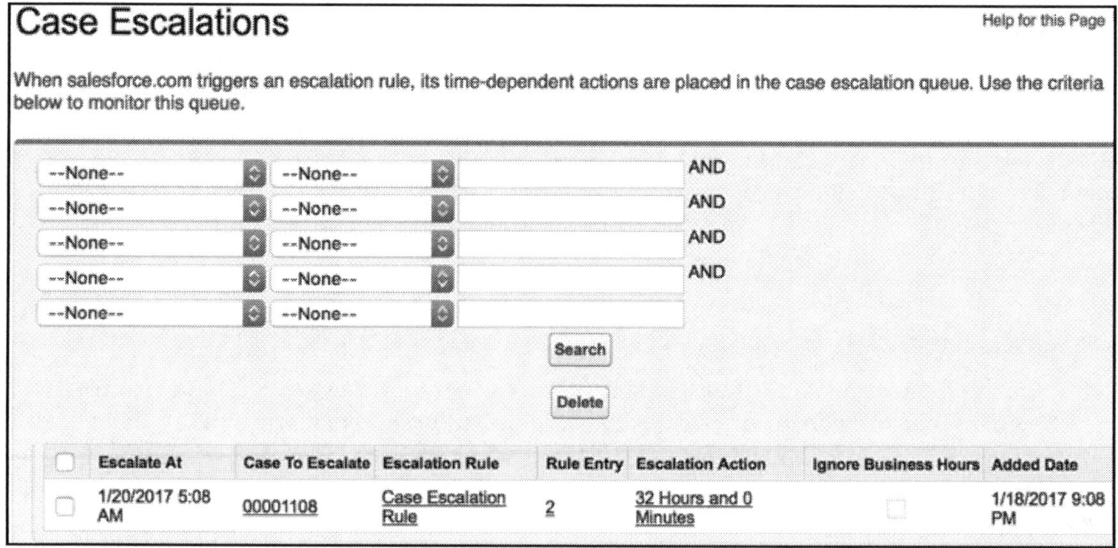

3. Once the support agent closes a case, it will automatically be removed from the case escalation queue.

The escalation rule will increase the productivity of service reps and decrease the case resolution time.

Entitlement management

Entitlement management helps an organization to provide the correct support to their customers. It helps a support agent to identify what all kind of service levels the customer is eligible for. There is a thin gap between an escalation rule and entitlement management. An escalation rule helps an organization to make sure that the cases do not remain open forever whereas entitlement management helps a support agent to identify what all kind of service levels the customer is entitled to, based on their service contract, asset, or account.

Let's start with an example: you have just opened a support ticket with your cellular operator to resolve the network issue. As we all know, cellular providers are not selling any support plan, such as Silver, Gold, or Platinum, separately. It means they are treating all support tickets equivalently; in this case, they can utilize an escalation rule to make sure that the cases do not remain open forever.

Here is another example: let's say that you have just purchased an iPhone 7 Plus 128 GB and one iPad Pro 9.7 128 GB. By default, it comes with 90 days of complimentary Apple care plan. Additionally, you have purchased an Apple care plan for iPad. Now you have a 90-day apple care plan for iPhone and a 3-year Apple care plan for iPad. Now, assume that after 100 days of your purchase, you call Apple's technical support to get some help regarding the iPhone. The support agent will first verify whether you are entitled for the iPhone support or not by checking the entitlement and service contract.

Choosing a correct entitlement model

Before proceeding with the entitlement setup process, make sure that you have chosen the correct model that suits your support process. There are three usual ways to set up entitlement management. Once you have decided what should determine the support eligibility, review the following three models and choose the model that best matches with your business needs:

Entitlement model	**What determines support eligibility**	**When to use this model**
Entitlement Only	Support agents will determine customer eligibility for support based on the entitlement defined at the account, contact, or asset level	If your entitlement doesn't have a renewal process. you are not selling entitlements separately; they're bundled with products (warranties). You don't want to manage the customers' entitlements as a part of the service contract. For example, a mattress firm like *DynanstyMattress* offers 30-years limited warranties to all their customers.

Entitlement + Service Contacts	Support agents will determine customer eligibility for support based on their service contract	Your customers' entitlements are renewed periodically at the service contract level. You are selling entitlements separately from the products, and they are part of the service contract. For example, you have purchased a *Dell* laptop including 1-year home site warranty. This 1-year warranty falls under the service contract.
Entitlement + Service Contacts + Contract Line Items	Support agents will determine customer eligibility for support, based on the products listed in their service contract	Entitlements are created and updated through a third-party system, such as ERP. Warranties, subscriptions, and other support products can appear as line items, and they are mapped to one or more entitlements. Your support team manages service contract transaction, such as, renewals, mergers, and transfers. For example, you have purchased an iPhone 7 Plus, iPad Pro 9.7 and iMac 21.5 from Apple store. You additionally purchased Apple care for iPad and iMac.

Service contracts are agreements between an organization and their customers for a type of customer support. It can represent different types of customer support, such as warranties, subscriptions, or service-level agreements. It is always possible to change the model later. In this chapter, we will discuss the first model, that is, entitlement only.

Setting up an entitlement process

Before creating an entitlement process, you must understand every step you need to configure correctly. To set up the entitlement process correctly, you need to perform the steps mentioned in the following screenshot:

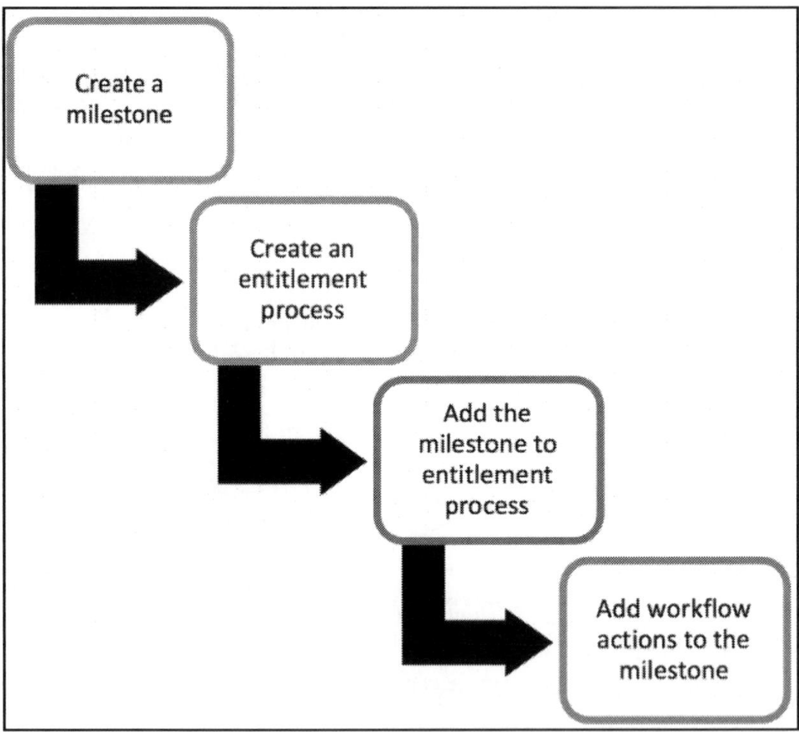

A business scenario: *David Guzman* is working as a *System Administrator* at Universal Containers. His manager, *Brigette Hyacinth,* asks him to implement an entitlement process (*Gold 24X7 Support*) in Salesforce, based on the following table:

Order	Milestone	Criteria	Minutes to complete milestone	Milestone action time	Milestone action (e-mail alerts to)
1	First Response	Case: Priority EQUALS High	60	Success: Immediate Warning: 30 minutes before Violation: 0 minutes after	Success: Case Owner Warning: Account Owner, Case Owner Violation: Account Owner, Case Owner
2	First Response	Case: Priority EQUALS Medium, Low	180	Success: Immediate Warning: 30 minutes before Violation: 0 minutes after	Success: Case Owner Warning: Account Owner, Case Owner Violation: Account Owner, Case Owner
3	Resolution Time	Case: Priority EQUALS High	960	Success: Immediate Warning: 30 minutes before Violation: 0 minutes after	Success: Case Owner Warning: Account Owner, Case Owner Violation: Account Owner, Case Owner

4	Resolution Time	Case: Priority EQUALS Medium, Low	1800	Success: Immediate Warning: 30 minutes before Violation: 0 minutes after	Success: Case Owner Warning: Account Owner, Case Owner Violation: Account Owner, Case Owner

As of *Spring'17* release, entitlement management is not supported by Lightning Experience. Perform the following steps to solve the preceding business requirement:

1. Click on **Setup** | **Build** | **Customize** | **Entitlement Management** | **Entitlement Settings.**
2. To enable entitlement management, select the **Enable Entitlement Management** checkbox.
3. Once you are done, click on the **Save** button.
4. Now, you will get some options, for example:
    1. Options to **Enable Entitlement Versioning** (It allows you to manage different version of an entitlement process).
    2. Limit the **Entitlement lookup** field to only return entitlements with **Active Stats**, **Same account on the case**, **Same asset on the case**, and **Same contact on the case**.
    3. Enable **Milestone Feed Items**, enable **Milestone Time Settings** **(The Stopped Time** field on milestones displays how long a support agent has been blocked from completing a milestone. **The Actual Elapsed Time** field on milestone shows how long it took to complete a milestone.).

Enable all these features, as shown in the following screenshot:

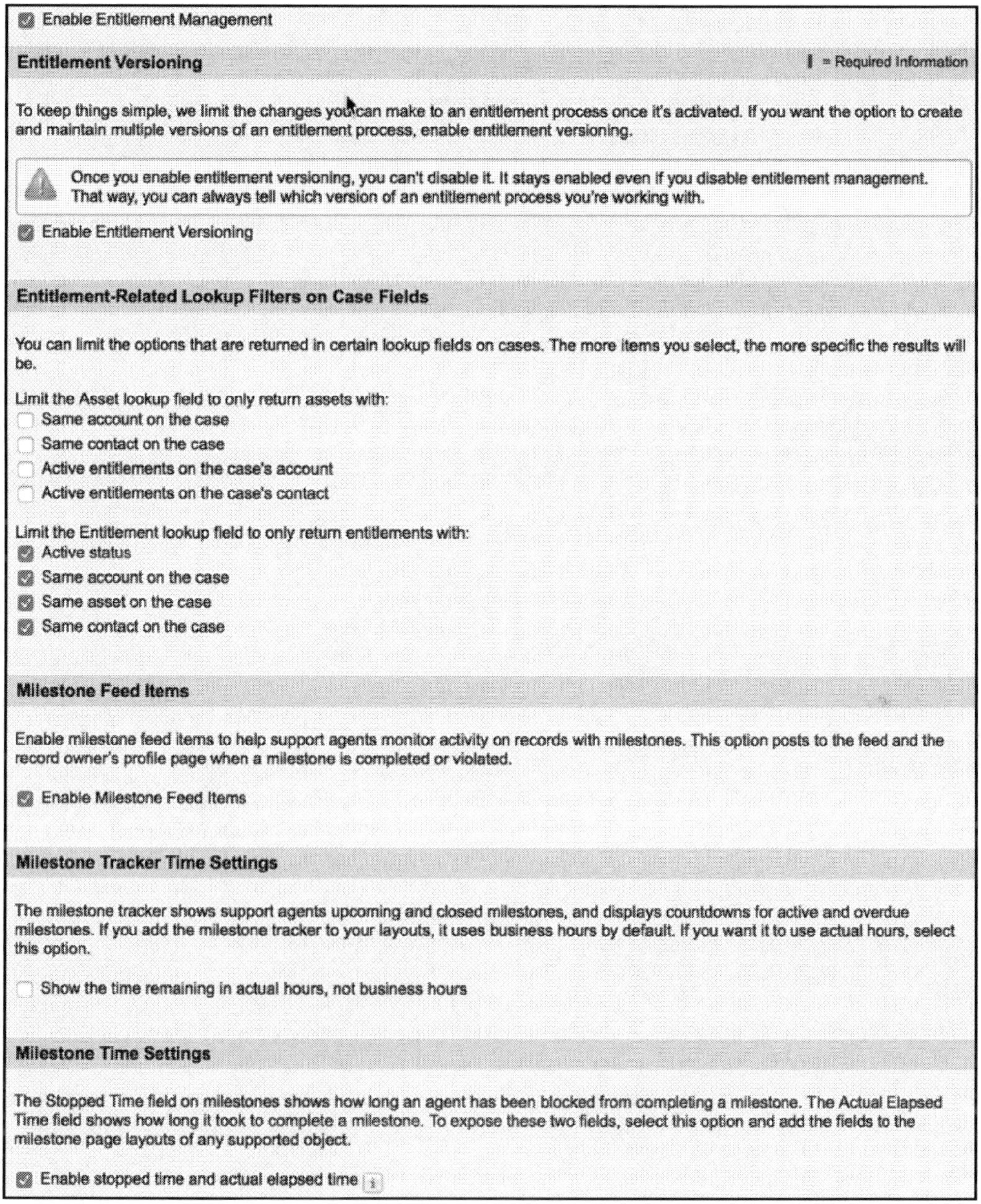

☑ Enable Entitlement Management

Entitlement Versioning | = Required Information

To keep things simple, we limit the changes you can make to an entitlement process once it's activated. If you want the option to create and maintain multiple versions of an entitlement process, enable entitlement versioning.

Once you enable entitlement versioning, you can't disable it. It stays enabled even if you disable entitlement management. That way, you can always tell which version of an entitlement process you're working with.

☑ Enable Entitlement Versioning

Entitlement-Related Lookup Filters on Case Fields

You can limit the options that are returned in certain lookup fields on cases. The more items you select, the more specific the results will be.

Limit the Asset lookup field to only return assets with:

☐ Same account on the case
☐ Same contact on the case
☐ Active entitlements on the case's account
☐ Active entitlements on the case's contact

Limit the Entitlement lookup field to only return entitlements with:

☑ Active status
☑ Same account on the case
☑ Same asset on the case
☑ Same contact on the case

Milestone Feed Items

Enable milestone feed items to help support agents monitor activity on records with milestones. This option posts to the feed and the record owner's profile page when a milestone is completed or violated.

☑ Enable Milestone Feed Items

Milestone Tracker Time Settings

The milestone tracker shows support agents upcoming and closed milestones, and displays countdowns for active and overdue milestones. If you add the milestone tracker to your layouts, it uses business hours by default. If you want it to use actual hours, select this option.

☐ Show the time remaining in actual hours, not business hours

Milestone Time Settings

The Stopped Time field on milestones shows how long an agent has been blocked from completing a milestone. The Actual Elapsed Time field shows how long it took to complete a milestone. To expose these two fields, select this option and add the fields to the milestone page layouts of any supported object.

☑ Enable stopped time and actual elapsed time

5. The next step is to set the field-level security for the following case fields so that you can view and edit it:
    1. **Entitlement Name**
    2. **Entitlement Process Start Time**
    3. **Entitlement Process End Time**
    4. **Milestone Status**
    5. **Milestone Status icon**
    6. **Stopped**
    7. **Stopped Since**
    8. **Asset**
    9. **Timeline (Minutes)**

    Also, add a new section, **Entitlement Information**, on the case page layout, as shown in the following screenshot:

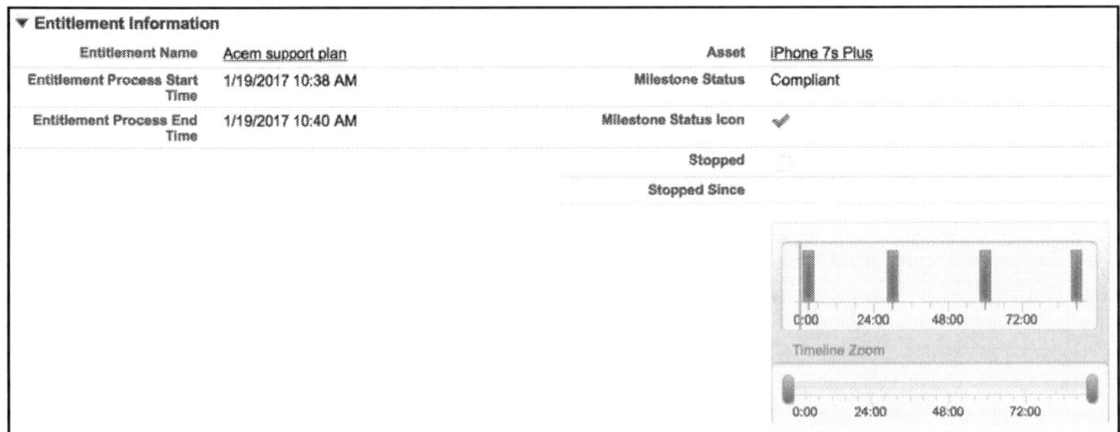

    Make sure to enable field history tracking for entitlement to see when the values were changed.

6. Now, the next step is to add the related list to different object page layouts, as per your business requirement:
    1. Add the **Entitlements** related list on the **Account** page layouts. It tells the support agent that any contacts on the account are eligible for support.
    2. Add the **Entitlements** related list on the **Contact** page layouts. It helps the support agent to understand which specific contacts are eligible for support.

3. Add the **Entitlements** related list on the **Asset** page layouts. It helps the support agent to understand which specific assets are eligible for support.
4. Add the **Entitlement Templates** related list to the **Product** page layouts. **Entitlement Templates** helps you to predefine the terms and conditions of support that the support users can add to the products.
5. Add the **Case Milestones** related list on the **Case** page layouts.
6. Add **Actual Elapsed Time**, **Entitlement**, **Elapsed Time**, **Stopped Time**, **Target Response**, **Target Remaining,** and **Time Since Target** on the **Case Milestones** page layouts into a new section called `Milestones Time Information`, as shown in the following screenshot:

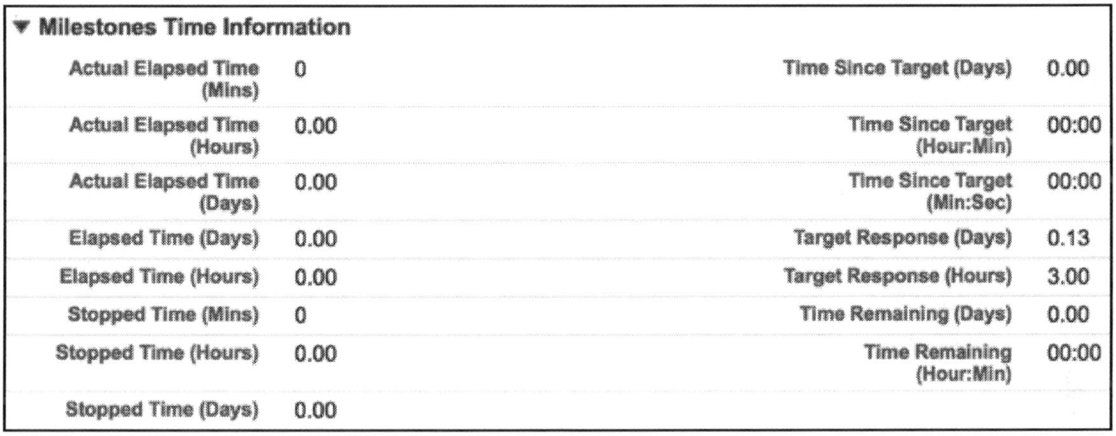

▼ Milestones Time Information			
Actual Elapsed Time (Mins)	0	Time Since Target (Days)	0.00
Actual Elapsed Time (Hours)	0.00	Time Since Target (Hour:Min)	00:00
Actual Elapsed Time (Days)	0.00	Time Since Target (Min:Sec)	00:00
Elapsed Time (Days)	0.00	Target Response (Days)	0.13
Elapsed Time (Hours)	0.00	Target Response (Hours)	3.00
Stopped Time (Mins)	0	Time Remaining (Days)	0.00
Stopped Time (Hours)	0.00	Time Remaining (Hour:Min)	00:00
Stopped Time (Days)	0.00		

Make sure that the **Entitlement** tab is visible in Salesforce and you have granted permissions to the respective users.

7. In case, going forward if you are planning to use a service contract and contract line items, then this is the right time to implement it.

Creating a milestone

Milestones represent mandatory steps in the support process, for example, case resolution time and first response time:

8. To create a milestone as per the preceding business requirement, click on **Setup** | **Build** | **Customize** | **Entitlement Management** | **Milestones** and then click on the **New Milestone** button

9. Enter the following information as mentioned:
    1. Enter `First Response` as **Name.**
    2. Enter the **Description**.
    3. For **Recurrence Type**, select **No Recurrence**. The different recurrence types are as follows:
        1. **No Recurrence**: The milestone will only occur once on the record.
        2. **Independent**: The milestone will occur whenever the milestone criteria are met on the record.
        3. **Sequential**: The milestone will occur repeatedly whenever the milestone criteria are met on the record.

    Your milestone page should look like the following screenshot:

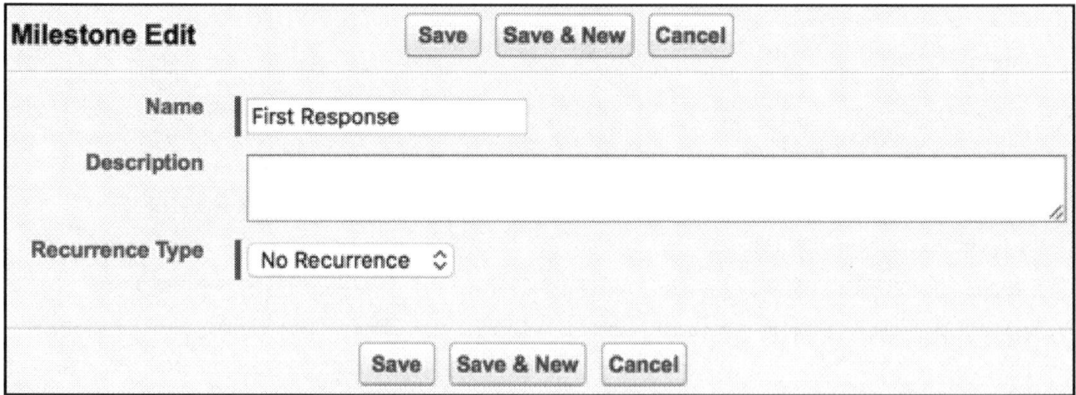

10. Once you are done, click on the **Save** button.
11. Repeat the steps 8, 9, and 10 to add one more milestone, **Resolution Time**.

Creating an entitlement process

Setting up an entitlement process gives the support agents a timeline of the required steps to follow when resolving support cases:

12. To create a milestone as per the preceding business requirement, click on **Setup** | **Build** | **Customize** | **Entitlement Management** | **Entitlement Processes** and then click on the **New Entitlement Process** button.
13. If you get the option to choose **Entitlement Process Type**, then select **Case**. Once you are done, click on the **Next** button.

14. Enter the details as follows:
    1. Enter `Gold 24X7 Support` as **Entitlement Process Name**.
    2. Enter the **Description**.
    3. Don't select the **Active** checkbox; we will activate the process after we add a milestone action to it.

    Leave the other fields as is; finally, it will look like the following screenshot:

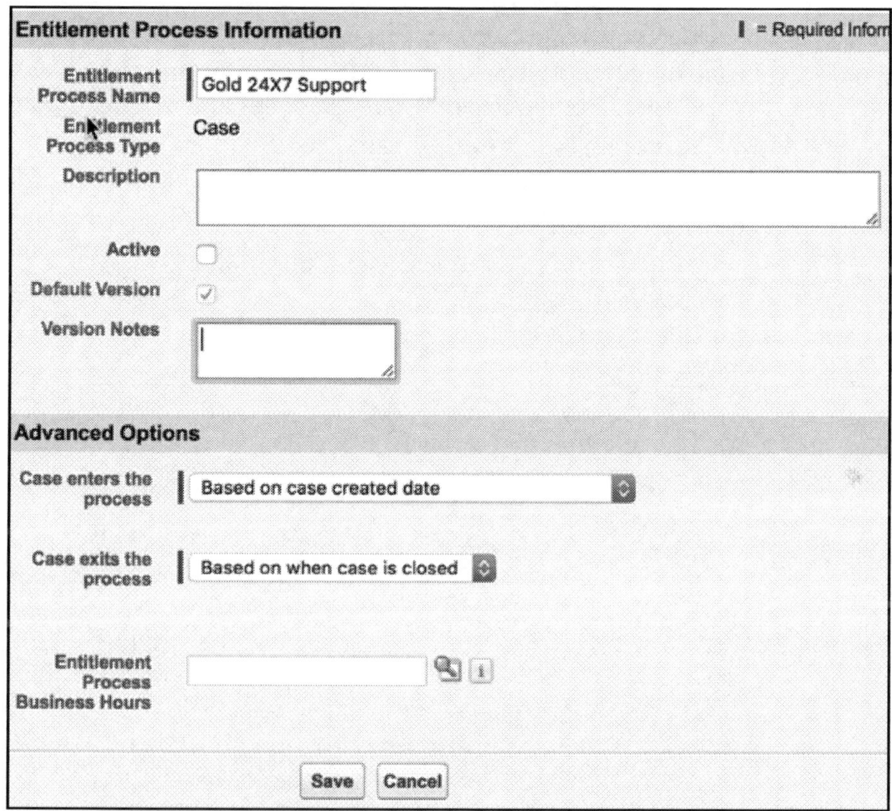

If you want to apply case business hours to the entitlement process, then don't populate **Entitlement Process Business Hours**, as shown in the preceding screenshot.

15. Once you are done, click on the **Save** button.

Adding a milestone to an entitlement process

Adding milestones to an entitlement process defines the required steps in your support process:

16. You should now be on the detail page of the entitlement process you created. To add a milestone to an entitlement process, navigate to the **Milestone** related list and click on the **New** button:
    1. For **Milestone Name**, choose **First Response.**
    2. For **Time Trigger (Minutes),** enter `60`. It means support agents will have 60 minutes to complete this action.
    3. Leave the **Enable Apex Class for the Time Trigger (Minutes)** unselected. This allows you to calculate the time trigger dynamically.
    4. For **Start Time**, select **Entitlement Process**.
    5. Leave the **Milestone Business Hours** field as is.
    6. For **Order**, enter `1`.
    7. For **Criteria**, select **Case: Priority** equals **High**.

It will look like the following screenshot:

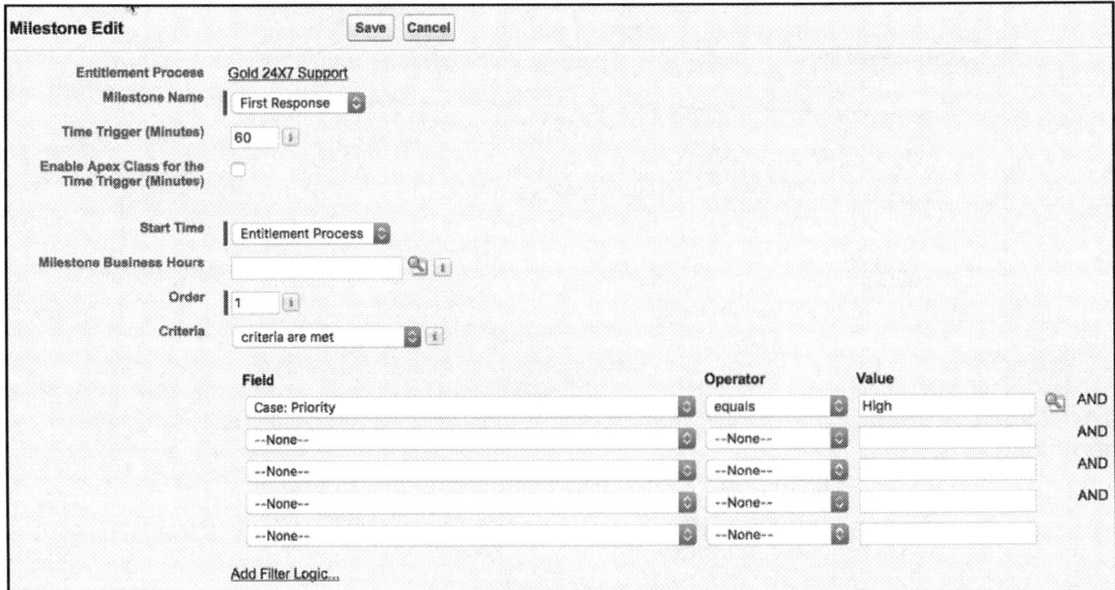

17. Once you are done, click on the **Save** button.
18. Repeat the steps 16 and 17, to add an additional milestone to the entitlement process as defined in the business requirement table. In the end, **Gold 24X7 Support** will have four milestones related to it.

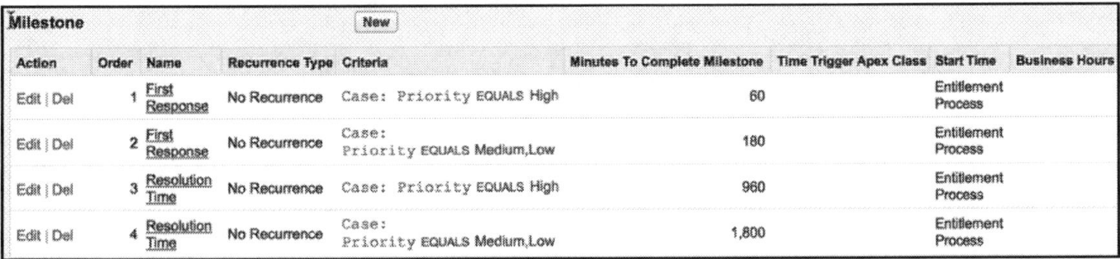

Milestone New

Action	Order	Name	Recurrence Type	Criteria	Minutes To Complete Milestone	Time Trigger Apex Class	Start Time	Business Hours
Edit | Del	1	First Response	No Recurrence	Case: Priority EQUALS High	60		Entitlement Process	
Edit | Del	2	First Response	No Recurrence	Case: Priority EQUALS Medium,Low	180		Entitlement Process	
Edit | Del	3	Resolution Time	No Recurrence	Case: Priority EQUALS High	960		Entitlement Process	
Edit | Del	4	Resolution Time	No Recurrence	Case: Priority EQUALS Medium,Low	1,800		Entitlement Process	

Milestones are calculated in minutes and seconds, but their start and end times are only precise to the minute. For example, suppose a milestone is triggered at *09:20:30 AM* and it took around 15 minutes for the support agent to complete the milestone, the milestone target time is 09:35:00 AM, *not 09:35:30 AM*. Thus, the remaining time for the support agent to complete the milestone is 14 minutes and 30 seconds, not complete 15 minutes. Now, the next step is to define the milestone actions for each milestone.

Adding a milestone action to an entitlement process

Milestone actions are immediate and time-dependent workflow actions (new task, new e-mail alert, new field update, and new outbound message) that occur at every milestone in an entitlement process. Once you have created an entitlement process and added a milestone to it, the next process is to add milestone actions to the milestone. A milestone action has three types of actions, as follows:

- **Success Actions**: This action will trigger only when a milestone is completed. This action will still fire for a milestone that is closed late.
- **Warning Actions**: This action will trigger only when a milestone is near violation.
- **Violation Actions**: This action will trigger only when a milestone is violated.

19. Let's start with defining a milestone action for milestone order 1, as per the requirements defined in the table. You should now be on the detail page of the entitlement process you created. Click on the name of **Milestone** (order 1) on the **Milestone** related list, as shown in the following screenshot:

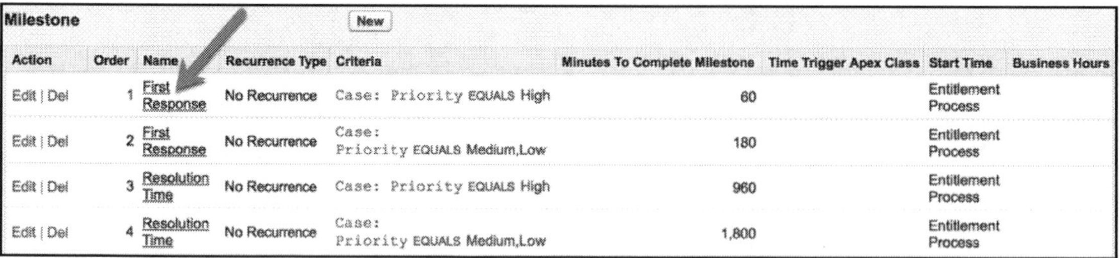

Milestone

Action	Order	Name	Recurrence Type	Criteria	Minutes To Complete Milestone	Time Trigger Apex Class	Start Time	Business Hours
Edit | Del	1	First Response	No Recurrence	Case: Priority EQUALS High	60		Entitlement Process	
Edit | Del	2	First Response	No Recurrence	Case: Priority EQUALS Medium,Low	180		Entitlement Process	
Edit | Del	3	Resolution Time	No Recurrence	Case: Priority EQUALS High	960		Entitlement Process	
Edit | Del	4	Resolution Time	No Recurrence	Case: Priority EQUALS Medium,Low	1,800		Entitlement Process	

20. Under **Warning Action**, click the **Add Time Trigger** button.
    1. Enter `30` and select **Minutes** to have the agents notified 30 minutes before the milestone time expires.
    2. Once you are done, click on the **Save** button.
    3. Navigate to the **Warning Actions** section, click **Add Workflow Action**, and select **New Email Alert** to add an e-mail alert action.

It should look like the following screenshot:

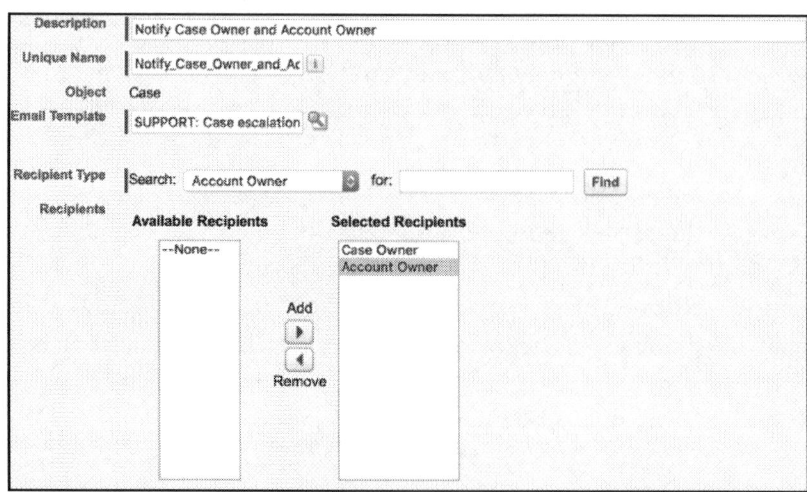

21. Once you are done, click on the **Save** button.

22. Likewise, repeat the steps 19, 20, and 21 to create e-mail alerts for **Success Actions** and **Violation Actions** as mentioned in the business requirement table. In the end, it should look like the following screenshot:

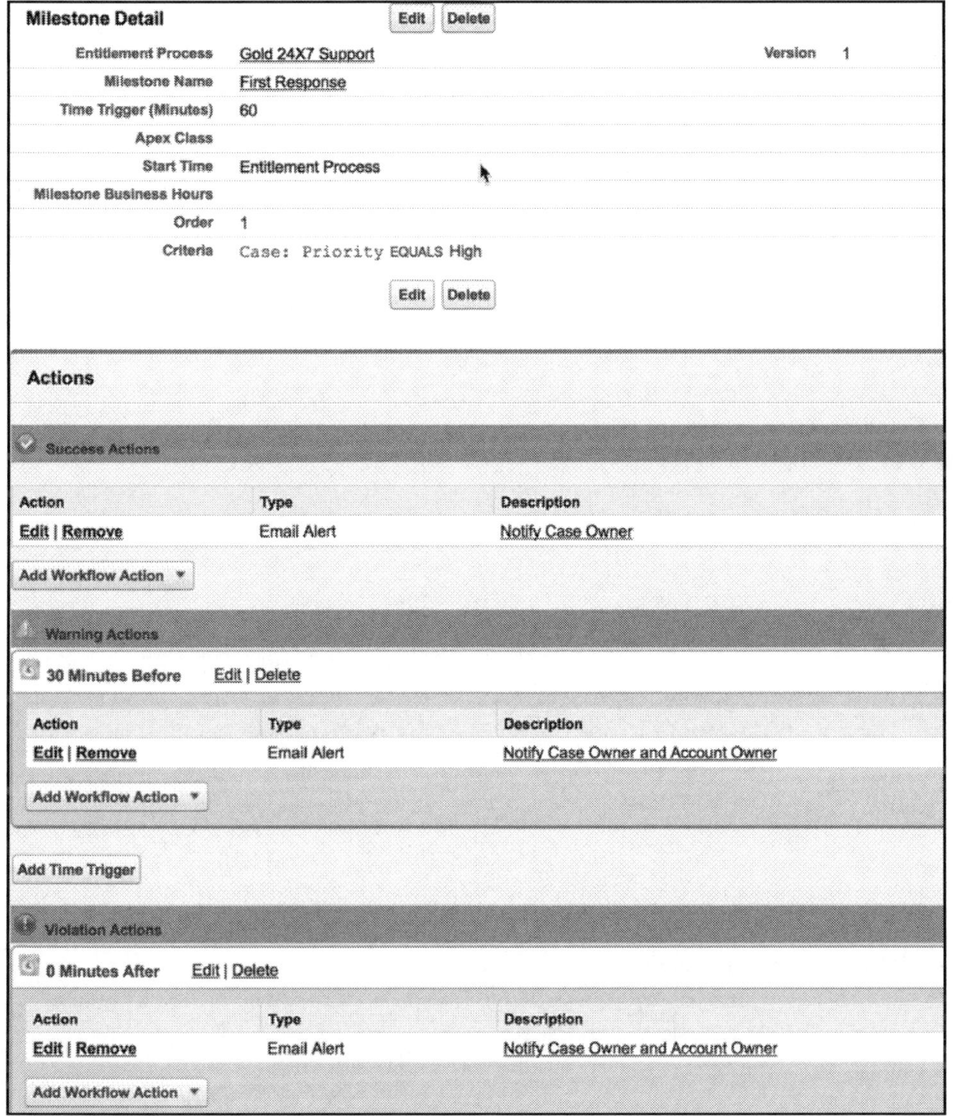

Likewise, repeat the steps 19, 20, and 21 to create e-mail alerts for three remaining milestones as mentioned in business requirement table.

Activating an entitlement process

The final step is to active your entitlement process. To do so, perform the following instructions:

23. Click on **Setup** | **Build** | **Customize** | **Entitlement Management** | **Entitlement Processes** and then click on the name of the entitlement process, that is, **Gold 24X7 Support**.
24. Click on the **Edit** button.
25. Select the **Active** checkbox.
26. Once you are done, click on the **Save** button.

Applying your entitlement process to an entitlement

Now that we have created an entitlement process, it's time to use it. First, create an entitlement for an asset and associate your entitlement process to it:

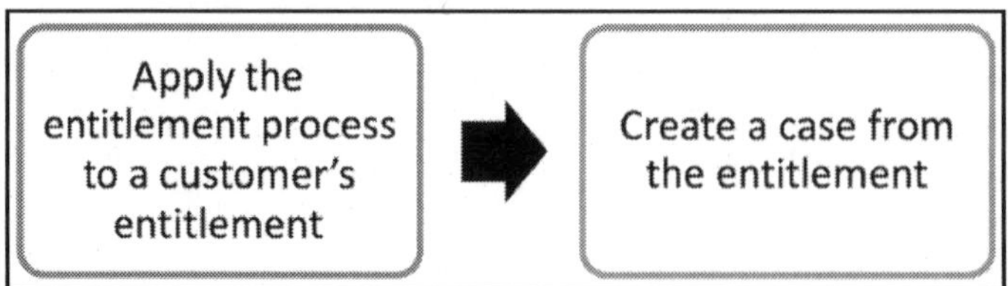

From the next time, creating a case from this entitlement will automatically apply your **Gold 24X7 Support** entitlement process. It means that the support agent will see the resolution time counting down on the case.

Knowledge management

Salesforce Knowledge gives you the capability to build a complete knowledge base inside Salesforce to service support agents, partners, and customers. Salesforce Knowledge is a placeholder where you can easily create and manage content, known as articles, and it is easy to find and view the articles you need. If you don't have any idea what a knowledge base is, it is basically a collection of articles with significant information about your products and services. The knowledge base is the most common way to provide a self-service portal to customers to solve their own queries, which helps the organization to decrease the case creation rate. This means hiring fewer support agents, and it helps customers to solve their queries a lot faster than calling up and waiting to ask a relatively common question.

For example, instead of calling the Apple customer care to ask about how to force restart an iPhone, it is very easy to read a knowledge article that describes the steps to force restart an iPhone.

Salesforce Knowledge is only included in Lightning Unlimited, Lightning Performance, and Developer editions org. Salesforce Knowledge is available as feature licenses; in most organizations, it is available as an add-on. This means that if you are using Lightning Enterprise edition org and you don't have Salesforce Knowledge available, you must purchase knowledge license.

You can only share the articles to these four channels. It is important to note that while publishing an article, you can define which channels the article should be shared through. The four different channels are as follows:

- Internal
- Partner Community
- Customer Community
- Public Knowledge Base

Creating an article type

Article types are containers for your articles. Every article you create should belong to a type that determines its content and structure. It is very relatable to objects or page layouts. To create a knowledge article, you must identify which fields you want to have on the page, for example, text, number, rich text, and so on. Article types also allow you to create different layouts for different kinds of articles.

A business scenario: *David Guzman* is working as a *System Administrator* at Universal Containers. His manager, *Brigette Hyacinth*, asked him to create an article type *FAQ* so that they can create different articles for Sales and Service Cloud later.

As of *Spring'17* release, the setup of Lightning Knowledge is not supported by Lightning Experience. Perform the following steps to solve the preceding business requirement:

1. Click on **Setup** | **Build** | **Customize** | **Knowledge** | **Knowledge Article Types**.
2. To create a new article type, click on the **New Article Type** button.
    1. For **Label**, enter `FAQ`
    2. For **Plural Label**, enter `FAQs`.
    3. **Object Name** will be autopopulated based on the **Label**.
    4. Enter the meaningful **Description** for the article type so that other administrators can easily understand why this article type has been created.
    5. For **Deployment Status**, select **Deployed**.
3. Once you are done, click on the **Save** button.

    It should look like the following screenshot:

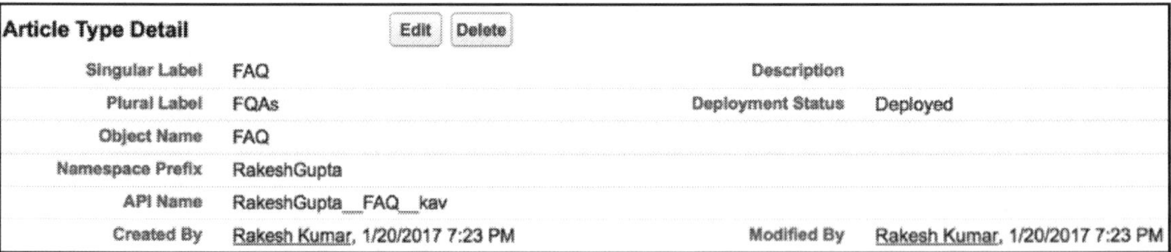

Look at the API Name of the article type; it should append `__kav`. It is now like another object in Salesforce; make sure to grant the FAQ article type permission to respective users on their profiles.

Enabling Salesforce Knowledge

The next step is to enable Salesforce Knowledge in your organization. Perform the following steps to enable Salesforce Knowledge:

1. Click on **Setup** | **Build** | **Customize** | **Knowledge** | **Knowledge Settings**.
2. Select the checkbox **Yes, I understand the impact of enabling Salesforce Knowledge**:

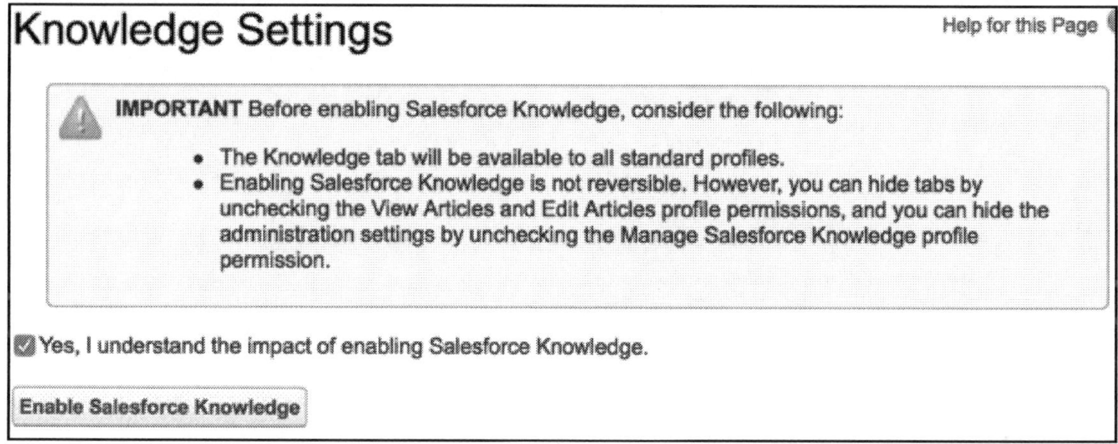

3. Once you are done, click on the **Enable Salesforce Knowledge** button.

Enabling Salesforce Knowledge cannot be undone.

If you are sure you want to enable Salesforce Knowledge, click OK. Otherwise, click Cancel.

Cancel OK

4. It will open a popup on your browser, to remind you that enabling Salesforce Knowledge is not a reversible process. Once you are ready, click on the **OK** button.

5. Once Salesforce Knowledge is enabled successfully, you can see that the different options are available under **Knowledge Settings**. Make sure that it looks like the following screenshot:

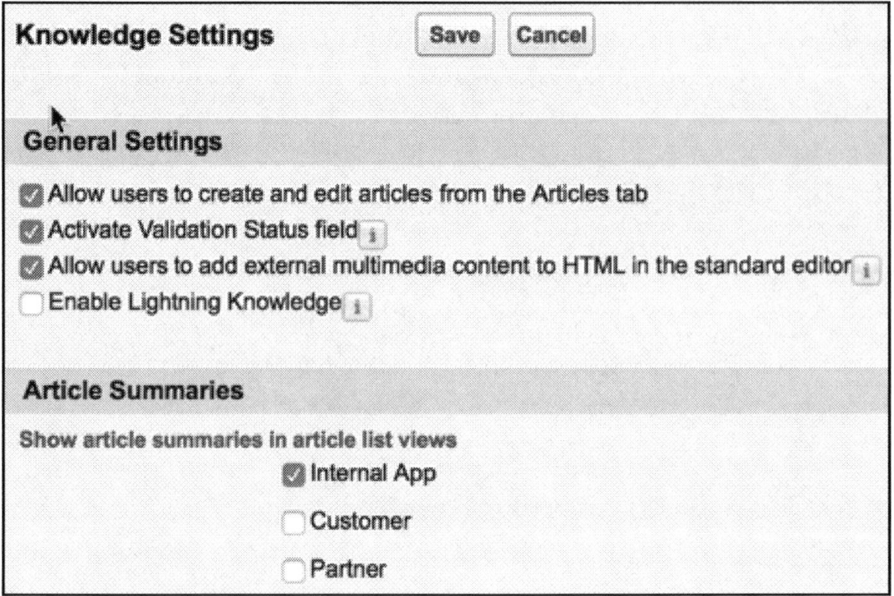

Before enabling the new Lightning Knowledge, remember that it uses files instead of old attachments.

Granting Salesforce Knowledge license to users

Now, it is time to grant the **Knowledge User** feature license to the users by editing their user records. Perform the following steps to grant a knowledge feature license to your users:

1. Click on **Setup** | **Build** | **Customize** | **Knowledge** | **Knowledge Settings**.
2. Click on the **Edit** link available next to the user's name.
3. Select the **Knowledge User** checkbox available under the **General Information** section.
4. Once you are done, click on the **Save** button.

Make sure to add the **Knowledge**, **Article**, and **Article Management** tabs to apps.

Configuring Data Categories

The **Data Categories** option allows you to organize articles into different categories. You can have a hierarchical structure for an article type, such as roles hierarchy. This allows you to assign articles to one or more categories that help in searching and increase the profile visibility of certain sets of articles. For example, if you have two data categories, Sales Cloud and Service Cloud, you can ensure that the Sales Cloud users do not see the Service Cloud articles.

A business scenario: *David Guzman* is working as a *System Administrator* at Universal Containers. His manager, *Brigette Hyacinth*, asks him to create two different data categories, as mentioned in the following table:

Data Category Group Name	Child Category
Sales Cloud	Accounts Assets Campaigns Contacts Leads Opportunities Orders Quotes
Service Cloud	Accounts Contacts Cases Articles Entitlements Service Contracts Ideas Live Agent

Perform the following steps to create the data categories:

1. Click on **Setup** | **Build** | **Customize** | **Data Categories** | **Data Categories Setup**.
2. Click on the **New** button available under **Category Groups**, and enter the following information:
    1. For **Group Name**, enter `Sales Cloud`.
    2. **Group Unique Name** will be auto populated based on the **Group Name**.
    3. Enter the meaningful **Description** for the **Data Category**, so other administrators can easily understand why this data category has been created.
    4. Once you are done, click on the **Save** button.

Adding categories to a data category group

The next step is to add categories to a data category. To add data categories to a Sales Cloud group as mentioned in the business requirement table. Perform the following steps:

3. Click on the **Sales Cloud** category, and then click on **Actions**. Select an action, **Add Child Category**, as shown in the following screenshot:

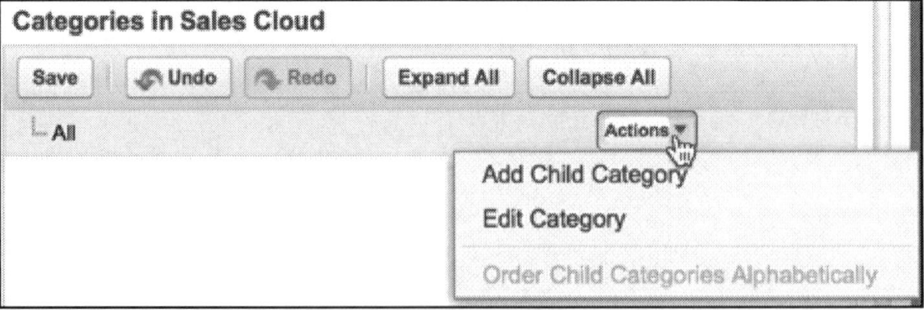

4. Enter a category name, that is, `Accounts`.
5. Once you are done, click on **Add** or press *Enter*.

6. Repeat the steps 3, 4, and 5 to add the remaining categories, **Assets**, **Campaigns**, **Contacts**, **Leads**, **Opportunities**, **Orders**, and **Quotes**, as mentioned in the business requirement table. In the end, it should look like the following screenshot:

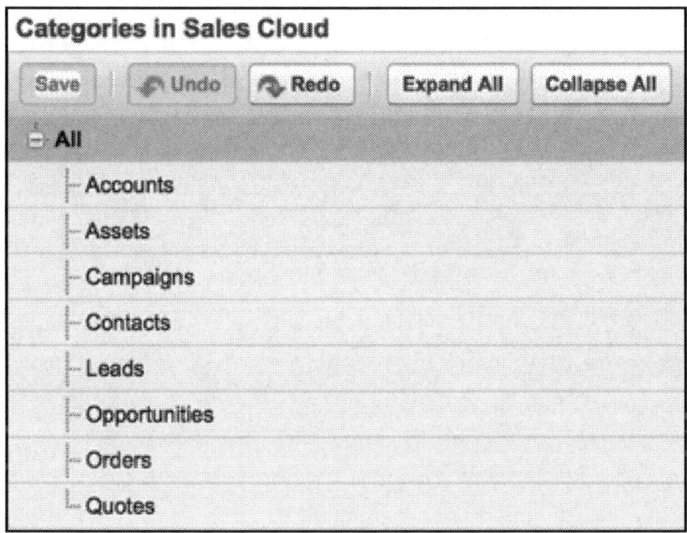

7. Once you are done, click on the **Save** button.
8. The next step is to activate a data category. To do so, hover on the **Sales Cloud** data category and click on the **Activate Category Group** icon, as shown in the following screenshot:

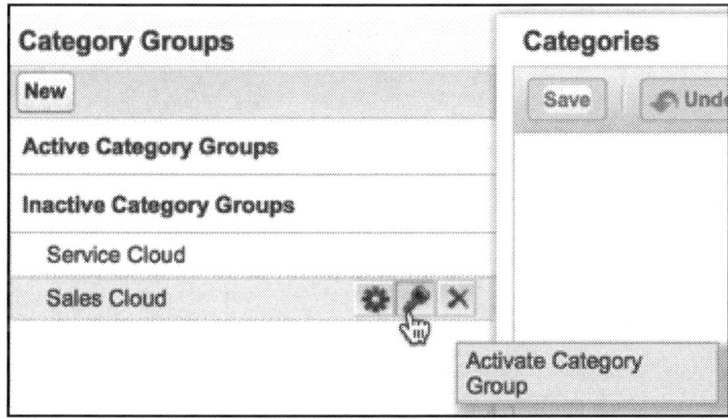

9. Repeat steps 2 through 9 to add one more data category **Service Cloud** and a child category to it, as mentioned in the business requirement table.

Controlling data categories visibility

If you want to make sure that Sales Cloud users do not see the Service Cloud articles and vice versa, then use the profile to control the data category visibility. Enable only those data categories on profiles that you want to allow users to access articles for, as shown in the following screenshot:

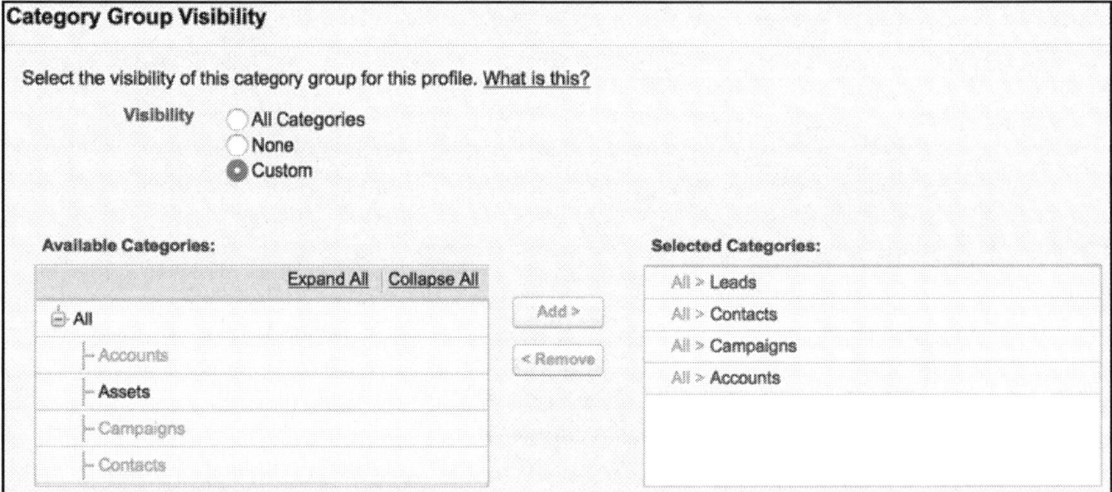

The preceding screenshot shows the custom data categories visibility for an **Inside Sales** profile. Now from the **Article Management** tab, article managers can create new articles and manage existing articles.

Live agent

Salesforce live agent is an out-of-the box feature that provides the power to communicate with your website visitors in real time. You may have noticed that there is a Need help? **Chat with us!** button on almost every company website, as shown in the following screenshot:

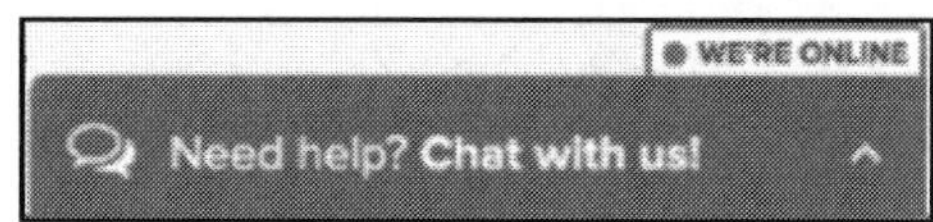

Live chat offers customers exactly what they are looking for from a customer support team, that is, real time interaction. Amazon, ExpressVPN, and Apple are a few companies that offer live chat as a channel of support for their customers. The following are a few benefits of having a live chat on the company website:

1. Real-time conversion with the customer and the ability to share files or screen.
2. Live chat is cost saving as one live chat agent can handle multiple customers simultaneously.
3. Studies prove that offering a live chat feature on the company website can bring more sales.
4. It also helps the organization to improve the call center deflection rates.
5. A live chat agent can drive both sales and service.

Use the following link to get the live chat implementation guide: `https://resources.docs.salesforce.com/sfdc/pdf/live_agent_administrator.pdf`

A few points to remember

1. Entitlements don't automatically apply to cases that are created using web-to-case, email-to-case, or communities. However, you can add entitlements to these features using Apex code.
2. Create a new version if you want to update an entitlement process.
3. Entitlement management is available for the case and work order object.
4. Entitlements don't automatically apply to cases created via web-to-case, email-to-case, or communities. If you want to apply entitlement automatically, then consider using Apex or Process Builder.
5. After you enable Lightning Knowledge, you can't disable it. Currently, it doesn't support multiple language translations.
6. You can have only one article type when enabling Lightning Knowledge.
7. By default, you can create a maximum of five category groups and three active category groups. Contact Salesforce to request additional category groups.

Test your knowledge

Q1. Universal Containers has service level agreements with clients that require an agent to respond within 3 hours of receiving a case. The agreement also states that the case must be resolved within 10 hours if the case priority is set to high. Which of the following features can they utilize to fulfill this requirement?

1. Workflow e-mail alert to send notification that a case was received
2. Case assignment rules to route the case to an escalation queue
3. Case comments to communicate updates to the client
4. Entitlements to define milestones to meet the SLAs

Q2. Which feature license needs to grant permission to a user to enable Salesforce Knowledge for them?

1. Allow Knowledge User
2. Allow forecasting
3. Marketing User
4. Knowledge User

Q3. Universal Containers leverage Service Cloud features to ensure that only specific individuals be allowed to contact support on behalf of the customer?

1. Utilize the case team feature to share case visibility
2. Configure the CTI adapter to block unknown numbers
3. Add the Entitlement related list contacts page layout to identify approved users
4. Grant the record owner field to manage record visibility

Q4. Universal Containers is now implementing communities for their customers. The company wants to grant customers access to service level agreements (SLA) via the community. Which of the following features can they utilize for this?

1. Milestones
2. Assets
3. Service Contracts
4. Cases

Q5. Universal Containers is migrating data from a legacy system into Salesforce Service Cloud. The company needs to migrate the account, contact, and cases data from its legacy system. What is the recommended order for data migration?

1. Account, Cases, Users, Contacts
2. Users, Contacts, Account, Cases
3. Account, Contacts, Cases, Users,
4. Users, Account, Contacts, Cases

Summary

In this chapter, we started with an explanation of support life cycle, and then we moved ahead with case management and discussed best practices to streamline customer support. We also discussed the escalation rule, email-to-case. We have also seen how to impose service level agreement into case by using entitlement and service contract. In the end, we discussed knowledge management and live agent. In the next chapter, you will go through and learn how to utilize visual workflow to streamline and optimize your business processes.

7

Optimizing Business Processes with Visual Workflow and Approval Processes

In the previous chapters, we discussed Salesforce Service Cloud. Service Cloud is a product designed to automate support processes. By implementing it, you can boost your support agents' productivity by allowing them to manage customer issues in a faster and simpler way. This chapter will start with an overview of Visual Workflow and its benefits. We will then take the discussion forward to the various business requirements where we can use Visual Workflow. Then, we will go through Visual Workflow's basic concepts. In addition to this, we will also look at how to set up an approval process in Salesforce. The following topics will be covered in this chapter:

- Business problems
- Benefits of Visual Workflow
- Overview of Visual Workflow's life cycle
- Overview of Cloud Flow Designer
- Creating a calculator to display summation of two numbers
- Approval process

A Visual Workflow is a drag and drop tool that allows you to automate business processes by creating an application that uses *click not code*. Using Visual Workflow, you can create records, update records, delete records, send an e-mail, submit a record for approval, post to Chatter, capture user input in Salesforce, and then make those flows available to business users. You can also execute logic with the help of record or fast elements, interact with the database, invoke an Apex class (an Apex class implements the `Process.Plugin` interface), and create a series of screens to capture user input for saving and processing data in Salesforce.

Business problems

As a Salesforce administrator or developer, you may get various requirements from the business to streamline the sales or support processes. As per our experience, we can say that many of them are achievable only if you make use of the **out-of-the box** features. For a few instances though, you would need to use either the Apex or Visualforce Page. Visual Workflow gives us a way to implement various business processes without using the Apex or Visualforce Page. We'll discuss more examples of this in a detailed manner in the subsequent subsections.

Business use case 1

A business scenario: *David Guzman* is working as a System Administrator at *Universal Containers*. He has received a requirement to create a survey page in Salesforce and expose it to the company's website for unauthenticated access.

There are several ways to solve the preceding business requirement; a few of them are mentioned next.

Solution 1 – Using a Visualforce Page, Apex class, and Force.com site

As the requirement is to capture users' feedback from the company website page, we can't use the standard out-of-the-box page to achieve it. We need to create a Visualforce Page to capture the data. We also need an Apex class to process that data and then expose a Visualforce Page to the Force.com site for unauthenticated access. This approach requires coding skills and is time consuming if you want to update logic in future. This is because here you will have to update both the Apex class as well as the test class.

Solution 2 – Using a Visual Workflow, Visualforce Page, and Force.com site

Another way to achieve the same business requirement is to use a combination of Visual Workflow, Visualforce Page, and Force.com site. Here is a description of the following screenshot:

- Section highlighted as 1 – This indicates a sample flow to capture the user's input and process data in Salesforce.
- Section highlighted as 2 – This indicates that you need to embed a Visual Workflow in a Visualforce Page.
- Section highlighted as 3 – Once you're done with Part 2, expose the Visualforce Page for unauthenticated access via the Force.com site.

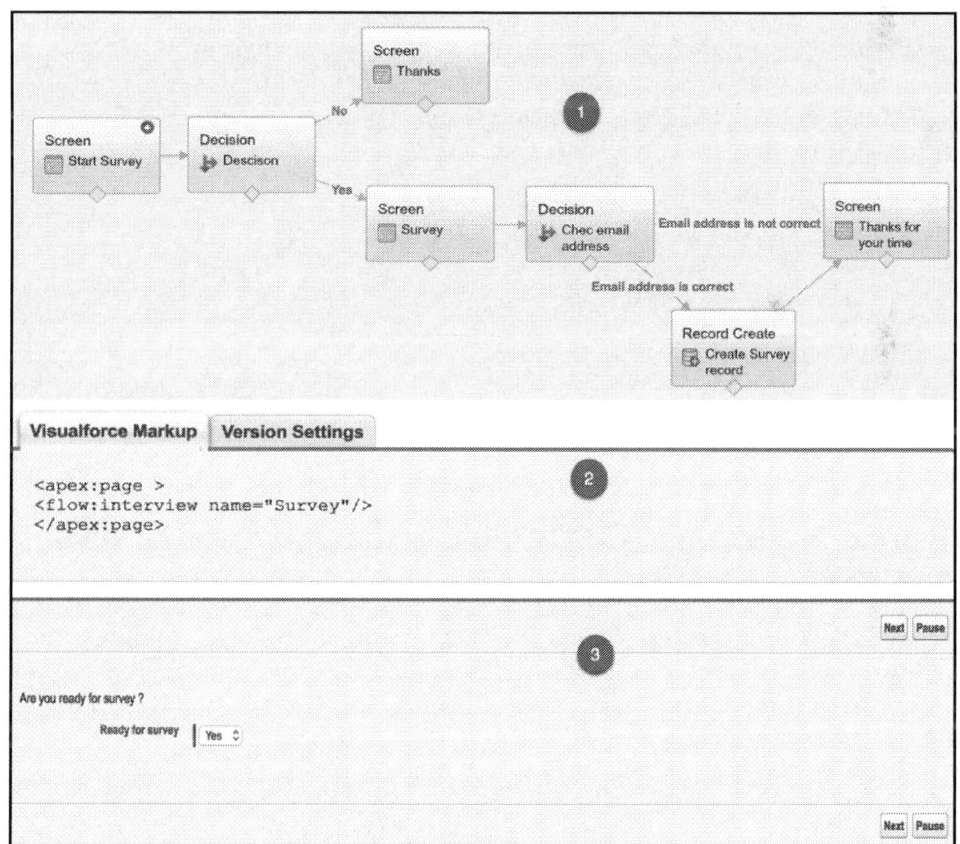

Visual Workflow is another way to automate business processes using *click not code*. To deploy a Visual Workflow in a production org, you don't need to write a test class for it.

Business use case 2

A business scenario: *David Guzman* is working as a system administrator at *Universal Containers*. He has received another requirement to auto-delete all **Closed Lost** opportunities when an account's **Active** fields (that is, custom fields) are updated as `False`.

There are several ways to solve the preceding business requirement. A few of them are mentioned in the subsequent subsection.

Solution 1 – Using an Apex trigger

As we can't achieve the preceding business requirement using the Workflow Rule, the next possible solution is to use an Apex trigger. A developer can write an Apex trigger on the `Account` object to delete all Closed Lost opportunities when an account's **Active** custom field gets updated to `True`. The following is a sample code:

```
trigger UpdateRelatedOpportunites on Account (after update) {
 for (Account AccountToUpdate : trigger.new)
    {
         If (AccountToUpdate.Active__c==False)
         {
         // Your logic;
         }
    }
}
```

Solution 2 – Using a Visual Workflow and Process Builder

Another way to achieve the preceding business requirement is to use a combination of a Visual Workflow and Process Builder. The following screenshot represents a solution for a similar business scenario using a Visual Workflow and Process Builder. Here is a description of the next screenshot:

- Section highlighted as 1 - It represents a sample flow to delete all the opportunities where stage equals to **Closed Lost**, which is related to an account that gets **Inactive**.

- Section highlighted as 2 - It represents a Process Builder on the `Account` object. It will fire when this is the case: `Active == False`.

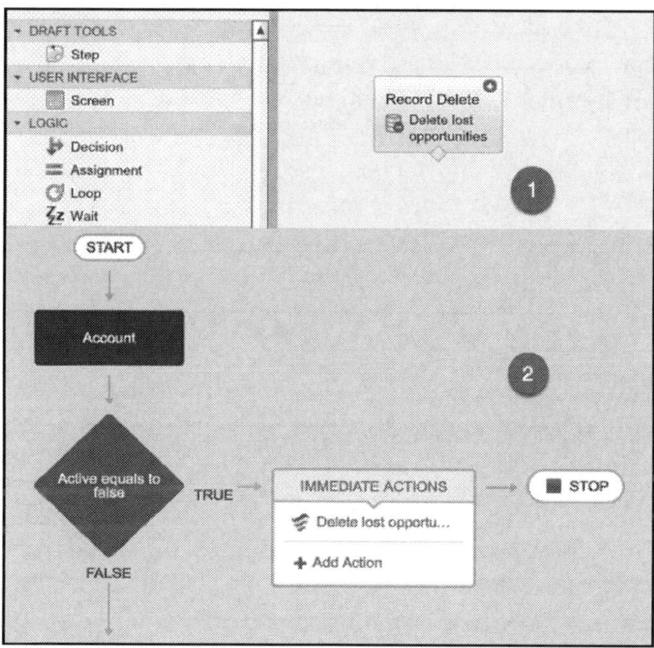

Process Builder is one of the ways to automate complex business processes using *click not code*, such as Visual Workflow. We will discuss more about it in `Chapter 8`, *Automating Complex Business Processes*.

Benefits of Visual Workflow

There are multiple benefits of using Visual Workflow instead of Visualforce Page or Apex code. They are as follows:

1. To use Visual Workflow, no coding is required. This means even if you don't have experience in writing Apex code, you can still develop an application.
2. You can share your application with peers by creating packages.
3. Using Screen, Record, Fast, Field, and Choice elements, you can implement a complex business process to make sure that your users are entering data in the right format.

4. It also allows you to auto-submit records for approval.
5. You can also post a message on Chatter. For example, If an opportunity status gets **Closed Won**, post a message on the **Account** feed.
6. It allows you to embed your flow into a Visualforce Page. Then, using Force.com site, you can expose it for unauthenticated access.
7. You don't need to write a unit test class, and this is one added advantage over Apex code.
8. Salesforce allows you to update your flow into production org, but you can't update Apex code there.

Overview of the Visual Workflow life cycle

Cloud Flow Designer is a tool for creating flows, configuring screen elements, and defining business logic for your flows without writing code. Visual Workflow has three different stages, which are as follows:

- **Design**: This allows you to create a flow using Flow Designer, which has a drag and drop user interface that allows you to draw the flow structure and configure how it would run, without writing code.
- **Administration**: Once you have developed a flow, you can manage it, update its properties, activate it, deactivate it, delete it, save it as a new version or new flow, or run it.
- **Runtime**: A flow user can run the active version of a flow from a custom button, link, and Visualforce Page or directly from the flow URL. If it is an autolaunched flow, then systems can run an active version of the flow through Process Builder, an Apex class.

Overview of Cloud Flow Designer

Cloud Flow Designer is a tool that allows you to implement business requirements by constructing a flow. It is a way to collect, create, update, and delete data in Salesforce. The Cloud Flow Designer user interface has different functional parts; they are as follows:

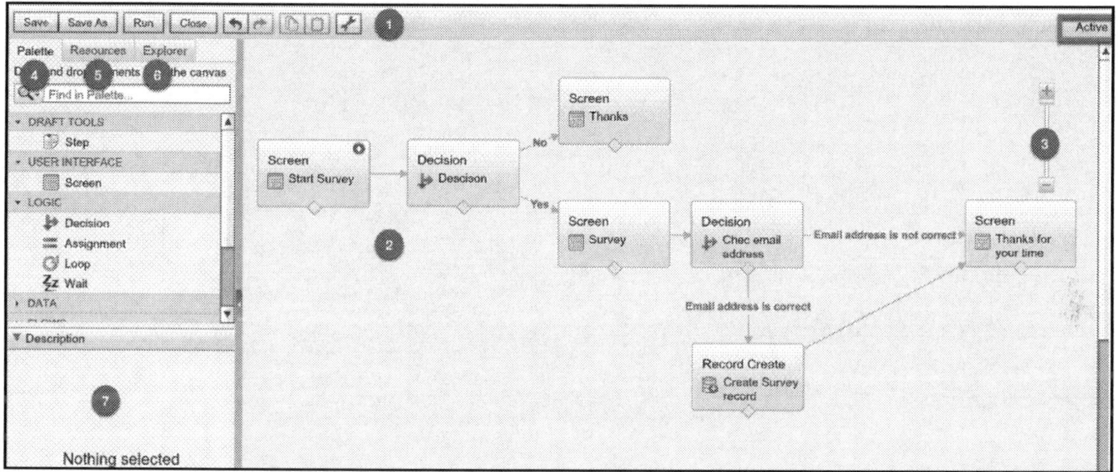

1. **Button bar**: You can use the buttons available in the **Button** bar to save, save as, run, run with latest, close, undo, or redo changes to run or view the properties of your flow. The status indicator marked with a red rectangle on the right-hand side of the bar shows the status of your flow.
    1. **Save**: Use this option to save a flow.
    2. **Save As**: If you want to clone the existing flow you are working in or want to save it as a new version, then use this option.
    3. **Run**: This runs the most recent version of the flow you are working in. If the flow comprises subflow elements, then each subflow refers to the active version of its referenced flow.
    4. **Run with latest**: This button will only appear if you are working in a flow that contains a subflow element.
    5. **Close**: If you are working on a flow and want to close it, then use this button.

6. Undo or **Redo**: Use this to *undo* or *redo* recent activities on the canvas.
7. **Flow Properties**: Click on the screwdriver ( ) icon to see information related to your flow, such as **Name**, **Unique Name**, **Description**, **Type** (**Autolaunched Flow** or **Flow**), **Interview Label**, **Version**, **Created By**, and **Last Modified By**:

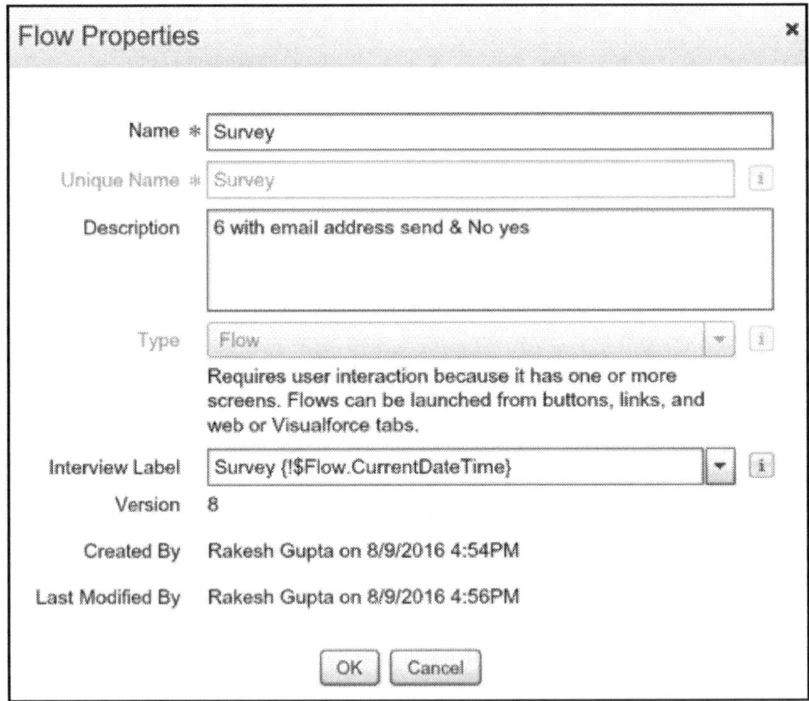

Interview Label helps us differentiate between the interviews of the same flow when an interview is paused.

2. **Flow canvas**: This is the area where you can drag and drop elements, for example, **Screen**, **Loop**, or **Decision**, and connect them through the line. To edit any element on the flow canvas, double-click on it.
3. **Zoom control**: This is a slider that helps you zoom in and out on the canvas so you can focus on specific areas. This feature is also combined with the search options in the **Explorer** tab, so it will highlight results on the canvas tab.

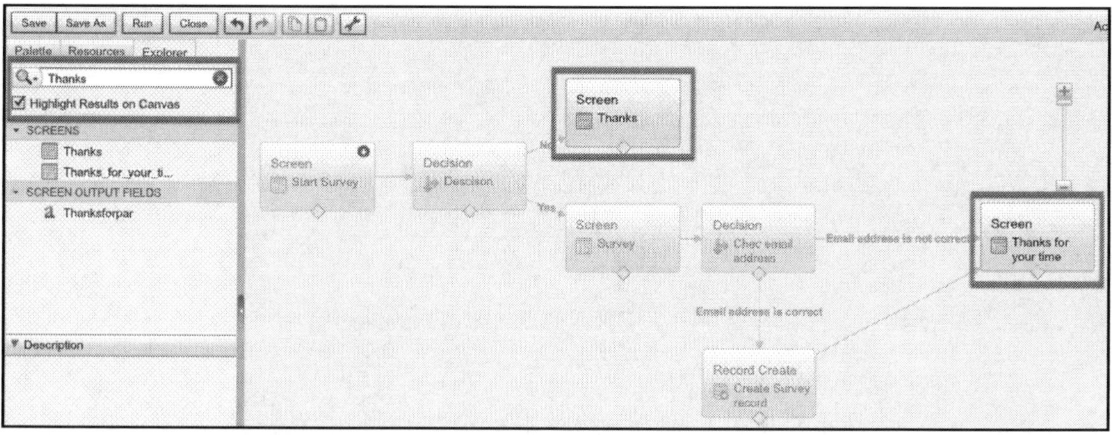

4. **Palette**: This is the area where you can find all the element types available for your flow. You must drag and drop elements from the palette onto the canvas to use it. To see the element description/properties in the **Description** pane (indicated by number 7), click on an element in the palette.
5. **Resources**: The **Resources** tab allows you to create new resources for your flow, for example, variables, formulas, and templates.
6. **Explorer**: The **Explorer** tab contains all the elements and resources added to the flow. Double-click on the items in the list to edit them and single-click to view their details and usage in the **Description** pane.
7. **Description**: The **Description** pane shows the item's description when you view an item in the **Palette** or **Resources** tab. It has two sub-tabs:

    1. **Properties**: This shows information such as **Unique Name**, **Description**, **Value Data Type**, **Default Value**, and input/output type of the element or resource you have selected.

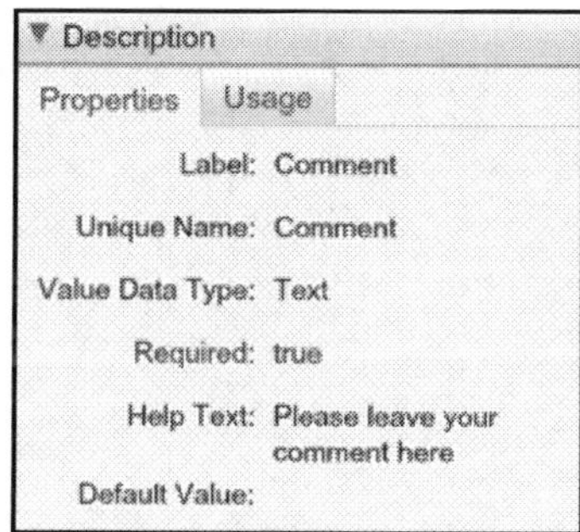

2. **Usage**: This lists the elements where the selected item is used.

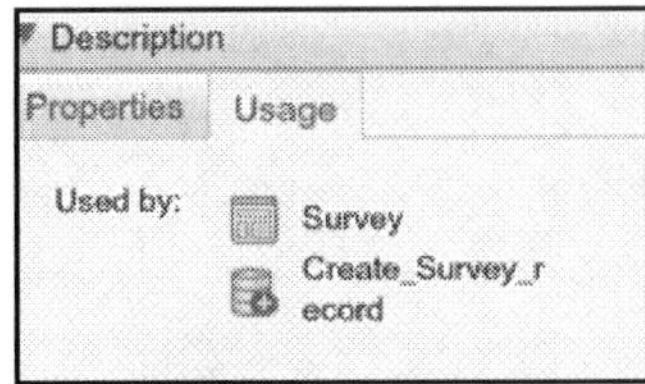

We will see how to use elements and variables later in this chapter.

Overview of Visual Workflow building blocks

The flow has three major building blocks known as **Element**, **Connector**, and **Resource**. With the help of these three, you can easily develop a flow:

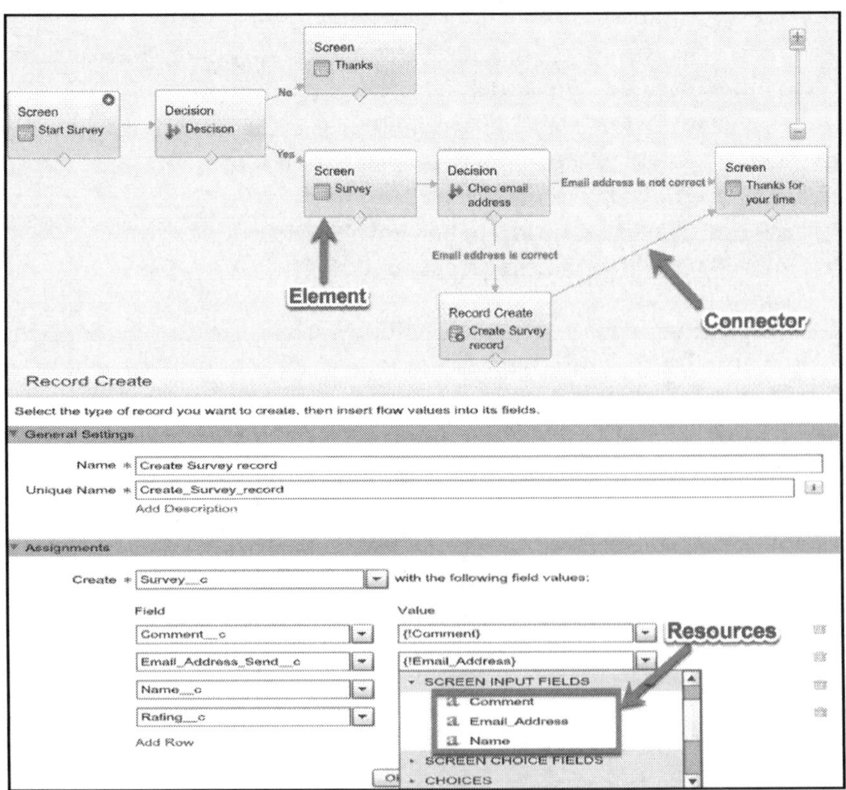

Element represents an action that the flow can execute, such as update records, delete records, or loop logic. It is basically used to manipulate data. **Connector** is used to establish the path between the elements so that the flow can take at runtime. **Resources** are used to hold the data that you can reference in your flow.

Flow elements

Flow elements represent an action that a flow can execute, which are illustrated as **Record update**, **Record lookup**, **Fast Lookup**, **Loop**, **Screen**, and **Decision**. They are used to read, update, or delete Salesforce data. Using element (the **Screen** element), you can also display data or capture input from users. Using the drag and drop function from the **Palette** tab, you can add a new element to your canvas, as follows:

Flow element	Description
Step	You can use this as a placeholder while designing your flow. Later, you can convert **Step** elements into **Screen** elements.
Screen	This will display a screen to the user who is running the flow. This screen contains **Input** or **Output** fields. It is mainly used to take input from users or display guided information.
Decision	This is used to evaluate the conditions that determine which flow path to take.
Assignment	This is used to set or change values in variables, collection variables, sObject variables, and sObject collection variables.
Loop	This iterates through an sObject collection variable and assigns an item's value to an sObject variable.
Wait	If you want your flow to wait for one or more defined events to occur, then use this element.
Record create	This is used to create one record using field values that you specify separately. You can assign these values from flow resources, such as variables, the sObject variable, and screen fields.
Record update	This is used to update records using field values that you specify separately. You can assign these values from flow resources, such as variables, the sObject variable, and screen fields.
Record Lookup	This is used to extract one record that meets the filter criteria you specify and then assign its field values to separate, individual flow variables or individual fields on sObject variables.

Record Delete	This is used to delete records from Salesforce that meet the filter criteria you specify in your flow.
Fast Create	This is used to create records using the field value from an sObject collection variable; alternatively, it is used to create one record using the field value from an sObject variable.
Fast Update	This is used to update records using the field value from an sObject collection variable or to update one record using the field value from an sObject variable.
Fast Lookup	This is used to extract records to assign their field values to an sObject collection variable or to query one record to assign its field values to an sObject variable.
Fast Delete	This is used to delete records using the ID value from an sObject collection variable or to delete one record by using an ID value from an sObject variable.
Apex Plug-in	This is used to call an Apex class that implements the `Process.Plugin` interface. If you use the tag property in the `PluginDescribeResult` class, the Apex class will appear under a customized section. Otherwise, it will appear under the Apex plug-in section.
Subflow	This is used to invoke another flow in the organization.
Other action	This is to call an object-specific or global action, such as `NewTask`, `LogACall`, and so on.
Email Alerts	This is used to send an e-mail by using a workflow e-mail alert specifying the e-mail template and recipients.
Post to Chatter	Using this element, you can post a message to the feed for a specific record, user, or Chatter group.
Send Email	This is used to sends an e-mail by using the flow to specify the subject, body, and recipients.
Submit for Approval	This is used to auto-submit one record for approval.

Flow resources

Resources are used to hold data that you can reference in your flow. The **Explorer** tab displays the resources that you had added to the flow. To create a new resource, double-click on it. Global constants and system variables are automatically provided by the system. There are several types of resources available under the **Resource** tab. They are as follows:

Flow resource	Description
Variable	This is used to store a value that can be updated as the flow is executed. It can be referenced throughout the flow and can be used as the value of a field in a record.
Global Variable	These are system-provided variables that can be referenced as resources, such as to know organization ID (`{!$Organization.Id}`) or running user Id (`{!$User.Id}`). Visual Workflow global variables are only available in flow formulae.
Collection Variable	This is used to store values with a single data type. You can use a collection variable as a container in the flow to store and reference multiple values at once.
SObject Variable	This is used to store a record for a specified object. Use an sObject variable as a container in the flow to store, update, and reference the field values for a record.
SObject Collection Variable	This is used to store multiple records for a specified object. Use an sObject collection variable as a container in the flow to store, update, and reference field values for multiple records.
Constant	This is used to store a fixed value.
Formula	This is used to calculate a value from other resources in the flow.
Text Templates	This is used to store formatted text with merge fields that reference flow resources.
Choice	This represents an individual value that can be used in choice screen fields.
Dynamic record choice	This looks up data from an object's record and dynamically generates a set of choices for screen fields at runtime. When referenced as a resource, a dynamic choice value is determined by the most recent user selection of a choice within the generated set. Let's take an example, display all contacts from an account if a user entered a valid account ID.
Element	Any element that you add to the flow is available as a resource with the visited operator in outcome criteria. An element is considered visited if the element has already been executed in the flow interview.
Global Constant	This is used to store fixed system-provided values, such as `EmptyString`, `True`, and `False`, which can be assigned as the values of flow resources.
Outcome	For the **Decision** element you have added to the flow, its outcomes are available as Boolean resources. If an outcome path has already been executed in the flow interview, the resource's value is `True`.

Picklist Values	These are system-provided values that are available as resources only in the **Assignment** and **Decision** elements when selecting values for or to comparing against picklist fields in sObject variables.
Picklist Choice	This is used to store picklist or multi-select picklist values, those are generated from standard or custom object picklist or multi-select picklist field.
Screen Field	This means the field that you add to the flow is available as a resource.
System Variable	These are system-provided values that can be referenced as resources, such as `{!$Flow.CurrentDate}`, `{!$Flow.CurrentDateTime}`, and `{!$Flow.FaultMessage}`.
Wait	**Wait** element events are always available as Boolean resources. If an event's waiting conditions are met, the resource's value is `True`. If the event has no waiting conditions set, the resource's value is always `True`.

Flow connectors

A connector is used to establish the path between the elements so that the flow can happen at runtime. It looks like an arrow that points from one element to another. There are several types of connectors available, as follows:

Label	**Sample**	**Description**
Unlabeled	→	This is used to identify which element to execute next.
Decision outcome name	Remove →	This is used to identify which element to execute when the criteria of a `decision` outcome is met.
Wait event name	10 days after Close →	This is used to identify which element to execute when an event that's defined in a **Wait** element occurs.
Fault	FAULT →	This is used to identify which element to execute if the previous element results in an error.
Next element	Next element →	This is used to identify the first element to execute for each iterations of a **Loop** element.
End of loop	End of loop →	This is used to identify which element to execute after a **Loop** element finishes iterating through a collection.

Creating a calculator to display the summation of two numbers

Let's start with an example. *David Guzman* is working as a system administrator at **Universal Containers**. He wants to develop an application using a flow to calculate the summation of two numbers. What he wants is this: on the first screen, he wants to allow users to enter two numbers and display the summation of it on the next screen. Perform the following instructions to develop a flow for the preceding business requirement:

1. Go to **Setup** (gear icon) | **Setup** | **PLATFORM TOOLS** | **Process Automation** | **Flows**.
2. Click on the **New Flow** button; it will open the flow canvas for you.
3. Then navigate to the **Palette** tab and drag and drop **Screen element** to the canvas; it will open a **Screen element** window for you.
4. Enter the name as `Sum of two numbers`. You can also add a description. Under the **Navigation options** section, select the **Don't show Previous** button from the dropdown. Also, select the **Show Pause** button checkbox and enter the pause message. This message will appear when a user pauses an interview of this flow. This will look like the following screenshot:

If you pause the interview data that you have entered the screen saved with the interview. So when you resume later, you will be able to use the data you had entered as long as the values were valid.

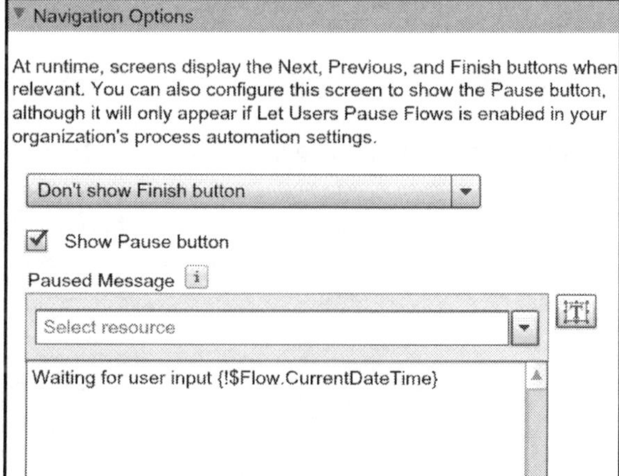

If you want to format the pause message, then click on and it will open the rich text editor for you. This text editor saves the content in HTML format:

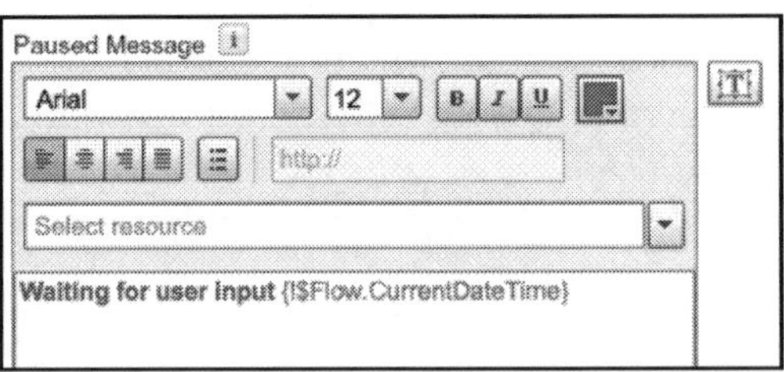

5. The next task is to add fields to the screen. From **Screen element**, navigate to the **Add a Field** tab, double-click on the **Number** field available under the **INPUTS** section to add it to the screen. In the **Screen overlays preview** pane, click on the **Number** field to configure its settings by entering **Label**, **Unique Name**, **Default Value**, and **Scale** (enter `0`). Select the **Required** checkbox under the **General Info** section, as shown in the following screenshot:

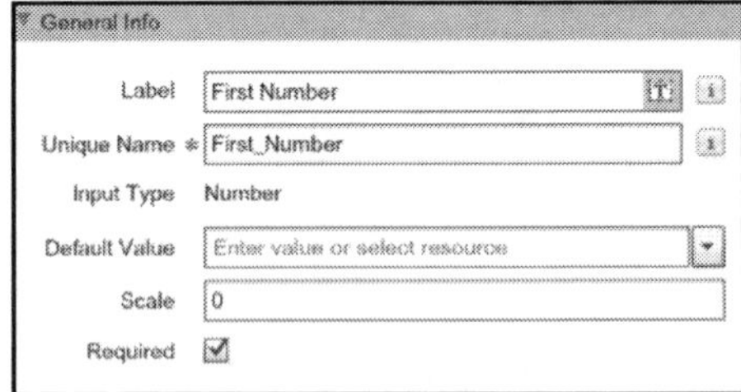

1) To make sure that a user always enters a property value greater than zero, we must add a validation rule to it. To do this, navigate to the **Input Validation** section under the **First Number** field setting and select the **Validate** checkbox. Then, it will open the formula editor for you where you can write a validation rule for this field. It also allows you to configure an error message for the validation rule. It will be displayed when the formula evaluates to `False`.

In the flow, if the formula statement evaluates to `True`, the input is valid. If the formula statement evaluates to `False`, an error message is displayed to the user.

It allows you to use a standard formula composition in a formula resource. You can also use it to validate user input in **Screen element**. But the flow formula doesn't support all the functions. A flow formula can't contain more than 3,000 characters. Formulas that are not supported by the flow include `ETRECORDIDS`, `IMAGE`, `INCLUDE`, `INCLUDES`, `ISCHANGED`, `ISNEW`, `ISPICKVAL`, `PARENTGROUPVAL`, `PREVGROUPVAL`, `PRIORVALUE`, `REQUIRE`, `SCRIPT`, and `VLOOKUP`. If you use these functions in your formula, they will always return `null`. The validation rule for the **Currency** field looks like the following screenshot:

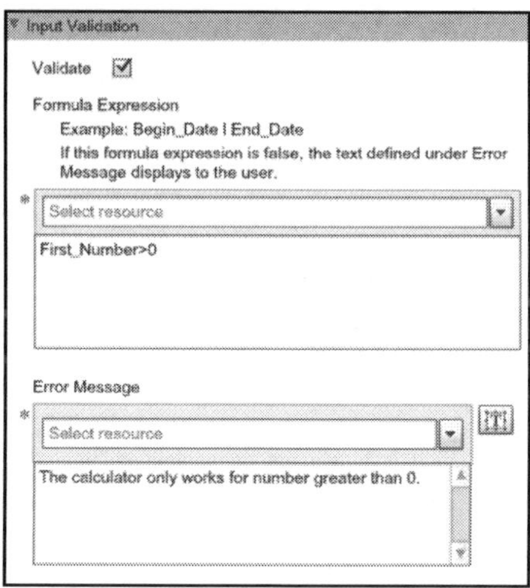

6. Likewise, add another number field to allow users to enter second number, as shown in the following screenshot:

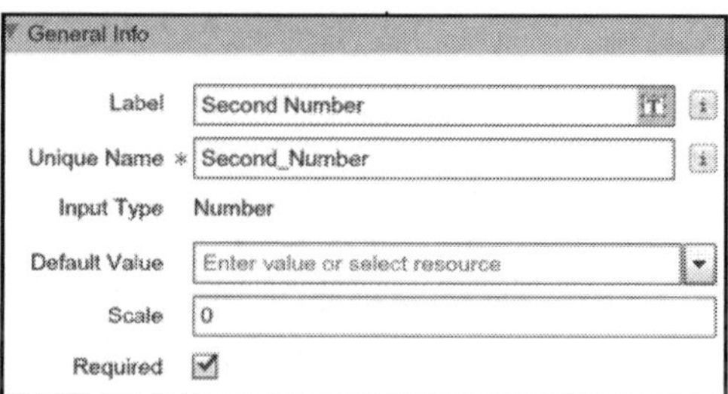

   1. Also, add a validation rule so the user will always enter commission that is greater than `0`. To achieve this, use `Second_Number > 0`.
   2. You can also configure help text for the screen under the **Help Text** section of **Screen element**.

7. Click on the **OK** button available on **Screen element**.
8. To calculate the summation of two numbers, create a formula. To do this, navigate to the **Resources** tab and double-click on **Formula**, available under the **Create new** section, and create a formula as shown in the following screenshot:

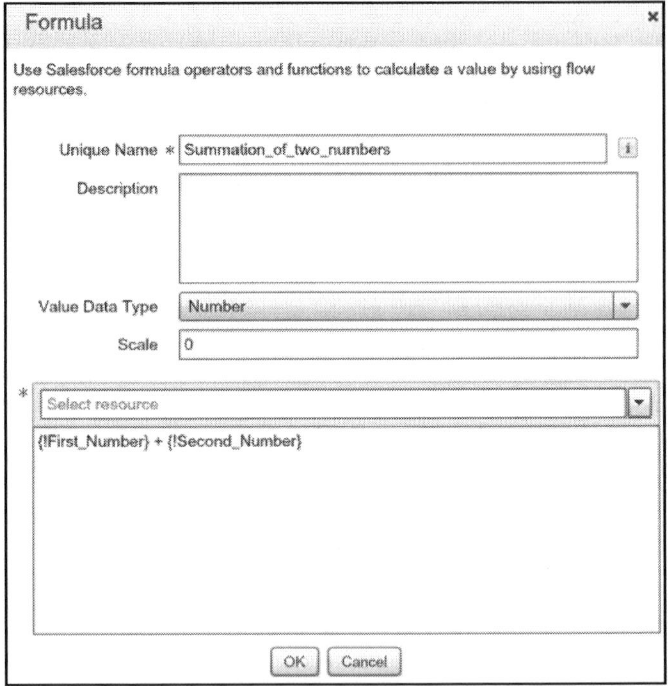

The `{!First_Number}` and `{!Second_Number }` are screen input fields that we created in steps 5 and 6.

9. The next task is to display the summation of two numbers on the screen. For this, drag and drop **Screen element** to the canvas; it will open a **Screen element** window for you. Here, you have to enter the name as `Display summation of two numbers`; you can also add a description. Under the **Navigation options** section, select **Don't show Previous button** from the dropdown.
10. Now navigate to the **Add a field** tab available under **Screen element**. Double-click on **Display Text** available under the **OUTPUTS** section.
11. In the **Screen overlays preview** pane, click on the **Display Text** field to configure its settings by entering `Unique Name`, for **Display Text** from drop-down select formula that we created in step 8. It will look like the following screenshot:

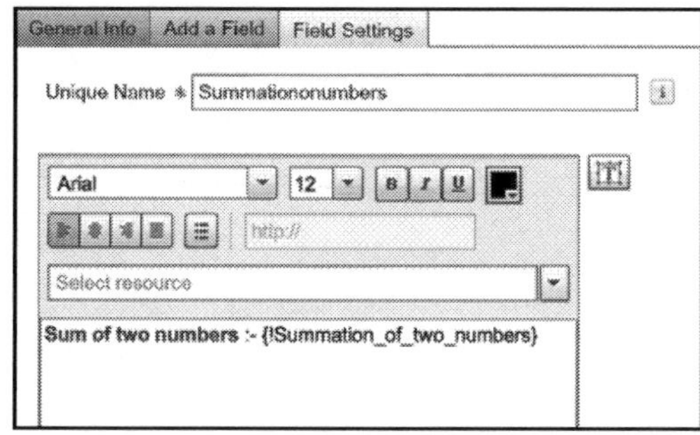

12. Once done, click on the **OK** button available on **Screen element**.

Connecting the flow elements

Until now, we have created two screens: one for getting input from a user and other to show the summation. Our next task is to connect both the elements so that at runtime, the flow could decide the order of execution of the elements. To do this, find the node at the bottom of the source element and drag it to the target element; it promptly selects which outcome you want to assign the path to. Also, set **Sum of two numbers** as the **Start** element, as shown in the following screenshot:

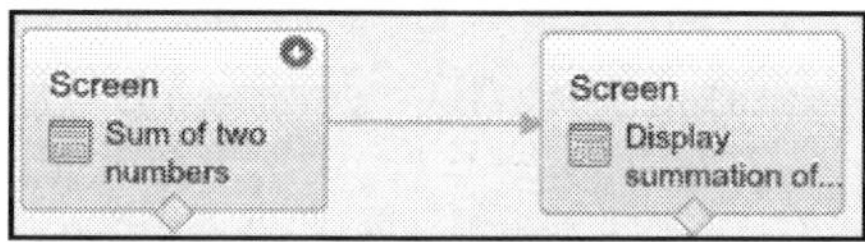

The next task is to save your flow. To do this, click on the **Save** button available in the top left-hand corner of the flow canvas and enter `Summation of two numbers` as the name and then fill in **Unique Name**, **Description**, **Flow**, and **Interview Label**. To test this flow, click on the **Run** button and enter **First Number** and **Second Number**, as shown in the following screenshot:

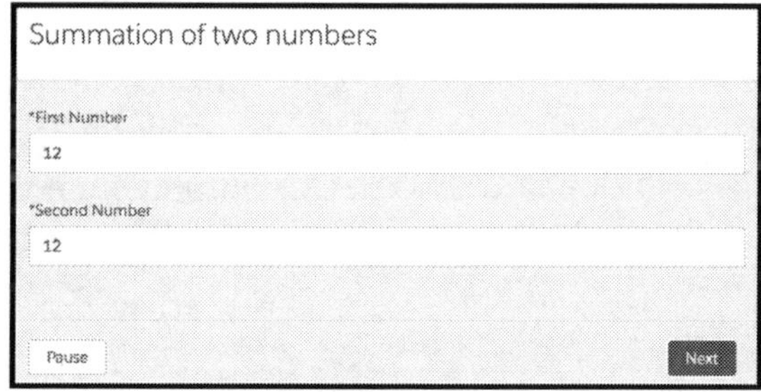

Click on the **Next** button, then it will display the summation on another screen:

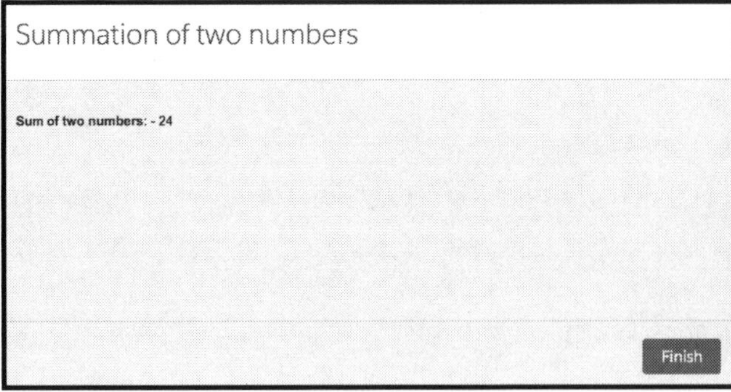

Finally, click on the **Finish** button and it will redirect you to the first screen.

Activating a version of a flow

Once you have activated a flow and you want to modify it, Salesforce will not allow you to modify the activated flow. There are two possibilities and they are mentioned as follows:

1. Create a new flow by copying the activated flow.
2. Modify the activated flow and save it as a **New version** or **Save** the activated flow as **New version** and modify it. Once you are done with the modification, activate the new version of the flow.

If you want to learn more about Visual Workflow, consider exploring *Learning Salesforce Visual Workflow*; refer to `https://www.packtpub.com/application-development/learning-salesforce-visual-workflow`.

Approval process

The approval process in Salesforce is an automated process for your organization that can be used to approve records in Salesforce. Here you can specify what happens when records are approved or rejected based upon your business requirement. After implementing the approval process, your business can run more efficiently. This process will take care of your business one step ahead, where you can define a sequence of steps that are essential to be approved for a record.

A business scenario: *David Guzman* is working as a system administrator at *Universal Containers*. He has received a requirement from higher management to create an approval process on the account object. Before activating any account, it must be approved by the *Sales Director* (Meish Johnson) and *CEO* (Rakesh Gupta). Initially, all accounts will be created with their statuses as **Inactive**.

Wizard to create an approval process

Salesforce offers two types of wizards to create an approval process. They are as follows:

- **Jump start wizard**: This wizard is used to create a one-step approval process. It allows you to quickly create the process as everything is available on the same screen; you do not have to navigate to different screens.
- **Standard wizard**: This wizard is used to create multistep approval processes. It consists of setup wizards that allow you to define your process and a specific setup wizard that allows you to define each step in the process.

We will use the standard wizard to create our approval process. Before you proceed, make sure that you have the **Status** picklist on the `Account` object, as follows:

Field Type	Label	Length/Values
Picklist	Status	Submitted Approved by the sales director Active Inactive

Creating a new approval process

Perform the following on Lightning Experience to create a new approval process on an account object:

1. Go to **Setup** (gear icon) | **Setup** | **PLATFORM TOOLS** | **Process Automation** | **Approval processes**.
2. From the **Manage Approval Processes For** dropdown, select **Account object**.
3. Click on the **Create new approval process** dropdown and select **Use Standard Setup Wizard**.

4. In the next screen, enter the following information:
    1. Enter **Process name** as `Account Approval Process`.
    2. **Unique Name** will be autopopulated based on **Process Name**.
    3. Enter a meaningful description for the approval process so other administrators can easily understand why this approval process was created.
    4. Once you are done, click on the **Next** button.
5. In the next screen, you have **Specify Entry Criteria**. In this scenario, make sure that it should look like the following screenshot:

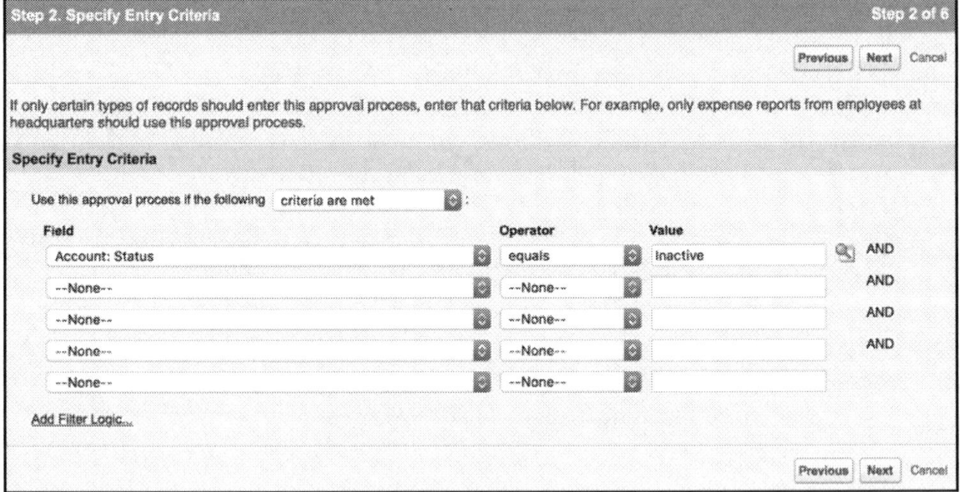

Once you are done, click on the **Next** button.

6. The next step is to define the following action items:
    1. **Select Field Used for Automated Approval Routing**: An approval process allows you to assign approval requests to any user. Another option is to use a user field to automatically route the approval request. The user field can be any custom hierarchical relationship field, such as an account manager or the manager standard user field. Leave this as is.
    2. **Record Editability Properties**: Once a record is submitted for approval, it gets locked. This allows you to define who all can edit records when a record is in the middle of an approval process. Select the **Administrators ONLY can edit records during the approval process** option.

It should look like the following screenshot:

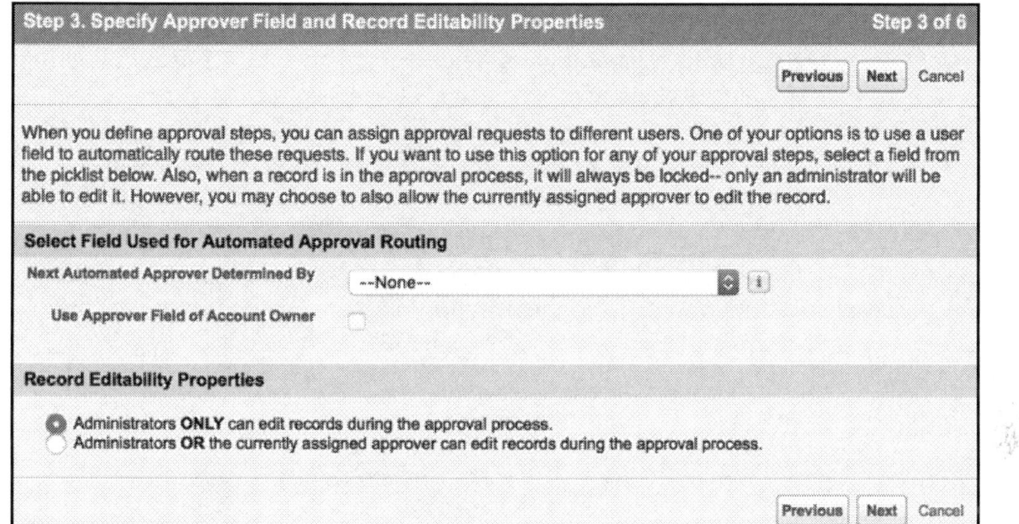

Once you are done, click on the **Next** button.

7. When an approval process assigns an approval request to a user, it automatically sends an e-mail notifying the user that it contains a link to the approval page. If you want to use a custom e-mail template, then choose a template or leave it blank so Salesforce could use the default e-mail template. Once you are done, click on the **Next** button.
8. In the next screen, click on **Select Fields to Display on Approval Page Layout** and do the following:
    1. Select the field that you want to display on the approval request page.
    2. Select the **Display approval history information in addition to the fields selected above** checkbox to display the **Approval History** list on the approval request page.
    3. Under the **Security Settings** section, select the option from where a user can approve or reject a request. In this scenario, select **Allow approvers to access the approval page from within the salesforce.com application, or externally from a wireless-enabled mobile device**.

    Once you are done, click on the **Next** button.

9. The next step is to specify initial submitters. For this, select the following:
    1. Select **Submitter Type** under **Account Owner**.
    2. Select the **Add the Approval History related list to all Booth Registration page layouts** checkbox to add the **Approval History** list to account page layouts.
    3. Make sure you select the **Allow submitters to recall approval requests** checkbox; it will allow the submitter to recall the approval process.
10. Once you are done, click on the **Save** button.

In the next screen, select the **No, I'll do this later, take me back to the listing of all approval processes for this object** option, then you will be redirected to the following screenshot:

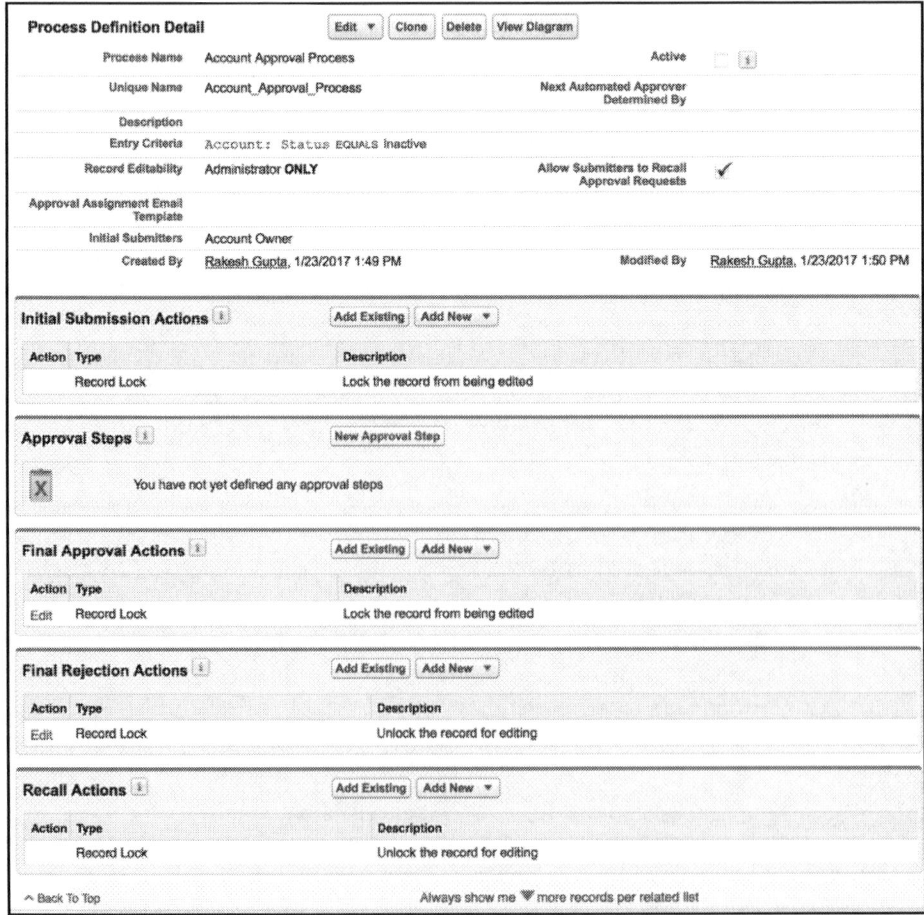

Final approval actions

The final approval action occurs only when a record has received all the required approvals. For the current business scenario, navigate to the **Final Approval Actions** section, click on the **Edit** link, and select **Unlock the record for editing**, as shown in the following screenshot:

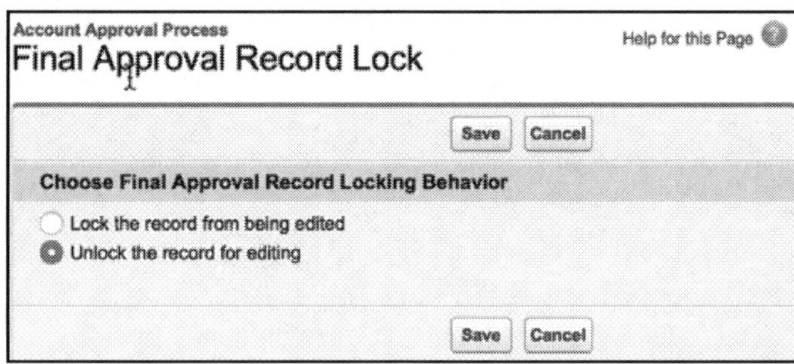

Once you are done, click on the **Save** button. Repeat this step for **Final Rejection Actions** and **Recall Actions**.

Initial submission actions

Initial action occurs only when a record is initially submitted for approval. Once a record is successfully submitted for approval, then the record gets locked. You can define actions such as **Field Update**, **Email Alert**, **Assign Task**, and **Outbound Message**. For example, you want to notify an account team or update a field to reflect the account status.

Add one initial submission action to update the status field to **Submitted**, as shown in the following screenshot:

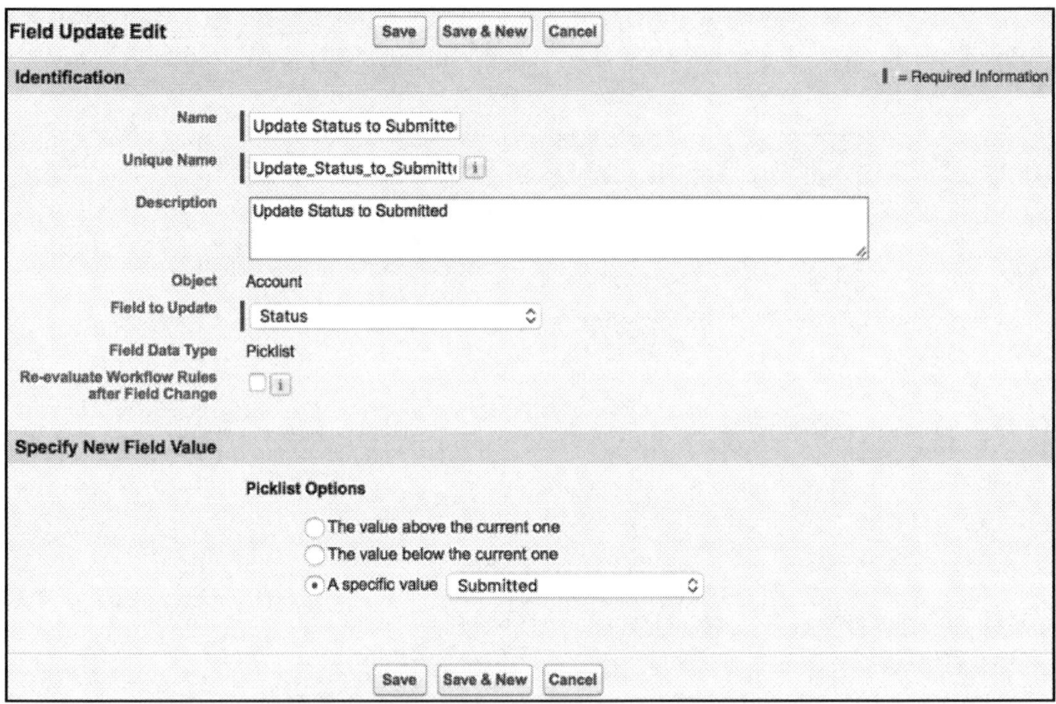

This field update will fire once an account record is submitted for approval.

Adding initial submission actions

Now we will add approval steps as per our requirement: first, for the *Sales Director* (Meish Johnson) and then for Rakesh Gupta (CEO).

Approval step 1

The first step is to get an approval process for the *Sales Director* (Meish Johnson). Perform the following actions to achieve this:

1. Navigate to the **Approval Steps** section, then click on the **New Approval Step** button.
2. In the next screen, enter the following details:
    1. Enter **Name** as `Approval from Sales Director`.
    2. **Unique Name** will be autopopulated based on the **Name**.
    3. Enter a meaningful description under the **Description** field for the approval step so other administrators can easily understand why this approval step was created.
    4. Once you are done, click on the **Next** button.
3. In the next screen, you can filter out records. This means you can decide which records should be entered in this approval step, for example, **Account Site** equals `New York`. For the current business scenario, select **All records should enter this step**, then click on the **Next** button.
4. The next step is to specify the approver. Salesforce offers a few combinations to define the approver:
    1. **Let the submitter choose the approver manually**: You can allow a submitter to approve records manually, but remember that this option will not be available if you select the **Allow approvers to access the approval page from within the salesforce.com application, or externally from a wireless-enabled mobile device** option in *step 8.3* while configuring approval process.
    2. **Automatically assign to queue**: Using this, you can auto-assign an approval request to a queue.
    3. **Automatically assign to approver(s)**: You can auto-assign an approval request to multiple users by selecting this option. You can select **User**, **Queue**, or **Related User**. It has two options:
        1. **Approve or reject based on the FIRST response**: The first response to the approval request controls whether the record is approved or rejected.
        2. **Require UNANIMOUS approval from all selected approvers**: The record is only approved if all the approvers approve the request. The approval request is rejected if any one of the approvers rejects the request.

For the current business scenario, select **Automatically assign to approver(s)** and then select **Meish Johnson**. It will look like the following screenshot:

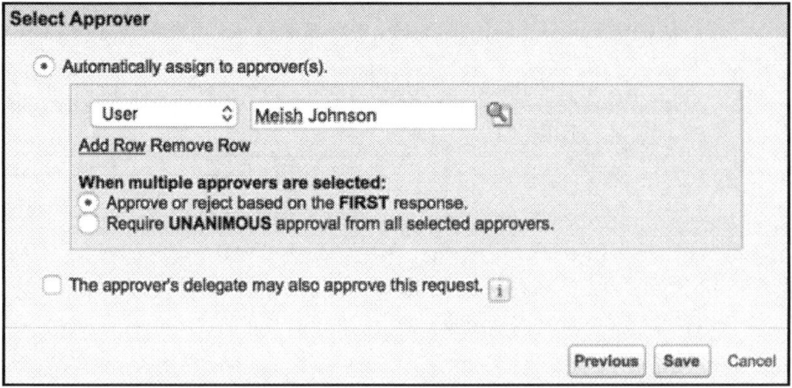

5. Once you are done, click on the **Save** button.
6. In the next screen, select the **No, I'll do this later. Take me to the approval process detail page to review what I've just created** option and you will be redirected to the approval process detail page.

Adding an action to approval step 1

For each step, Salesforce allows you to add two types of action, as follows:

- Approval actions
- Rejection actions

Perform the following steps to add an approval action, that is, a field status update:

1. Navigate to **Approval Steps**, then click on the **Show Action** link available in front of step 1.
2. It will open a small window from where you can add actions for approval or rejection actions, as shown in the following screenshot:

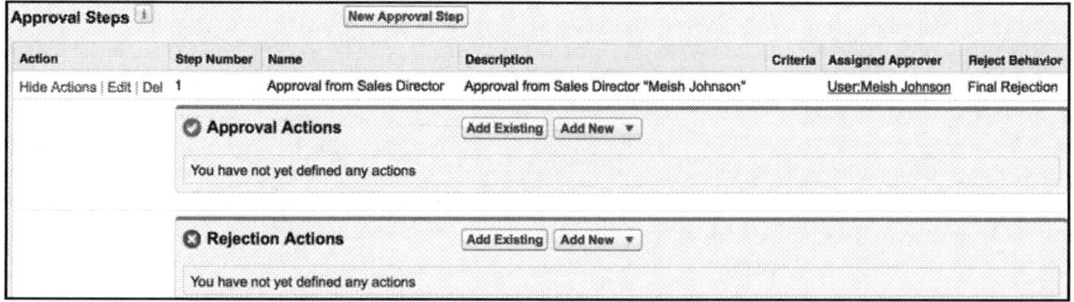

3. Move to the **Approval Actions** section and click on the **Add New** dropdown and select **Field Update**. Add one initial **Approval Action** to update the status field to **Approved by Sales Director**, as shown in the following screenshot:

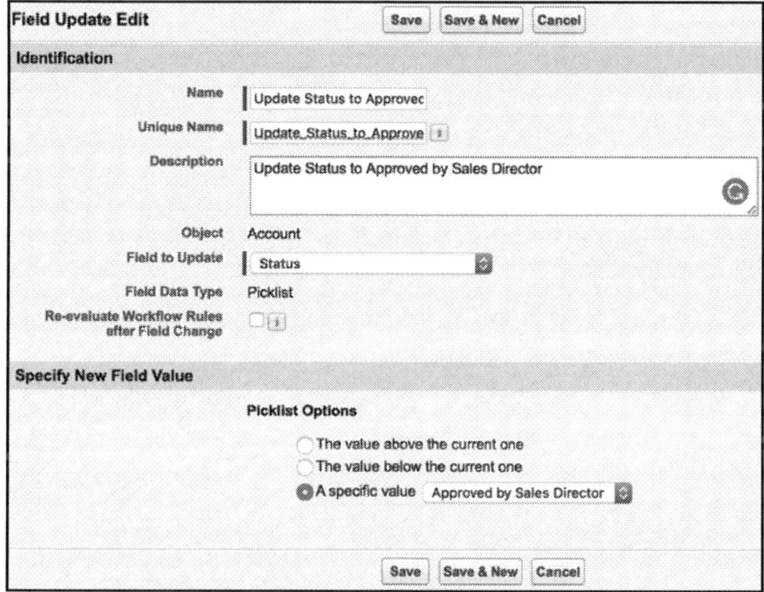

4. Once you are done, click on the **Save** button.

This field update will fire once the account record is approved by the sales director, Meish Johnson.

Approval step 2

The second step is to get the approval process from company's *CEO* (Rakesh Gupta). Perform the following actions to achieve this:

1. Navigate to the **Approval Steps** section, then click on the **New Approval Step** button.
2. In the next screen, enter the following details:
    1. Enter **Name** as `Approval from CEO`.
    2. **Unique Name** will be autopopulated based on the name.
    3. Enter a meaningful description in the **Description** field for the approval step so other administrators can easily understand why this second approval step was created.
    4. Once you are done, click on the **Next** button.
3. In the next screen, you can filter out records, so you can decide which records should be entered in this approval step, for example, **Account Site** equals `New York`. For the current business scenario, select **All records should enter this step**, then click on the **Next** button.
4. In the next screen, select **Rakesh Gupta**, then select the rejection behavior (what happens in case an approval request is rejected by Rakesh Gupta). Select the **Perform all rejection actions for this step AND all final rejection actions. (Final Rejection)** option for the current business scenario. It will look like the following screenshot:

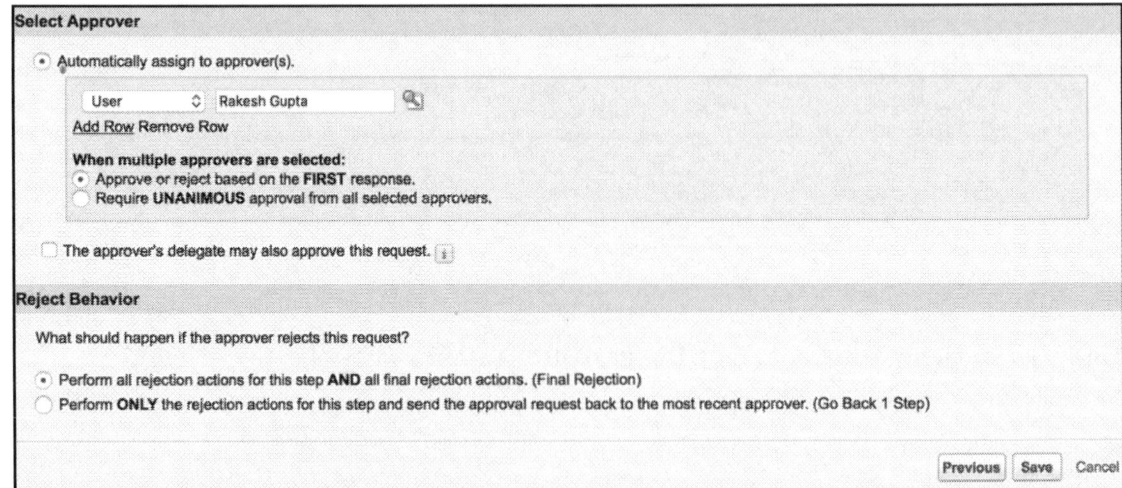

5. Once you are done, click on the **Save** button.
6. In the next screen, select the **No, I'll do this later. Take me to the approval process detail page to review what I've just created** option and you will be redirected to the approval process detail page.
7. Add one initial **Approval Actions** for step 2 to update the status field to **Active**, as shown in the following screenshot:

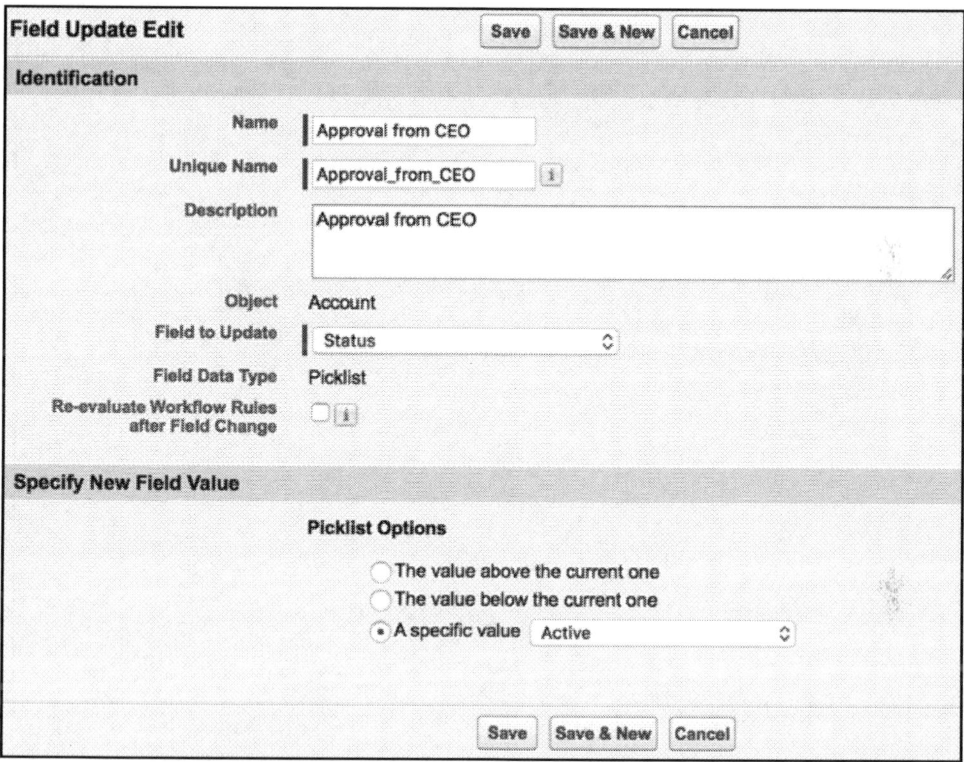

This is how you can create a multistep approval process. You view the process diagram of the approval process by clicking on **View Diagram**. It will look like the following screenshot:

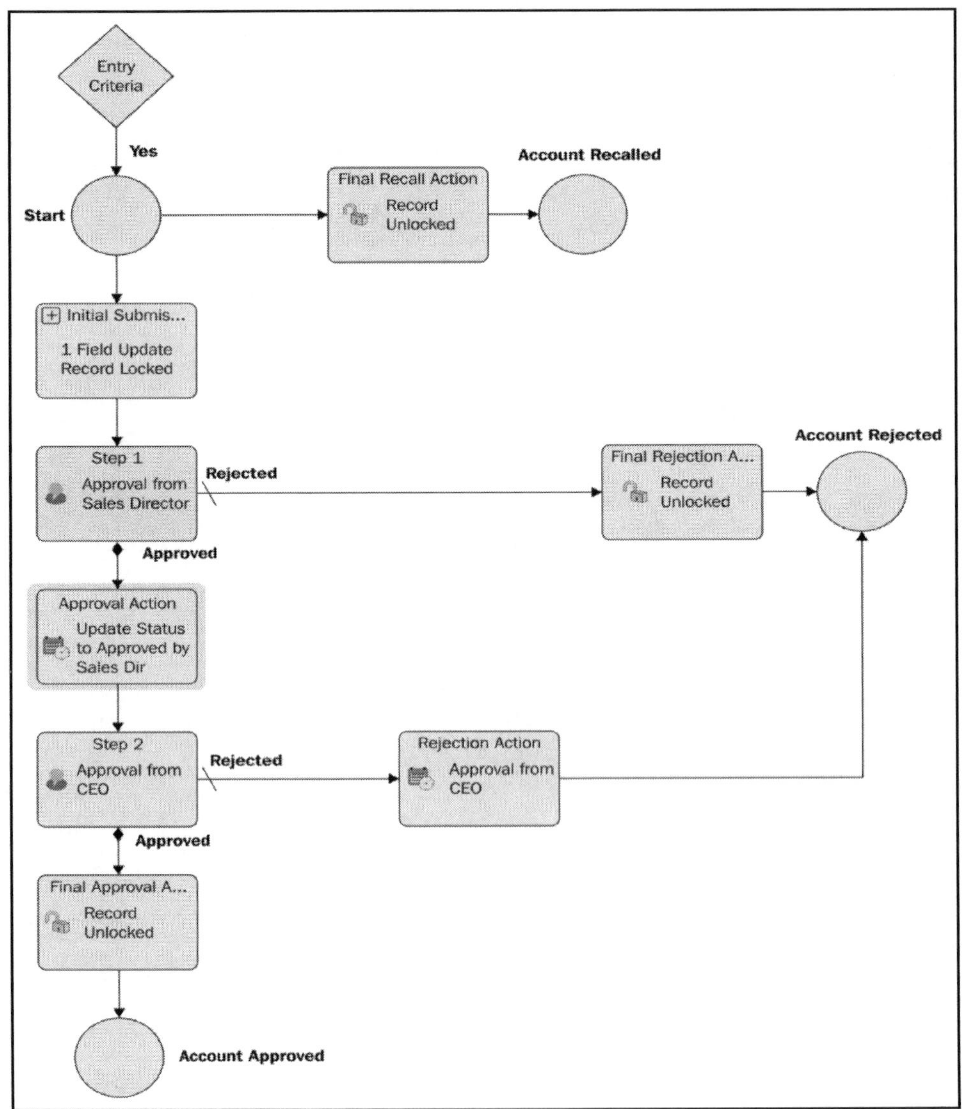

Activating an approval process

You can activate an approval process by clicking on the **Activate** button available on top of the approval process page, as shown in the following screenshot:

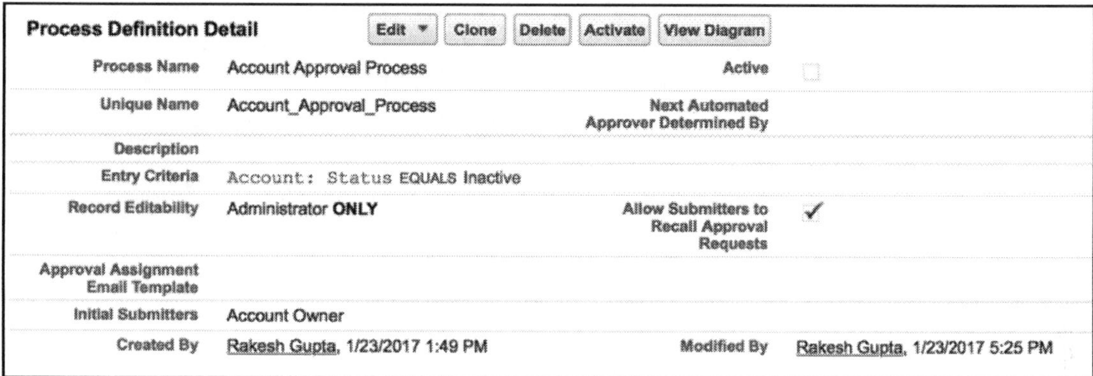

Before activating an approval process, make sure that no more changes or modifications are required, because once an approval process is active, it not possible to add more steps to it.

A few points to remember

1. If you leave the **Next Automated Approver Determined By** field blank, you can't automatically assign approval requests to the manager in any step you create for this approval process.
2. For both enterprise and unlimited editions, there is a limit of 15 steps per process.
3. Process visualizer allows you to export data in PDF format or print it as a flowchart.
4. Advise your users that they must click on **Submit for Approval** to enter records into the approval process.
5. You can have multiple versions of a flow, but you can activate only one version of a flow at a time. From the flow detail page, activate or deactivate one version of a flow. Click on the **Activate** link available next to version 1 of the flow.
6. If the flow doesn't have a **start** item, the **Activate** link will not be available.

7. Consider using a process, Visual Workflow, or an Apex trigger to submit a record to the approval process.
8. Use the **Mass Transfer Approval Requests** wizard to mass transfer pending approval requests from one user to another.
9. Create and run approval history reports to check progress and completed approval processes and their steps.
10. Users with the manage Force.com flow permission can open Visual Workflow.
11. The limit on the number of executed elements in Visual Workflow at runtime is 2,000.
12. One organization can have a maximum of 500 active flows and processes.

Summary

In this chapter, we have gone through various concepts related to Visual Workflow. We started with the business scenario where you can use Visual Workflow, followed by the benefits of using Flow. Then we discussed the Visual Workflow development life cycle and had an overview of Cloud Flow Designer. At the end, we discussed steps to creating a multistep approval process. In the next chapter, we will go through the basic concepts of Process Builder and a few use cases where you can use it.

8
Automating Complex Business Processes

In the previous chapters, we discussed the overview of Visual Workflow. We also talked about the benefits of using Visual Workflow and a few use cases where we can use it. We also learned the way of setting up an approval process. This chapter starts with an overview of the Process Builder. We will take the discussion forward to discuss the difference between various automation tools and when to use what. Then, we will go through step-by-step instructions to create a process using Process Builder. The following topics will be covered in this chapter:

- Process Builder overview
- Difference between Process Builder and other tools
- Auto-creating a child record
- Auto-updating child records
- Posting messages to a Chatter group
- Auto-submitting records into the approval process

Process Builder overview

Process Builder is an alternate way of automating your business processes by writing code. It is an advanced version of the Workflow Rule. Process Builder is created on top of **Visual Workflow** and **Flow Trigger** (Deprecated). Whenever you create a process by using the Process Builder, it will automatically create a Flow and a Flow Trigger (Deprecated) to call this Flow; this happens behind the scenes and users don't need to interact with these Flows.

Workflow Rule comes with several limitations, for example, it doesn't have an action to update child records, post to Chatter, and create a child record. Process Builder is available for the Lightning Enterprise, Lightning Unlimited, and Developer editions. It is also available for the Lightning Professional edition with a few limitations, for example, you can only have five active processes in the Lightning Professional edition. There are a few advantages of Process Builder, as follows:

- You can define the complete process in a single screen, unlike Workflow Rule where you have to move from screen to screen to create a complete rule
- It allows you to create the complete process using point-and-click
- By using it, you can minimize Apex code usage in your Salesforce org
- It is also possible to call an Apex class from a process

Business problems

As a Salesforce administrator or developer, you may get various requirements from the business to streamline the internal sales or support processes. As per our experience, we can say that many of them are achievable by using **out-of-the box** (**OOB**) features, and for a few, we must use Apex or Visualforce Page. Visual Workflow gives us another way of implementing various business processes without using Apex or Visualforce Page. The following are a few examples of it, explained in further subsections.

Business use case

A business scenario: *David Guzman* is working as a system administrator at *Universal Containers*. He has received a requirement to auto-add new users to a Chatter group, *Universal Containers Notice Board*.

There are several ways to solve the preceding business requirement; a few of them are mentioned in the subsequent subsections.

Solution 1 – using an Apex trigger

As the requirement is to add new users to a Chatter group, we can't use Workflow Rule to achieve it. One possible solution is to write an Apex trigger on a user object to add new users to the Chatter group, *Universal Containers Notice Board*, as soon as the user gets created.

The following is the sample code:

```
trigger AutoAddNewUsertoChatter Group on User (after insert) {
List<CollaborationGroup> chatterGroups=[select id, Name from
CollaborationGroup where name =' Universal Containers Notice Board];
  for(user user: Trigger.new)
              {
                 //your logic
              }
}
```

Solution 2 – using an Apex trigger

Another way to achieve the same business requirement is to create a process by using the Process Builder. Check out the following screenshot:

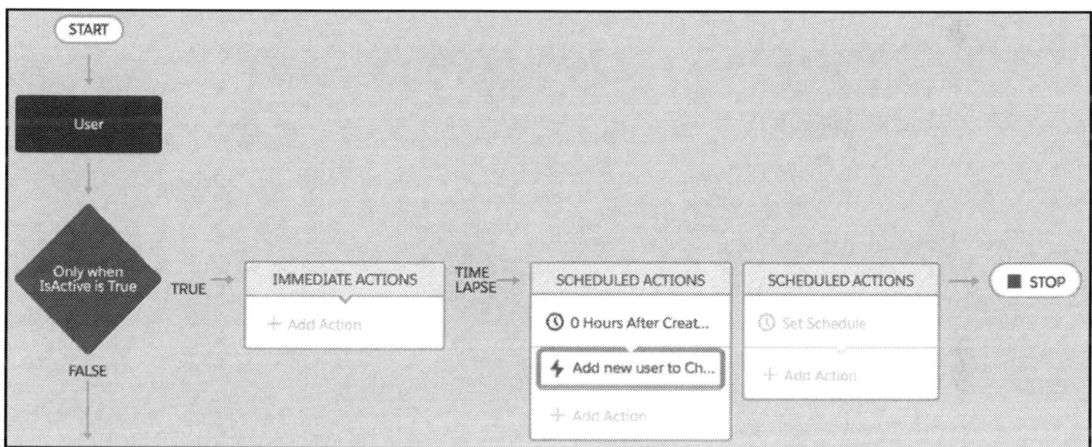

Here is the description for the preceding screenshot:

- A sample process on user object; it will only trigger at the time of user creation
- Add one schedule action; it will trigger after 0 hours of user creation
- Then, add a quick action to add new users to the Chatter group, *Universal Containers Notice Board*

Process Builder is another way to automate business processes using *click not code*. To deploy a process in production org, you don't need to write a test class for it.

Overview of Process Builder user interface

The Process Builder is a point-and-click wizard that allows you to completely automate a business requirement by creating a process. It has almost all the features offered by Workflow Rule, including a few extra features such as post to Chatter, call a Flow, create a record, and more. The Process Builder user interface has different functional parts, as follows:

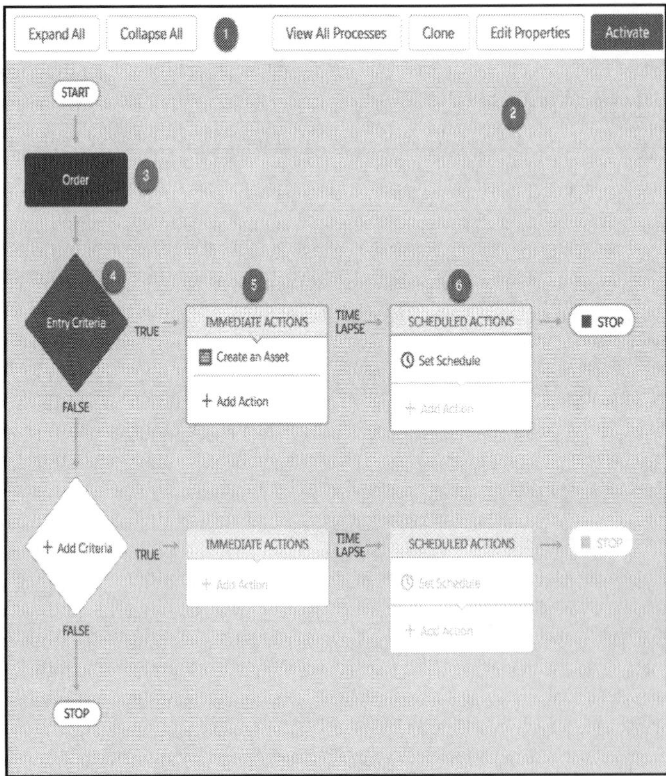

1. **Button Bar**: The following are the buttons available in the **Button Bar**.
    1. **Activate:** Use this button to activate a process. You can't make any changes once a process is activated.
    2. **Deactivate**: This button is only available if a process is activated. Use this button to deactivate a process.
    3. **Edit properties**: It will show you **Name**, **API Name**, and **Description** of your process. It allows changing the process name and description till the process is not activated. However, you can't change **API Name** after you have saved it for the first time.

4. **Clone**: The cloud Flow designer has a **Save As** button to either save a Flow as **New Version** or create a **New Flow**. Likewise, Process Builder has a **Clone** button for the following activities:
    - The version of the current process
    - New process

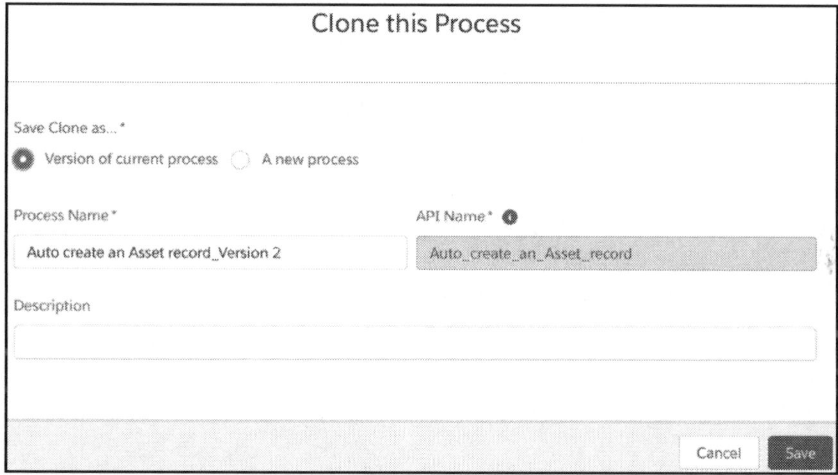

5. **View All Processes**: Once you click on this button, it will redirect you to the **Processes Management** page. On the **Process Management** page, it will display all the processes.
6. **Collapse All**: Collapse actions on the process canvas.
7. **Expand All**: Expand actions on the process canvas.

2. **Process Canvas**: This is the point-and-click area to develop a process. To edit any element in the process canvas, double-click on it.
3. **Add Object**: Choose the object on which you want to create a process and choose **Evaluation Criteria**.
4. **Add Criteria**: Use this to define the entry criteria and set the filter conditions.
5. **Immediate Actions**: Use this to define immediate actions for the process.
6. **Scheduled Actions**: Use this to define scheduled actions for the process.

Actions available in Process Builder

Process Builder can perform almost all actions that are available for Workflow Rule and it also contains a few extra actions, but it doesn't support outbound messages. With Process Builder, you can perform the following actions:

1. **Apex**: Using this action, you can call an Apex class that contains an invocable method.
2. **Create a Record**: Using this action, you can create a record.
3. **Email Alerts**: Using this action, you can send out an e-mail alert.
4. **Flows**: Using this action, you can call a Flow from a process.
5. **Post to Chatter**: Using this action, you can post TextPost on Chatter group, Record, or User Chatter profile.
6. **Processes**: Using this action, you can invoke another process.
7. **Quick Actions**: Using this action, you can use object-specific or global actions to create a record, update a record, or log a call.
8. **Submit for Approval**: Using this action, you can auto-submit a record into **Approval Process**.
9. **Update Records**: Using this action, you can update any related records.

Difference between Process Builder and other tools

Salesforce offers different tools to automate the business process, for example, Visual Workflow, Workflow Rule, and Process Builder. So, it is important to understand the difference between these tools and when to use which. The following table describes the difference between these tools:

	Workflow	Flow	Process Builder
Visual Designer	Not available	Available	Available
Start When	– A record is created or edited – It can by invoked by another process	– User clicks on custom button/link – A process starts – Apex is called – Inline Visualforce Page – The user accesses a custom tab	A record is created or edited
Supported Time-based actions	Yes	Yes	Yes
Call Apex Code	No	Yes	Yes
Create Records	Only task	Yes	Yes
Update Records	Yes (only fields from the same record or parent)	Yes, any record	Yes, any related record
Delete Records		Yes	
Launch a Flow	No	Yes	Yes
Post To Chatter	No	Yes	Yes
Send an Email	Yes	Yes	Yes
Submit for Approval	No	Yes	Yes
Send Outbound Message	Yes	No	No
Support User Interaction	No	Yes	No
Version Control	No	Yes	Yes
Support User Input on Runtime	No	Yes (through screen element)	No
Supported Unauthenticated access	No	Yes (through Force.com sites)	No
Can pause on Runtime	No	Yes	No

Allow modification	After deactivation, you can modify the Workflow Rule.	Once a Flow is activated, you can't modify it; create a new version to modify a Flow	Once a process is activated, you can't modify it; create a new version to modify a process.

Creating applications with Process Builder

To automate the complex business process in Salesforce, it is required that you must have Apex and Visualforce understanding. After completing this chapter, you will get an understanding of how to automate business processes using Process Builder without code.

Hands on 1 – auto creating a child record

It's a very common scenario to auto create a child record when a parent record gets updated and meets specific criteria. For example, as soon as an order gets delivered it will auto create an asset record it. To resolve these types of business scenarios, a developer usually writes an Apex trigger, but there are alternate ways through which you can achieve it, and that too, without writing the code, as follows:

- Apex Trigger
- Combination of Flow and Process Builder
- Combination of Flow and Inline Visualforce Page on the **Order Detail** page
- Process Builder

A business scenario: *David Guzman* is working as a system administrator at *Universal Containers*. He has received a requirement to auto create an opportunity as soon as an account, `Status__c`, gets updated as **Active** after the approval process completion (refer to `Chapter 7`, *Optimizing Business Processes with Visual Workflow and Approval Processes*). Use the following values to create a new action:

- **Name**: Account name
- Stage: Prospecting
- **Close Date**: Today + 90 days
- Associate it with account record.

Perform the instructions given in the subsequent subsections to fulfill the preceding business requirement using Process Builder.

Creating a process

The next step is to create a process for auto creating an opportunity record once an account record `Status__c` updated as **Active**.

1. Click on **Setup** (gear icon) | **Setup** | **PLATFORM TOOLS** | **Process Automation** | **Process Builder**.
2. Click on the **New** Button and enter the following details:
    1. **Name**: Enter the name for the process. Enter `Auto Create new Opportunity` as **Name**. It must be within 255 characters.
    2. **API Name**: This will be autopopulated based on the **Name**.
    3. **Description**: Write some meaningful text, so other developers/administrators can easily understand why this process is created.
    4. **The process starts when**: For this, select when **A record changes**. In case you want to invoke the process by another process, then select **It's invoked by another process**.

    It will look like the following screenshot:

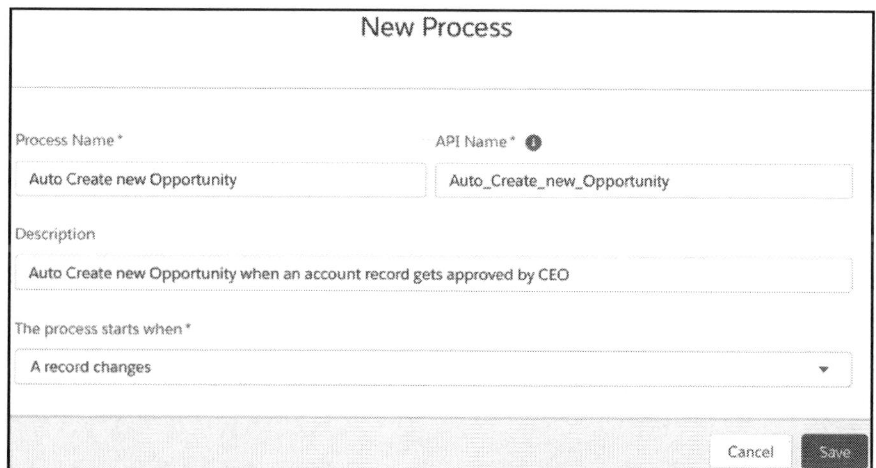

Click on the **Save** button once you are done; it will redirect you to the process canvas, which allows you to create the complete process.

Adding evaluation criteria

Once you are done with process property definitions, the next task is to select the object on which you want to create a process and define the evaluation criteria:

3. Click on the **Add Object** node, as shown in the following screenshot:

It will open a window on the right-hand side, which allows you to select the object on which you want to create the process. Enter the following details:

1. **Object**: Select the **Account** object.
2. **Start the process**: For **Start the process**, select **when a record is created or edited**. It means the process will only execute at the time of record creation.
3. **Recursion – Allow process to evaluate a record multiple times in a single transaction?**: Select this checkbox only when you want the process to evaluate the same record for up to five times in a single transaction. It might be possible that the same record is updated by another process, Workflow Rule, or Visual Workflow in the same transaction. It will look like the following screenshot:

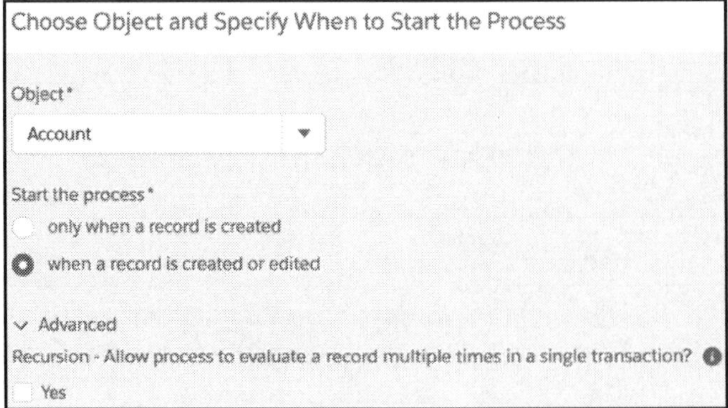

Once you are done, click on the **Save** button. Similar to the Workflow Rule, once you save the panel, it doesn't allow you to change the selected object.

Adding process criteria

Once you are done with defining the evaluation criteria, the next step is to define the process criteria. It is like the Rule Criteria in Workflow Rule. The process will execute the associated actions once when the process criteria are true:

4. To define the process criteria, click on the **Add Criteria** node, as shown in the following screenshot:

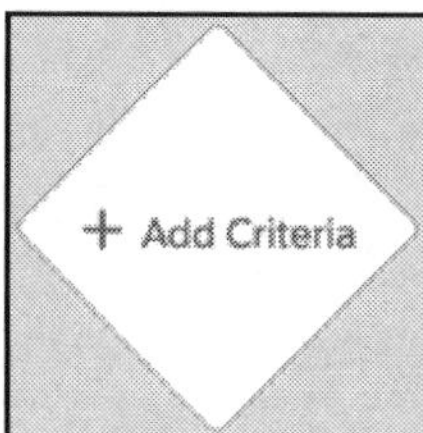

Enter the following details to define the process criteria:

1. **Criteria Name**: Enter a name for the criteria node. Enter `Only for Active account` as **Criteria Name**.
2. **Criteria for Executing Actions**: Select the type of criteria you want to define. You can either use formula or filter to define the process criteria or no criteria. In this scenario, select **Conditions are met**.
3. **Set Conditions**: Here, you can define the filter condition for your process. In this scenario, select `Status__C` equals picklist **Active**. It means the process will fire only when account `Status__c` is **Active**.
4. **Do you want to execute the actions only when specified changes are made to the record?**: Select this checkbox if you want the actions to be executed only if the record meets the criteria now but the values the record had immediately before it was saved didn't meet the criteria. Select this checkbox for the current business scenario.

It will look like the following screenshot:

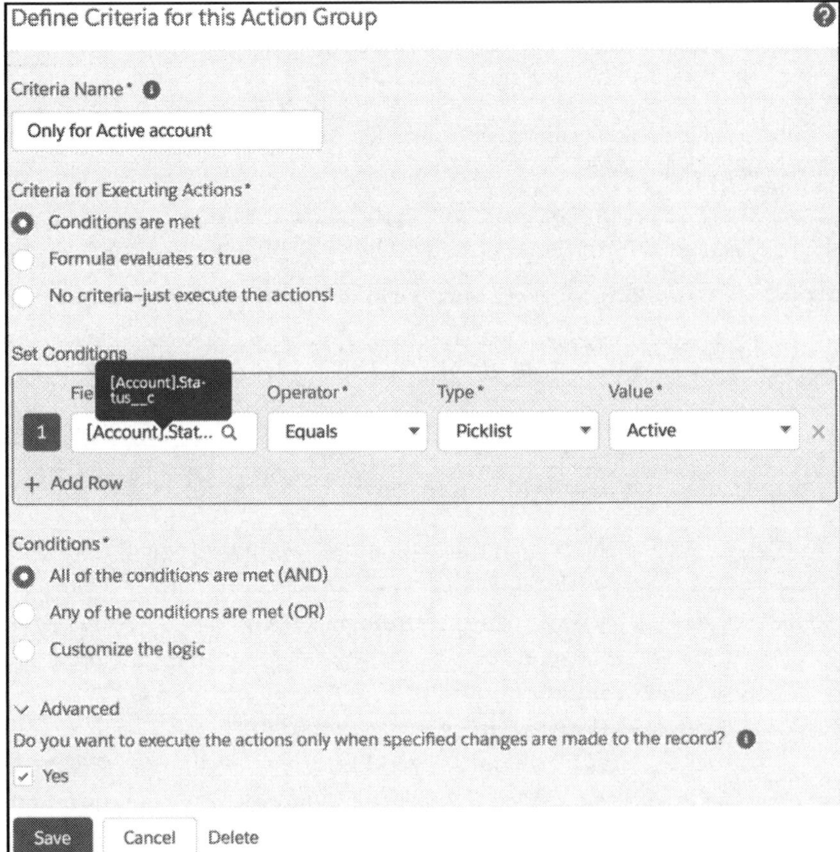

Once you are done, click on the **Save** button.

Adding an action to a process

Once you are done with defining the process criteria, the next step is to add one immediate action to create an Opportunity. To do this use **Create a Record** action. Immediate actions are executed as soon as evaluation criteria are met whereas scheduled actions are executed at a specified time.

The next step is to add an immediate action.

5. Click on **Add Action** available under **IMMEDIATE ACTIONS**, as shown in the following screenshot: Enter the following details to define the immediate action:

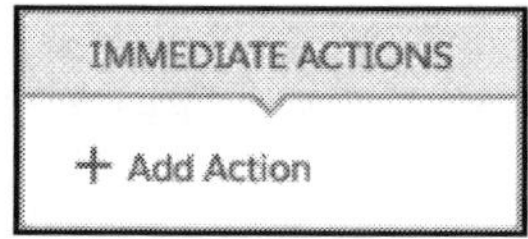

   1. **Action Type**: Select the type of action you want to perform. In this scenario, select **Create a Record**.
   2. **Action Name**: Enter a name for this action. Enter `Create an Opportunity record` as **Action Name**.
   3. **Record Type**: Start typing and then select the **Opportunity** object.

Then, map the fields according to the following screenshot:

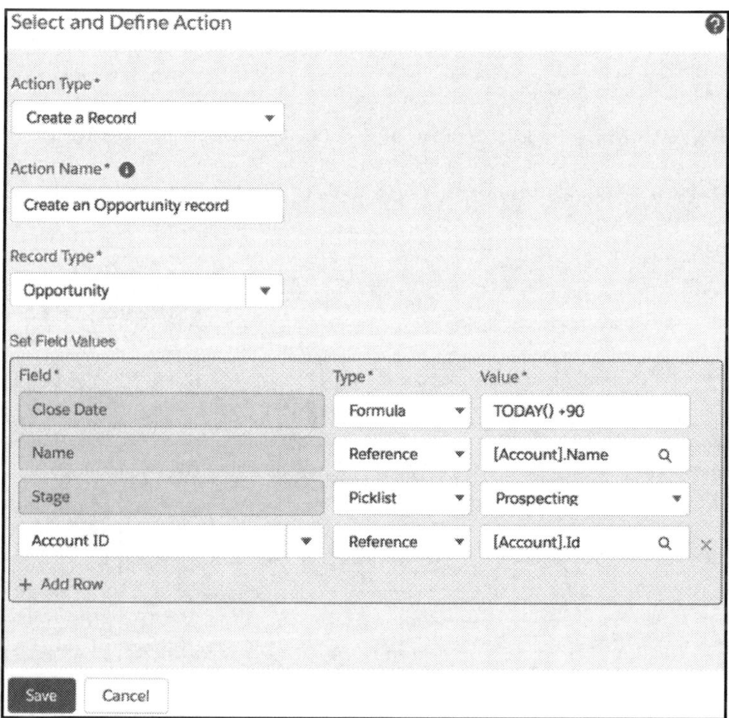

To select the field, you can use **Field Picker**. To enter the value, use the **Text Entry** field. Once you are done, click on the **Save** button. In the end, your process should look like the following screenshot:

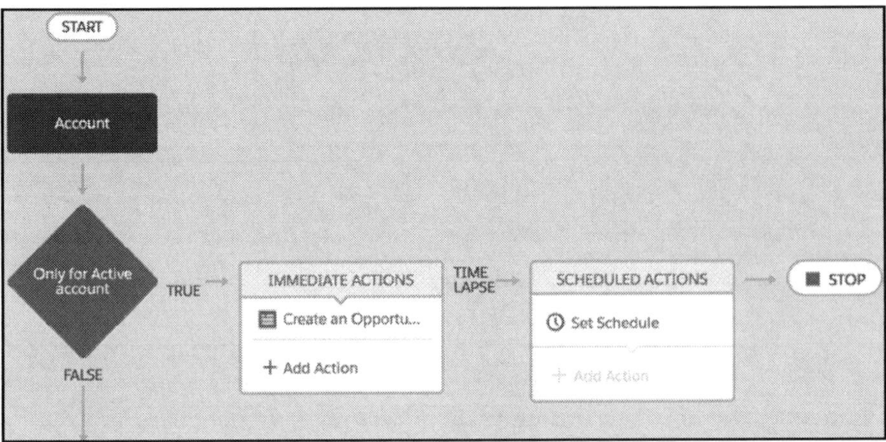

Activating a process

Once you are done with the process creation, the next step is to activate it:

6. To activate a process, click on the **Activate** button, as shown in the following screenshot:

A warning message will appear on the screen; read it carefully and then click on the **Confirm** button, as shown in the following screenshot:

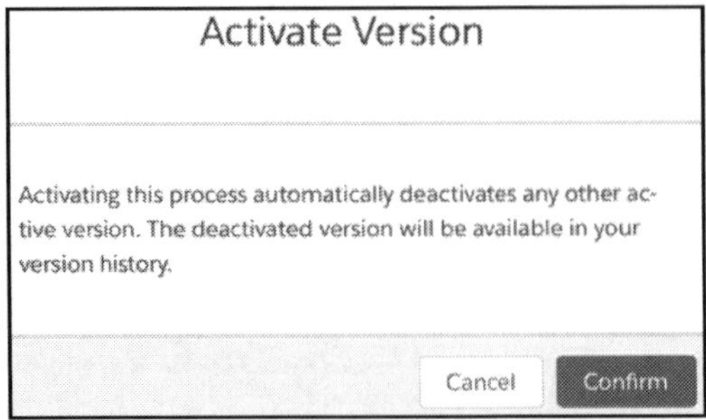

Once you click on the **Confirm** button, it will activate the process. Once the process is activated, it is not possible to make any changes to it. If you want to do so, you must clone it and save it as either a new version or a new process.

Now onwards, if you try to create a new account manually, set `Status__c` to **Active**; the process will fire and it will create an opportunity. However, if you want to auto create an opportunity record after the completion of the account approval defined in `Chapter 7`, *Optimizing Business Processes with Visual Workflow and Approval Processes* then make sure that you have selected **Re-evaluate Workflow Rules after Field Change** for the final **Approval Action** field update:

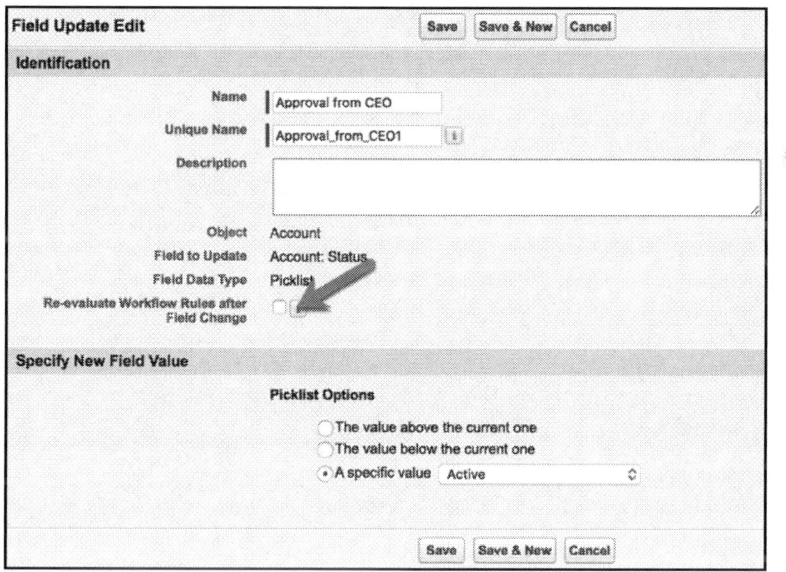

Deactivating a process

If some of the processes are not required, then you can deactivate those. To deactivate an activated Flow, open the activated Flow and click on the **Deactivate** button, as shown in the following screenshot:

Once the process is deactivated, Salesforce stops using a to evaluate it, when any record is created or edited.

Deleting a process

If a process is no longer in use, then you can delete it. You can only delete those processes that are in **Status Draft**, **Inactive**, or **Invalid Draft**; it means that you can't delete an active process. If you want to delete an active process, first deactivate it and then you can immediately delete it. If a process has scheduled actions, then you can't delete it; for this, you must wait until those pending actions have been completed or deleted. To delete a process, follow the given instructions:

7. Click on **Setup** | **Build** | **Create** | **Workflow & Approvals** | **Process Builder**.
8. It will redirect you to the **Process Management** page. Identify the process that you want to delete and click on **Arrow** as shown in the following screenshot:

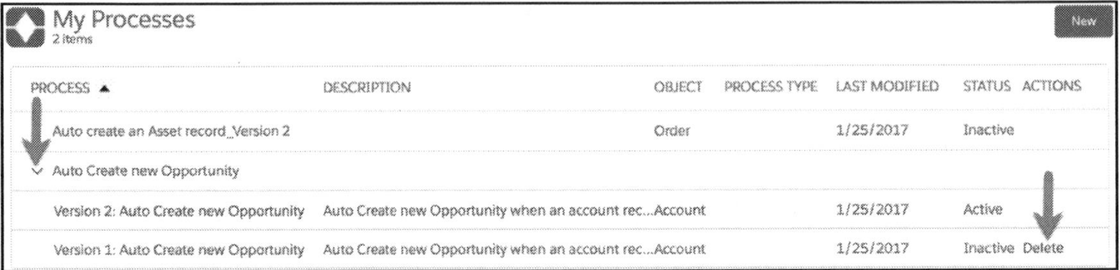

9. It will open a popup for you from where you can delete a process. Click on the **Confirm** button:

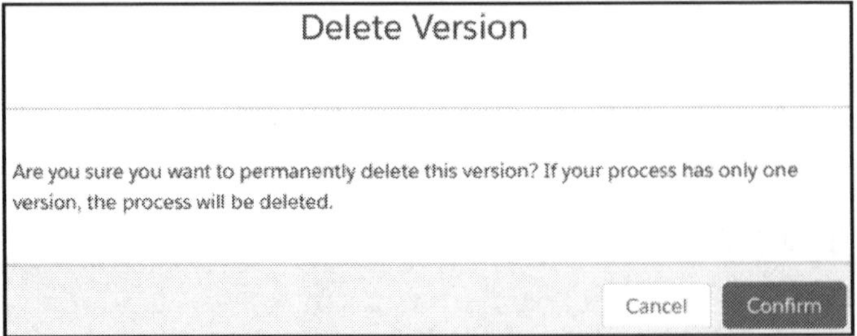

Once you have successfully deleted a version or process, it will be removed from the **Process Management** page.

Hands on 2 – auto-updating child records

Another common scenario is to update child records when a parent record gets updated and fulfill the entry criteria. For example, as soon as a **Stage** opportunity is updated as **Closed Lost**, auto-update all the related **Quote Status** to **Denied**. To resolve these types of business scenario, a developer usually writes an Apex trigger, but there are alternate ways through which you can achieve it, and that too without writing the code, as follows:

- Apex Trigger
- Combination of Flow and Process Builder
- Combination of Flow and Inline Visualforce Page on Order detail page
- Process Builder

A business scenario: *David Guzman* is working as a system administrator at *Universal Containers*. He has received a requirement to auto-update a related open opportunity (except **Closed Won**) **Stage** to **Closed Lost** as soon as the account `Status__c` is marked as **Out of business**. Use the following values to create a new action:

Before proceeding ahead, update the `Status__c` field on the account object and add the value, out of business.

Perform the following instructions to fulfill the preceding business requirement using Process Builder:

1. Click on **Setup** (gear icon) | **Setup** | **PLATFORM TOOLS** | **Process Automation** | **Process Builder**.
2. Click on the **New** button and enter the following details:
    1. **Name**: Enter the name for the process. Enter `Auto update open Opportunities to lost` as **Name**. It must be within 255 characters.
    2. **API Name**: This will be autopopulated based on the **Name**.
    3. **Description**: Write some meaningful text, so other developers/administrators can easily understand why this process is created.
    4. **The process starts when**: For this, select when **A record changes**.

It will look like the following screenshot:

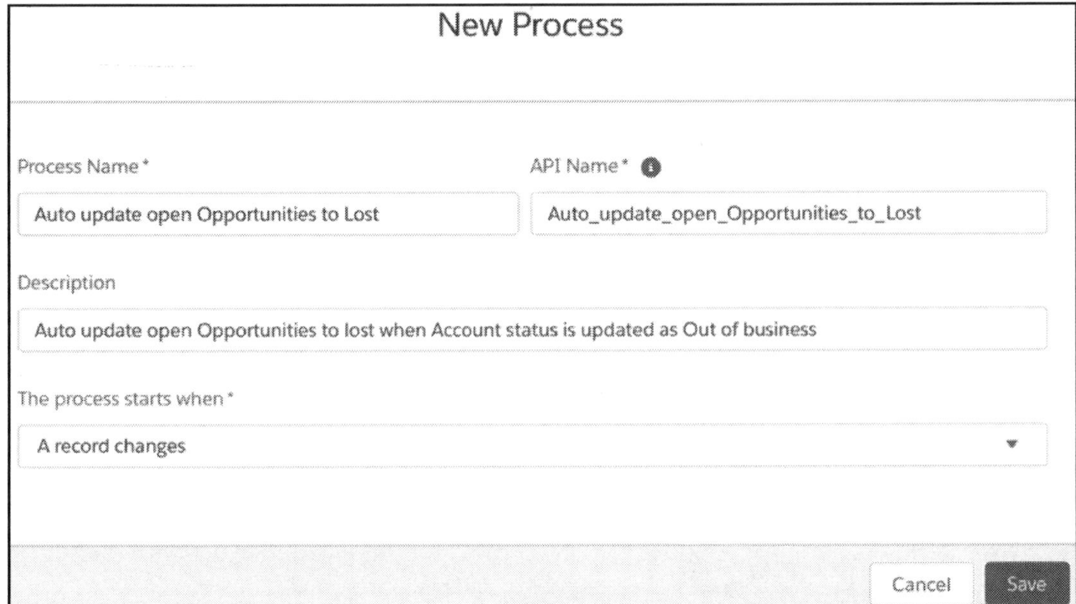

Once you are done, click on the **Save** button.

3. Once you are done with the process property definitions, then the next task is to select the object on which you want to create a process and define the evaluation criteria. For this, click on the **Add Object** node and enter the following details:
    1. **Object**: Select **Account** object.
    2. **Start the process**: For **Start the process**, select **when a record is created or edited**.
    3. **Allow process to evaluate a record multiple times in a single transaction**: Select this checkbox only when you want a process to evaluate the same record for up to five times in a single transaction. Don't select this option for a current business scenario.

It will look like the following screenshot:

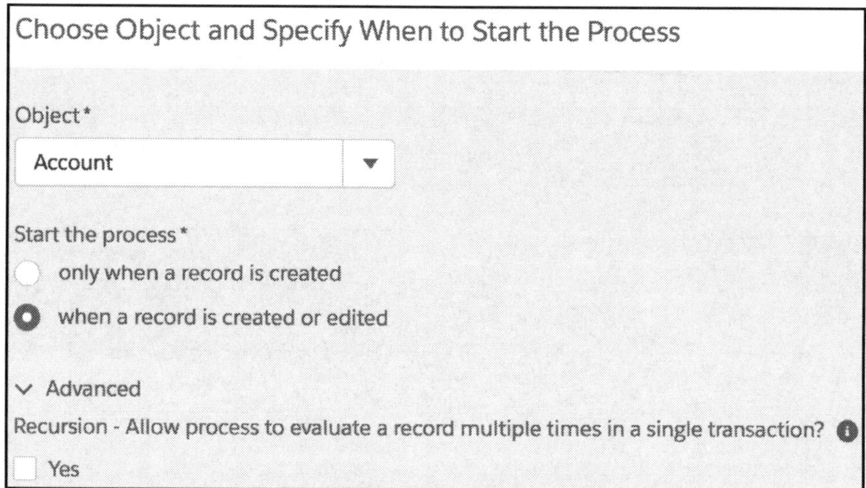

Once you are done, click on the **Save** button.

4. Once you are done with defining the evaluation criteria, the next step is to define the process criteria. To define the process criteria, click on the **Add Criteria** node; it will open an additional window on the right-hand side of the process canvas screen where you have to enter the following details:
    1. **Criteria Name**: Enter a name for the criteria node. Enter `Only for Out of business accounts` as **Criteria Name**.
    2. **Criteria for Executing Actions**: Select the type of criteria you want to define. You can either use formula or filter to define the process criteria or no criteria. In this scenario, select **Conditions are met**.
    3. **Set Conditions**: Here you can define the filter condition for your process. In this scenario, select `Status__C` equals picklist **Out of business**.
    4. **Do you want to execute the actions only when specified changes are made to the record?**: Select this checkbox if you want actions to be executed only if the record meets the criteria now but the values that the record had immediately before it was saved didn't meet the criteria. Select this checkbox for the current business scenario.

It will look like the following screenshot:

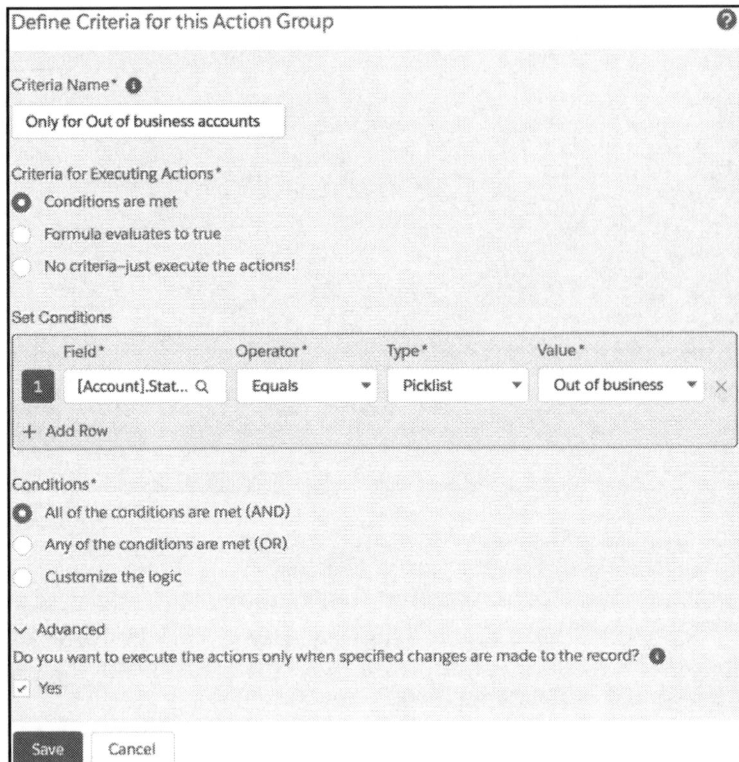

Once you are done, click on the **Save** button.

5. The next step is to add one immediate action to update the related opportunities. To do this, use the **Update Records** action available under the process. Click on **Add Action** available under **IMMEDIATE ACTIONS**. It will open an additional window on the right-hand side of the process canvas screen, where you have to enter the following details:
    1. **Action Type**: Select the type of action you want to perform. In this scenario, select **Update Records**.
    2. **Action Name**: Enter a name for this action. Enter `Update open opportunities to closed lost` as **Action Name**.
    3. **Record Type**: Choose **Select a record related to the Account** and then select the **Opportunities** object.

Map the fields as per the following screenshot:

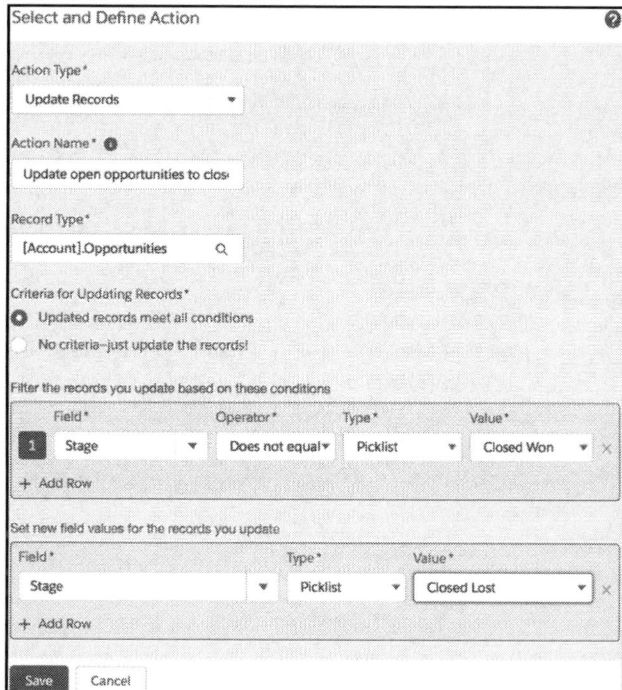

To select the field, you can use **Field Picker**. To enter the value, use the **Text Entry** field. Once you are done, click on the **Save** button. In the end, your process should look like the following screenshot:

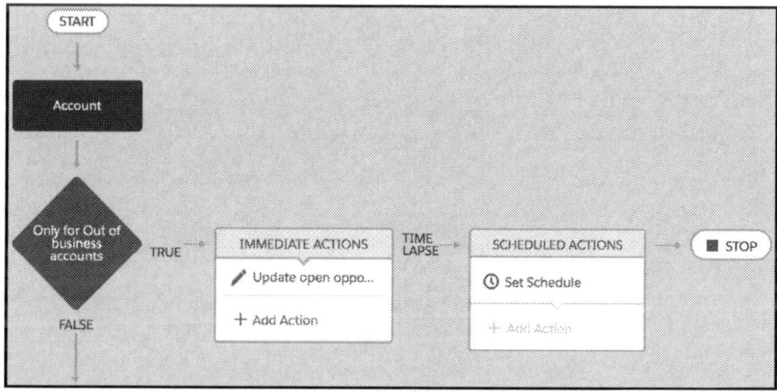

6. The last step is to activate it. To activate a process, click on the **Activate** button.

Now onwards, if someone updates the account `Status__c` to **Out of business**, the process will fire and it will update all open opportunities (except **Closed Won**) to **Closed Lost**.

Hands on 3 – posting message to Chatter group

Organizations are using Chatter as collaboration and company social networking tool. There are many scenarios when sales reps want to auto post new account acquire details to a Chatter group. This is possible through Apex code, but there is another way through which you can achieve it without code, that is, Process Builder. Process Builder has a specific action for it, that is, Post to Chatter.

A business scenario: *David Guzman* is working as a system administrator at *Universal Containers*. He has received a requirement from the sales team to auto post a message to the Chatter group, *Universal Containers Sales Team*, once an opportunity is successfully closed.

Before proceeding ahead make sure to create a Chatter group named *Universal Containers Sales Team*.

Perform the following instructions to fulfill the preceding business requirement using Process Builder:

1. Click on **Setup** (gear icon) | **Setup** | **PLATFORM TOOLS** | **Process Automation** | **Process Builder**.
2. Click on the **New** Button and enter the following details:
    1. **Name**: Enter the name for the process. Enter `Auto post message to Chatter Group` as **Name**.
    2. **API Name**: This will be autopopulated based on **Name**.
    3. **Description**: Write some meaningful text, so other developers/administrators can easily understand why this process is created.
    4. **The process starts when**: For this, select when **A record changes**.

It will look like the following screenshot:

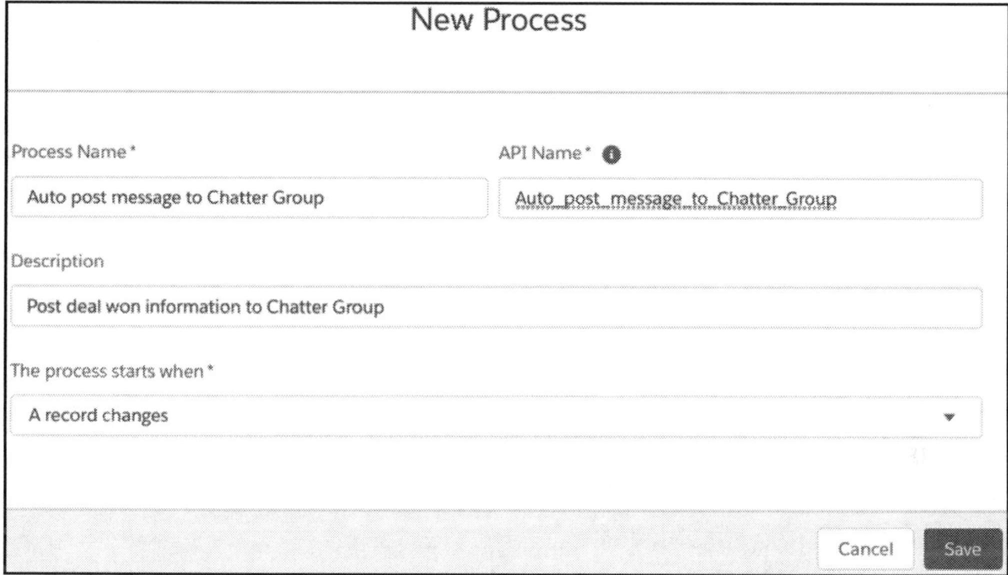

Once you are done, click on the **Save** button.

3. Once you are done with the process property definitions, the next task is to select the object on which you want to create a process and define the evaluation criteria. For this, click on the **Add Object** node and enter the following details:
    1. **Object**: Select the **Opportunity** object.
    2. **Start the process**: For **Start the process**, select **when a record is created or edited**.
    3. **Allow process to evaluate a record multiple times in a single transaction**: Select this checkbox only when you want a process to evaluate the same record for up to five times in a single transaction. Don't select this option for the current business scenario.

It will look like the following screenshot:

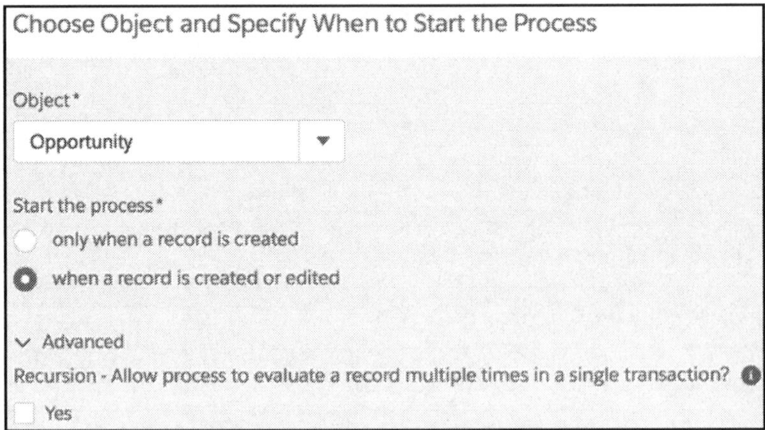

Once you are done, click on the **Save** button.

4. Once you are done with defining the evaluation criteria, the next step is to define the process criteria. To define the process criteria, click on the **Add Criteria** node. It will open an additional window on the right-hand side of the process canvas screen where you have to enter the following details:
    1. **Criteria Name**: Enter a name for the criteria node. Enter `Only for Closed Won Opportunities` as **Criteria Name**.
    2. **Criteria for Executing Actions**: Select the type of criteria you want to define. You can either use a formula or filter to define the process criteria or no criteria. In this scenario, select **Conditions are met**.
    3. **Set Conditions**: Here you can define the filter condition for your process. In this scenario, select **Stage** equals picklist **Closed Won**.
    4. **Do you want to execute the actions only when specified changes are made to the record?**: Select this checkbox if you want the actions to be executed only if the record meets the criteria now but the values that the record had immediately before it was saved didn't meet the criteria. Select this checkbox for the current business scenario.

It will look like the following screenshot:

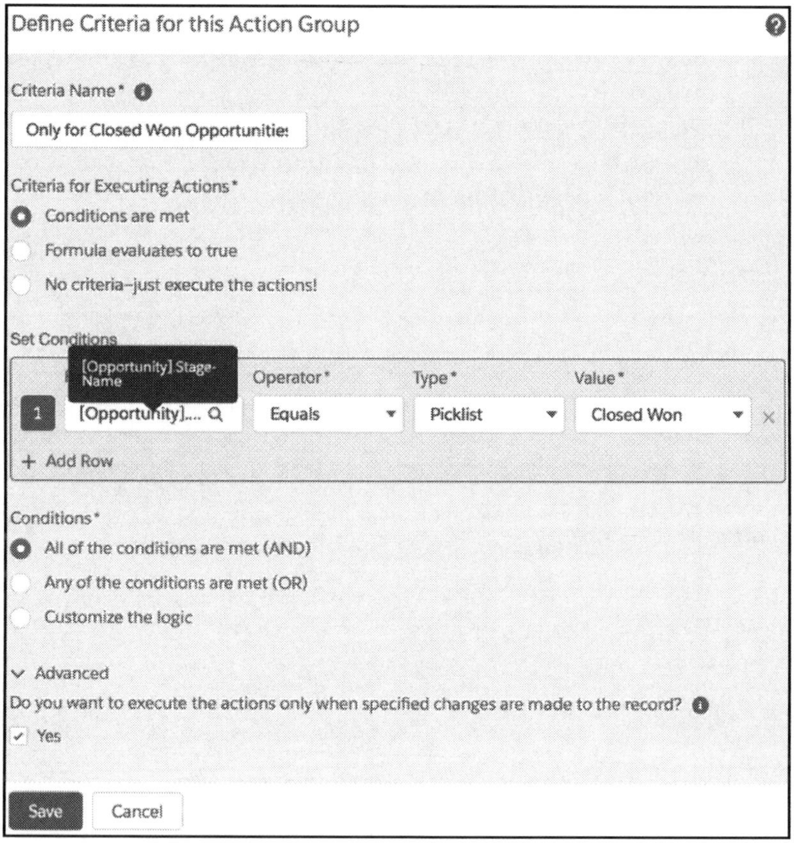

Once you are done, click on the **Save** button.

5. The next step is to add one immediate action to post a message to Chatter group. For this, we will use the **Post to Chatter** action available in process. Click on **AddAction** available under **IMMEDIATE ACTIONS**. It will open an additional window on the right-hand side of the process canvas screen, where you have to enter the following details:
    1. **Action Type**: Select the type of action; in this case, select **Post to Chatter**.
    2. **Action Name**: Enter a name for this action. Enter `Post message to Universal Containers Sales Team Chatter Group` as **Action Name**.

3. **Post to Chatter**: It allows you to select the area (means Chatter group, user, or current record) where you want to post opportunity details. From the drop-down menu, select **Chatter Group**, start typing on the textbox, and then select the Chatter group, **Universal Containers Sales Team**.
4. **Message**: Enter the message that you want to post. You can use the fields above the text box to mention a user or group, add a topic, or insert a merge field into the message.

It will look like the following screenshot:

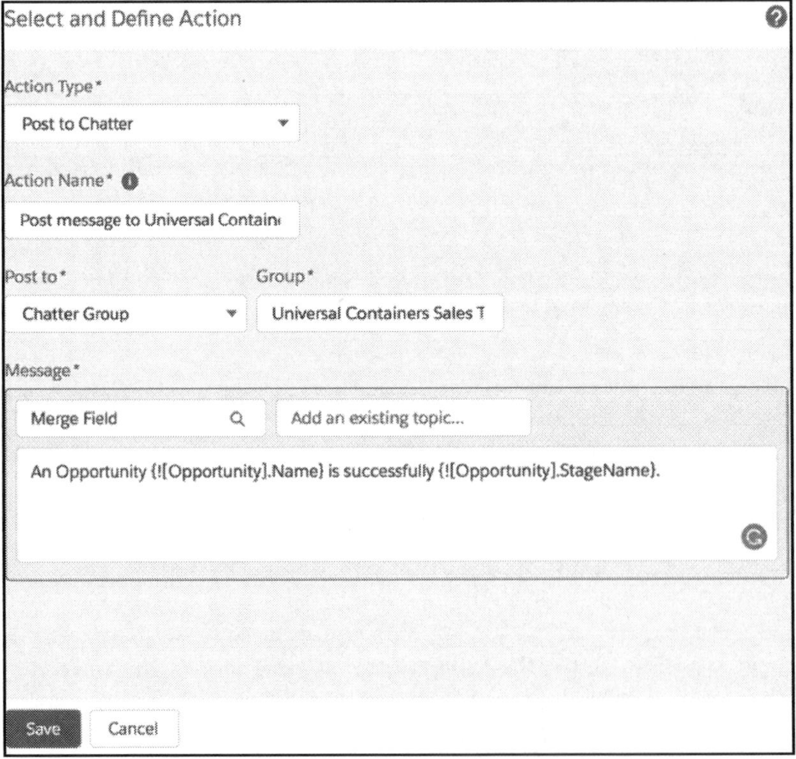

Use **Merge Field** to add fields from **Opportunity** and the related object. To add the topic, use **Add an existing topic** textbox. Once you are done, click on the **Save** button. In the end, your process should look like the following screenshot:

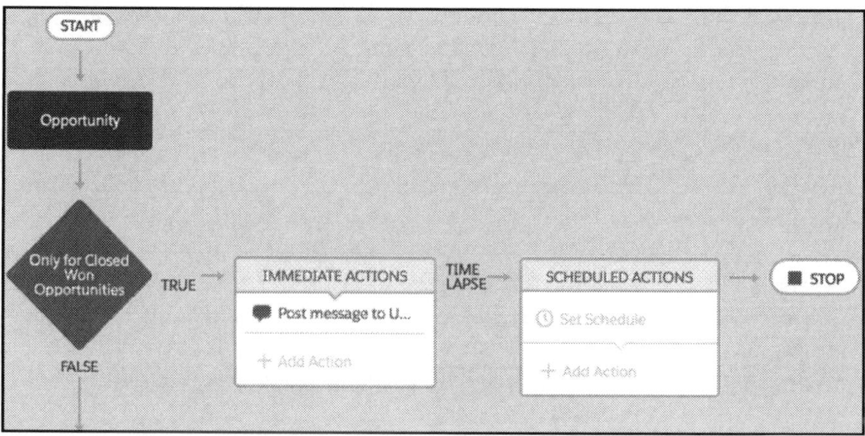

6. The last step is to activate it. To activate a process, click on the **Activate** button.

Now onwards, if someone updates the Opportunity **Stage** as **Closed Won**, the process will fire and post a message to the Chatter Group, and it will look like the following screenshot:

It is also possible to include the link of the opportunity record. To do so, construct the URL and include in the Chatter post message.

Hands on 4 – auto submitting record into approval process

Using Process Builder, you can auto-submit a record into an approval process. Now, the user must submit a record for approval manually. To resolve these types of business scenarios a developer usually writes an Apex trigger, but there are alternate ways through which you can achieve it, and that too, without writing the code, as follows:

- Apex Trigger
- Combination of Flow and Process Builder
- Process Builder

A business scenario: *David Guzman* is working as a system administrator at *Universal Containers*. He has received a requirement to auto-submit a new account for approval if `Status__c` equals to **Inactive**. He has already created a two-step approval process for this in `Chapter 7`, *Optimizing Business Processes with Visual Workflow and Approval Processes.*

Perform the following instructions to fulfill the preceding business requirement using Process Builder:

1. Click on **Setup** (gear icon) | **Setup** | **PLATFORM TOOLS** | **Process Automation** | **Process Builder**.
2. Click on the **New** button and enter the following details:
   1. **Name**: Enter the name for the process. Enter `Auto submit account record for approval` as **Name**.
   2. **API Name**: This will be autopopulated based on the **Name**.
   3. **Description**: Write some meaningful text, so other developers/administrators can easily understand why this process is created.
   4. **The process starts when**: For this, select when **A record changes**.

   It will look like the following screenshot:

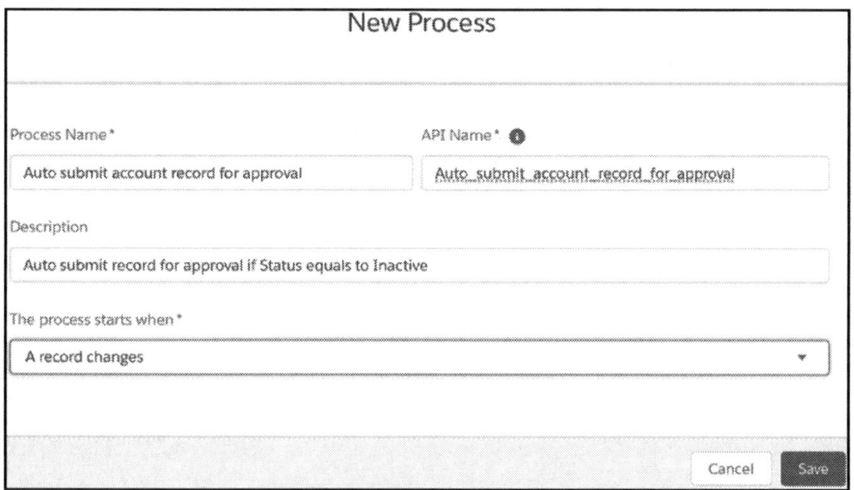

3. Once you are done with the process property definitions, then the next task is to select the object on which you want to create a process and define the evaluation criteria. For this, click on the **Add Object** node and enter the following details:
    1. **Object**: Select the **Account** object.
    2. **Start the process**: To **Start the process**, select only when a record is created.
    3. **Allow process to evaluate a record multiple times in a single transaction**: Select this checkbox only when you want the process to evaluate the same record for up to five times in a single transaction. Don't select this option for the current business scenario.

It will look like the following screenshot:

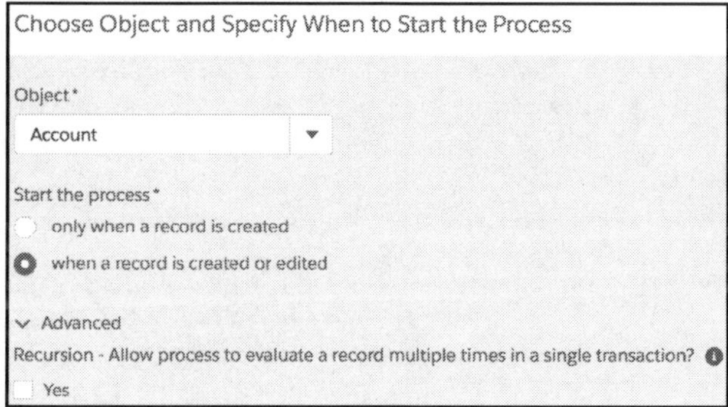

Once you are done, click on the **Save** button.

4. Once you are done with defining the evaluation criteria the next step is to define the process criteria. To define the process criteria, click on the **Add Criteria** node. It will open an additional window on the right-hand side of the process canvas screen, where you have to enter the following details:
    1. **Criteria Name**: Enter a name for the criteria node. Enter `Only for new accounts` as **Criteria Name**.
    2. **Criteria for Executing Actions**: Select the type of criteria you want to define. You can either use a formula or filter to define the process criteria or no criteria. In this scenario, select **Conditions are met**.
    3. **Set Conditions**: Here, you can define the filter condition for your process. In this scenario, select `Status__C` equals picklist **Inactive**.

It will look like the following screenshot:

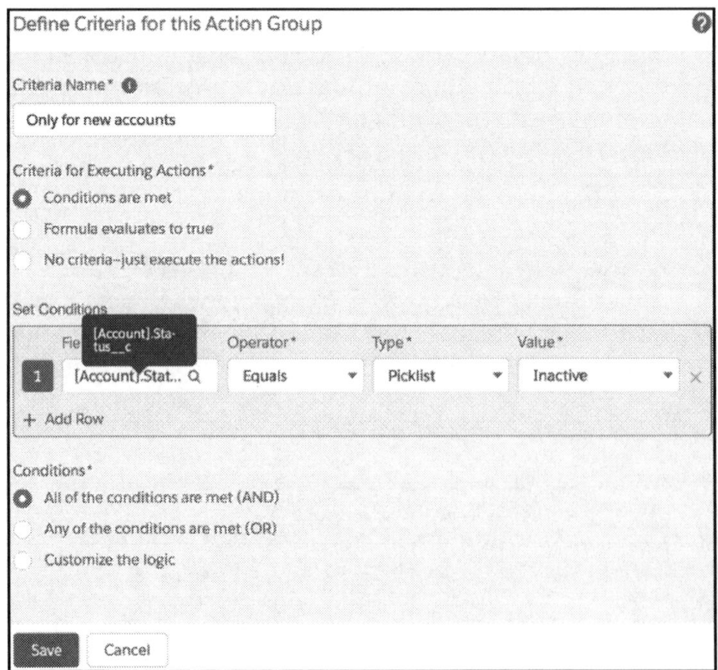

Once you are done, click on the **Save** button.

5. The next step is to add one immediate action to auto-submit records into the approval process. For this, we will use the **Submit for Approval** action available under process. Click on **Add Action** available under **IMMEDIATE ACTIONS**. It will open an additional window on the right-hand side of the process canvas screen, where you have to enter the following details:
    1. **Action Type**: Select the type of action you want to perform. In this scenario, select **Submit for Approval**.
    2. **Action Name**: Enter a name for this action. Enter `Auto submit account records into approval` as **Action Name**.
    3. **Object**: It will automatically populate from the object you have created in the process.
    4. **Approval Process**: You can either select **Default approval process**, or if the object contains more than one approval process, then you can use the **Specific approval process** option from the drop-down menu. Select **Default approval process**.
    5. **Skip the entry criteria for this process?**: If you want to submit the record for approval regardless of the approval process entry criteria, then select this option. In this scenario, leave it as is.
    6. **Submitter**: It allows you to choose the user for auto-submitting records into the approval process and receives all the related notifications. In this scenario, select **Current User**.
    7. **Submission Comments**: Optionally, you can enter submission comments; It will appear in the approval history for the specified record. Enter `Auto submit from Process` in this case.

It will look like the following screenshot:

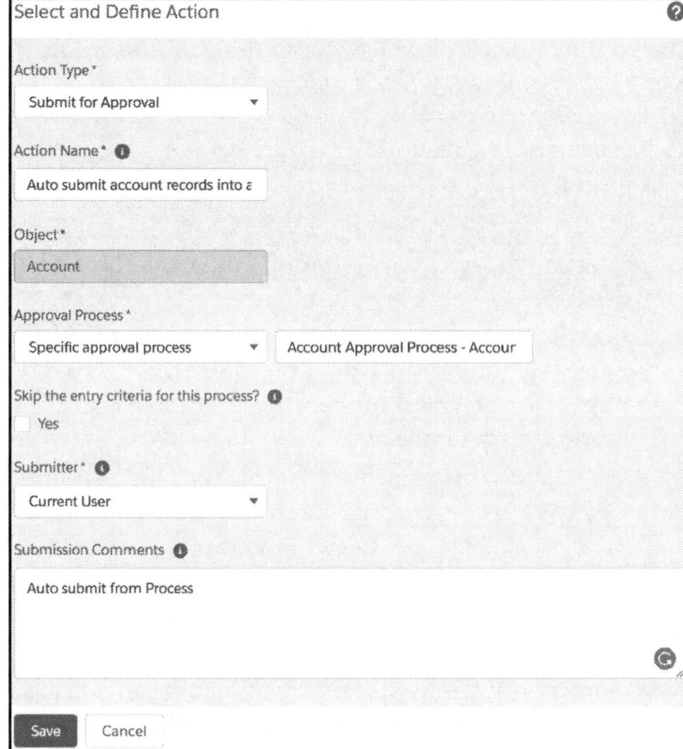

Once you are done, click on the **Save** button.

6. The last step is to activate it. To activate a process, click on the **Activate** button.

Now onwards, if someone creates an account with status, the process will fire and auto-submit records for approval.

Time-dependent actions from Process Builder

In a similar manner, if you want to send an e-mail after one day of account creation to an account owner, or if you want to send a reminder to your customers about a pending order, then use the scheduled action instead of using immediate action. The same set of actions are available under both the immediate and scheduled actions.

Steps to check time-dependent action queue for Process Builder

To monitor a time-dependent action queue for Process Builder, follow the given instructions:

1. Click on **Setup** (gear icon) | **Setup** | **PLATFORM TOOLS** | **Process Automation** | **Flow**.
2. Navigate to the **Paused and Waiting Interviews** section; it will display the time-dependent action queue for Process Builder.

A few points to remember

1. A process's API name must be less than or equal to 79 characters.
2. To activate a process, it must have an action added to it.
3. The process will fail at runtime if it allows initial submitters to manually select the next approver in the approval process.
4. Process Builder doesn't have an option to delete the records; if you want to do so you must use the combination of Visual Workflow with Process Builder.
5. The process owner will receive an e-mail from Salesforce; if it fails on runtime or any fault occurs, the error or warning messages might refer to a Flow instead of a process.
6. Process has same governor limits that apply to Apex.
7. Process actions are executed in the same order in which they appear in the Process Builder Canvas.
8. You can't delete an active process; if you want to do so, first deactivate it.

Summary

In this chapter, we have gone through various concepts related to the Process Builder–starting from a business scenario where you can use a Process Builder, followed by the Process Builder user interface. Then, we moved forward and discussed the differences between various automation tools. We also went through a couple of hands-on exercises to see how we can use the Process Builder to automate business processes. In the next chapter, we will go through the report and dashboard concepts.

9
Analyzing Productivity with Reports and Dashboards

In the previous chapter, we had an overview of Process Builder. We learned the difference between automation tools such as Visual Workflow, Workflow Rule, and Process Builder. We also discussed the various actions available in Process Builder.

In this chapter, we will discuss various concepts related to a report and dashboard. We will also explain the different ways to share reports and dashboards, followed by a few advanced concepts such as cross filters in reports and formulas. We'll cover the following topics in this chapter:

- Understanding report types
- Different types of report formats
- Dashboard components and their types
- Reporting snapshot

A report provides you a way to analyze how efficiently your organization is performing. For example, the VP of Sales of Universal Containers wants either a list of opportunities closed-won in the current quarter or the number of leads passed by web-to-lead form embedded on the company website in the current fiscal year, to check its effectiveness. Salesforce offers various types of options that we can utilize to create reports as per our requirements. Reports always generate data in real time. When we save them in a folder, Salesforce saves their configuration parameters but not the generated data. Reports will always show data as per the running user's security access. Creating them on both standard and custom objects is possible. They are stored in folders, and only those users who have access to these folders would be able to run the reports.

Understanding report types

Report types are a predetermined amalgamation of related objects and their fields that we can use as starting points when building new custom reports. In other words, report types are containers that contain data and fields on which we can create custom reports. The following screenshot represent a Venn diagram of outer join report type in Salesforce:

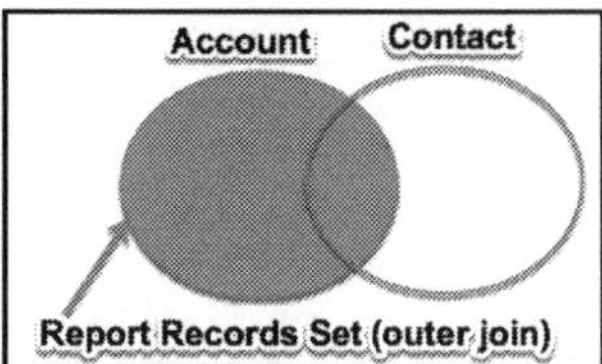

The different kinds of report types are as follows:

- Standard report types
- Custom report types

Standard report types

Standard report types are available for building reports on standard and custom objects and their related objects by default. When you are creating a new custom field, it is automatically added to standard report types. The following screenshot displays a standard report type that shows **Leads with converted lead information**:

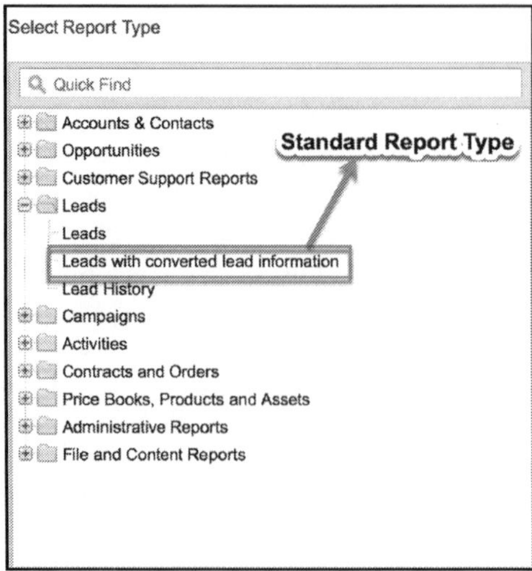

Custom report types

Custom report types allow us to build our own report framework in the report wizard; through this, users can create custom reports. While creating custom report types, keep the following things in mind:

1. Select combinations of up to four related objects and create with or without relationships.
2. Select which objects fields can be used as columns in reports.
3. Add fields that are related via lookup.

Creating a custom report type

Salesforce provides the out-of-the box simple wizard for defining custom report type. Let's start with a business use case.

Say *David Guzman* is working as a *System Administrator* at Universal Containers. As part of day-to-day admin activity, he has received a requirement from the management to create a report to list all the accounts that have at least one order record and each order record must have at least one related activities record.

As we all are aware that it is not possible to achieve the preceding business requirement using a standard report type, we will go ahead and create a custom report type. Perform the following steps to create a custom report type for the preceding business requirement:

1. Navigate to **Setup** (gear icon) | **Setup** | **PLATFORM TOOLS** | **Feature Settings** | **Analytics** | **Report & Dashboards** | **Report Types**.

2. To create a new custom report type, click on the **New Custom Report Types** button, as shown in the following screenshot:

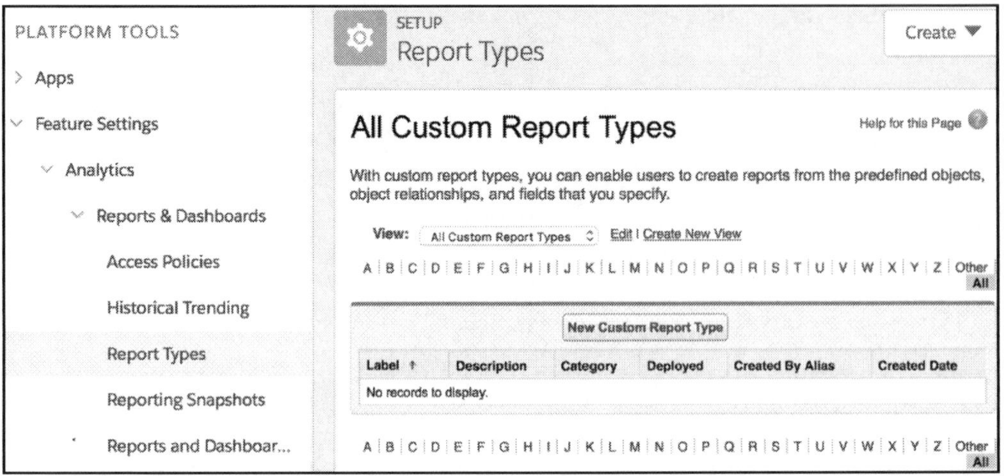

3. This will open a window for you where you will have to enter the following details:
    1. **Primary Object**: Select the primary object from all the objects available in your organization, even those that you don't have the permission to view. In our case, select the **Account** object.
    2. **Report Type Label**: Enter a meaningful name for the report type label. Use `Accounts with Order and Activities` as **Report Type Label**.
    3. **Report Type Name**: This will be auto populated based on **Report Type Label**.
    4. **Description**: Name it using some meaningful text so other developers/administrators can easily understand why this custom report type was created.
    5. **Store in Category**: Select the category to store the custom report type. In this case, select the **Account & Contacts** folder.

6. Deployment Status: Select **Deployment Status**. In this case, select **Deployed**.

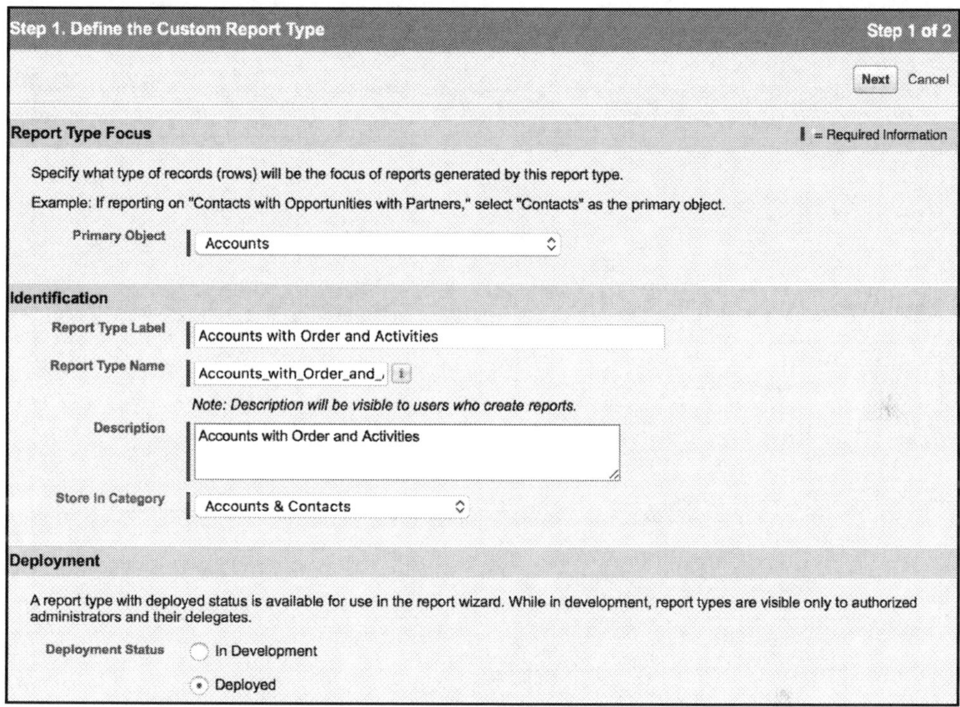

7. Once you are done, click on **Next**.

8. The next step is to define related objects. To do this, click on the **(Click to relate another object)** box, as shown in the following screenshot:

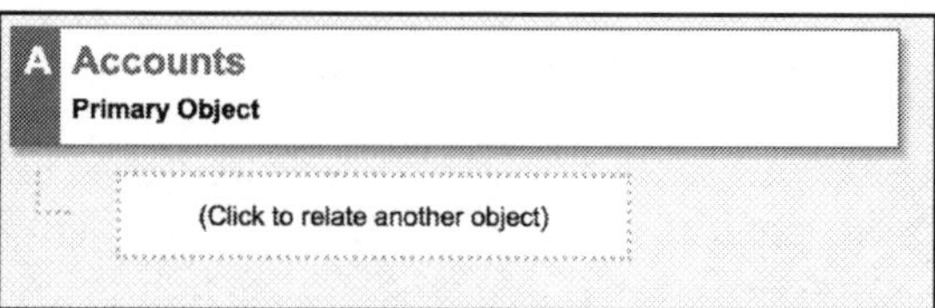

9. Object references can be used as the four main objects, as sources of fields via lookup or as objects used to traverse relationships.

4. Select **Orders** as the secondary object and then select the **Each "A" record must have at least one related "B" records** checkbox. Then select **Activities** as the tertiary object and select the **Each "B" record must have at least one related "C" record** checkbox as well, as shown in the following screenshot:

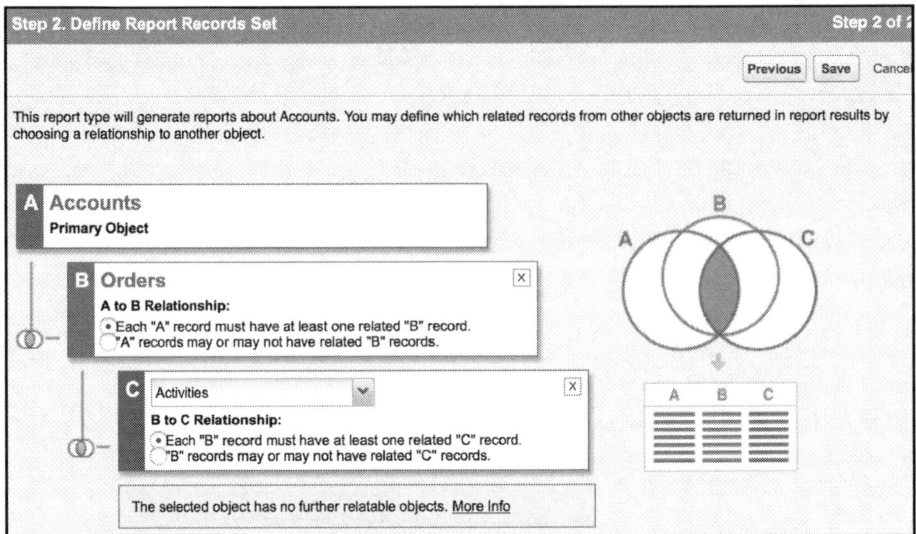

5. Once you are done, click on **Save**.

You can't use product schedule fields, person account fields, history fields, or the age field on cases and opportunities to custom report types. You can add up to 1,000 fields to each custom report type.

Adding fields related via Lookup

Custom report types also allow us to add fields from related objects that are not included in the report types. For example, custom fields are automatically included in standard report types but not custom report types. We have to add it to a custom report type manually. Let's start with a business use case.

Say *David Guzman* is working as a *System Administrator* at Universal Containers. He has created a custom report type called **Accounts with Order and Activities**. Now he wants to add the **Account's Owner City** field to it.

Perform the following steps to solve the preceding business requirement:

1. Navigate to **Setup** (gear icon) | **Setup** | **PLATFORM TOOLS** | **Feature Settings** | **Analytics** | **Report & Dashboards** | **Report Types**.
2. Open the **Accounts with Order and Activities** report type.
3. Navigate to the **Fields available for Reports** section, then click on the **Edit Layout** button.
4. The next step is to select the object from the **View** drop-down field from the right-hand side of the page. In this case, select the **Account Fields** as shown in the following screenshot:

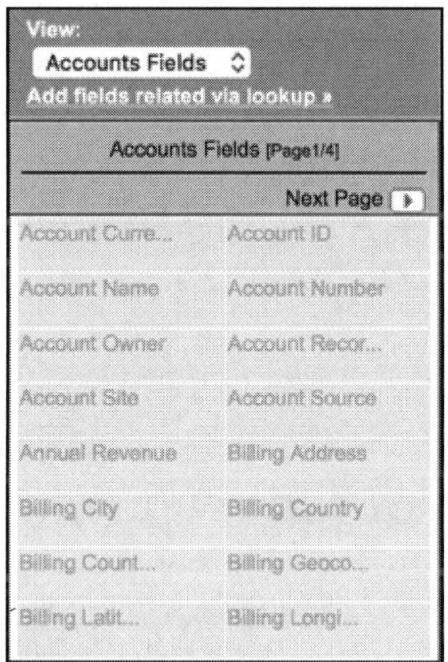

5. To select the **Account** field, click on the **Add fields related via lookup** link available below the **View** field.

6. The final step is to select the appropriate field, that is, **City** in this case:

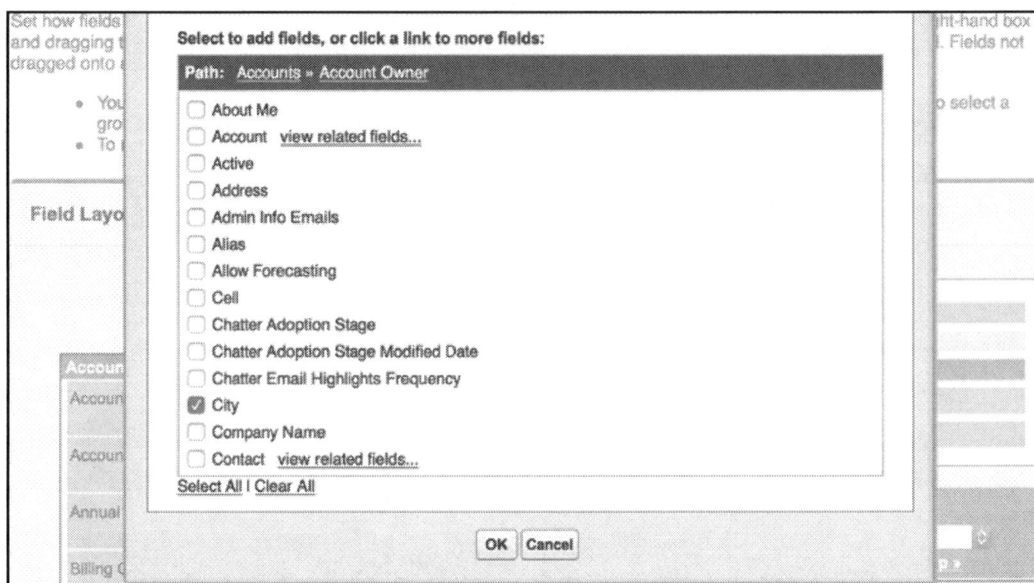

7. Once you are done, click on **OK** and then click on **Save**.

Different types of report formats

Salesforce allows us to generate reports on different predefined formats based on business requirement. Salesforce offers four different report formats that you can use. They are as follows:

- Tabular
- Summary
- Matrix
- Joined

Tabular report

You can use this type of report to display a row of records in a table without any subtotal. Let's start with a business use case.

Say *David Guzman* is working as *System Administrator* at Universal Containers. As part of day-to-day admin activity, he has received a requirement from the management to create a report to list all the accounts that have at least one order record and each order record must have at least one related activities record.

Perform the following steps to create a custom report for the preceding business requirement:

1. Navigate to the **Reports** tab and click on the **New Report** button.
2. It will redirect you to a page where you have to select **report types**. In this case, select the `Accounts with Order and Activities` report type and then click on **Create**, as shown in the following screenshot:

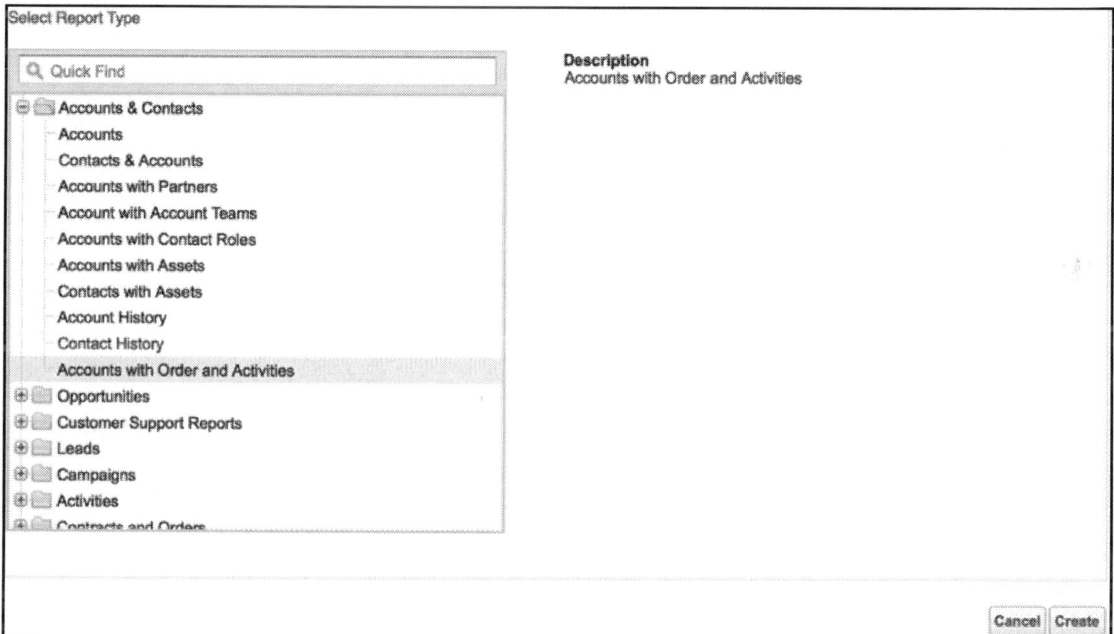

3. It allows you to adjust the filter as you want. For the **Date Field** filter, select the **Created date** range, that is, **All Time**. At the end, the report will look like the following:

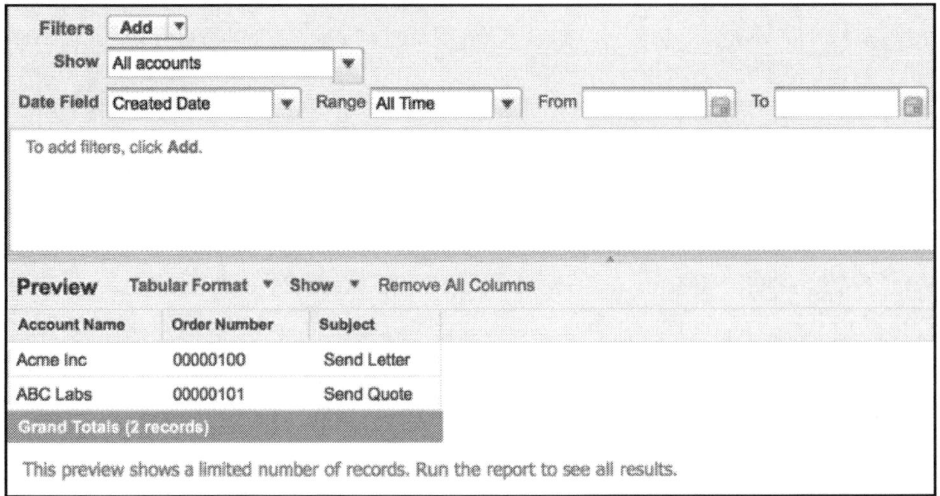

4. Once you're done, click on **Save**. Make sure to save the report in the appropriate folder and also check the report folder sharing settings.

Summary report

This type of report is used to display groupings of rows of data. Let's start with a business use case.

Say *David Guzman* is working as *System Administrator* at Universal Containers. He has received a requirement from the VP of Sales to create a custom report that would display only those accounts that do not have related contacts, and he or she wants you to group the result by account type.

Perform the following steps to create a custom report for the preceding business requirement:

1. Navigate to the **Reports** tab and click on the **New Report** button.
2. It will redirect you to a page where you have to select **Report Types**; in this case, select the **Accounts** report type and then click on **Create**.

3. The next step is to change the format. To do so, click on **Tabular Format** and select **Summary**, as shown in the following screenshot:

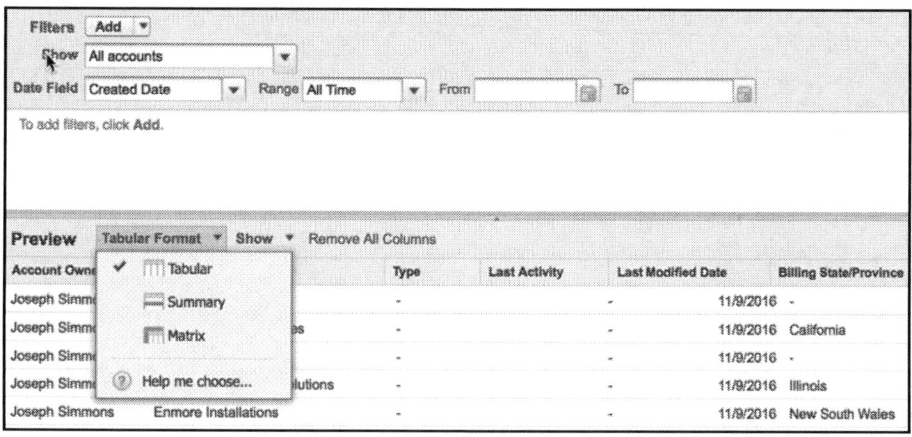

Using cross filters in reports

Cross filters allow us to filter the parent records in a report by their related child records, using the **with** or **without** condition.

1. In the filters section, go to **Add** | **Cross Filter**.
2. The next step is to select a parent object from the drop-down list. In this case, select the **Account** object.
3. Then choose either **with** or **without**. In this case, select **without**.
4. Then, select a child object from the drop-down list. Select **Contacts** in this case. The drop-down list will display all the eligible child objects of the **Account** object.

   It will look like the following:

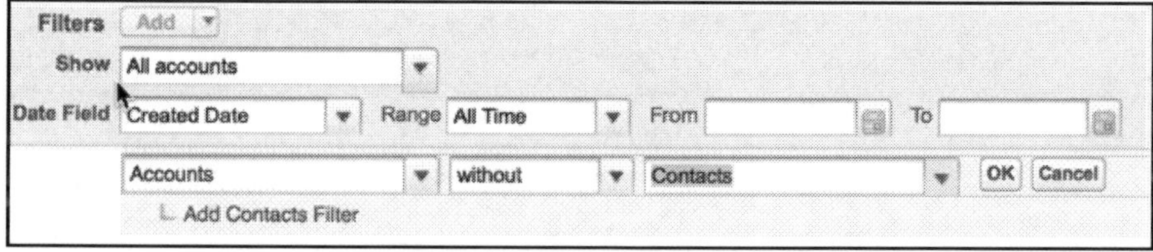

5. Once you are done, click on **OK**.
6. After applying the cross filter, your report will look like the following:

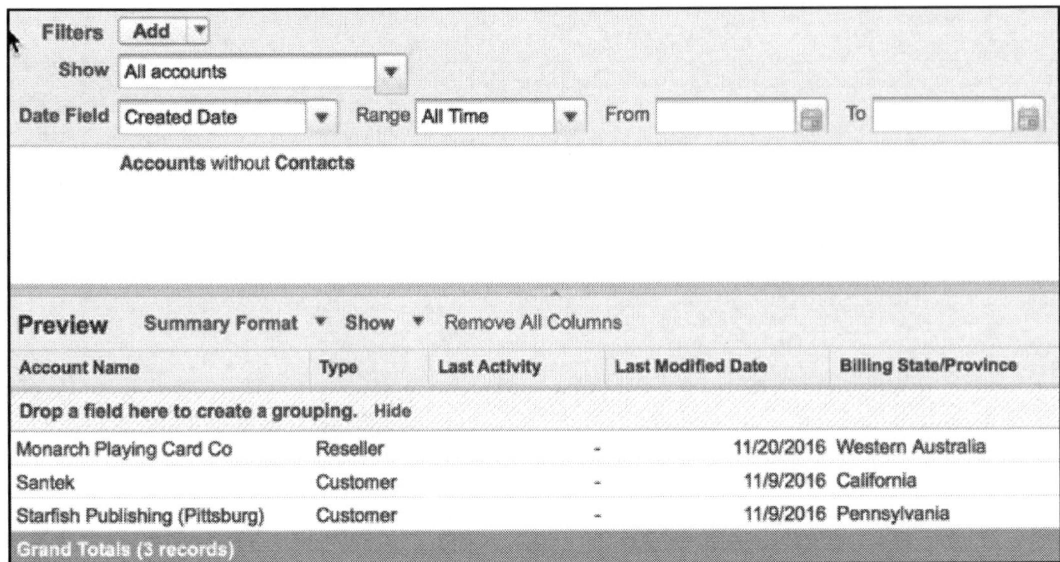

7. The final step is to apply grouping based on **Type**. To do so, go to column **Type** | **Group by this Field**, as shown in the following screenshot:

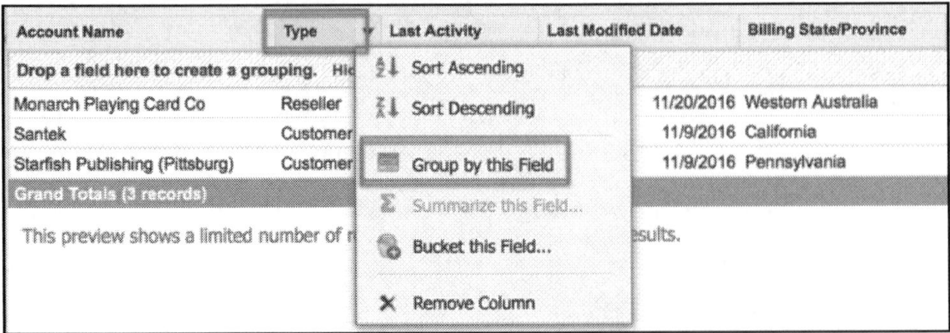

8. Once you are done, click on **Save**.
9. Save the report with the name `Account without Contacts` in the `Unfiled Public Reports` folder:

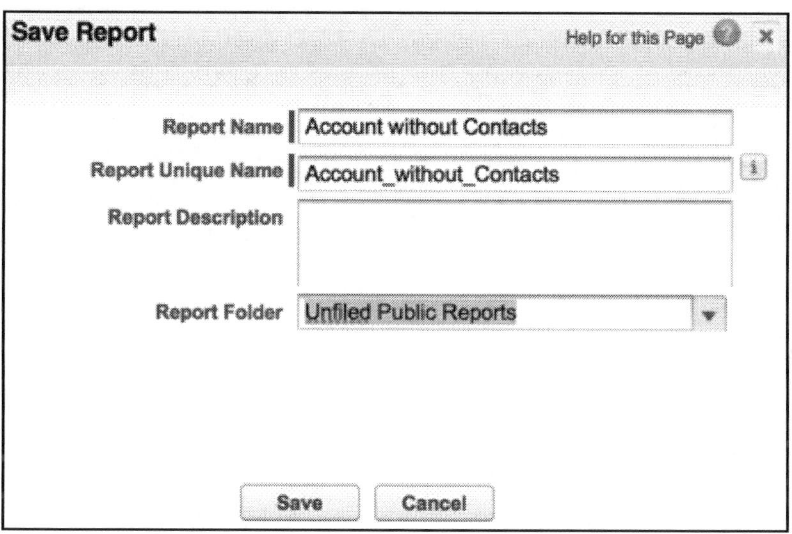

10. Once you are done, click on **Save**.

Matrix report

Matrix report is the most complex report format. It allows us to summarize data in grid format. It allows records to be grouped by both columns and rows.

Joined report

Joined reports allow us to combine multiple views of related information in a single report; for example, you want to display the comparison between sales in the current quarter and last quarter.

Categorizing report data with bucketing

This process allows us to segment report data on the fly. It does so by defining a set of categories or buckets to sort, group, or filter records. Let's start with a business use case.

Say *David Guzman* is working as *System Administrator* at Universal Containers. He has created a summary report in the account object group as per the industry, as shown in the following screenshot:

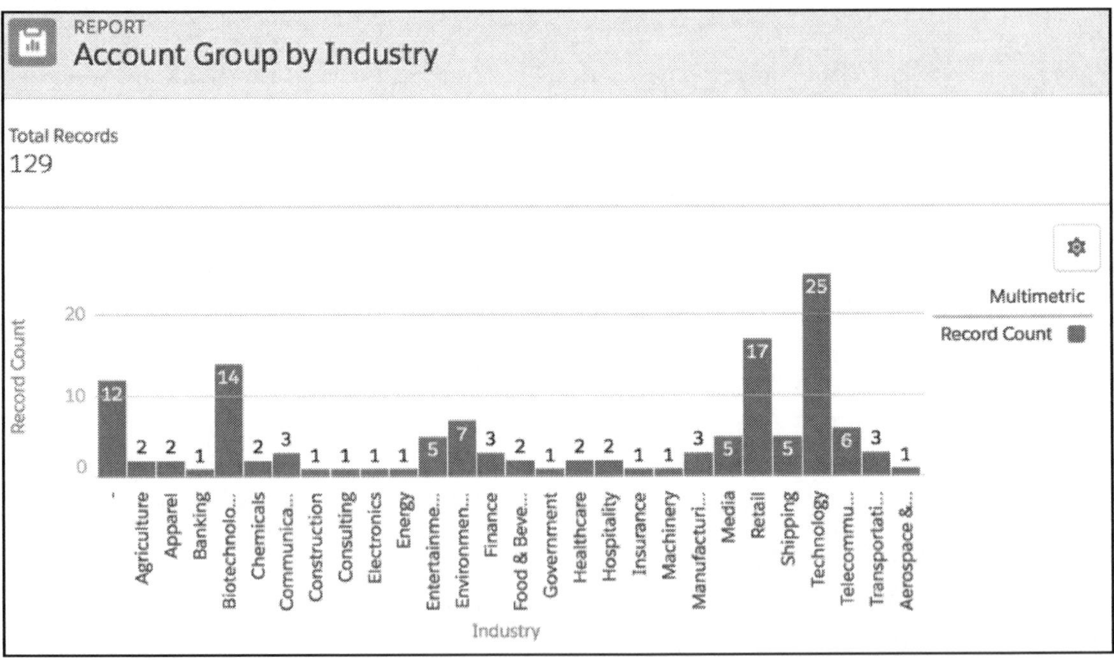

At Universal Containers, they are currently using 31 industries. Their VP of Sales finds it very difficult to analyze the data. He or she wants to categorize industries in two parts: profit and non-profit.

Perform the following steps to create a bucket field for the preceding business requirement:

1. Navigate to the **Reports** tab and click on the **New Report** button. Create summary report group by the industry. Next is step is to create bucket field for an industry, to do so navigate to **Industry** | **Bucket this Field**, as shown in the following screenshot:

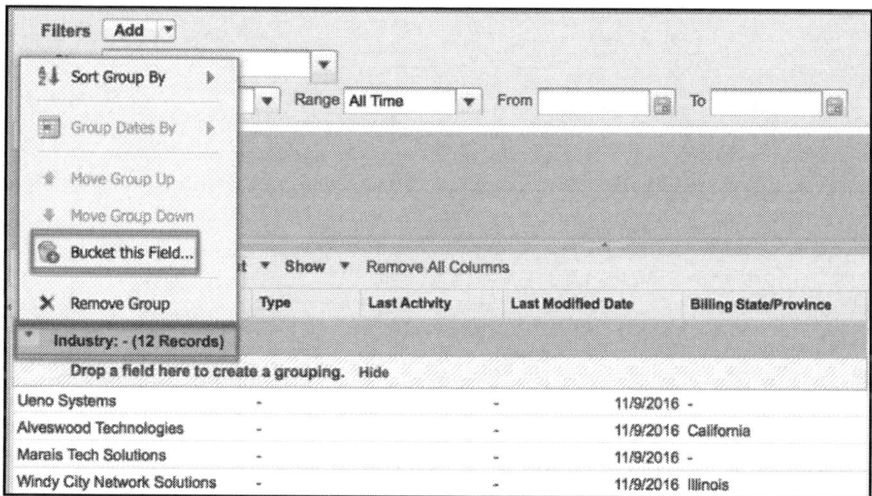

2. Enter `Industry Bucket Field` as **Bucket Field Name**.
3. Click on **New Bucket**; enter `Profit` and hit enter and do the following:
    1. Select **Banking, Transportation, Telecommunication, Technology, Shipping, Retail, Media, Manufacturing, Machinery, Finance, Environmental, Engineering, Energy, Electronics, Consulting, Construction, Communication, Agriculture, and Apparel**.
    2. Click on **Move To**, and from the drop-down list, select **Profit**.
4. Click on **New Bucket**; enter `Non Profit` and hit enter and do:
    1. Select **Biotechnology, Chemicals, Education, Entertainment, Food & Beverage, Healthcare, Hospitality, Insurance, Other, Recreation, Utilities, Banking, and Government**.
    2. Click on **Move To**, and from the drop-down list, select **Non Profit**.
5. Make sure you select **Show unbucketed values** as **Other**.
6. Click on **OK**.
7. Make sure to add **Industry Bucket Field** (that is, the bucket field you have just created) on report.
8. The next step is to remove the old group (that is, based on the industry).

9. Now set the group based on **Bucket Field**, that is, **Industry Bucket Field**, as shown in the following screenshot:

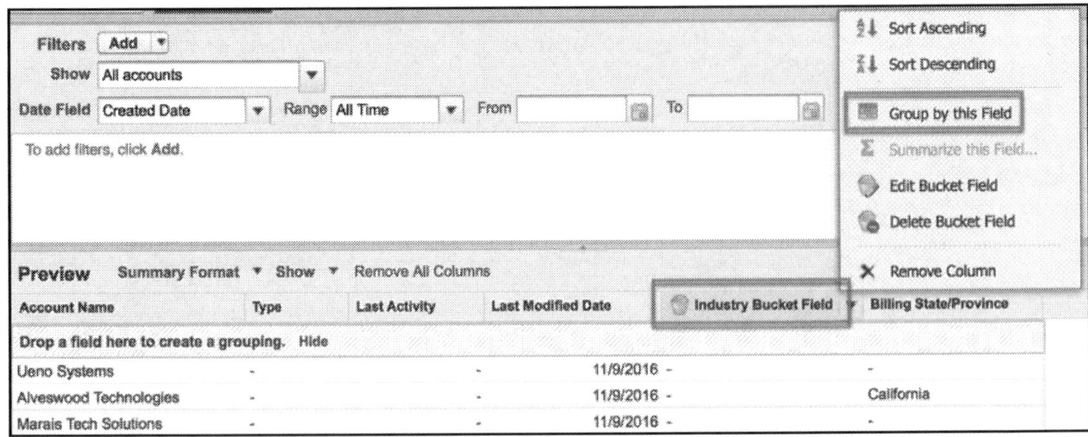

10. Once you are done, click on **Save**.

Create a dashboard and run the **Account** group as per the industry report; it will look much clearer and easy to understand.

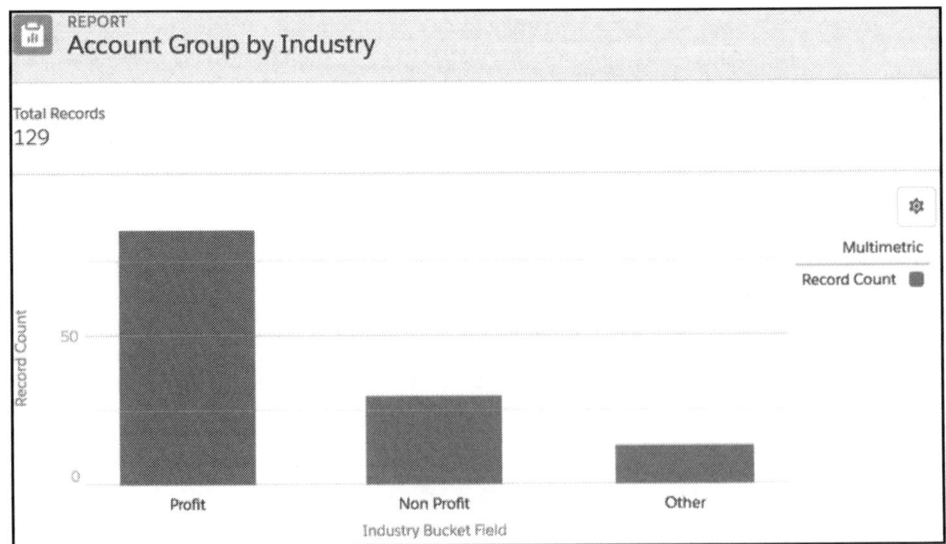

In one bucket, you can have a maximum of 20 values.

Dashboard component and its types

The dashboard is a graphical representation of a report. It will show data from the source report as a graphical component, which can be a metric chart, gauge, donut chart, and so on. Components provide a glimpse of the key metrics and performance meters of your organization. Use this when you are interested in knowing about the numbers and comparisons based on the same fields.

A user will be able to see all the details in a dashboard whether they have access to the records or not; however, once they drill down to the report, they will only be able to see records that he or she has access to. Dashboard components can be a metric chart, gauge, donut chart, table, or another component that you can create with Visualforce. A description of each component is as follows:

- **Chart**: You can use a chart when you want to display data graphically. It also allows you to choose from a variety of chart types.
- **Gauge**: You can use a gauge when you have a single value that you want to show within a range of custom values. For example, to create a dashboard that would measure where your current lead amounts would fall within a range of values, set **Minimum Value**, **Breakpoint #1 Value**, **Breakpoint #2Value**, and **Maximum Value** for the gauge. The ranges that you set can indicate poor, acceptable, or good performance. You can set appropriate colors for each of these ranges to visually indicate progress.
- **Metric**: You can use a metric when you have one key value to display. For example, consider you have a report that shows the total amount of all the leads from the origin web, phone, or newspaper for the current month. If this is the case, you can name this value and use it as a potential revenue target for the month displayed on the dashboard.
- **Table**: You can use a table to show a set of report data in column form, similar to what you see in Microsoft Excel, for example, to see the top 20 accounts based on revenue.
- **Visualforce Page**: You can use a Visualforce page when you want to create a custom component or when your requirement is not fulfilled by the component available.

- **Custom S-control**: Use **Custom S-control** when you want to display any type of content in a browser, for example, a Java applet, an Active-X control, an Excel file, or a custom HTML web form.

Dynamic dashboard

Dynamic dashboards display the data of the users viewing it, rather than the data of a specified running user. The system administrator or users who have **Run Reports** and **Manage Dashboards** permission can create dashboards. We can only create dashboards from the **Summary** and **Matrix** report. Let's start with a business use case.

Say *David Guzman* is working as a *System Administrator* at Universal Containers. He has created a summary report called **Account without Contacts**. Now he wants to create a dynamic dashboard for it.

1. Navigate to the **Dashboards** tab and click on the **New Dashboard** button.
2. It will redirect you to a page where you will need to enter the dashboard name. In this case, enter `Accounts without Contacts`, select the folder to store the dashboard as **Company Dashboard**, then click on **Create**, as shown in the following screenshot:

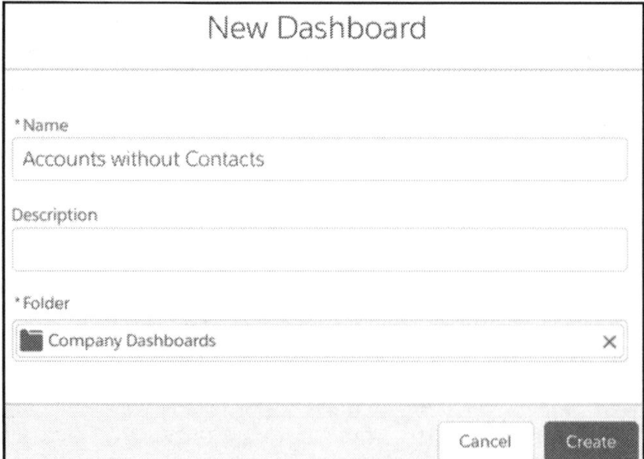

3. Click on **+ Add** to insert a component into your dashboard.
4. It will prompt you a window to select the **Report** and **Chart** type for the new component. For **Report**, select **Accounts without Contacts**, and for **Chart**, select **Horizontal Bar Chart**, as shown in the following screenshot:

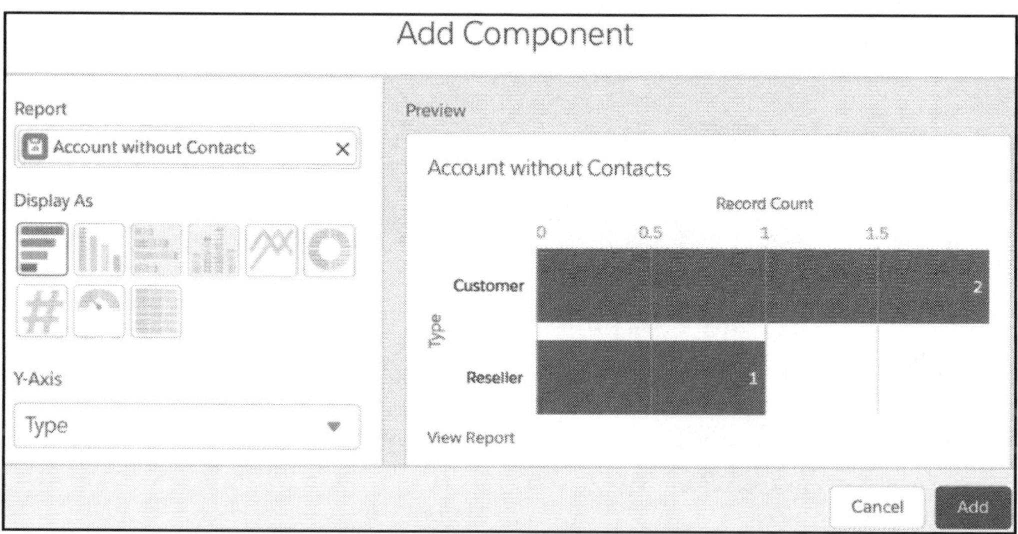

5. Once you are done, click on **Add**. Once you add a component, it will also allow you to resize it, change its position, and delete or change it from the report.
6. You can add multiple components to your dashboard. Each component will show data from one report. Add one more donut chart component to your dashboard. Use the drag-and-drop feature to reposition your components.

7. Once you are done, click on **Save**.

   At the end, it will look like the following:

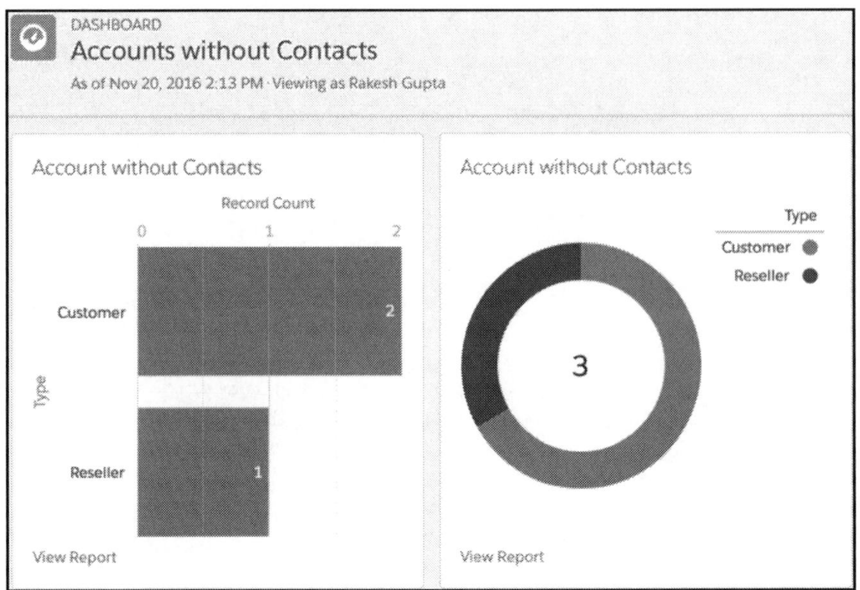

8. To create a dynamic dashboard, click on the **Edit** | **Gear Icon** button available on the dashboard page.
9. You can set **View dashboard as filter**; there are three possible options provided by Salesforce:
   1. **Me**: Dashboard readers see data in the dashboard according to your access to data.
   2. **A specified user**: By using this setting, all users will see data in the dashboard according to the data access level of whomever you specify.
   3. **The logged in user**: If you select this, the user will see data according to their access. If you select this option, you will not be able to schedule a dashboard.

In this case, select **The logged in user** option, as shown in the following screenshot:

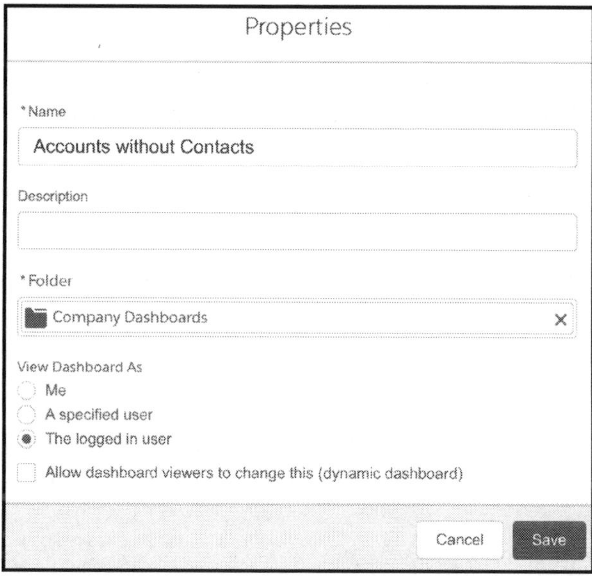

10. Once you are done, click on **Save**. Then click on **Save**.

Dashboard filter

A dashboard filter allows users to change the data visible on the dashboard by selecting a filter value from a drop-down list. You can have maximum three fitters in a dashboard, each with up to ten filter values. Let's start with a business use case.

Say *David Guzman* is working as a *System Administrator* at Universal Containers. He has created a dashboard for the **Accounts without Contacts Aloha** summary report. Now he wants to add dashboard filters based on the **Account Annual Revenue** field, mentioned as follows:

- Less than 50,000
- Between 50,000 and 10,000,000

As of *Spring'17* release, the dashboard filter feature is not available in Salesforce Lightning Experience. You can't dashboards filters in Lightning Experience. Lightning Experience users can view filtered dashboards. It's possible to apply or clear filters that were added in Salesforce Classic.

To create a dashboard filter, we would need to switch back to Salesforce Classic UI. Use the switcher to switch back to Salesforce Classic. Perform the following steps to solve the preceding business requirement:

1. Navigate to the **Reports** tab and create a new dashboard with the same chart (which we created in *Creating a dynamic dashboard* section) in Salesforce Classic. Use `Accounts without Contacts Aloha` as the new dashboard name.

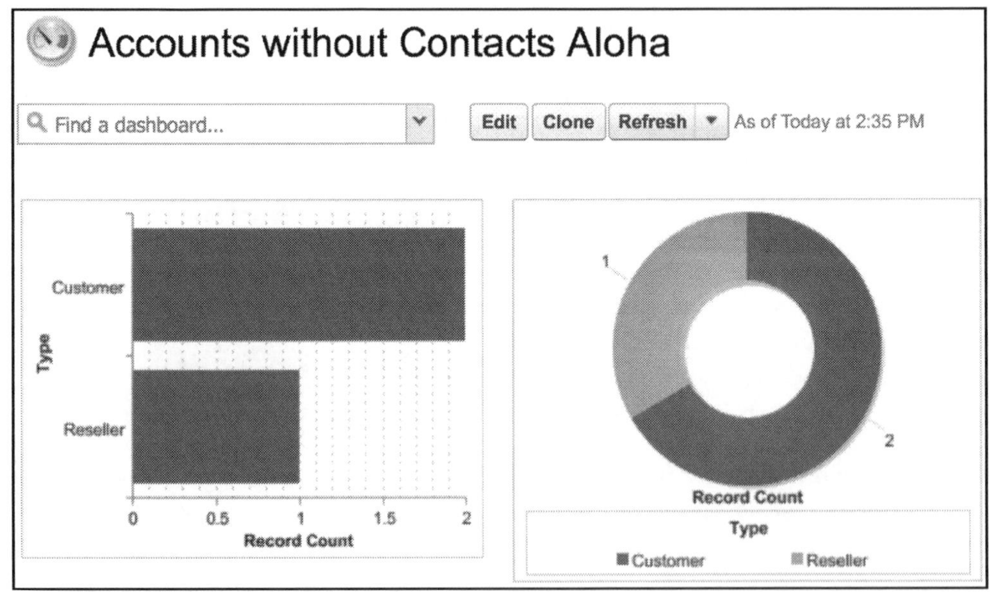

2. Navigate to the **Reports** tab and click on **Edit** for the **Accounts without Contacts Aloha** dashboard in Salesforce Classic.
3. To add a filter to the dashboard, click on the **Add Filter** button.
4. Now select the field to filter on from the **Field** dropdown, that is, **Annual Revenue** in this case.

5. The next step is to define the condition as shown in the following screenshot:

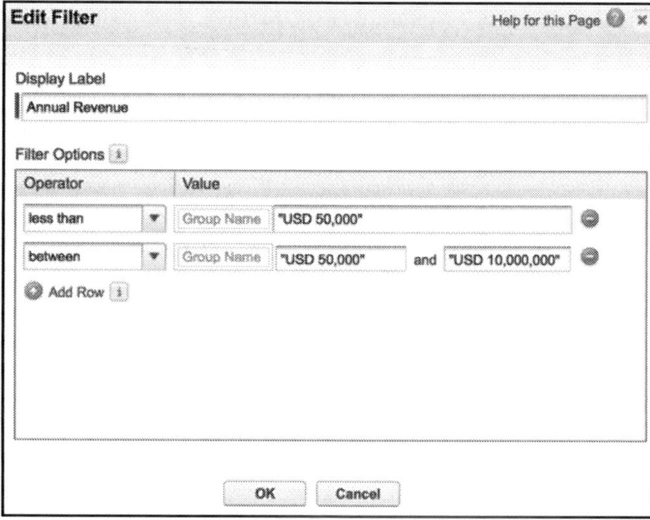

6. Once you are done, click on **OK**. Then click on **Save**.

From the next time onward, whenever this dashboard is run, the user will see the option to filter dashboard data, similar to the following screenshot:

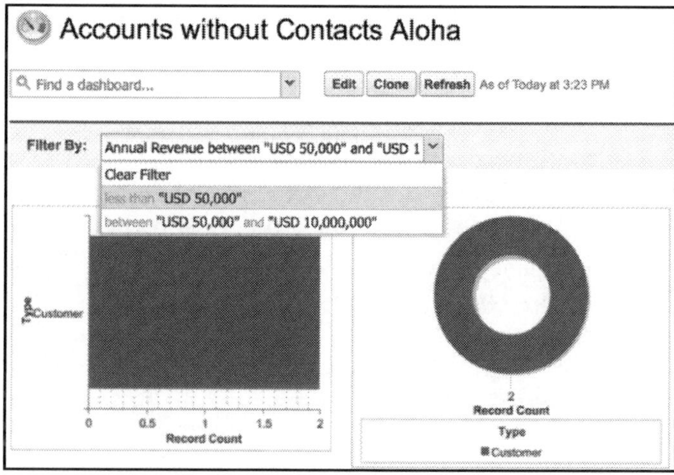

We can have maximum three filters in a dashboard, and each filter can have up to 10 filter values.

Reporting snapshot

Reporting or Analytics Snapshot allows us to build trend reports that are based upon historical data. We can either use a tabular or summary report to create a reporting snapshot. The column from the report is mapped to the fields in the custom object. Let's start with a business use case.

Say *David Guzman* is working as a *System Administrator* at Universal Containers. He has created a summary report called **Accounts without Contacts**. He has received a requirement to build a monthly historical trend report based upon the **Accounts with Order and Activities summary** report to check data improvement. Perform the following steps to solve the preceding business requirement:

1. We already have a summary report build, that is, **Accounts without Contacts**.
2. Create a custom object named **Account HB** (HB stands for historical backup).
3. Create a few custom fields in the **Account HB** custom object, **Account Name**, **Type**, and **Billing City** with the data type text.
4. Go to **Setup** (gear icon) | **Setup** | **PLATFORM TOOLS** | **Feature Settings** | **Analytics** | **Report & Dashboards** | **Reporting Snapshots**.
5. Click on the **New Reporting Snapshot** button, It will redirect you to the **New Analytic Snapshot** page where you will have to enter a few details mentioned as follows:

    - **Reporting Snapshot Name**: Enter a meaningful name for the reporting snapshot. In this case, enter `Account With Contact HB`.
    - **Reporting Snapshot Unique Name**: This will be auto-populated based on **Reporting Snapshot Name**.
    - **Description**: Name it with some meaningful text so other developers/administrators can easily understand why this reporting snapshot was created.
    - **Running User**: Choose a user in the **Running User** field by clicking on the lookup icon. The user in the **Running User** field determines the source report's level of access to data. This bypasses all security settings, giving all the users who can view the results of the source report in the target object access to data they might not be able to see otherwise.
    - **Source Report**: Select a source report from the drop-down list. In our case, select the **Account without Contacts** report.
    - **Target Object**: Select a custom object from the **Target Object** drop-down list. In our case, select the custom object `Account HB`.

The new reporting snapshot will look like the following screenshot:

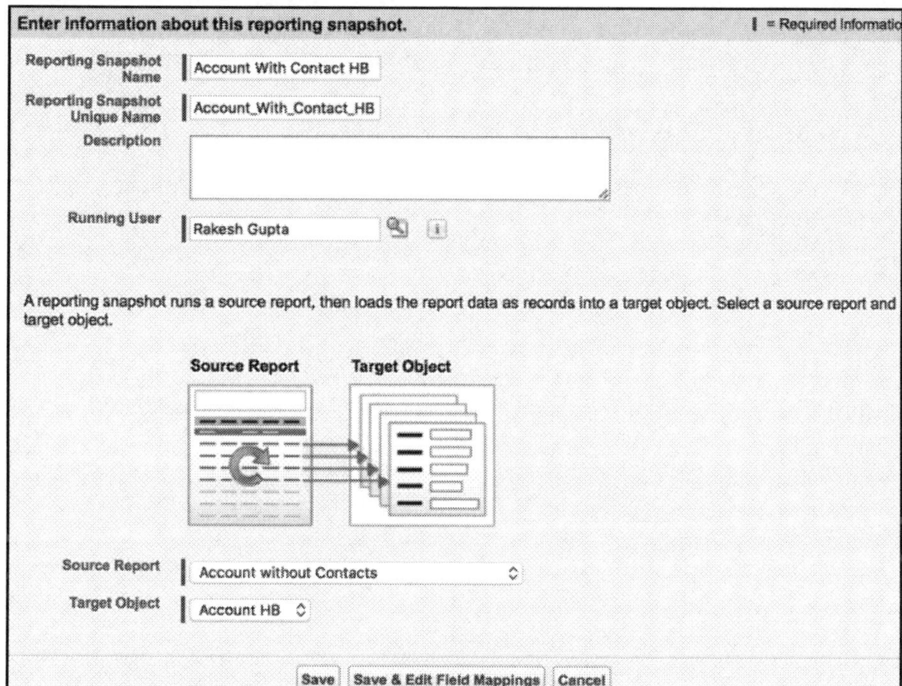

6. Once you are done, click on the **Save & Edit Field Mappings** button.
7. The next step is to map the report columns to custom object fields. Map it as you want.
8. The final step is to schedule the reporting snapshot. Navigate to the list related to **Schedule Reporting Snapshot** and click on **Edit**. It will allow you to set the schedule and frequency of the snapshot so that historical data could be captured as records in the custom object.
    1. Select the **Email reporting snapshot** setting. Then select the **To me** option to receive the e-mail when schedule will run in future.
    2. Set the frequency, duration, and time for running the report. In the **Frequency** field, select **Daily, Weekly, or Monthly** and then refine the frequency criteria. In our case, select **Monthly** and **last day of every month**.
    3. Use the **Start** and **End** date fields to specify the dates during which you want to schedule the report.

4. Next, to set **Preferred Start Time**, click on **Find available options...** to choose a start time. Your preferred start time might not be available if other users have already selected that time to schedule a report. Set **Preferred Start Time** to `12:00AM`.

Scheduling Reporting Snapshot will look like the following screenshot:

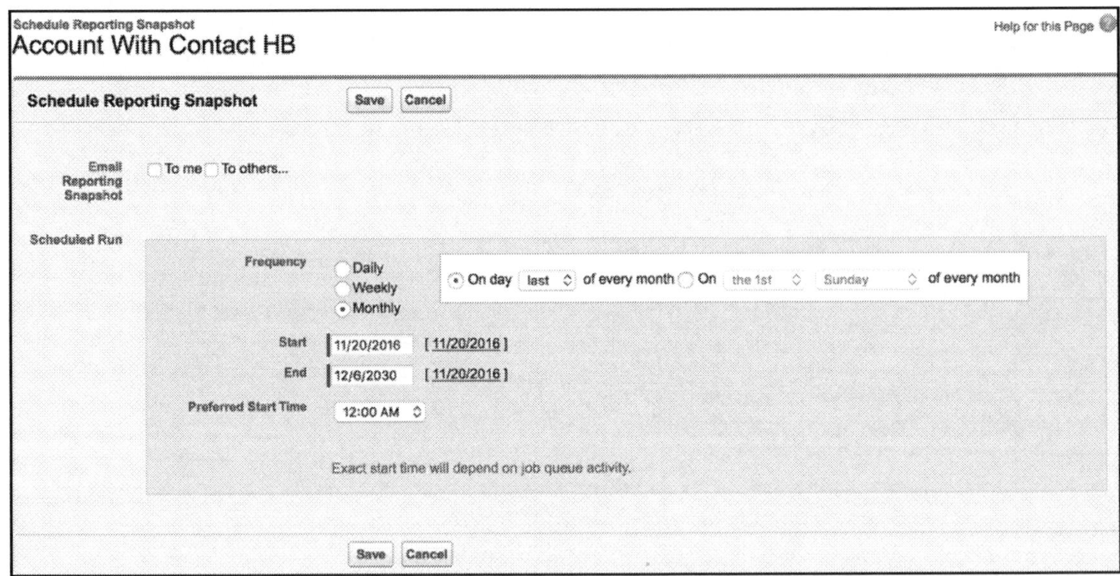

9. Once you are done, click on **OK**.

Now onward, on the last day of every month, at 12 AM, the reporting snapshot will run and store the data from the source report to the custom object as in records. Upon completion of this process, an e-mail will be sent to you with details of how many records were captured into the reporting snapshot.

A few points to remember

1. We can create a dashboard from a matrix or summary report.
2. A maximum of 2,000 rows will be displayed in a report. To view all the rows, export the report to Excel or use the printable view for tabular and summary reports. For joined reports, export is not available, and printable view will display a maximum of 20,000 rows.

3. In the report builder, up to 20 rows for summary and matrix reports and 50 rows for tabular reports will be displayed.
4. We can have up to 20 field filters in a report.
5. By default, reports time out after 10 minutes. You can contact Salesforce.com support to extend the timeout limit to 20 minutes for tabular, summary, and matrix reports, but no extension is possible for joined reports. It will continue to time out after every 10 minutes.
6. The maximum number of source report columns you can map to target fields is 100.
7. A reporting snapshot will fail during a scheduled run if the source report includes more than 100 fields.
8. A reporting snapshot will fail during a scheduled run if the target object is included in a workflow.
9. You can't use custom formula fields in a dashboard filter.
10. Filters aren't applied when you schedule or e-mail a dashboard.

Test your knowledge

Q1. A developer needs to create a trending report. What should he/she use to get the historical data?

1. Reports
2. Reporting snapshots
3. Roll-up summary
4. Report types
5. Audit history records

Q2. What will cause a reporting snapshot run to fail? Select three choices:

1. The source report has been deleted
2. The target object has a trigger on it
3. The running user has been deactivated
4. The target object is a custom object
5. The source report is saved as a matrix report

Q3. Which components of the dashboard use grand totals? Select two choices:

1. Metric
2. Table
3. Gauge
4. Chart

Q4. An application designed without considering requirements for reports are known as dashboards. Which of the following statements is correct?

1. The data model will support all the requirements of the application, including reports and dashboards
2. Reports are part of the application and application design will take care of it
3. No special considerations for reports or dashboards are required as Salesforce can natively take care of the requirements
4. The data model and the application will not cater to reports and dashboards

Q5. Dashboard refresh can be monitored using:

1. Apex jobs
2. Scheduled jobs
3. Dashboard jobs
4. Report jobs

Q6. The VP of Sales at Universal Container wants to monitor sales data from some period A to B. How could he/she achieve this?

1. With the help of a matrix report
2. Using reporting snapshot
3. Creating a record type for a report
4. Using a joined report

Q7. Which report type is used to group rows of data and show their subtotals?

1. Summary
2. Matrix
3. Tabular
4. Detailed

Q8. Which report type is used to group rows and columns of data and show their subtotals?

1. Summary
2. Matrix
3. Tabular
4. Detailed

Summary

In this chapter, first you learned about report types and how to create custom report types. Then, we moved ahead and discussed the different report formats available in Salesforce. We also spoke about building an exception report with cross filters and bucket fields, followed by dynamic dashboards and dashboard filters. At the end, we went through the concept of a reporting snapshot. In the next chapter, we will discuss various concepts related to mobile and e-mail administration in Salesforce.

10
E-mail and Mobile Administration

In the previous chapter, we went through various reports and dashboard concepts. We discussed different report types, ways to create custom report types, and how to create a dynamic dashboard. We followed this up with concepts such as dashboard filters and reporting snapshot. In this chapter, we will start a discussion on the key concepts of e-mail administration, such as deliverability, to make sure that a company or individual's e-mails reach the target audience. In addition to this, we will look at methods to configure compliance BCC e-mail address in your Salesforce organization. We will also cover the various mobile applications offered by Salesforce Inc. so you could learn how to better manage your Salesforce system. Finally, we will discuss ways of configuring these apps for your internal users. The following topics will be covered in this chapter:

- Deliverability
- Compliance BCC e-mail
- E-mail to Salesforce
- Overview of a SalesforceA application
- Overview of a Salesforce Authenticator application
- Overview of a Salesforce1 application

Deliverability

If you want to make sure the e-mails you send to your customers from Salesforce are delivered without issues, then configure deliverability settings. E-mail deliverability is a way to confirm that a company's or user's e-mails will reach their target recipient. It helps you reduce cycle time and erroneous e-mail traffic.

Access to send e-mails

Salesforce allows you to control outbound e-mail messages to better manage bounces and e-mail security compliance.

A business scenario: *David Guzman* is working as a *System Administrator* at Universal Containers. As part of the release management process, he has created a full copy sandbox. Now he wants to make sure that only system e-mails are allowed to be sent from the sandbox.

Perform the following steps to solve the preceding business requirement:

1. Go to **Setup** (gear icon) | **Setup** | **ADMINISTRATION** | **Email** | **Deliverability**.
2. Navigate to the **Access to Send Email** section and select the **Access level** dropdown.

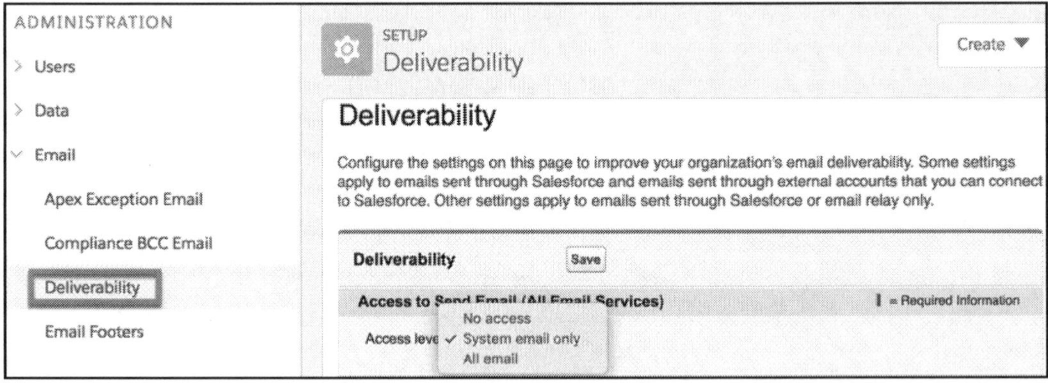

The following are the various types of access levels available along with their descriptions:

- **No access**: This will prevent all the outbound e-mails to and from users. Workflow e-mail alerts will not work if you select this option.
- **System email only**: This option will allow you to send autogenerated e-mails, such as new user and password reset e-mails. These settings are very useful for controlling the e-mails sent from sandboxes so that testing and development-related test e-mails are not sent to your users.
- **All email**: This option will allow you to send all types of outbound e-mails.

3. Select the **System email only** access level, as shown in the preceding screenshot.
4. Once you are done, click on **Save**.

Bounce administration

Bounce e-mail administration features help you make sure that the e-mail addresses you have for your leads, contacts, and person accounts are valid. They also help you ensure that the e-mail your users send to these e-mail addresses are not blocked due to extreme e-mail bounces.

A business scenario: *David Guzman* is working as a *System Administrator* at Universal Containers. His company has thousands of sales and service reps who are sending e-mails to their customers. His manager, *Brigette Hyacinth,* would like to activate bounce management at Universal Containers. She also wants to make sure that if an e-mail is bounced for any reason, an alert would be displayed to all the records of the e-mail address.

Perform the following steps to solve the preceding business requirement:

1. Go to **Setup** (gear icon) | **Setup** | **ADMINISTRATION** | **Email** | **Deliverability**.
2. Navigate to the **Bounce Management** section and then select the **Activate bounce management** checkbox to enable bounce management.

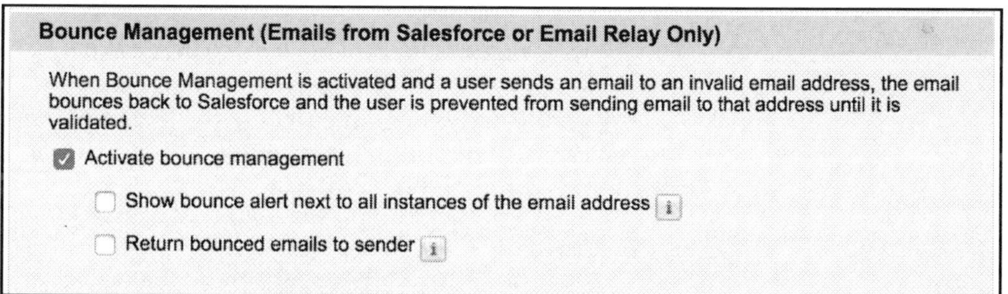

From now onwards, if users try to send an e-mail to a lead, contact, or person account with an invalid e-mail address in their record, the e-mail will bounce to Salesforce and the user will be banned from sending another e-mail to that particular lead, contact, or person account until the address is updated or confirmed.

Bounce administration also allows you to select what happens when an e-mail is bounced by selecting the following checkboxes available under **Activate bounce management**:

- **Show bounce alert next to all instances of the email address**: If this checkbox is not selected, Salesforce will only display a bounce alert to the record from where the e-mail was originally sent.
- **Return bounced emails to sender**: If this checkbox is not selected, then Salesforce will display the bounce alert but discard the bounce message. This feature is not recommended if you are using an e-mail relay.

3. Select the **Show bounce alert next to all instances of the email address** checkbox to fulfil the business requirement, as shown in the following screenshot:

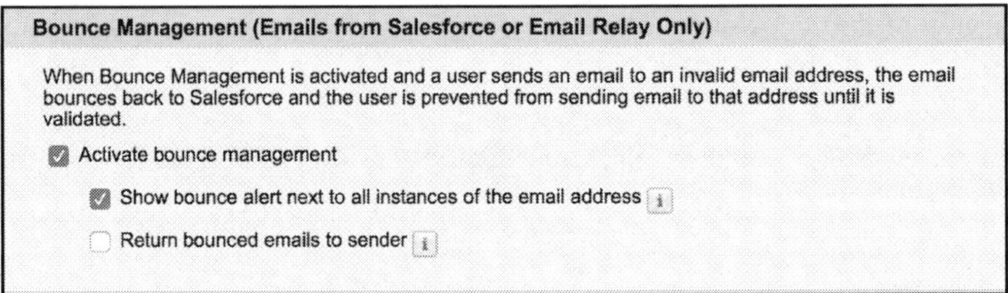

Bounce alert means this, for example. If you are sending an e-mail to your contact or lead, it is possible the e-mail address you have in Salesforce is incorrect. If Salesforce is unable to deliver an e-mail to the recipient, an alert will show up next to the address and other users will not be able to send an e-mail to the address until it's updated or confirmed.

4. Once you are done, click on **Save**.

E-mail security compliance

E-mail security compliance increases the chance of delivering an e-mail to recipients. Also, it automatically modifies the "from" address of every e-mail you send from Salesforce to comply with the e-mail security framework that your recipients might have implemented, such as **Sender Policy Framework** (**SPF**).

If you enable sender ID compliance, it would mean that the e-mails your users would send to your customers from Salesforce will come from an authorized IP address. Perform the following steps to enable e-mail security compliance for your Salesforce organization:

1. Go to **Setup** (gear icon) | **Setup** | **ADMINISTRATION** | **Email** | **Deliverability**.
2. Navigate to the **Email Security Compliance** section, then select the checkboxes as shown in the following screenshot to enable them:

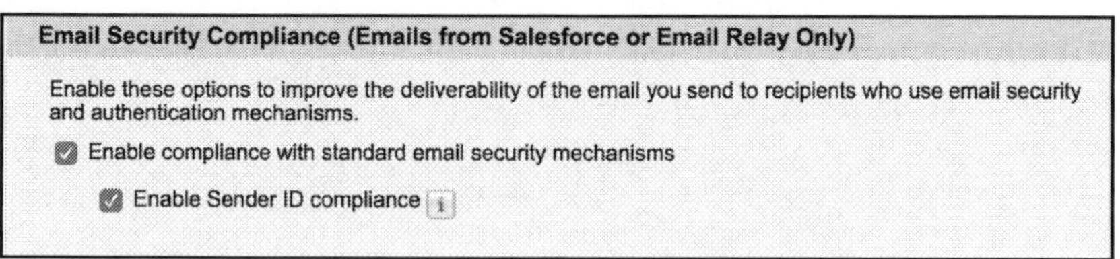

   This modifies the Sender field in the e-mails that are sent out from Salesforce to automatically include `no-reply@Salesforce.com`. For example, if you are sending out an e-mail, all the replies from your customers would still be delivered to your e-mail address. The customer's e-mail client (not Salesforce) may append the phrase *Sent on behalf of* to the **From** field of e-mails sent from Salesforce.

3. Once you are done, click on **Save**.

Compliance BCC e-mail

Compliance BCC e-mail helps your organization forward a copy of outgoing e-mails to a specific e-mail address. This is so that you have all your e-mails in one place for security and compliance purposes. In Salesforce, you can easily set up Compliance BCC e-mails to automatically send a copy of each outbound e-mail to a specific e-mail address.

A business scenario: *David Guzman* is working as *System Administrator* at Universal Containers. He has received a requirement from the company's legal team: they would like to have all the outgoing e-mails sent by sales or service reps from Salesforce forwarded to a particular e-mail address, say, `legal@universalcontainers.com`.

Perform the following steps to solve the preceding business requirement:

1. Go to **Setup** (gear icon) | **Setup** | **ADMINISTRATION** | **Email** | **Compliance BCC Email**.
2. Select the **Enable** checkbox and then enter the e-mail address, as shown in the screenshot:

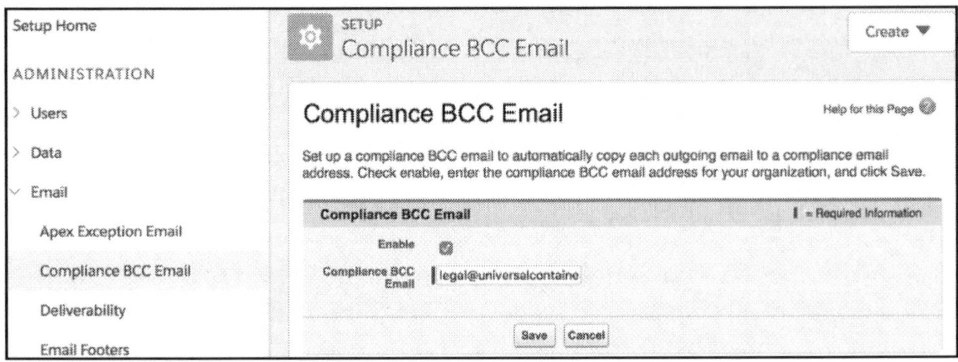

3. Once you are done, click on **Save**.

Compliance BCC Email excludes system generated e-mails, such as password reset or import completion notifications.

Compliance BCC e-mails prevent users from editing the BCC field on any e-mail and disables their automatic BCC setting under **My Email Settings**.

E-mail to Salesforce

Salesforce allows your reps to send an e-mail to leads, contacts, and person accounts. Some of them prefer Salesforce to send e-mails, but some prefer the company-provided third-party e-mail client to send e-mails, for example, *Outlook 365*, *Google for Work*, and so on.

If your reps send e-mails from Salesforce, then a copy of the e-mail will be saved as a record. If they use a third-party e-mail client, say, Outlook 365, to send e-mails to customers, then those e-mails will not be saved in Salesforce. If you want to keep a record of each e-mail sent from a third-party e-mail client to the leads, contacts, opportunities, and other records, use **Email to Salesforce**.

This allows you to keep a copy of each e-mail in Salesforce, for e-mails, those are sent from the third-party e-mail client. You simply need to BCC your e-mail to the Salesforce organization-specific e-mail address while sending an e-mail from a third-party e-mail client. If the e-mail address in the **to** section of your e-mail matches the e-mail address of the lead, contacts, or opportunities, then Salesforce will create a task with the corresponding record, and it will be shown under the activity history of the record. Alternatively, you can keep this as an unresolved item and later assign it to some other user.

A business scenario: *David Guzman* is working as *System Administrator* at Universal Containers. His manager, *Brigette Hyacinth,* would like to activate **Email to Salesforce** at Universal Containers. *David Guzman* is an experienced Salesforce administrator; he also wants to set up **Email to Salesforce** for himself.

Perform the following steps to solve the preceding business requirement:

1. Go to **Setup** (gear icon) | **Setup** | **ADMINISTRATION** | **Email** | **Email to Salesforce**.
2. On the **Email to Salesforce** page, click on the **Edit** button:

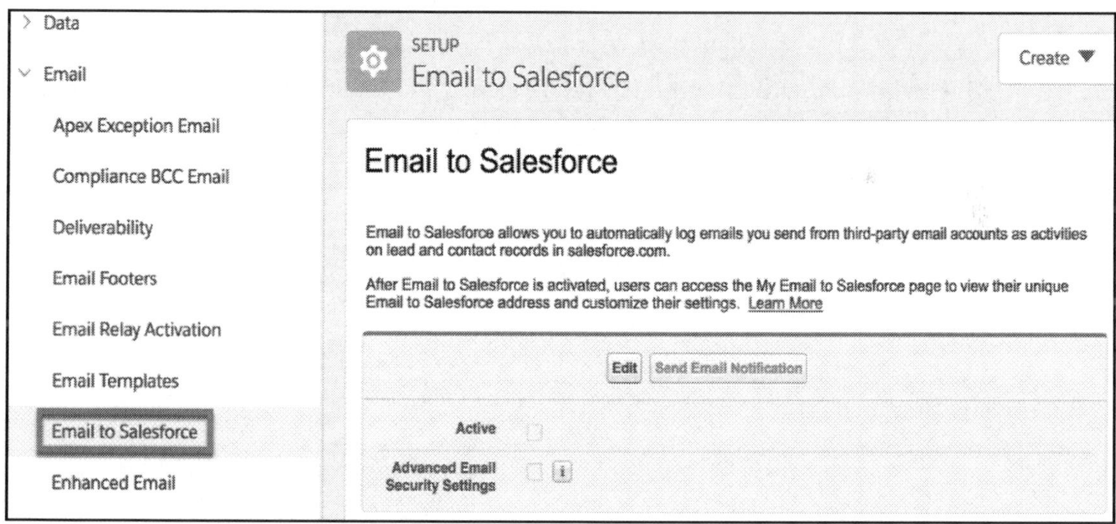

3. Select the **Active** checkbox. Optionally, you can select the **Advanced Email Security Settings** checkbox to configure **Email to Salesforce**; this will verify the legitimacy of the sending server before processing a message:

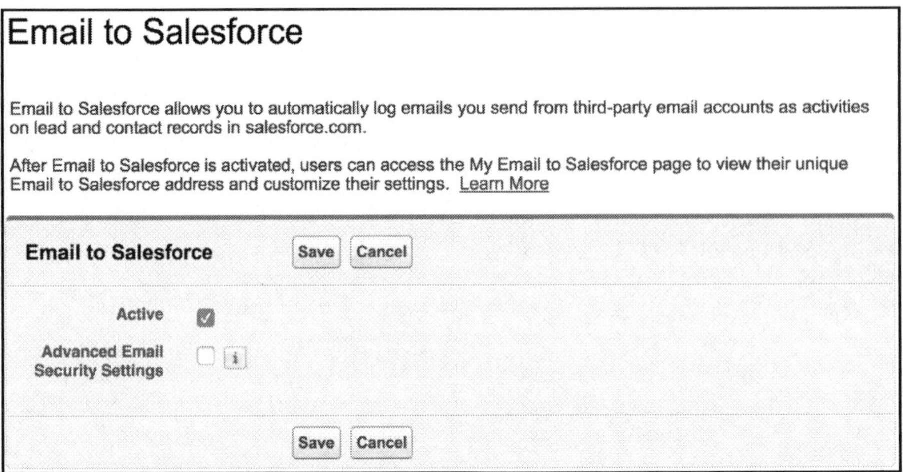

4. Once you are done, click on **Save**.
5. Now Salesforce will ask you to send a notification to all the users indicating that the administrator has enabled **Email to Salesforce**, and it will include a link to get started with the **Email to** setup for individual users:

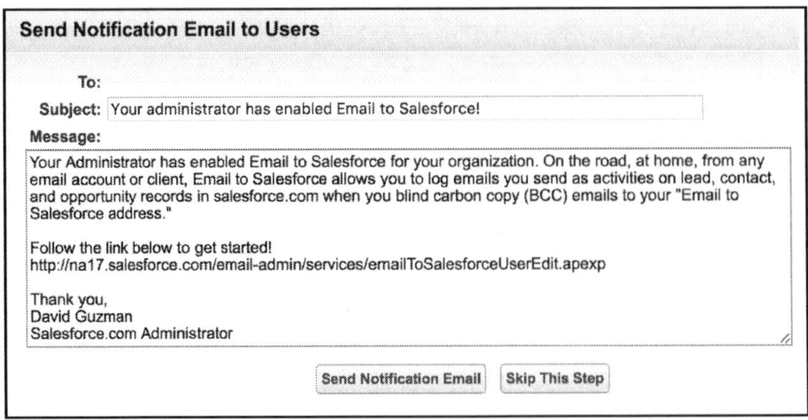

6. Once you are done, click on the **Send Notification** or **Skip This Step** button.

Autogenerating the Email to Salesforce e-mail address

Each user has to set up their own **Email to Salesforce** URL. Salesforce generates a unique user-specific **Email to Salesforce** e-mail address that is to be used by the user to send e-mails as BCC.

Perform the following steps to configure **Email to Salesforce** for own use:

1. Click **Switcher** | **Settings**:

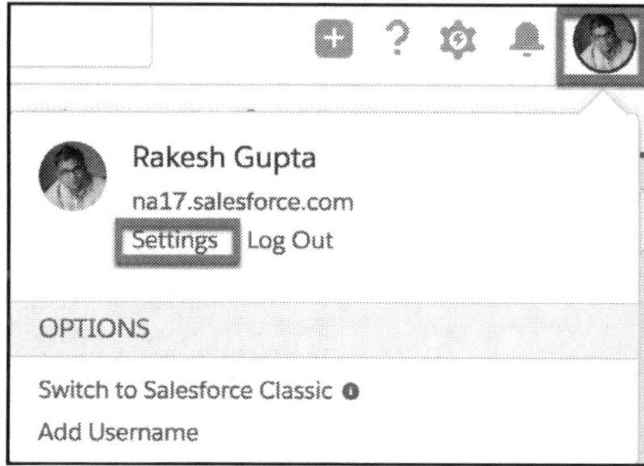

2. Then go to **Email** | **My Email to Salesforce**.
3. Now you will be able to see **Your Email to Salesforce addresses** in the **My Email to Salesforce** section of the page:

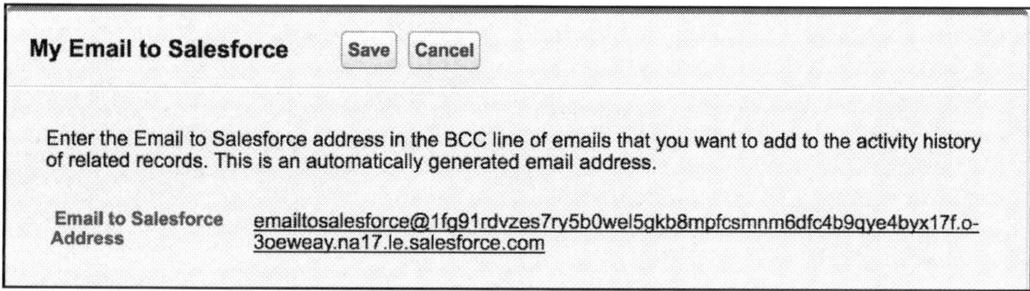

4. You can set the e-mail addresses you will use to send e-mails from **Email to Salesforce address** in the **My Acceptable Email Addresses** field separated by commas. Only e-mails received from an e-mail address you specify under **Email to Salesforce address** will be added to the activity history of related records. Unauthorized sender error will be bounced otherwise.

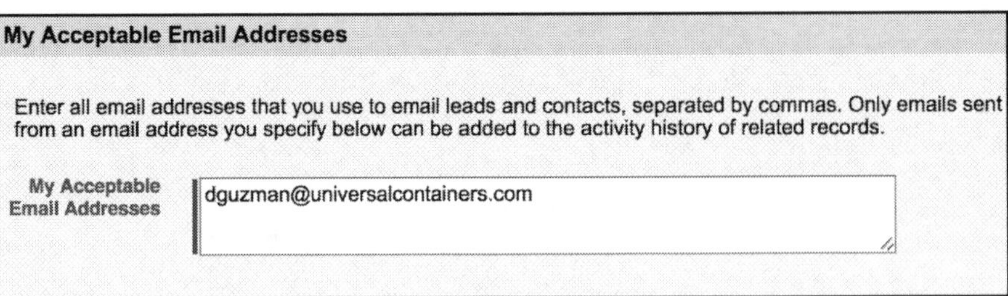

5. Additionally, you can decide the association of e-mails that are sent to Salesforce with a record. By default, it is set to **Automatically assign them to related salesforce.com records**. You can also select the **Always save email attachment** and **Email me confirmation of creation** checkboxes:

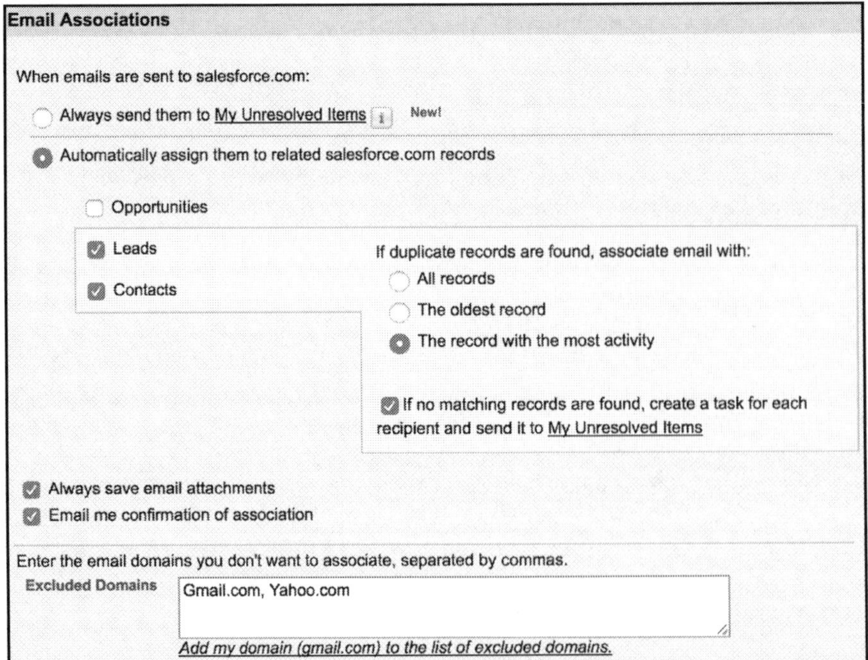

6. Once you are done, click on **Save**.

From the next time, if you send an e-mail to a lead or contacts from your third-party e-mail client and BCC your **Email to Salesforce** address, an e-mail will automatically be associated with the records under the Activity-related list. You will also get a confirmation e-mail from Salesforce with a link of the record where the e-mail is attached under the list related to **Activity History**.

Overview of the SalesforceA mobile application

SalesforceA is a mobile application for system administrators. It allows them to do their work on the fly while walking on the road or travelling in a bus or train.

Options available in the SalesforceA mobile application

A SalesforceA mobile comes with various features. Here are the actions that a Salesforce administrator can perform through the SalesforceA mobile application:

1. Get the current system status
2. Check a user's login history
3. Freeze a user's action
4. Unlock and deactivate a user's account
5. Edit a user's account
6. Reset password
7. Add and remove permission sets
8. Create a new user
9. Access to Trailhead, Success Community, Release Notes and Admin News
10. Reassigning licenses

Installing the SalesforceA mobile application

Users can download the SalesforceA mobile application from iTunes or Google Play. It is supported by the following devices:

- Android phone or tablet with OS 4.4 or higher
- Apple iPhone, iPad, and iPod Touch with iOS 8.0 or higher

Use the following links to download the SalesforceA application for your device:

- **iTunes**: `https://itunes.apple.com/in/app/salesforcea/id731117958?mt=8`.
- **Play Store**: `https://play.google.com/store/apps/details?id=com.salesforce.admin1&hl=en`.

Logging in to the SalesforceA mobile application

Perform the following steps to login into the SalesforceA mobile application:

1. Click on the **SalesforceA** mobile app icon on your device.
2. Enter your login credentials and verification code.
3. Allow the SalesforceA application to access your Salesforce basic information.
4. The first time it will ask you to set a passcode, and from the next time, you just have to enter this passcode to access the SalesforceA application.
5. It will redirect you to the application home page, which will look like the following screenshot:

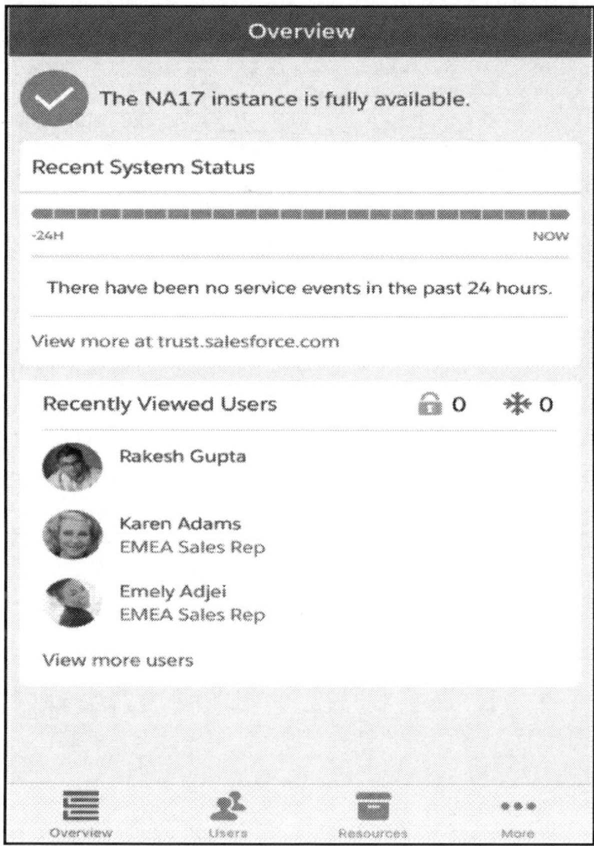

6. Now start administrating your Salesforce organization from anywhere.

Overview of the Salesforce Authenticator application

The Salesforce Authenticator application allows you to generate a time-based token. It will help you implement two factor authentications for your account.

Installing the Salesforce Authenticator mobile application

You can download the Salesforce Authenticator mobile application from iTunes or Google Play. It is supported by the following devices:

- Android phone or tablet with OS 4.2 or higher
- Apple iPhone and iPod Touch with iOS 7.0 or higher

Use the following links to download the Salesforce Authenticator application for your device:

- **iTunes**: `https://itunes.apple.com/us/app/salesforce/id782057975?ls=1&mt=8.`
- **Play Store**: `https://play.google.com/store/apps/details?id=com.salesforce.authenticator.`

Overview of the Salesforce1 mobile application

Salesforce1 is a mobile application for users to create, update, and delete records from anywhere. It also allows users to view reports and dashboards and access Chatter functionality through it.

Features of the Salesforce1 mobile application

Salesforce1 comes with various features. The following are a few actions that a user can perform through it: read, create, update, and delete records, including changing the owner of records. Using this application, you can create and edit records offline as well and also perform the following:

- Send push notifications
- Submit a record for approval
- Access a list view and related list
- Access all your custom objects and apps through the navigation menu
- Access Visualforce pages and components in the navigation menu

- Access Salesforce files
- Access reports, dashboards, and Lightning charts
- Get insights into accounts and opportunities through a news app

Installing the Salesforce1 mobile application

You can download the Salesforce1 mobile application from iTunes or Google Play. It is supported by the following devices:

- Android phone or tablet with OS 4.4 or higher
- Apple iPhone and iPod Touch with iOS 9.2 or higher

Use the following links to download the Salesforce1 application for your device:

- **iTunes:** `https://itunes.apple.com/in/app/salesforce1/id404249815?mt=8.`
- **Play Store:** `https://play.google.com/store/apps/details?id=com.salesforce.chatter&hl=en.`

Enabling Salesforce1 for a mobile browser

Let's see how to allow your user to access the Salesforce1 application through a supported mobile browser. Perform the following steps to enable Salesforce1 for a mobile browser:

1. Go to **Setup** (gear icon) | **Setup** | **PLATFORM TOOLS** | **Apps** | **Mobile Apps** | **Salesforce1 Settings**.
2. Navigate to **Mobile Browser App Settings** and select the **Enable the Salesforce1 mobile browser app** checkbox, as shown in the following screenshot:

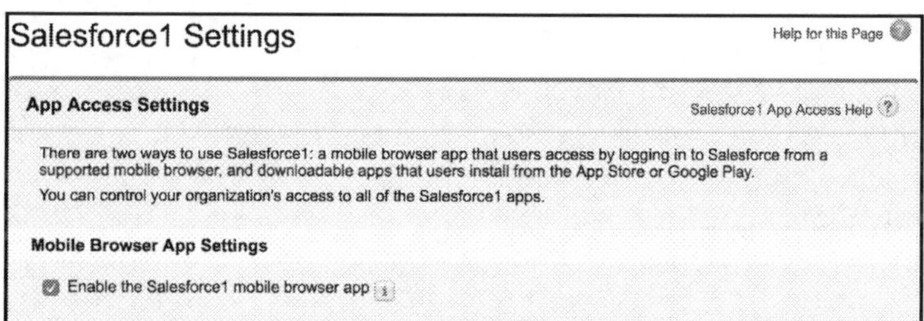

3. Once you are done, click on **Save**.

Granting Salesforce1 access to users

If you are looking for a way to automatically redirect your user to the Salesforce1 mobile browser app when they log in to Salesforce from a supported mobile browser, perform the following steps:

1. Go to **Setup** (gear icon) | **Setup** | **ADMINISTRATION** | **Users** | **Users**.
2. Edit your user record and select the **Salesforce1 User** checkbox, as shown in the following screenshot:

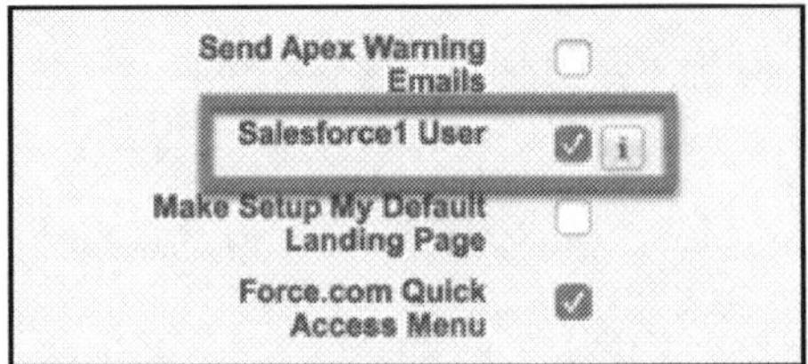

   If you turn this option off, your mobile browser would be directed to the full Salesforce site instead.

3. Once you are done, click on **Save**.

Controlling which users can use the Salesforce1 application

Salesforce1- and SalesforceA-downloadable apps are connected apps. It means, Salesforce allows you to control the users who have access to these apps, including other security policies. By default, all the users in your organization can use Salesforce1-downloadable apps. As these are connected apps, the system administrator will have control over security and access policies of each of the Salesforce1-downloadable apps. He or she will be able to do this using the settings components that are installed from the managed Salesforce1-connected apps package. When one of your users installs a Salesforce1 app from *iTunes Store* or *Google Play Store* on a mobile device and authenticates by logging in to the mobile app, then these components will automatically get installed. The same is applicable for a SalesforceA-downloadable app.

Setting up connected apps for Salesforce1

Salesforce1-downloadable apps are connected apps and they allow the system administrator to control security and access policies.

A business scenario: *David Guzman* is working as *System Administrator* at Universal Containers. As part of a pilot program, his manager, *Brigette Hyacinth*, would like to enable Salesforce1 for an iOS-downloadable application access only to the *Contract Manager* profile.

To solve the preceding business requirement, first we will have to limit Salesforce1-downloadable apps and then use the profile or permission set to grant access. Perform the following steps to do this:

1. Go to **Setup** (gear icon) | **Setup** | **PLATFORM TOOLS** | **Apps** | **Connected Apps** | **Manage Connected Apps**.
2. Now click on **Edit** next to **Salesforce1 for iOS**, as shown in the following screenshot:

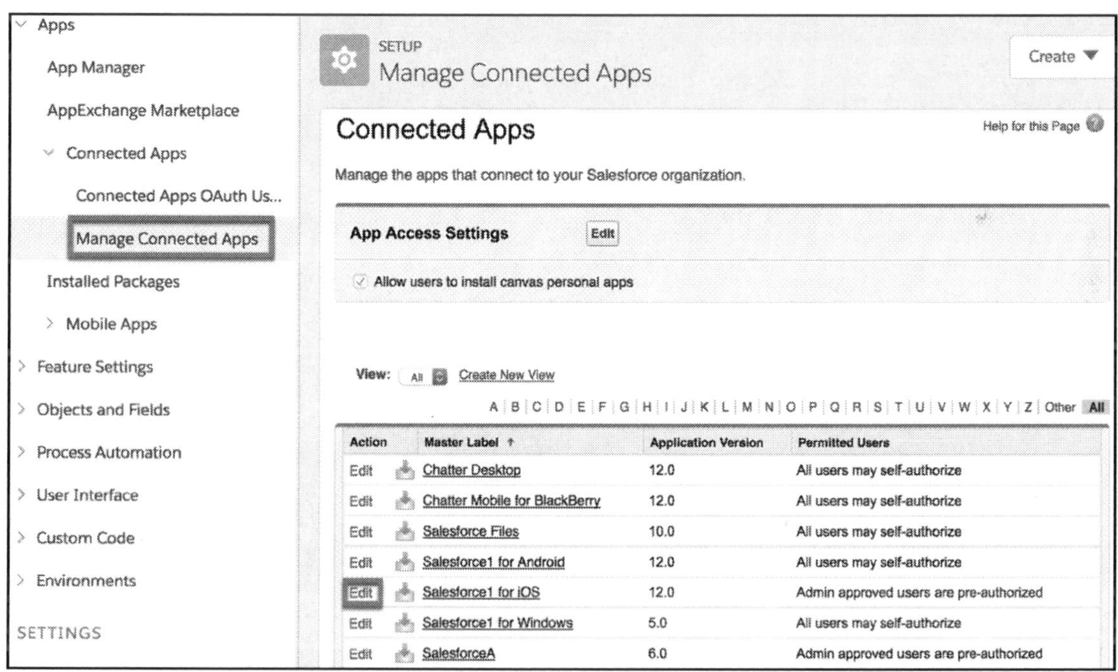

3. The next step is to change the **Permitted Users** dropdown from **All Users may self-authorize** to **Admin-approved users are pre-authorized**:
    - **All Users may self-authorize**: This means any user in the org can self-authorize the app first time they access it.
    - **Admin-approved users are pre-authorized**: This means access is limited to users who have the correct permission to access it via a profile or permission set.
4. For better security management, change **IP Relaxation** from **Relax IP Restrictions** to **Enforce IP restrictions** (user running a Salesforce1 app is subject to the organization's IP restrictions, for example, IP ranges set in the user's profile) and set the **Refresh Token Policy** validity.
5. To enhance security, make sure you set **Timeout Value** and enforce the PIN for it.

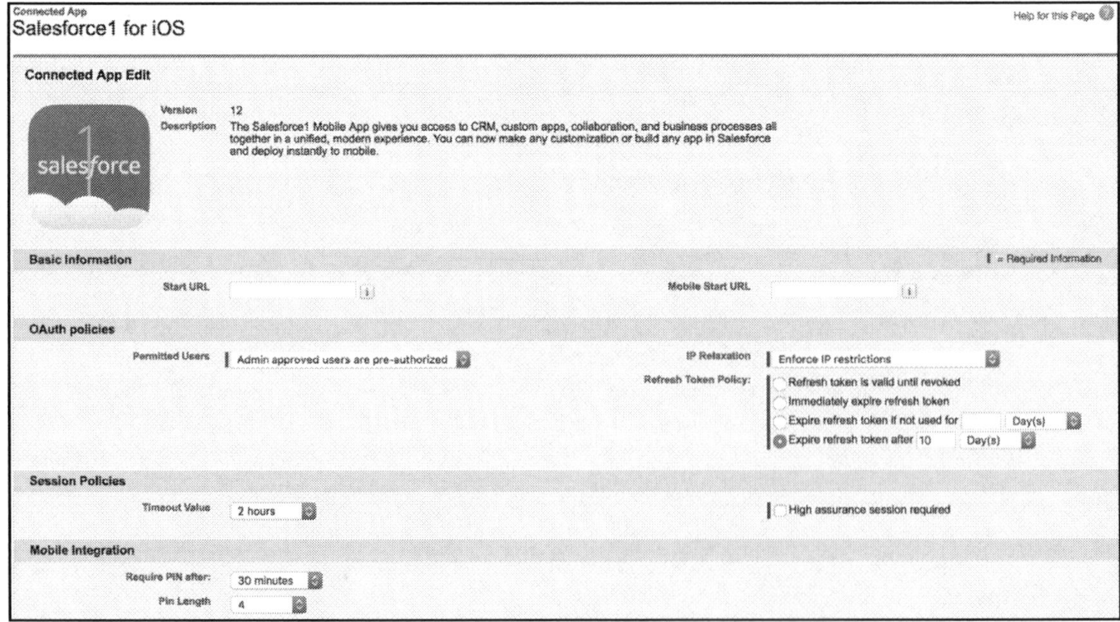

At the end, it will look like the preceding screenshot.

6. Once you are done, click on **Save**.

Granting a Salesforce1-downloadable app access to users

To grant a Salesforce1-downloadable app access to **Contract Manager** profile users, we have the following options:

- **Grant Permission through Profile**
- **Grant Permission through Permission Sets**

We will use Profile to grant the Salesforce1-downloadable app access, for the preceding business requirement we will use **Contract Manager** profile. Perform the following steps to grant permission through a profile:

1. Go to **Setup** (gear icon) | **Setup** | **PLATFORM TOOLS** | **Apps** | **Connected Apps** | **Manage Connected Apps**.
2. Click on the app connected to **Salesforce1 for iOS**; as **Permitted Users** is now set to **Admin approved users are pre-authorized Profile and Permission Sets,** related lists are automatically added to it.
3. Now navigate to the list related to **Profiles** and click on the **Manage Profiles** button.
4. The next step is to select the **Contract Manager** profile.
5. Once you are done, click on **Save**.

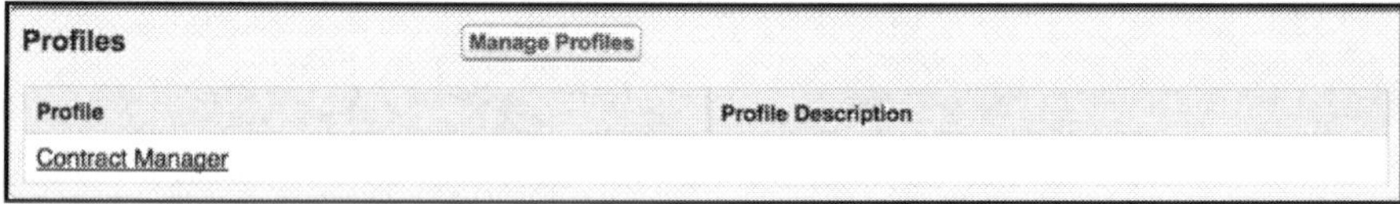

At the end, it will look like the preceding screenshot. Repeat the same step if you want to enable **Salesforce1 for Android** and **Salesforce1 for Windows** for the **Contract Manager** profile.

Logging in to a Salesforce1 application

Perform the following steps to log in to a Salesforce1 mobile application:

1. Click on the **Salesforce1** mobile app icon on your device.
2. Enter your login credentials and activation code.
3. The next step is to allow the Salesforce1 application access your Salesforce basic information.

4. The first time it will ask you to set **passcode**, and from the next time, you just have to enter this passcode to access the Salesforce1 application.
5. At the end, it will redirect you to the application home page. It will look like the following screenshot:

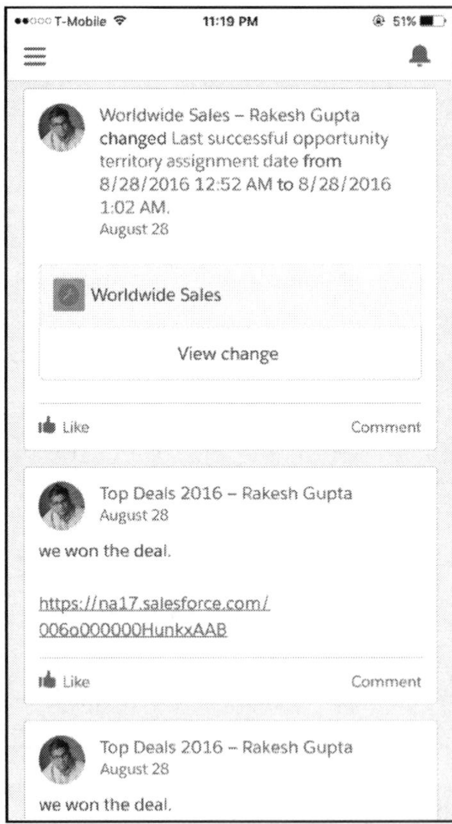

If a user does not belong to the **Contract Manager** profile and tries to access Salesforce from a Salesforce1-downloadable app, then he or she will get an error. This will be similar to the following screenshot:

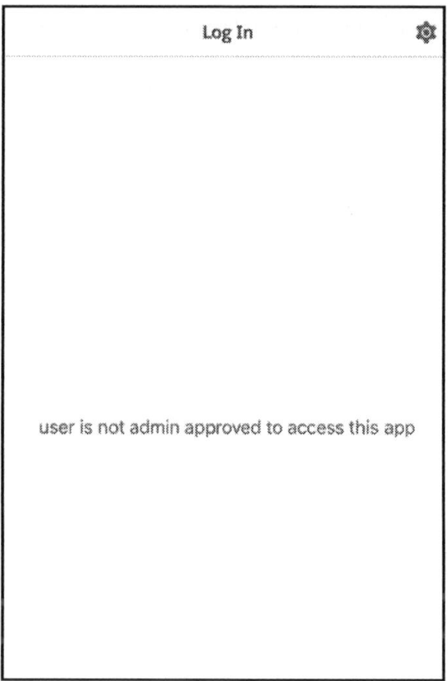

6. Now start creating, updating, or deleting records or collaborating with your user.

Branding of the Salesforce1 application

You can now brand the Salesforce1 mobile application that matches your company's branding. For example, you can now change the Salesforce1 app's loading page logo and loading page background color and brand color. Perform the following steps to brand the Salesforce1 mobile application:

1. Go to **Setup** (gear icon) | **Setup** | **PLATFORM TOOLS** | **Apps** | **Mobile Apps** | **Salesforce1 Branding**.
2. Navigate to the **Salesforce1 Branding Settings** section, then click on the **Edit** button.
3. To customize **Brand Color** for key user interface elements, including the header, click on **Brand Color** and then select a color.
4. To customize **Loading Page Color** of the loading page, click on **Loading Page Color** and then select a color.

5. To customize **Loading Page Logo**, select an image of the type `.jpg`, `.gif`, or `.png` files up to 200 KB in size. The maximum image size is 460 pixels by 560 pixels.

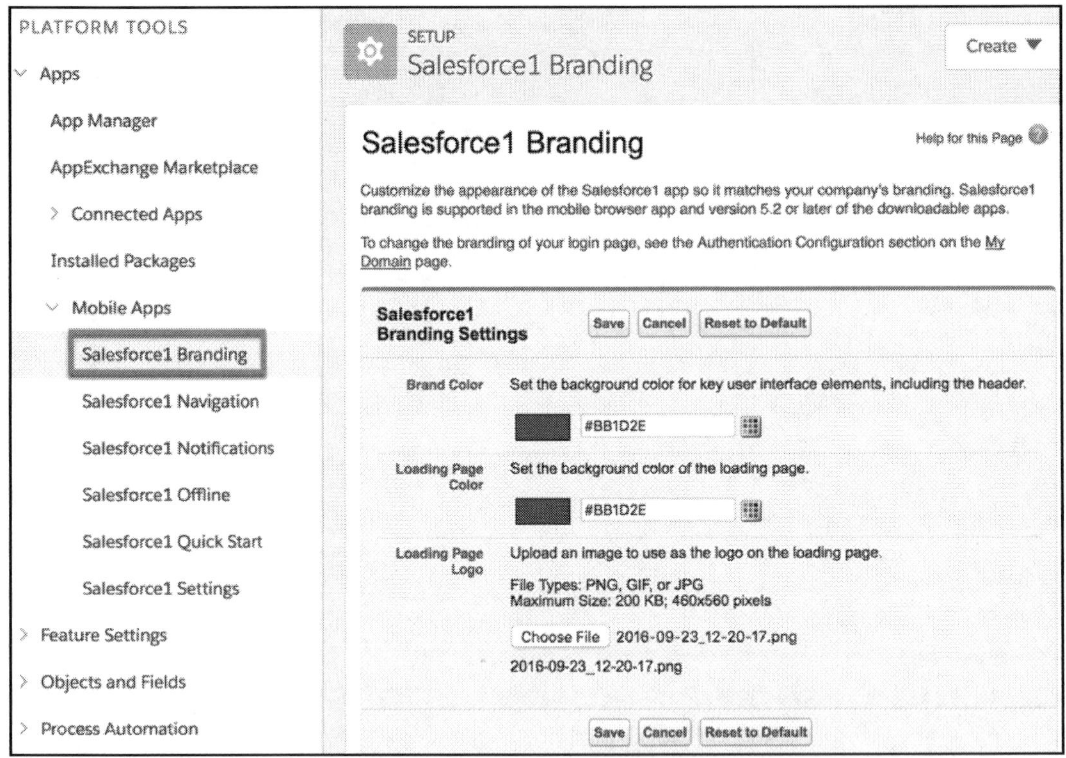

6. Once you are done, click on **Save**.

Enabling offline access for Salesforce1

Now you can safeguard Salesforce1 users against the whims of mobile connectivity. This allows you to enable two levels of offline access:

1. Enable caching for frequently accessed records so users can view data when offline.
2. Enable the option through which users could create, edit, and delete records even when offline. Offline access is available in Salesforce1-downloadable apps only.

Perform the following steps to enable Salesforce1 offline access for your Salesforce organization:

1. Go to **Setup** (gear icon) | **Setup** | **PLATFORM TOOLS** | **Apps** | **Mobile Apps** | **Salesforce1 Offline**.
2. Navigate to the **Offline Settings** section, then select the **Enable offline create, edit, and delete in Salesforce1** checkbox as shown in the following screenshot:

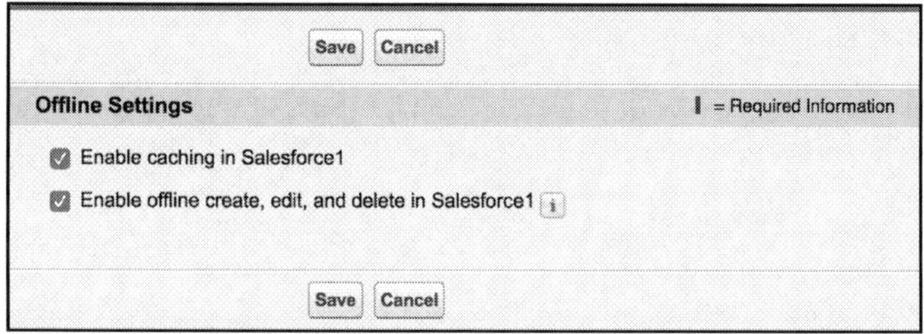

   The **Enable caching in Salesforce1** checkbox is automatically enabled when the first time someone from your organization installs one of the Salesforce1-downloadable application.

3. Once you are done, click on **Save**.

A few points to remember

1. E-mail deliverability is a way to confirm that your company's or user's e-mails reach their target recipient.
2. If you want to keep a record of each e-mail sent to the leads, contacts, opportunities, and other records from a third-party e-mail client, then use **Email to Salesforce**.
3. Use connected apps to restrict Salesforce1-downloadable apps from accessing specific users.
4. Using a SalesforceA downloadable app, you can check a user's login history.

Test your knowledge

Q1. When you want to restrict a Salesforce1-downloadable app from accessing specific users, which of the following sharing model will you use? Choose two options:

1. Profile
2. Permission set
3. Connected apps
4. Restrict IP address

Q2. Using a SalesforceA-downloadable app, which of the following actions we can't perform?

1. Resetting a user's password
2. Assigning permission sets
3. Creating a new user
4. Freezing a user account

Q3. Enabling caching in Salesforce1 allows users to access records offline. Is this:

1. True
2. False

Q4. What are the different Salesforce-downloadable applications available for business users?

1. Salesforce1
2. SalesforceA
3. Salesforce Authenticator
4. Salesforce Chatter

Summary

In this chapter, we started with enabling e-mail deliverability. Then we moved ahead and discussed how to set up BCC e-mail and e-mail to Salesforce. We also learned how to enable a Salesforce1-downloadable app for a particular profile. At the end, we discussed how to enable Salesforce1 offline access.

In the next chapter, we will go through various ways to deploy applications or changes between Salesforce organizations.

11
Different Ways of Deploying an Application between Environments

In the previous chapter, we discussed different techniques to manage e-mail administration, including e-mail deliverability and bounce management. We also discussed Salesforce-downloadable applications: SalesforceA, Salesforce Authenticator, and Salesforce1. In this chapter, we will discuss different ways of deploying an application or changes between Salesforce environments. We'll cover the following topics:

- Deploying using change sets
- Deploying using the Force.com IDE
- Deploying using packages
- Deploying using Force.com migration tool

Once you start working on any application from scratch or enhancement, you mainly have to develop a schema, that is, metadata. It means you have to deploy the new metadata into production org as soon as development and testing are over. In another scenario, if you are working on a migration project from a legacy system to Salesforce. In such cases, you will have to deploy the newly developed metadata as well as the existing data (records from the legacy system) into production org. To deploy metadata between Salesforce environments, you can use change sets, Force.com IDE, packages, or Force.com migration tool. To deploy data from a legacy system into Salesforce, you can use data import wizard; Apex data loader; or a third-party tool such as Jitterbit data loader, dataloader.io, or Informatica Cloud Data Wizard. In this book, we are going to discuss various ways to deploy metadata between Salesforce environments.

Deploying using change sets

Using change sets is a classic way of deploying metadata from a Sandbox to a production org. It means if both the orgs are connected, you can use change sets to deploy the metadata. Change sets are containers that are used to send metadata from a Sandbox to a production org or to other Sandboxes. They can only hold metadata, meaning they will allow you to move or deploy only those changes or customizations that you would have made through the **Setup** menu. They don't allow you to migrate records from one organization to another. To use change sets, make sure that both the organizations have a deployment connection set up. There are two types of change sets available, and they are as follows:

- Outbound change sets
- Inbound change sets

Outbound change sets

Outbound change sets are those change sets that can be used to send metadata from a Sandbox to a production org or other Sandboxes.

A business scenario: *David Guzman* is working as a *System Administrator* at Universal Containers. In `Chapter 4`, *Extending Salesforce with Custom Objects and Applications* he created a custom object called **registration** in Sandbox. Now he wants to migrate this object to a production org.

Perform the following steps to create an outbound change set for the preceding business requirement:

1. Log in to your Sandbox org by visiting `https://test.salesforce.com.`
2. Go to **Setup** (gear icon) | **Setup** | **PLATFORM TOOLS** | **Environments** | **Change Sets** | **Outbound Change Sets** as shown in the following screenshot:

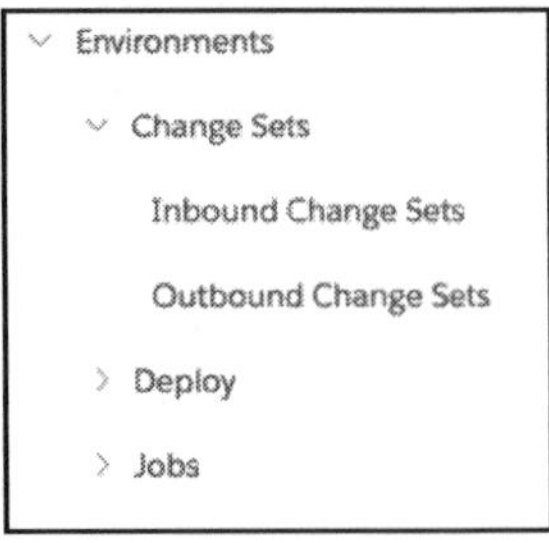

3. If you are accessing **Outbound Change Sets** for the first time, click on the **Continue** button.
4. Navigate to the **Change Sets** section, then click on the **New** button to create a new outbound change set, as shown in the following screenshot:

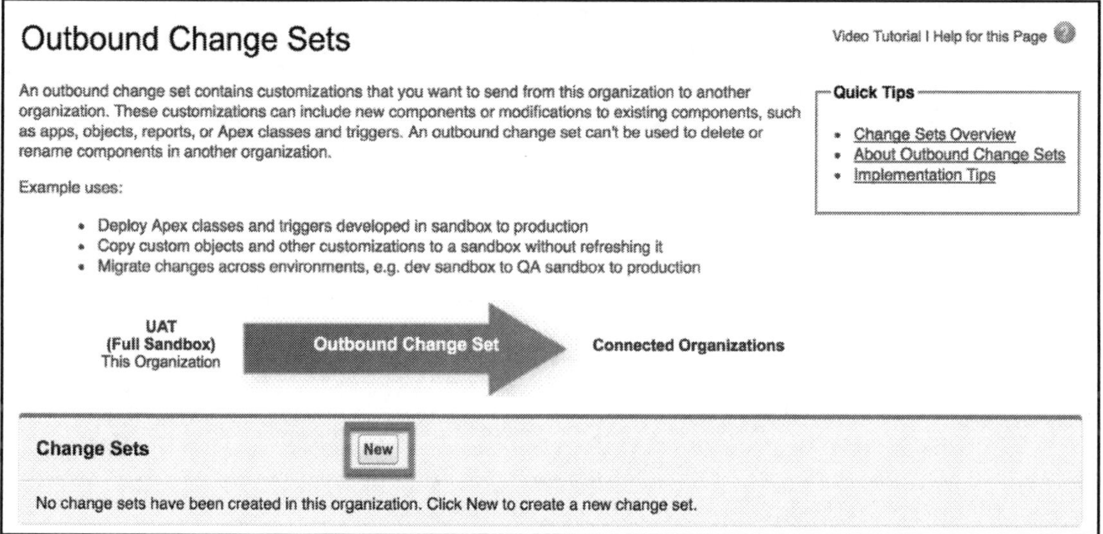

5. This will open a window for you where you have to enter the following details:
    1. **Name**: Enter a meaningful name for the outbound change set. Use `Registration App` as the name.
    2. **Description**: Write some meaningful text so other developers/administrators can easily understand why this outbound change set was created.

This will look like the following screenshot:

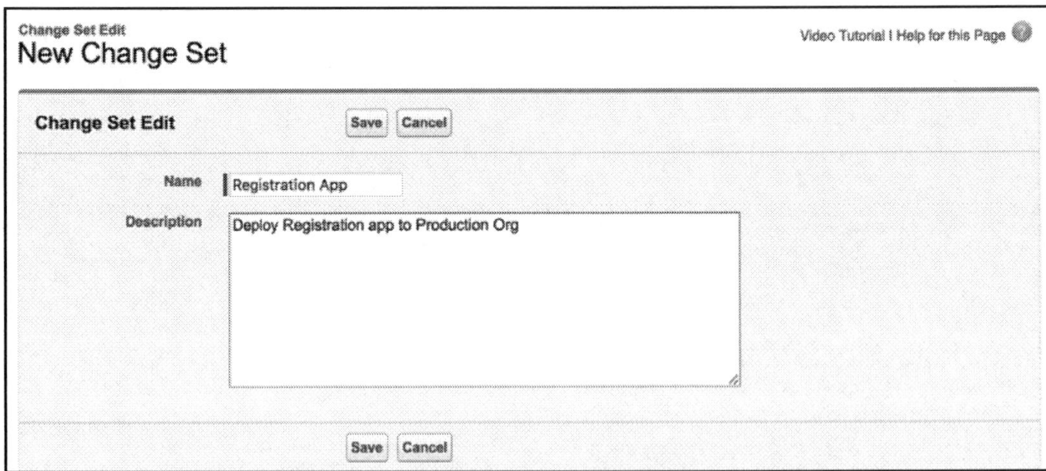

6. Once you are done, click on **Save**.
7. The next step is to add the components you want to deploy to a production org. To do this, navigate to the **Change Set Components** section and click on the **Add** button, as shown in the following screenshot:

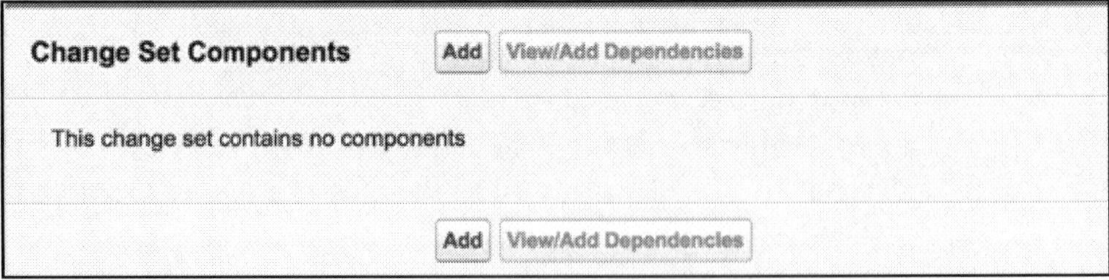

8. For **Component Type**, select **Custom Object** and then select the **Registration** custom object from the list:

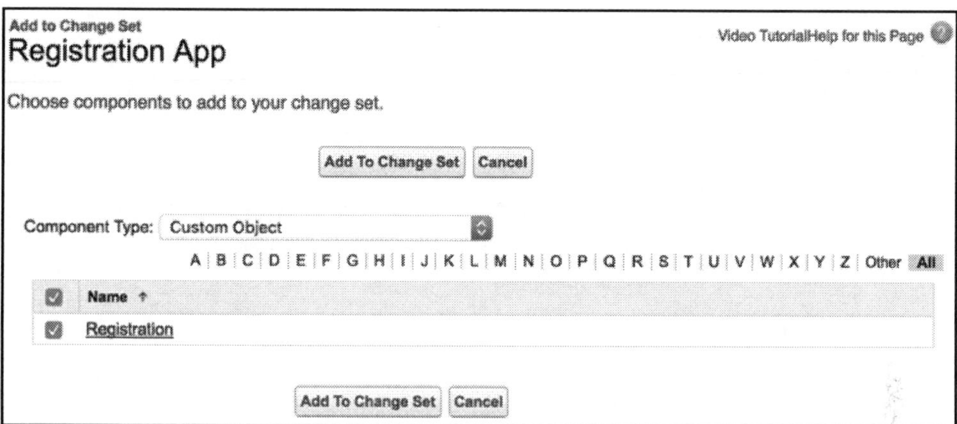

9. Repeat the preceding step if you want to add different components to the outbound change set. Once you are done, click on **Add To Change Set**.
10. Once you've added all your components to the outbound change set, the next step is to upload them. To do this, navigate to the **Change Set Detail** section and then click on **Upload**, as shown in the following screenshot:

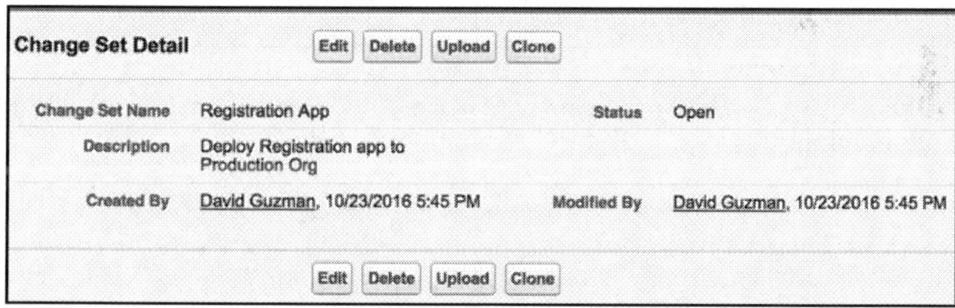

11. The final step is to select the target organization, under the **Upload Details** section, where you want to upload the change set. In this case, select **Production**, as shown in the following screenshot:

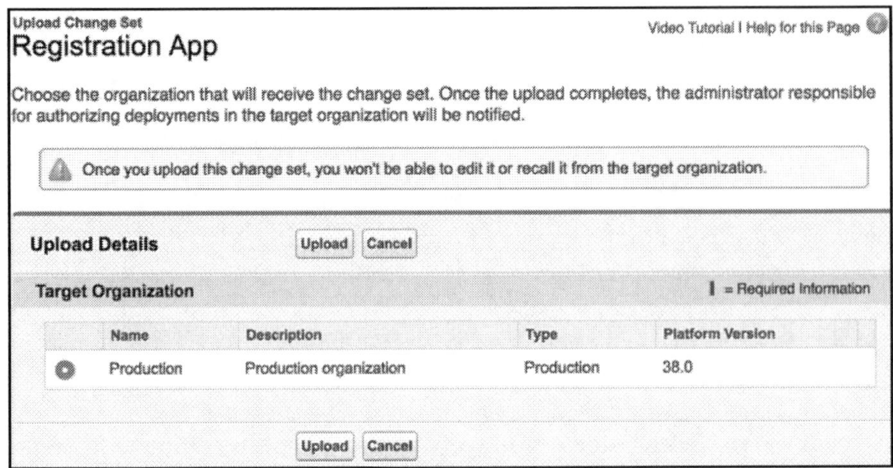

12. Once you are done, click on **Upload**. If it were successful, you will see a message as shown in the following screenshot:

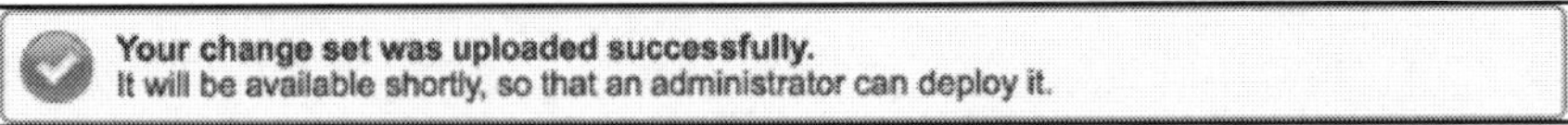

You will also receive an e-mail from Salesforce stating that your change set upload was successful, which would be similar to the following screenshot:

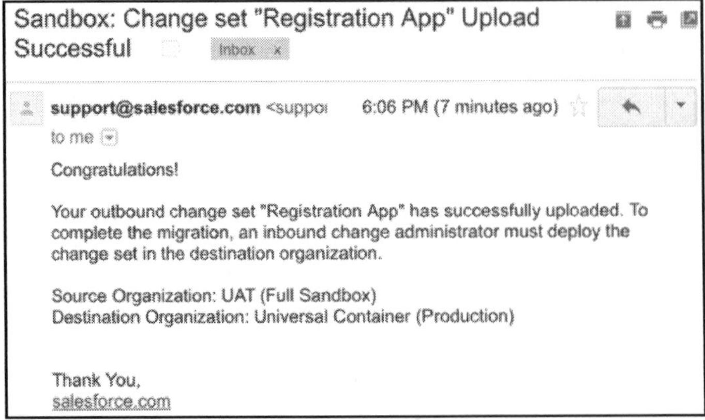

Inbound change sets

Inbound change sets are those change sets that can be used to receive metadata from a Sandbox to Production or another Sandboxes.

Perform the following steps to deploy an Inbound change set that you would send from your Sandbox:

1. Log in to your Sandbox org by visiting `https://login.salesforce.com`.
2. Navigate to **Setup** (gear icon) | **Setup** | **PLATFORM TOOLS** | **Environments** | **Change Sets** | **Inbound Change Sets**.
3. If you are accessing **Inbound Change Sets** for the first time, click on the **Continue** button.
4. Navigate to the **Change Sets Awaiting Deployment** section; you will see the list of inbound change sets that came from your Sandbox organization and are waiting for deployment.

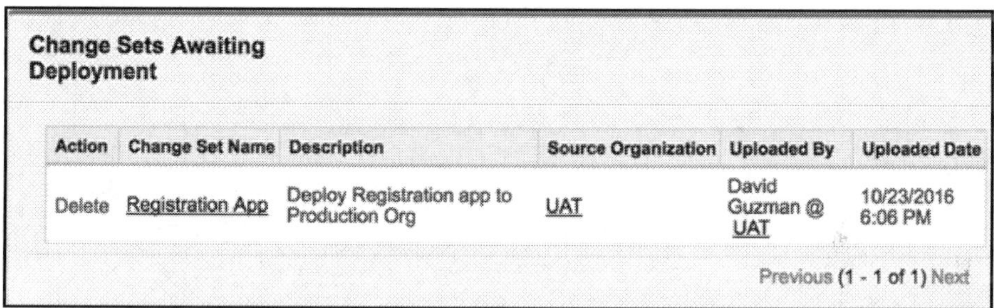

5. Click on the inbound change set to view its details. In this case, click on the **Registration App** change set.
6. In the **Change Set Detail** page, you will find the **Validate** and **Deploy** buttons:

    - **Validate**: This is nothing but a simulation of the actual deployment. Validating a change set means you can view the success or failure messages that you would otherwise receive during the actual deployment process.

- **Deploy**: This allows you to deploy a change set. A change set is deployed in a single operation. If the deployment remains incomplete or fails for any reason, then the entire transaction is rolled back.

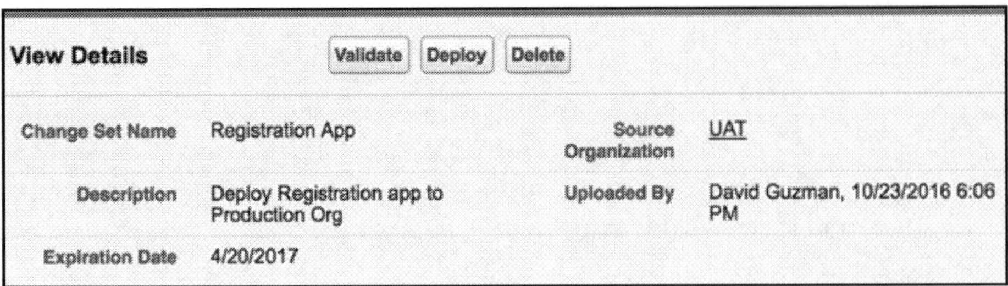

7. It is a best practice to validate the deployment first; once you do this, you just need to go ahead and deploy it. If the validate process is successful, the next step is to deploy it by clicking on **Deploy**. At the time of deployment, it allows you to select the test class you want to run. Let it be **Default**, then again click on **Deploy**. It will pop up a warning message stating that a change set once deployed would not be rolled back:

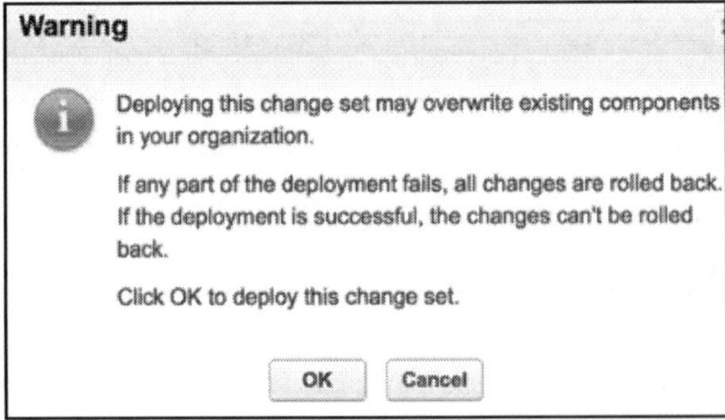

8. Click on **OK**. You will see the following message while the upload is in progress:

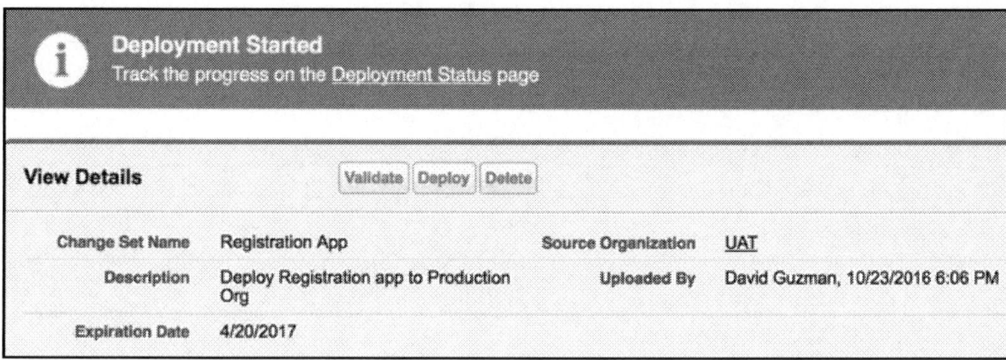

9. Once the upload is finished, either successful or not, you will see it under the **Deployment History** list:

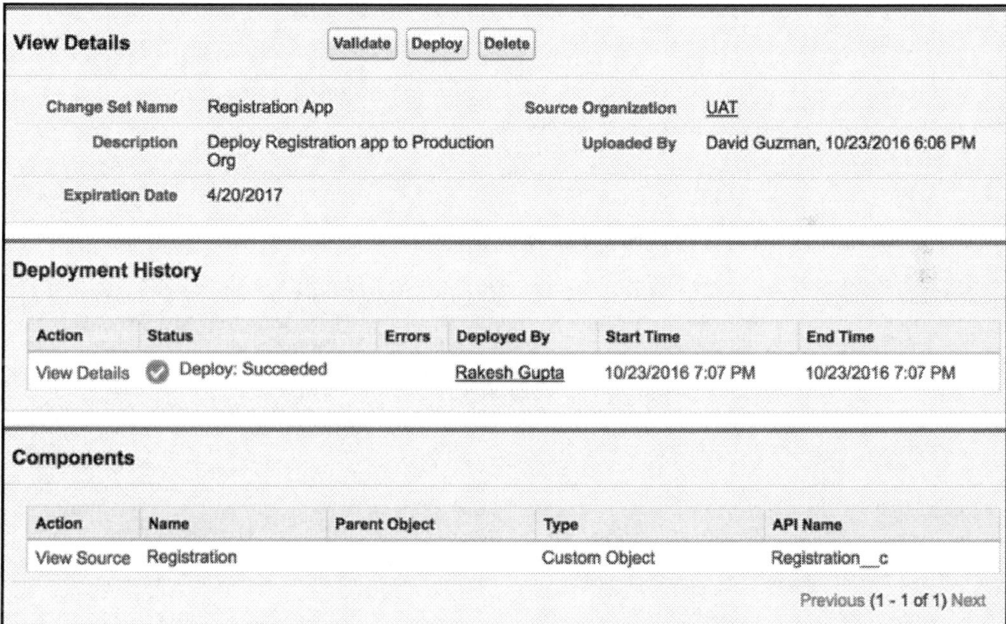

If the status of the change set shows **Success**, it would mean the change set was successfully deployed.

Benefits of using change sets

There are a few advantages of using a change set for deployment, and they are as follows:

- It will provide you with a neat and clean user interface for picking up changes that need to be deployed.
- It allows you to validate the change set before you deploy it.
- It is an out-of-the-box feature of Salesforce; you don't need to install any other app to use it.
- Change set deployment can be tracked by Audit Trail; this means you can check which components have been deployed and when.
- It is easy to clone a change set.
- It can be used to deploy similar components into multiple Salesforce orgs.

Deploying using Force.com IDE

Force.com IDE is a Salesforce-provided development tool that can be used to write Apex classes, Apex triggers, Lightning Components, and Visualforce Pages. It also allows you to download and edit the metadata of components.

Force.com IDE Installation

Before you install *Force.com IDE*, you need the following to be available and installed on your machine:

- Java SE Runtime Environment (v1.5 or higher)
- Eclipse IDE for Java Developers (Helios 3.6 or Galileo 3.5)

Perform the following steps to install the Force.com IDE for Eclipse Helios:

1. Open the Eclipse IDE on your machine.
2. Go to **Help | Install New Software**:

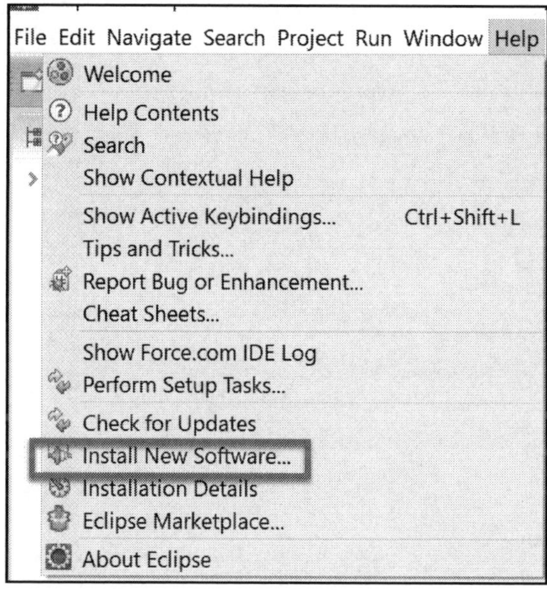

3. In the next window, click on the **Add** button. In the dialog box, enter `Force.com IDE` as the name and `https://developer.salesforce.com/media/force-ide/eclipse42/` as the location. Then click on **OK**:

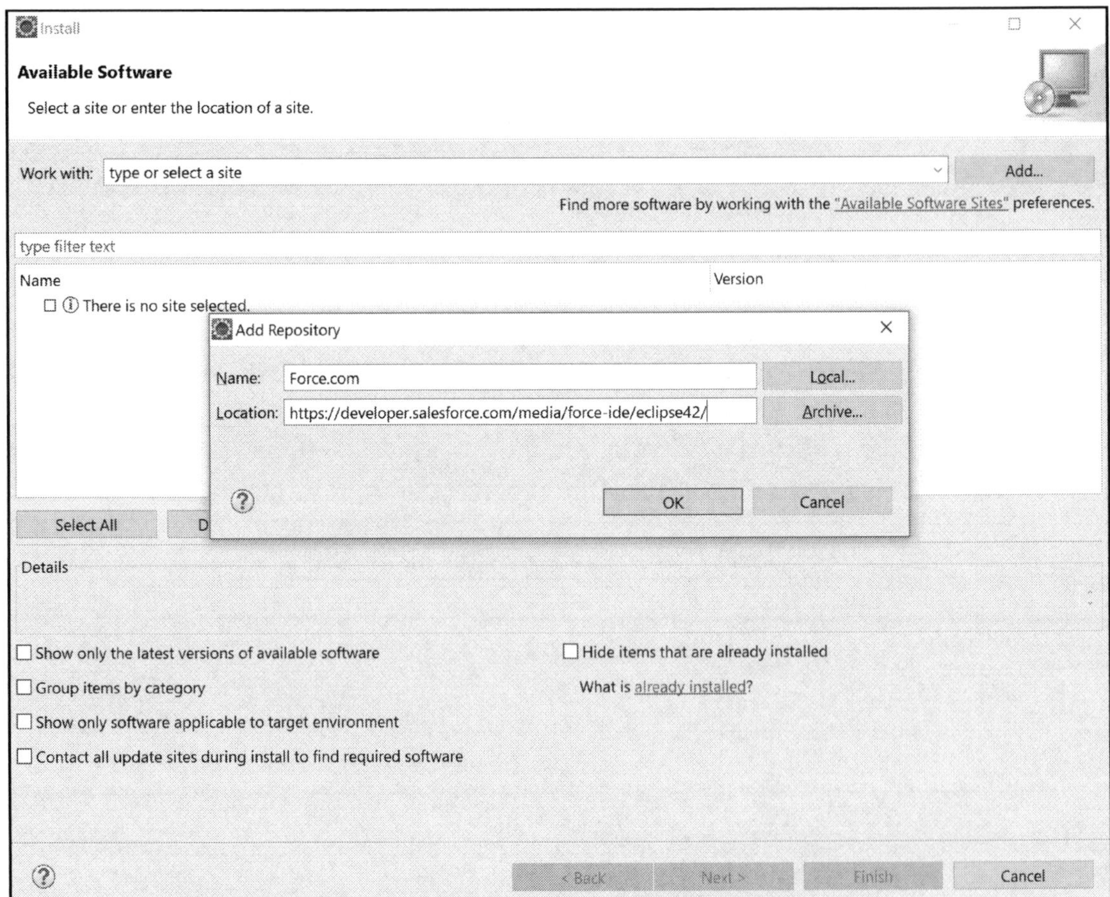

Once you add the new repository, Eclipse will download the list of available plugins and display them in the **Available Software** section.

4. Select the checkbox in front of Force.com IDE version 36.0, as shown in the following screenshot:

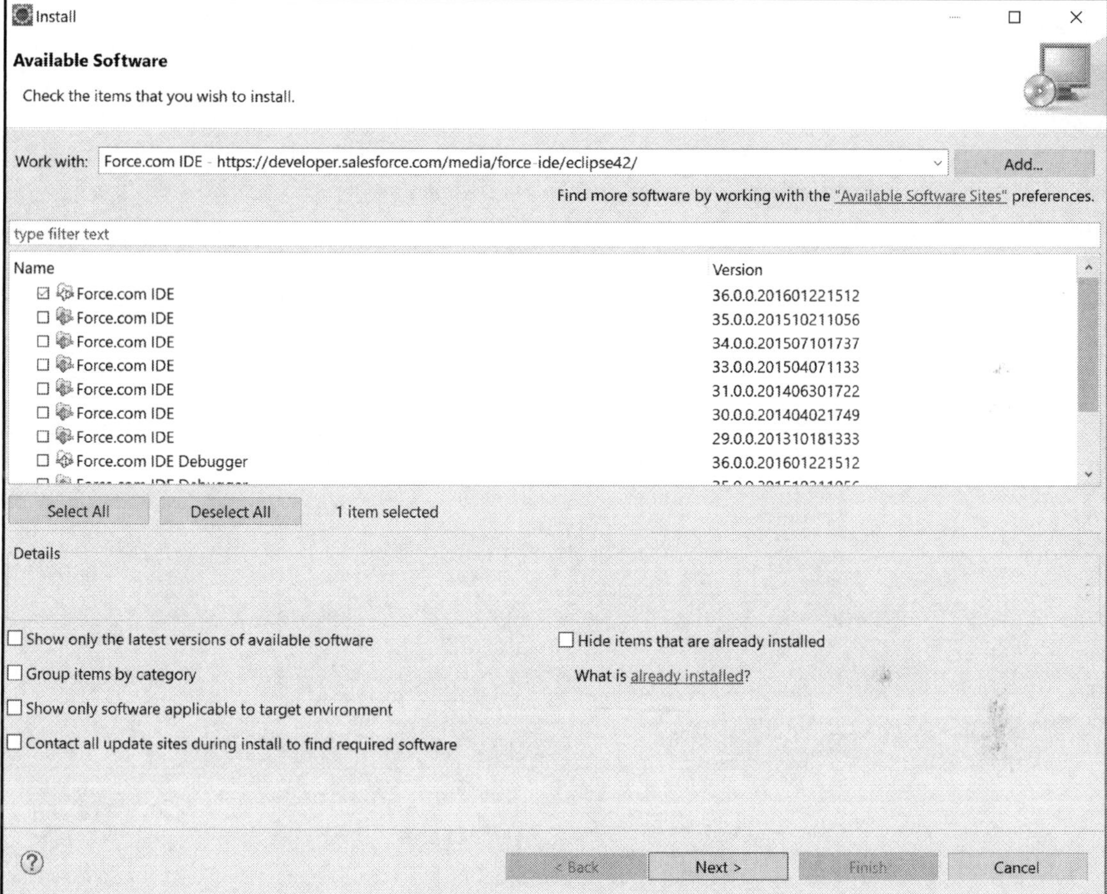

5. Once you are done, click on **Next**.
6. In the **Review Licenses** dialog, accept the terms and then click on **Finish**.
7. Once the installation is complete, you will be asked to restart Eclipse. Click on **Yes**.

Creating a project and deploying it using Force.com IDE

Projects allow you implement version control and keep a backup of your work on a local machine.

A business scenario: *David Guzman* is working as a *System Administrator* at Universal Containers. In `Chapter 2`, *Security Settings in Salesforce* he created a permission set called *Modify all Opportunities*. Now he wants to migrate this object to a production org though Force.com IDE.

Perform the following steps to deploy components using Force.com IDE:

1. Open Eclipse IDE on your machine and then go to **File** | **New** | **Force.com project**. To create a new project, enter the project name and Sandbox credentials, as shown in the following screenshot:

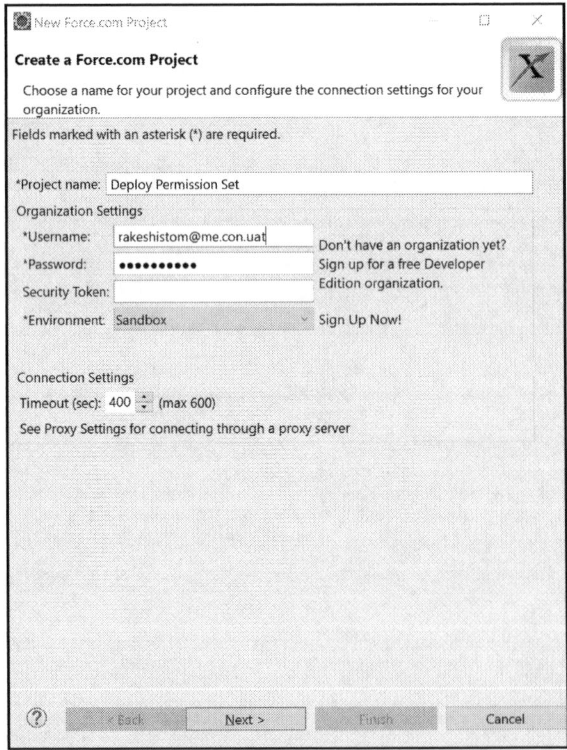

2. The next step is to select the metadata components. Click on **Selected metadata components:** and then click on **Choose** to select the components that you want to include in the project, as shown in the following screenshot:

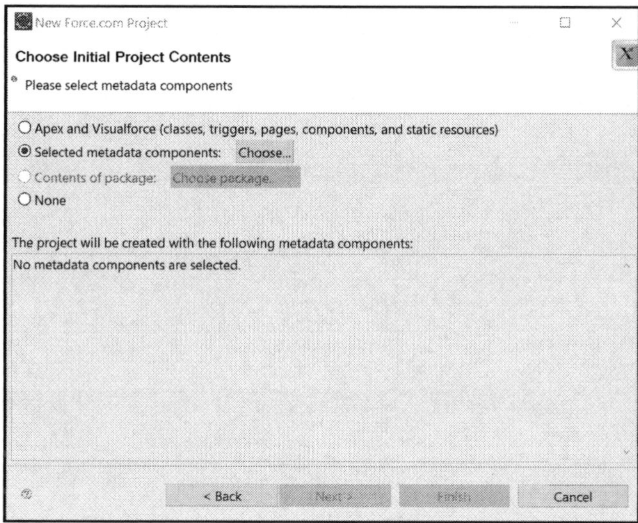

3. The next step is to retrieve the components that you want to deploy to the production org. In this case, select the **Modify_all_Opportunities** permission sets, as shown in the following screenshot:

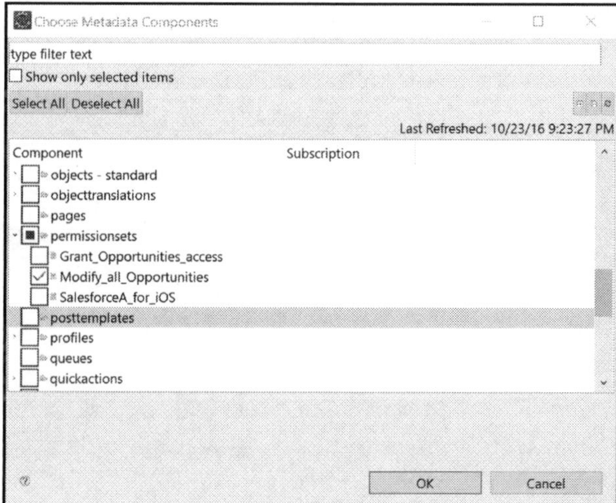

4. Once you're done with the components selection, click on **OK**.
5. The confirmation screen will display all your selected metadata components. Click on **Finish** and you will get all your selected metadata components on your local machine:

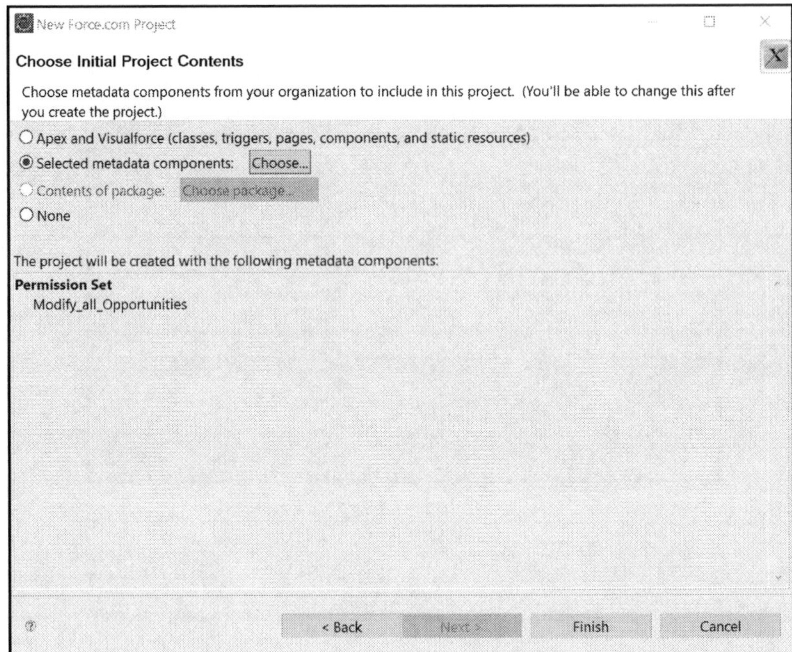

6. The next step is to deploy the project to the production org. To do this, right-click on **Project Name** and then go to **Force.com** | **Deploy to Server**, as shown in the following screenshot:

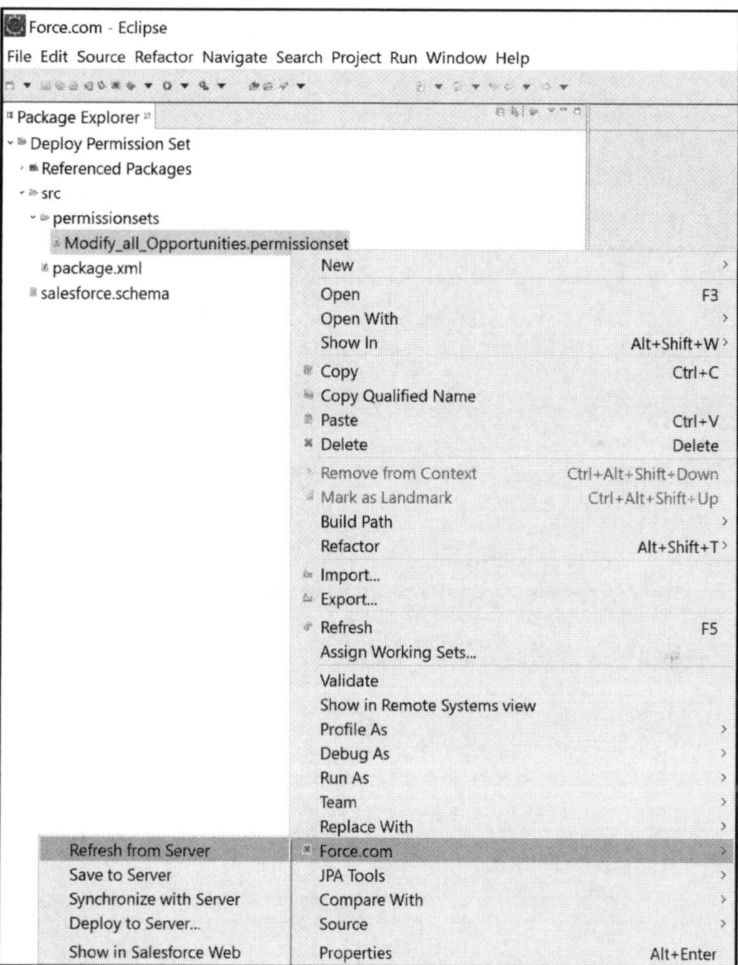

7. Then, the next step is to enter your production credentials and click on **Next**, as shown in the following screenshot:

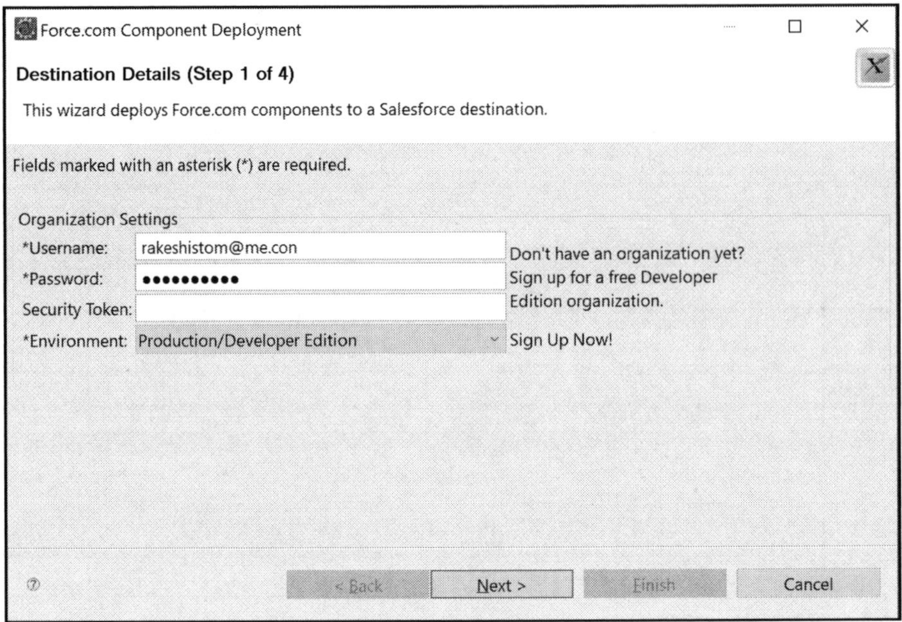

8. The next step is to select the components that you want to deploy to the production org. For the current business scenario, select the **Modify_all_Opportunities** component, as shown in the following screenshot:

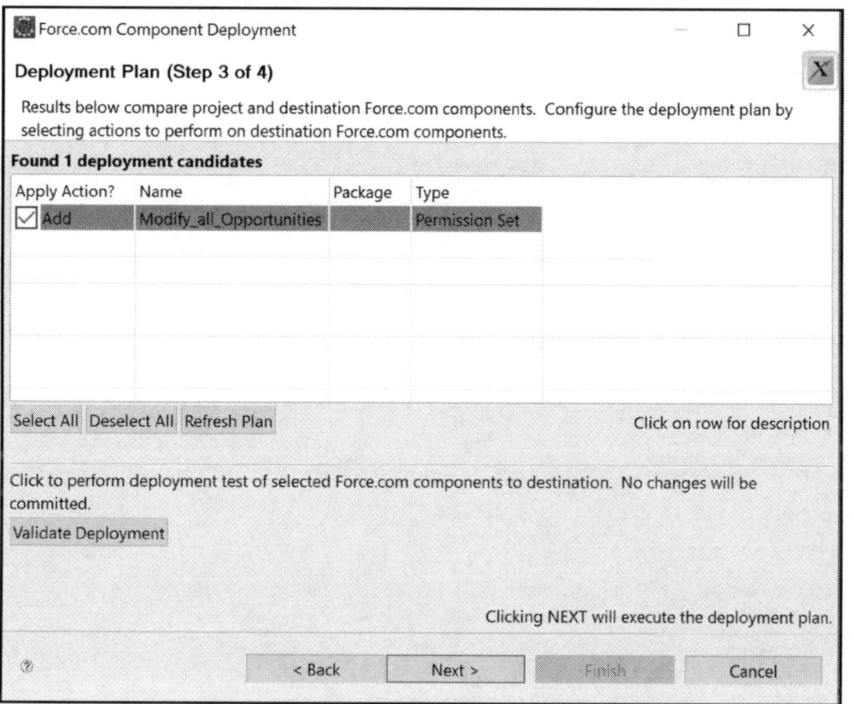

9. As soon as you're done with component selection, the final step is to click on **Next** to deploy the metadata components to Production. If the deployment is successful, you will get a message as shown in the following screenshot:

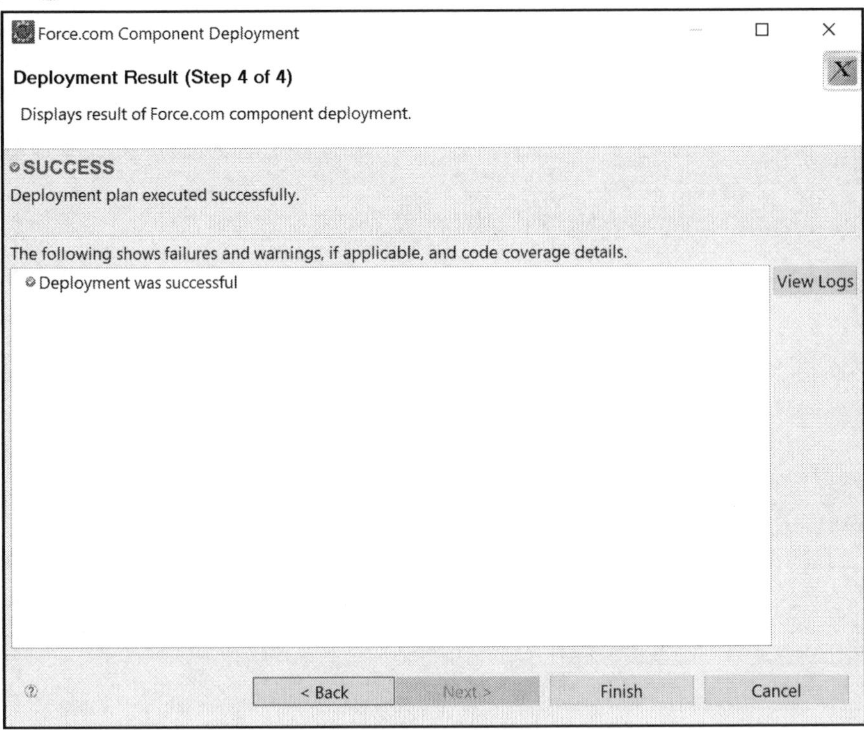

10. To close the popup, click on **Finish**.

Benefits of using Force.com IDE

There are a few advantages of using Force.com for deployment, and they are as follows:

- Eclipse can be used to move metadata between orgs, for example, the Developer Edition org to a Sandbox.
- You can use Force.com IDE to delete metadata from a production org, for example, deleting the Apex class or trigger.
- It can be used to take a backup of the components as well as version control on your local machine.

- It allows you to deploy only the components selected from your Force.com project.
- It allows you to merge code with other developers to reduce deployment effort.
- Force.com IDE can be used to deploy all types of metadata components.
- You can easily integrate it with version control systems such as GitHub.

Deploying using packages

Packages are containers that can hold metadata components, either one component or a group of components. They are mainly used to distribute an app; the best example of this is Salesforce AppExchange. Packages are also used to deploy the metadata components between any orgs, for example, Salesforce Developer Edition to one of your Sandboxes. There are two types of Packages available and they are as follows:

Unmanaged Packages	**Managed Packages**
Developers can view and modify the Apex code of components included in an unmanaged package.	It is not possible to view the code of components, for example, Apex class or Apex trigger, in this package.
Components can be edited in the organization after the installation.	Components cannot be edited in the organization after the installation.
The source organization has no control over the package once it is installed in the customer org; this is because the code can be altered in the target organization.	The code can only be altered in the source organization, where the package components were developed.
These are used for module distribution among developers.	These are used by Salesforce.com partners to distribute the app to their customers primarily through the AppExchange marketplace.

The third type of package is called as **unpackaged**. It refers the components that exist natively in your organization, such as standard objects, go into the unpackaged package.

Deploy using Force.com Migration Tool

Force.com Migration Tool is Java ANT based command line tool to deploy metadata components from one Salesforce org to another org or deploy same metadata components to multiple Salesforce org's like **Developer org –> UAT org –> Pre-Production org –> Production org**. It allows you to deploy metadata components likes Objects, Communities, Apex classes, Apex triggers, Lightning Components and Visualforce Pages, and so on. The advantage of using Force.com Migration Tool is, it allows you to schedule a deployment over the weekend or non-business hours. This use Metadata API to deploy the components. It is very useful and time-saving to use Force.com Migration Tool in following scenarios

- Migrate components from development org to a test org with large amounts of metadata quickly.
- In the case of multistage release processes using this tool deployment of components can make this activity much more efficient.
- When IT does deploy from staging org to production org.
- Deploying metadata components from a local repository to Salesforce org.

Force.com Migration Tool pre-requisite

Before installing Force.com Migration Tool you need the following to be available and installed on your machine:

1. **Java SE Runtime Environment (v1.7 or higher)**: To verify that you have properly installed Java, run the following command on Mac Terminal or Windows command line:

   ```
   Java -version
   ```

   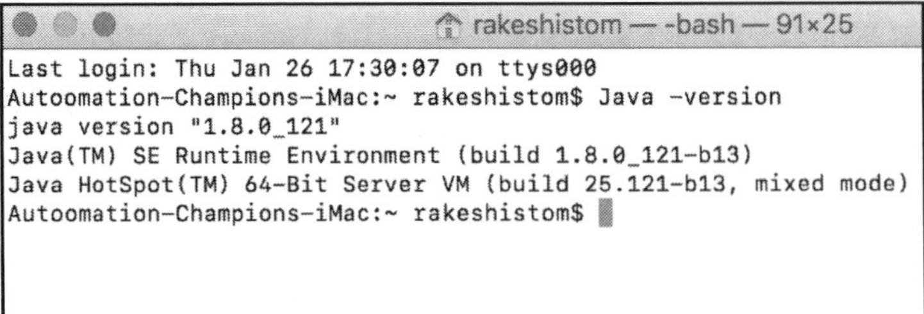

   Make sure that the output should look something like the preceding screenshot.

2. **Apache ANT installation (v1.6 or higher):** Open the following URL in your browser, then installed ANT version 1.6 or higher `http://ant.apache.org/bindownload.cgi`. Once you have installed the ANT, the next step is to set the environment variables `ANT_HOME` and `JAVA_HOME`. `Set ANT_HOME` environment variable value to pointing to the directory where you have installed ANT. Set `JAVA_HOME` environment variable value to pointing to the location of your JDK. On a Mac, it should look like the following screenshot:

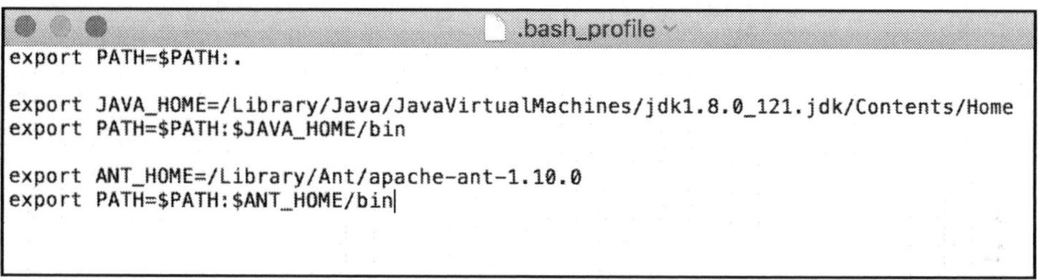

To verify that you have properly installed and setup environment variables for Ant, run the following command on Mac Terminal or Windows command line:

```
ant -version
```

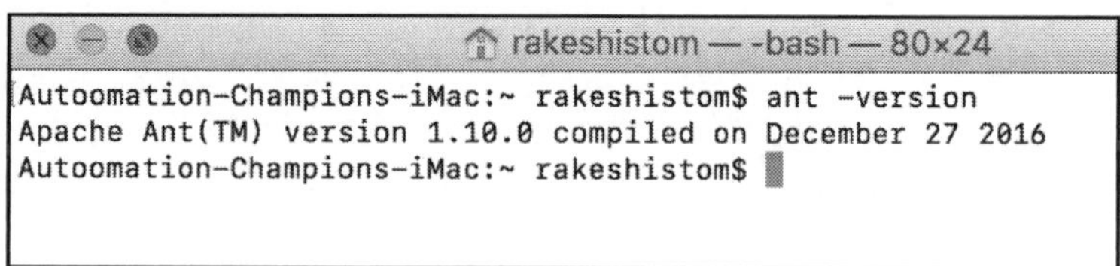

Make sure that the output should look something like the preceding screenshot.

Installing Force.com Migration Tool

Perform the following steps to install Force.com Migration Tool

1. Open the following URL in your browser, then installed Force.com Migration Tool in your local machine `https://gs0.salesforce.com/dwnld/SfdcAnt/salesforce_ant_39.0.zip`

2. Save the ZIP file on your local machine and extract the contents to the directory where you want to store it. It should look something like the following screenshot

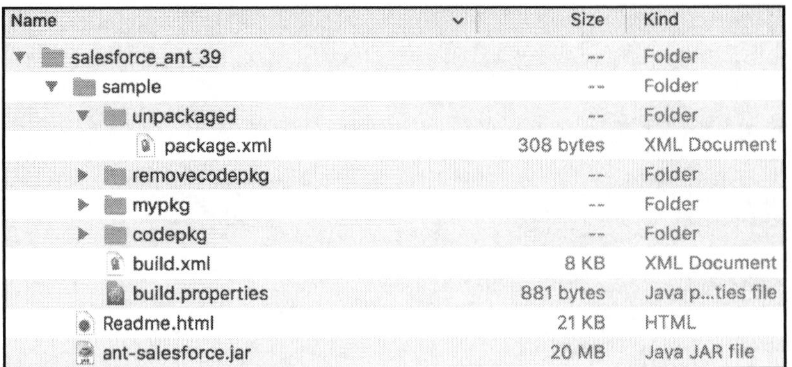

3. Following are the details of folders and files extracted by Force.com Migration Tool
    1. `Readme.html` contains the instructions how to use Force.com Migration Tool.
    2. `Ant-salesforce.jar` is a JAR file containing the ANT task.
    3. Sample folder contains the following items:
        1. A `codepkg` folder contains sample Apex class and Apex trigger.
        2. A `mypkg` folder contains sample custom object.
        3. A `removecodepkg` folder that contains XML files for removing the preceding metadata components from your org if deployed.
        4. A sample `build.properties` file is used to store your Salesforce credentials, to run the task.
        5. A sample `build.xml` file, that used to deploy and retrieve API calls.
4. You are now all set to use Force.com Migration Tool.

Creating a project and deploy using Force.com Migration Tool

Force.com Migration Tool allows you to manage version control and keep a backup of your work on your local machine. It also allows you to create folders based on your project or deployment strategy.

A business scenario: David Guzman is working as System Administrator at Universal Containers. In `Chapter 7`, *Optimizing Business Processes with Visual Workflow and Approval Processes* he has created a custom field on `Account` object called as `Status__c`. Now he wants to migrate this field to his personal developer org using Force.com Migration Tool.

Perform the following steps to deploy metadata components using Force.com Migration Tool

1. Create few folders in your ANT directory that is `UAT-Metadata` and `Version 1` inside `UAT-Metadata`. Then copy `build.properties` and `build.xml` files inside `UAT-Metadata` folder, as shown in the following screenshot:

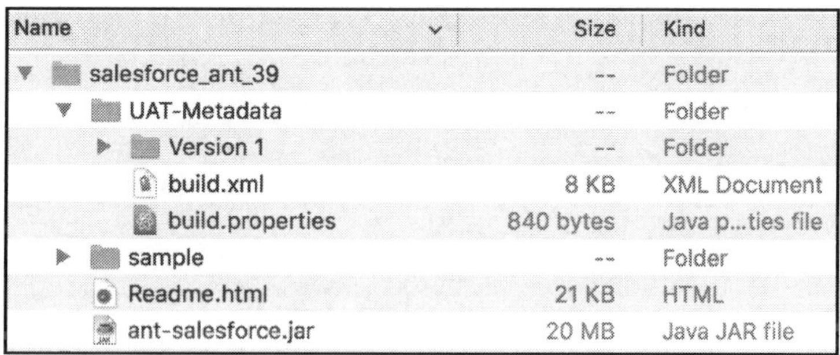

2. The next step is to edit `build.properties` file and enter `Salesforce credentials` for source org to retrieve the metadata components based on the schema defined inside the `package.xml` (we will create `package.xml` in next step):

```
build.properties
# build.properties
#

# Specify the login credentials for the desired Salesforce organization
sf.username = rakesh.gupta@uat.com
sf.password = 785^%^$#%%jB9g4f6SPXImGMLtsamw78SO
sf.serverurl = https://test.salesforce.com
sf.maxPoll = 20
#
```

3. The next step is to build a `package.xml` file that contains account's custom field `Status__c`. Either you can create it manually with the help of Metadata API developers guide or use Force.com IDE to do so. Once you have the `package.xml` file moves it to inside the `Version 1` folder. Then it should look something like the following screenshot:

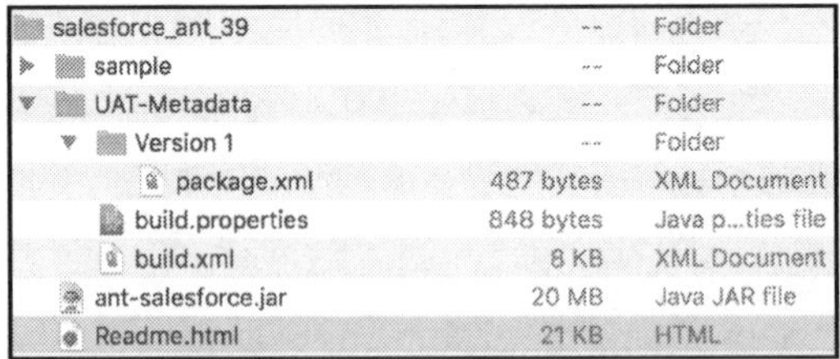

Your `package.xml` should look like the following screenshot:

```
package.xml
<?xml version="1.0" encoding="UTF-8" standalone="yes"?>
<Package xmlns="http://soap.sforce.com/2006/04/metadata">
    <types>
        <members>Account.Status__c</members>
        <name>CustomField</name>
    </types>
    <version>38.0</version>
</Package>
```

4. Then edit the `build.xml` file and set the `package.xml` location, inside target `retrieveUnpackaged` tag, as shown in the following screenshot:

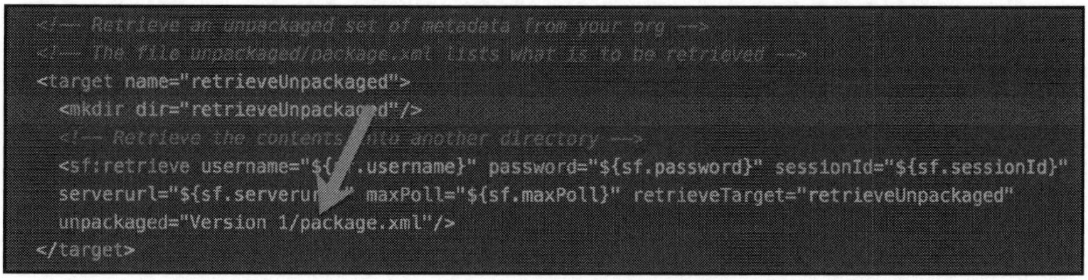

```
<!-- Retrieve an unpackaged set of metadata from your org -->
<!-- The file unpackaged/package.xml lists what is to be retrieved -->
<target name="retrieveUnpackaged">
  <mkdir dir="retrieveUnpackaged"/>
  <!-- Retrieve the contents into another directory -->
  <sf:retrieve username="${sf.username}" password="${sf.password}" sessionId="${sf.sessionId}"
  serverurl="${sf.serverurl}" maxPoll="${sf.maxPoll}" retrieveTarget="retrieveUnpackaged"
  unpackaged="Version 1/package.xml"/>
</target>
```

5. Open the Terminal on Mac and navigate to the directory of the UAT-metadata for the current scenario. Then run the following command on Mac Terminal or Windows command line to retrieve the metadata components from source org for schema defined inside `package.xml`:

```
ant "retrieveUnpackaged"
```

```
UAT-Metadata — -bash — 80×24
Autoomation-Champions-iMac:UAT-Metadata rakeshistom$ ant "retrieveUnpackaged"
Buildfile: /Users/rakeshistom/Downloads/salesforce_ant_39/UAT-Metadata/build.xml

retrieveUnpackaged:
    [mkdir] Created dir: /Users/rakeshistom/Downloads/salesforce_ant_39/UAT-Meta
data/retrieveUnpackaged
[sf:retrieve] Request for a retrieve submitted successfully.
[sf:retrieve] Request ID for the current retrieve task: 09SV000000153xFMAQ
[sf:retrieve] Waiting for server to finish processing the request...
[sf:retrieve] Request Status: InProgress
[sf:retrieve] Request Status: Succeeded
[sf:retrieve] Finished request 09SV000000153xFMAQ successfully.

BUILD SUCCESSFUL
Total time: 13 seconds
Autoomation-Champions-iMac:UAT-Metadata rakeshistom$
```

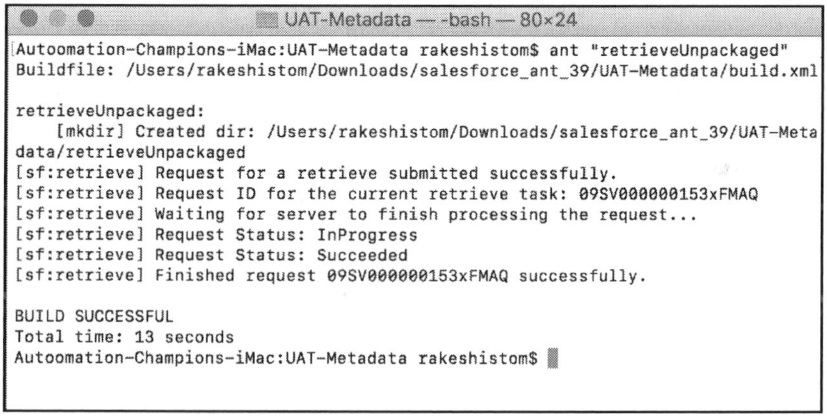

If the retrieval or build is successful, then you will get success message on the screen. It should look like something the preceding screenshot. The next step is to navigate to `UAT-Metadata` folder on your local machine. After successful retrieval of metadata components from source org, it should contain a folder `object` inside `retrieveUnpackaged` folder, as shown in the following screenshot:

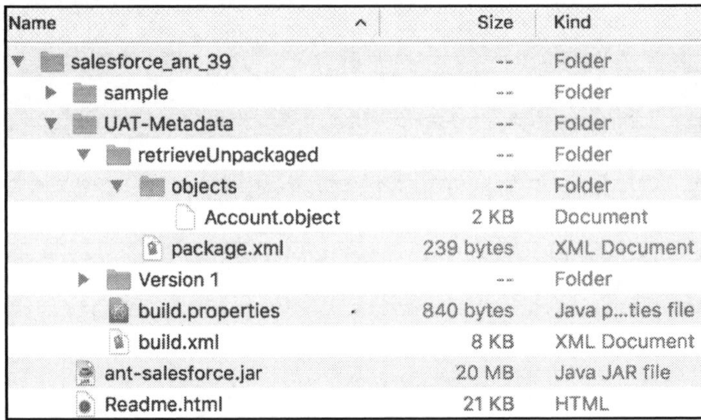

Inside `object` folder, you can find the document `Account.Object` that contains complete schema of account's custom field `Status__c`:

```
<?xml version="1.0" encoding="UTF-8"?>
<CustomObject xmlns="http://soap.sforce.com/2006/04/metadata">
    <fields>
        <fullName>Status__c</fullName>
        <description></description>
        <externalId>false</externalId>
        <inlineHelpText></inlineHelpText>
        <label>Status</label>
        <required>false</required>
        <trackFeedHistory>false</trackFeedHistory>
        <type>Picklist</type>
        <valueSet>
            <valueSetDefinition>
                <sorted>false</sorted>
                <value>
                    <fullName>Active</fullName>
                    <default>true</default>
                </value>
                <value>
                    <fullName>Inactive</fullName>
                    <default>false</default>
                </value>
                <value>
                    <fullName>Archived</fullName>
                    <default>false</default>
                </value>
                <value>
                    <fullName>Submitted</fullName>
                    <default>false</default>
                </value>
                <value>
                    <fullName>Approved by Sales Director</fullName>
                    <default>false</default>
                </value>
                <value>
                    <fullName>Out of business</fullName>
                    <default>false</default>
                </value>
            </valueSetDefinition>
        </valueSet>
    </fields>
</CustomObject>
```

6. To deploy metadata components to target org, navigate to `UAT-Metadata` folder on your local machine and edit the `build.properties` file to change the Salesforce credentials pointing to target org.

7. Open the Terminal on Mac and make sure that you are still inside `UAT-Metadata` folder. Then run the following command on Mac Terminal or Windows command line to deploy metadata components to target Salesforce org `ant "deployUnpackaged"`:

```
UAT-Metadata — -bash — 80×24
Autoomation-Champions-iMac:UAT-Metadata rakeshistom$ ant "deployUnpackaged"
Buildfile: /Users/rakeshistom/Downloads/salesforce_ant_39/UAT-Metadata/build.xml

deployUnpackaged:
[sf:deploy] Request for a deploy submitted successfully.
[sf:deploy] Request ID for the current deploy task: 0AfB0000009Lth1KAC
[sf:deploy] Waiting for server to finish processing the request...
[sf:deploy] Request Status: Pending
[sf:deploy] Request Status: Succeeded
[sf:deploy] *********** DEPLOYMENT SUCCEEDED ***********
[sf:deploy] Finished request 0AfB0000009Lth1KAC successfully.

BUILD SUCCESSFUL
Total time: 12 seconds
Autoomation-Champions-iMac:UAT-Metadata rakeshistom$
```

If the deployment is successful, then you will get success message on the screen. It should look like something the preceding screenshot.

8. The final step is to login into your target org and verifies the deployment.

Design the folder structure as your want. Make sure to update the folder structure in `build.xml` file.

A few points to remember

1. Change sets are limited to 5,000 components and 400 MB.
2. You can't use change sets to delete or rename components.
3. When deploying using a change set, note that it will run all the tests of Apex code. If you have low code coverage, you will not be able to deploy it; it will fail every time. With Force.com IDE though, you can push code without coverage.
4. Change sets deployment track by Audit Trail means you can check which components have been deployed and when.
5. Use packages when you want to distribute your metadata components to customers across the globe.
6. To deploy metadata components through any tools, it is necessary that you have system administrator permission.

Test your knowledge

Q1. When using change sets to deploy an application, which of the following you do not have to do?

1. Installing Force.com IDE
2. Creating an outbound change set using click
3. Deploying to GitHub
4. Deploying an Inbound change set

Q2. Which of the following tools can be used to delete components from a production org?

1. Change set
2. Force.com IDE
3. Package
4. Force.com Workbench

Q3. How can you delete a component from a production org?

1. Change set
2. Force.com IDE
3. Package
4. Force.com Workbench

Q4. Which of the following deployment tool activities is tracked by Audit Trail?

1. Change set
2. Force.com IDE
3. Package
4. Force.com Workbench

Q5. It is possible to create a trigger directly in a production org:

1. True
2. False

Summary

In this chapter, we started with change sets that allow you to easily deploy components from a Sandbox to production org. Then, we moved ahead and discussed how to set up Force.com IDE for Eclipse, followed by project creation and deployment. We also learned about packages in Salesforce. At the end, we have gone through Force.com Migration Tool. In the next chapter, we will discuss the basic concepts of Apex and Visualforce Pages that will help you troubleshoot common business problems.

12
Basics of Apex and Visualforce Page

In the previous chapter, we discussed different methods to deploy an application to different organizations. We also discussed the method of deploying component metadata using Force.com IDE, Force.com Migration Tools and followed it up with the process of distributing an application using packages.

In this chapter, we will discuss the basics of Apex programming and Visualforce page concepts. We'll cover the following topics:

- Introducing Apex
- Apex data types
- Creating an Apex class
- Introducing a Visualforce page
- Understanding the MVC model

Until now, you have used an out-of-the-box feature–that is, *point and click* development–to customize your Salesforce org. For example, creating the object's structure, relationships between objects, Process Builders, and approval process to customize it according to your business needs. The *point and click* development method doesn't require any coding skill.

Introducing Apex

Apex is the world's first on-demand programming language that allows you to implement complex business requirements and transactions on the Force.com platform. There are two types of application development in Salesforce and they are as follows:

- Declarative development
- Programmatic development

Apex falls under programmatic development. It is a strongly typed object-based language. It remains well connected with your data, schema, and data manipulation using the query and search language. Apex is included in Developer Edition, Lightning Enterprise Edition, Lightning Unlimited Edition and Database.com. You can write Apex classes or triggers in a developer or sandbox organization. As soon as you finish the development of Apex code, you have to write test methods to cover the implemented Apex code. Once you have greater than 75 percent code coverage, you can deploy the particular Apex code to the production organization. The Apex programming language has the following features:

- It offers **data manipulation language** (**DML**) with built-in exception handling.
- **Salesforce Object Query Language** (**SOQL**) and **Salesforce Object Search Language** (**SOSL**) are used to query and retrieve the list of sObject records.
- Apex has a built-in record-locking mechanism to prevent conflict of record updates.
- It runs in a multitenant environment. This means the same resource is used by multiple Salesforce.com. customers across the globe. It prevents the monopolizing of shared resources using governor limits. If any particular Apex code violates the limits, error messages are displayed.
- Apex code is stored as metadata. Therefore, they are automatically upgraded with every release. You don't need to rewrite your code when the platform gets updated.
- Apex is similar to Java syntax and variables. Syntaxes and semantics of Apex are easy to understand and write code.
- It provides a built-in feature for unit testing and test execution with code coverage.

You can write Apex logic in the following ways:

- **Apex class**: An Apex class includes methods that are related to logic implementation. It can be called from a trigger; you can also associate it with a Visualforce page. Also, it can act as a supporting class, for example, API, Helper classes, or Batch Apex.
- **Apex trigger**: A trigger is executed in relation to a particular database action. For example, you can create a trigger on the account object that is executed whenever an account record is deleted. Therefore, triggers are implicitly called from a database action.

Apex data types

Variables are used to store data in a programming language. In Apex classes and triggers, we can use variables that contain data values. Variables must be similar to a data type, and a particular variable should hold the values of the same data type, for example, integer data types should store integer values. All variables and expressions can have a data type mentioned as follows:

- **Primitives**: It may appear that Apex primitive variables are passed by values, but they actually use absolute references, similar to Java string behavior. They include the following data types: integer, double, decimal, long, date, time, datetime, string, ID, object, blob, or Boolean.
- **sObjects**: The sObject represents standard or custom Salesforce objects that store record data in the database. There is also an sObject data type in Apex; it is a programmatic representation of sObjects and their data in the code.
- **Enums**: Enum stands for enumerated list and it is an abstract data type that stores one value of a finite set of specified identifiers. To define an Enum, you have to use the `enum` keyword in the variable declaration and then define the list of values.

- **Collections**: A collection represents a group of objects. There are three different types of collections in Apex, and they are:
    - **List**: A list is an ordered collection of the primitive's data types dignified by its index. Each element in a list contains two sets of information: an index (this is an integer) and a value (the data). The index of the first element is zero. You can define a list as follows:

```
List<DataType> listName = new List<DataType>();
List<String> sList = new List<String>();
```

- **Set**: A set is an unordered collection of data of one primitive data type or sObject that must have unique values. You can define a set as follows:

```
Set<DataType> setName = new Set<DataType>();
Set<String> setName = new Set<String>();
```

- **Map**: A map is an unordered collection of unique keys of one primitive data type and their corresponding values. You can define a map as follows:

```
Map<PrimitiveKeyDataType, DataType> = mapName =
    newMap<PrimitiveKeyDataType, DataType>();
Map<Integer, String> mapName = new Map<Integer, String>();
Map<Integer, List<String>> sMap =
    new Map<Integer,List<String>>();
```

- An object created from user or system-defined classes.
- Null (for the `null` constant)

Creating an Apex class

You can create and modify an Apex class through the **Setup** menu of the Salesforce organization, Force.com IDE, or Developer Console. You can also do this using third-party development tools, for example, MavensMate IDE for Force.com, Welkin Suite IDE, and so on. The best way to interact with Apex classes via the **Setup** page is by navigating to **Setup** (gear icon) | **Setup** | **PLATFORM TOOLS** | **Custom Code** | **Apex Classes**. It will look like the following screenshot:

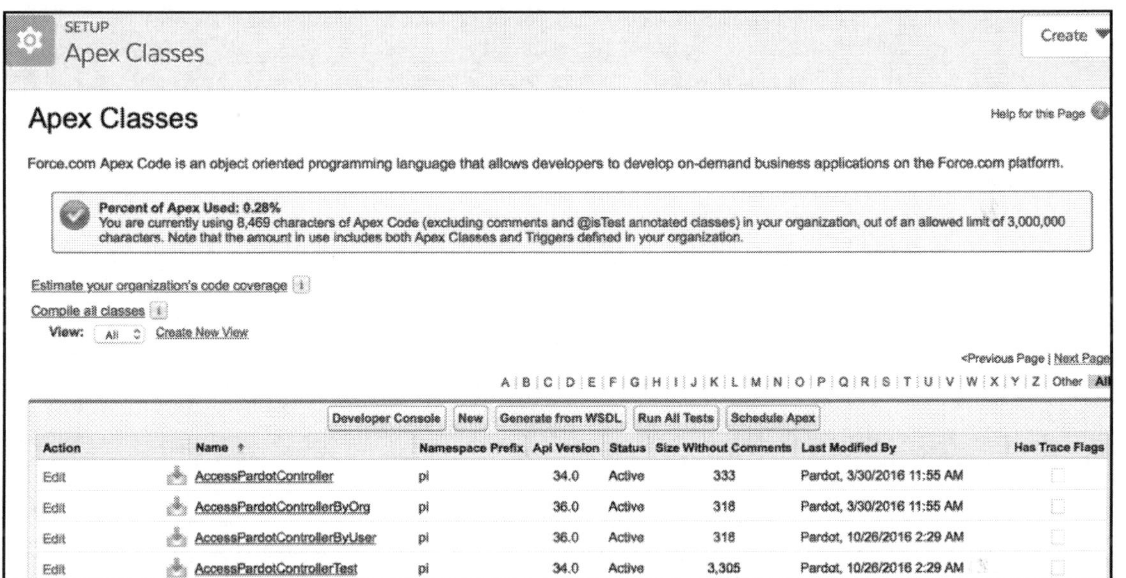

The preceding screenshot displays the currently available classes in the org. This page allows you to create new classes, edit and delete existing classes, assign security to existing classes, generate an Apex class from a WSDL file, and schedule an Apex class for future run.

Another way to view, create, and modify a class through the Developer Console is by navigating to **Setup** (gear icon) | **Developer Console**. It will look like the following screenshot:

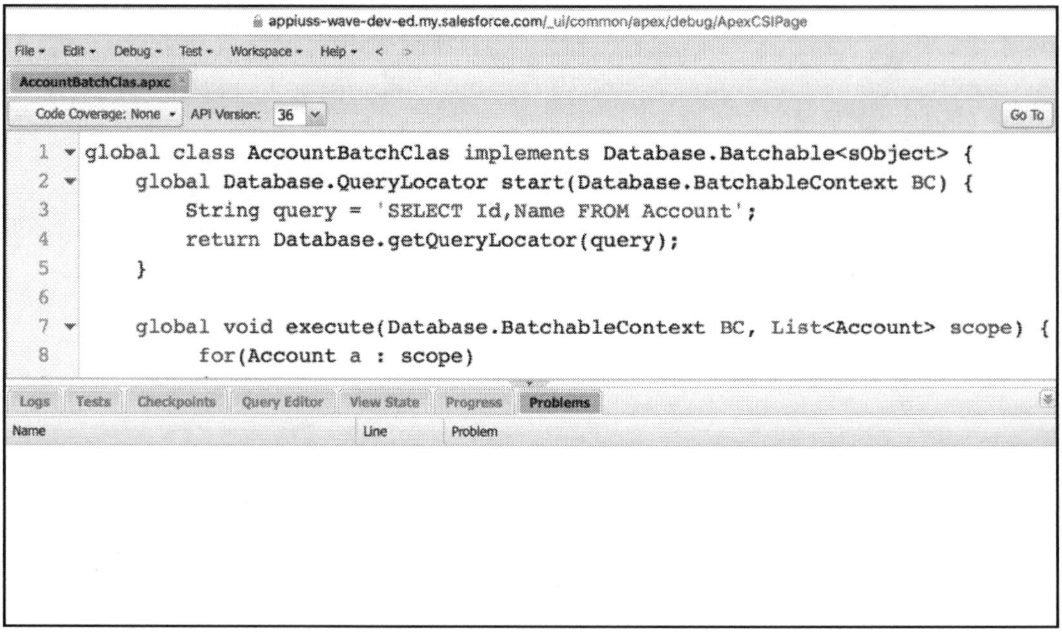
appiuss-wave-dev-ed.my.salesforce.com/_ui/common/apex/debug/ApexCSIPage
File Edit Debug Test Workspace Help < >
AccountBatchClas.apxc
Code Coverage: None API Version: 36
Go To
global class AccountBatchClas implements Database.Batchable<sObject> {
global Database.QueryLocator start(Database.BatchableContext BC) {
String query = 'SELECT Id,Name FROM Account';
return Database.getQueryLocator(query);
}
global void execute(Database.BatchableContext BC, List<Account> scope) {
for(Account a : scope)
Logs Tests Checkpoints Query Editor View State Progress Problems
Name Line Problem

Similar to Apex classes, you can create a new Apex trigger from the **Setup** page, the Force.com IDE, or the Developer Console. When you are using the **Setup** page, you must navigate to **Setup** (gear icon) | **Setup** | **PLATFORM TOOLS** | **Custom Code** | **Apex Triggers**.

Introducing a Visualforce page

In Salesforce, it is very easy to build powerful applications using only declarative methods; however, there are some situations where declarative methods aren't enough if you want to build an application. In Salesforce, standard and custom objects have their own standard user interface, either classic or Lightning Experience. You can easily customize a standard user interface by creating multiple page layouts using "clicks not code." A standard user interface has its own limitations; for example, you can't create three column pages or generate a PDF out of it. This is where the Visualforce markup language comes into play.

Similar to HTML, Visualforce is a markup-based user interface design language. Visualforce is a framework that includes a tag-based markup language that allows you to build sophisticated, attractive, and dynamic custom user interfaces. You can use almost all the standard web technologies, for example, CSS, jQuery, HTML5, and so on, along with a Visualforce page. This means you can build rich user interfaces for any device, including mobile or tablet.

The best way to view, create, and modify a Visualforce page is via the **Setup** page; just navigate to **Setup** (gear icon) | **Setup** | **PLATFORM TOOLS** | **Custom Code** | **Visualforce Pages**. It will look like the following screenshot:

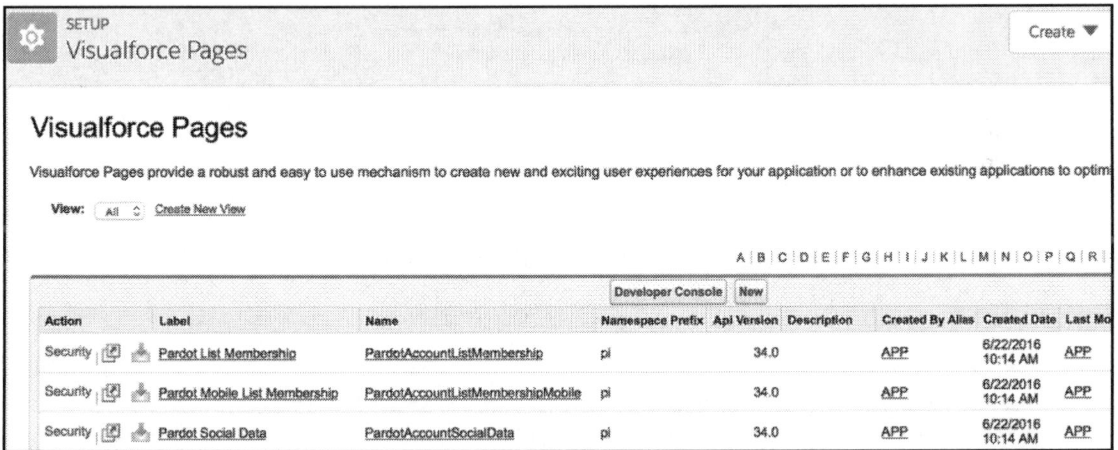

Another way to create a Visualforce page is by entering the page names in your browser's address bar. To use this, make sure that **Development Mode** is enabled in the particular user record. You will be redirected to a blank Visualforce page and you can specify the name of the page there.

Understanding the MVC model

Visualforce pages are rendered on the Salesforce server, and they display the output on a client machine, typically a web browser. As such, Visualforce has server-side access to data and logic. Modern platforms will separate the model, view, and database into distinct layers. This gives you modularity and containment for making your application easier to code and maintain. The following figure highlights the various layers of the MVC pattern:

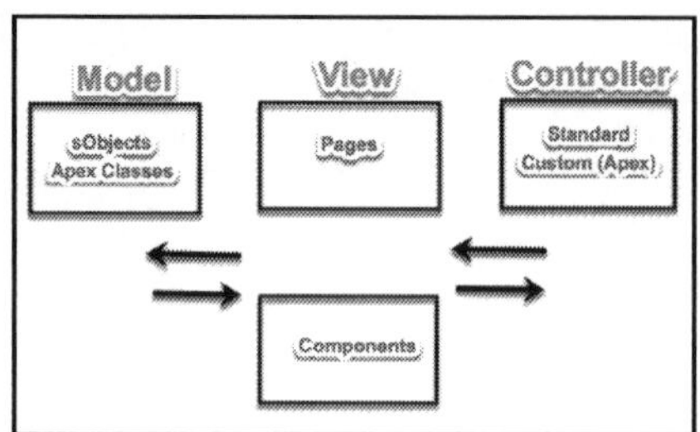

- **Model**: This defines the structure of the data. In Salesforce, objects define the data model. In other words, it can be defined as either sObjects or classes in Apex.
- **View**: This defines how data is represented. In Salesforce, page layouts and Visualforce pages fall under this category.
- **Controller**: This defines business logic. The rules and actions which manipulate the data controls the view. In Salesforce, Apex classes, Apex triggers, Process Builders, and approval processes fall under this category.

A few points to remember

1. Apex is a case-insensitive language.
2. The **New**, **Edit**, and **Delete** options of Apex classes are not available in the production organization.
3. As a best practice, start class names with an uppercase letter and method names with a lowercase letter.
4. When deploying using a change set, it runs all the tests of Apex code. If you have low code coverage, you will not be able to deploy it and it will fail every time; however, with Force.com IDE, you can push code without coverage.
5. The blob data type represented as binary data is stored in a single object.
6. If you want to execute code repeatedly, use `do...while`, `while`, or `for` loops.
7. Rolling back transactions is also supported by Apex.

Test your knowledge

Q1. Is it possible to create a trigger directly in a production org?

1. True
2. False

Q2. Which layer of the MVC architecture are standard or custom objects associated with?

1. View
2. Model
3. Controller
4. View and Controller

Q3. Which of the following cannot be used on a user page layout?

1. Tags
2. Links
3. Buttons
4. Custom Fields
5. Inline Visualforce

Q4. In an MVC architecture, which of the following corresponds to View?

1. Page layouts
2. Validation rules
3. Tabs
4. Process Builders

Q5. Which of the following statements is true about page layouts?

1. They can have one or two columns per section
2. We can add a list button using a page layout editor
3. We can hide a section header detail view or edit view or both the views
4. We can add blank spaces instead of fields
5. We can preview a single layout for different profiles

Q6. Which edition supports Apex and Visualforce?

1. Unlimited Edition
2. Enterprise Edition
3. Apex Edition
4. Professional Edition
5. Group Edition

Q7. Apex is executed when Data Manipulation Language events occur on the Force.com platform:

1. True
2. False

Q8. sObjects is a data type:

1. True
2. False

Q9. Classes can be enabled or disabled for profiles:

1. True
2. False

Q10. A Visualforce page consists of which primary elements?

1. An Apex class
2. A Visualforce controller
3. A trigger
4. S-Controls
5. Visualforce markup
6. None of the above

Summary

In this chapter, we learned about the basics of developing custom pages using Visualforce. We also learned the basics of Apex coding. Then, we moved ahead and discussed the MVC design pattern for a Visualforce page. We also discussed Apex data types.

After completing this chapter, you will have a good knowledge of Salesforce's advanced configuration concept, and should you wish, you can appear for the advanced administrator certification examination. If you want to explore Apex and Visualforce further, refer to the following blogs:

- `http://www.jitendrazaa.com`
- `http://bobbuzzard.blogspot.com`
- `http://blog.jeffdouglas.com`
- `http://www.tgerm.com`
- `https://andyinthecloud.com`

Index

D

E

F

H

I

J

K

L

M

O

P

Q

R

S

T

U

V

W